MW01702699

WEST ACADEMIC PUBLISHING'S LAW SCHOOL ADVISORY BOARD

JESSE H. CHOPER
Professor of Law and Dean Emeritus,
University of California, Berkeley

JOSHUA DRESSLER
Distinguished University Professor, Frank R. Strong Chair in Law
Michael E. Moritz College of Law, The Ohio State University

YALE KAMISAR
Professor of Law Emeritus, University of San Diego
Professor of Law Emeritus, University of Michigan

MARY KAY KANE
Professor of Law, Chancellor and Dean Emeritus,
University of California, Hastings College of the Law

LARRY D. KRAMER
President, William and Flora Hewlett Foundation

JONATHAN R. MACEY
Professor of Law, Yale Law School

ARTHUR R. MILLER
University Professor, New York University
Formerly Bruce Bromley Professor of Law, Harvard University

GRANT S. NELSON
Professor of Law, Pepperdine University
Professor of Law Emeritus, University of California, Los Angeles

A. BENJAMIN SPENCER
Earle K. Shawe Professor of Law,
University of Virginia School of Law

JAMES J. WHITE
Robert A. Sullivan Professor of Law Emeritus,
University of Michigan

LEGISLATION AND REGULATION

IN A NUTSHELL®

STEVEN F. HUEFNER
Alumni Society Designated Professor of Law
The Ohio State University
Moritz College of Law

WEST ACADEMIC PUBLISHING

The publisher is not engaged in rendering legal or other professional advice, and this publication is not a substitute for the advice of an attorney. If you require legal or other expert advice, you should seek the services of a competent attorney or other professional.

Nutshell Series, In a Nutshell and the Nutshell Logo are trademarks registered in the U.S. Patent and Trademark Office.

© 2017 LEG, Inc. d/b/a West Academic
444 Cedar Street, Suite 700
St. Paul, MN 55101
1-877-888-1330

West, West Academic Publishing, and West Academic are trademarks of West Publishing Corporation, used under license.

Printed in the United States of America

ISBN: 978-1-62810-210-9

ACKNOWLEDGMENTS

Teaching Legislation & Regulation as a first-year course at the Ohio State University Moritz College of Law, as well as teaching our elective Legislation Clinic for second- and third-year students, have been immensely satisfying experiences. They form the backbone of this volume and I am grateful to my many wonderful colleagues who have collaborated or otherwise shared these teaching experiences with me over the past two decades: Doug Berman, Jim Brudney, Sandy Caust-Ellenbogen, Ruth Colker, Terri Enns, Dakota Rudesill, Peter Shane, Donald Tobin, Dan Tokaji, & Chris Walker.

In addition, my involvements since 2004 with the *Election Law @ Moritz* program, and in the past several years with the related OSU Democracy Studies Program, have further enriched my perspective on the legislative and regulatory processes treated in this volume. My activities with these programs have confirmed for me the importance of promoting a better understanding of these processes. I am grateful for my OSU colleague Ned Foley, Director of *Election Law @ Moritz*, for his vision and leadership in this regard.

In preparing this volume I have been fortunate to have the assistance of a cadre of excellent research assistants: Ryan Agee, Hailey Akah, Jedidiah Bressman, Kris Chandler, Ben Fogle, Ethan McNaghten, Zach Soehnlen, & Ben Wallace. I also owe an especially great debt of gratitude to my former student Keith Darsee, who in addition to his own fabulous service as a research assistant has also been a steadfast supporter of the project and an invaluable advisor about content and organization.

My parents, Bob and Dixie; my children, Diana, Emmy, and Kate; and my partner, Julianne, have also been immensely supportive, each in distinctive ways, of all my efforts to study, improve, and teach about the institutions and processes of American law and government. I am deeply grateful not only for their love and encouragement, but also to be able to share our lives—and citizenship—together.

STEVE HUEFNER

Columbus, Ohio
March 2017

OUTLINE

TABLE OF CASES

References are to Pages

LEGISLATION AND REGULATION

IN A NUTSHELL®

INTRODUCTION

WHY STUDY LEGISLATION AND REGULATION?

Traditionally, American legal education has focused primarily on the role, function, and doctrinal pronouncements of the judicial branch of government. Since the adoption of the case method almost a century and a half ago, lawyers have learned the law primarily through the close reading and analysis of hundreds of representative appellate court decisions, a pedagogy familiar to all first-year law students. Yet for most of the past hundred years, legislatures and administrative agencies have created and implemented every bit as much law in the United States as have state and federal courts.

Furthermore, the contemporary practice of American law now takes place against a backdrop of increasingly complex interactions between the institutions of all three branches of government, namely, legislatures, executive and administrative agencies, and courts. At both the state and federal levels, legislatures enact sweeping measures that touch almost every aspect of citizens' lives in myriad ways, from health insurance, to motor vehicle operation, to the mechanics of voting, to stimulating the economy, to the criminalization of internet piracy, to the distribution of tax burdens, to name only a few specific areas of government regulation. Administrative agencies and executive branch officials in turn must enforce many of these legislative measures through the creation of their own subsidiary regulations, as well as through their own adjudication of particular controversies. Meanwhile, citizens often turn to courts for clarification of the scope and meaning of complicated statutes or dense administrative regulations, as well as to challenge the underlying validity of these statutes and regulations.

Accordingly, twenty-first century attorneys need to possess not only a thorough understanding of the judicial branch, its operation, and doctrinal output, but also a comprehensive grounding in the lawmaking activities of each of the three branches of government, including the interactions among these branches. These interbranch relationships sometimes may be truly collaborative; at other times they may be merely cooperative; and on yet other occasions they may even be genuinely conflicting or competitive. In this context, as a matter of both law creation and law implementation, opportunities for thoughtful, creative lawyering abound. Clients today may seek legal assistance in advancing a legislative agenda, appearing before an administrative agency, or persuading a court to adopt a favorable construction of a statutory or regulatory provision—all legal tasks that require in-depth knowledge of the legislative and regulatory processes and of the various theories about their proper relationship.

Reflecting this reality, in recent years an increasing number of U.S. law schools have included in their first-year curriculum a course in Legislation and Regulation, or in Legislation alone. As a result, a rich supply of new course materials on legislative processes, regulatory agencies, and statutory interpretation is now available to students and practitioners, in addition to an explosion of academic research concerning the complexities of modern American lawmaking. Upper level courses that build on these foundations also have expanded into specific areas of regulatory policy, courses in election law and the law of democracy, and clinical and experiential learning opportunities in legislative and regulatory settings.

This Nutshell is designed to accompany this trove of new learning, serving as an aid to law students and practicing lawyers who are seeking to refine and deepen their basic mastery of the functioning of the legislative bodies and regulatory institutions in which the vast majority of American law today is made, updated, and applied. The Nutshell discusses state as well as federal institutions and processes, addressing not only the U.S. Congress and today's vast federal regulatory bureaucracy, but also state legislatures and administrative agencies. As part of its treatment of this subject, it considers the settled practice of delegating lawmaking authority from the legislative branch to the executive branch, and it explores the complicated relationship between these two branches. It also examines the interplay between the legislative and executive institutions that draft the text of the law, on the one hand, and the state and federal courts that frequently must serve as the interpreters of that legislative and regulatory output, on the other.

The Nutshell is divided into two principal but closely related parts. Part I describes the functioning of modern-day legislatures and administrative agencies. In addition to analyzing the various stages and inputs in the processes of law creation and implementation, it identifies the primary participants in these processes and discusses their motives and influences. The topics of this first part include: the sources and hierarchy of lawmaking authority (Chapter 1); theories of democratic representation (Chapter 2); rules governing the election processes that shape and populate the legislative institutions of representative democracy (Chapter 3); anti-corruption measures, including campaign financing and lobbying regulations, which further shape and influence our representative institutions (Chapter 4); the essential mechanics of how legislatures craft laws (Chapter 5); and the basic structure and function of governmental agencies, including the tools of legislative and judicial oversight of agencies (Chapter 6).

Part II then develops in detail the dominant theories, doctrines, and practices of statutory and regulatory interpretation. Statutory and regulatory language can be fraught with ambiguity, despite the drafters' best efforts. The results lead to questions like these: How is an implementing agency or court to deal with statutory ambiguity? What latitude is appropriate? What interpretive tools or aids can or should guide this process? How might the responses to these questions be different for agencies than for courts? How do, or ought, courts differ in how they approach the interpretation of regulatory text rather than statutory text? And what are the most salient differences between the federal and state systems regarding the interpretation of statutes and regulatory language?

In addressing these essential questions about American law today, the second part of the Nutshell builds directly on the first part, illustrating that a sophisticated understanding of the challenges and problems of statutory and regulatory interpretation must be predicated on an equally nuanced understanding of the processes by which the words of the law come into being. The topics in this second part include: the challenge of textual interpretation (Chapter 7); theories of statutory interpretation (Chapter 8); canons of construction and other intrinsic tools of interpretation (Chapter 9); legislative history and other extrinsic tools of interpretation (Chapter 10); agency interpretation of legislative text (Chapter 11); and judicial review of agency interpretations (Chapter 12). An Appendix of Representative Canons of Statutory Interpretation follows.

PART 1

UNDERSTANDING LEGISLATURES AND AGENCIES

CHAPTER 1

SOURCES AND HIERARCHY OF LAWMAKING AUTHORITY

Today, a thorough grounding in legislative and regulatory processes is an essential component of an understanding of the sources and authority of American law. While the court-centric common-law tradition to which American law traces its roots continues to profoundly shape the U.S. legal system, state and federal legislatures have long displaced courts as the primary creators of law. In turn, as

American society and government have grown more complex, legislatures have increasingly shared their lawmaking authority with administrative agencies, whose regulations now comprise another substantial layer of American law. Accordingly, this chapter briefly identifies the sources and hierarchy of legislative and regulatory lawmaking authority. The remaining chapters of Part I then provide more detail concerning the function and operation of contemporary legislatures and administrative agencies.

A. CONSTITUTIONAL DEMOCRACY: LAWMAKING AUTHORITY DERIVES FROM THE PEOPLE

In the United States, the foundational legal document of both the state and federal levels of government is a written constitution that defines the scope of governmental powers and duties. But the constitutions themselves derive their ultimate authority from the citizenry, who either through their designated representatives, or through processes of direct democracy, have the authority to ratify, amend, or replace altogether these foundational documents. Each of these state and federal constitutions in turn then establishes a legislative body as the primary lawmaking institution of their respective systems of government; many state constitutions also establish mechanisms of direct democracy that allow the citizens themselves to enact state statutes in supplement of their state legislature.

1. THE UNITED STATES CONSTITUTION

The United States Constitution stands as a model of the democratic principle, explicitly articulated in the Declaration of Independence, that governments must derive their just powers "from the consent of the governed." Decl. of Indep. The U.S. Constitution's framework for a set of government powers and institutions for the new federal republic—including the commitment to a government of separated legislative, executive, and judicial powers—resulted not only from the collective wisdom of the group of drafters drawn from twelve of the thirteen original states, but also from a ratification process through which the citizens of each of the thirteen states accepted the document and imbued it with authority. As new states have been added to the Union, each in turn has recognized the Constitution's place as the country's foundational legal document.

As further confirmation that the people of the nation remain the ultimate sovereign over the federal government, the Constitution itself establishes a process for its own amendment that depends on popular approval. This process provides that amendments to the Constitution will take effect only upon the assent of state conventions or state legislatures representing three-fourths of the several states. *See* U.S. Const. art. V. The amendment process is deliberately difficult, reflecting the judgment that the national constitution should not undergo frequent change, but should express the country's foundational principles with a relatively high degree of permanence and stability.

To date, some twenty-seven amendments have been added to the U.S. Constitution, and only one has ever been repealed. Some of these amendments have altered the manner in which the federal government operates, as for instance by limiting the President to two elected terms, U.S. Const. amend. XXII; granting presidential electors to the District of Columbia, U.S. Const. amend. XXIII; or specifying when members of Congress can receive pay increases, U.S. Const. amend. XVII. But many of these twenty-seven amendments, including the first ten amendments constituting the Bill of Rights, as well as the Fourteenth Amendment's guarantees of due process and equal protection of law, and the Twenty-Fourth Amendment's prohibition of poll taxes, impose constraints on the reach of government power over the lives of U.S. citizens.

From the outset, it is important to recognize that even without these amendments, the U.S. Government is a government of limited powers, having only those powers and authorities that the people, through the Constitution, have given it. This stands in direct contrast to state governments, which are understood to possess plenary power to control and regulate all aspects of society, unless some provision of either the U.S. Constitution or the pertinent state constitution disables the state from exercising power in some specified arena. These limits on the legislative powers of the federal and state governments will be discussed further in section B below.

Nevertheless, the U.S. Constitution gives Congress broad authority to legislate in many areas. For instance, among other powers, the Constitution permits Congress to: impose taxes and spend the proceeds thereof; establish a national military; develop a body of law to protect copyrights and other intellectual property; regulate commerce among the states; admit additional states into the Union; and enforce the Fourteenth Amendment's guarantees of due process and equal protection of law for all citizens. Whenever Congress legislates, it must rely, at least implicitly, on some particular grant of authority in the Constitution.

2. STATE CONSTITUTIONS

As a second foundational legal document, functioning in tandem with the U.S. Constitution, all fifty states have a written state constitution that structures the operation of state government. Like their federal counterpart, these state constitutions establish a legislative, executive, and judicial branch of government and have been adopted through some process that required the assent of that state's citizens. Each state constitution, with the exception of Delaware's, can be amended by an action of the people.

A state-by-state description of the differences between federal and state procedures of constitutional amendment would be impractical to detail here, given the range of state processes. It is helpful, however, to outline some typical structural features, as well as to highlight a few noteworthy outliers.

As a general matter, every state except Delaware provides for some method of constitutional amendment by legislative initiative. These legislatively-referred amendments must first be proposed and passed by a state's legislature, and then be presented to the voting public for approval on a general election ballot. In four states—Connecticut, Hawaii, New Jersey, and Pennsylvania—legislative approval requires either super-majority approval of one legislative session, or simple-majority approvals of two consecutive legislative sessions, prior to a proposed amendment going to the ballot for popular ratification in a general election. Eleven other states require majority legislative approval to occur in two consecutive legislative sessions. The Delaware Constitution's Article XVI is unique in that it requires two consecutive super-majority legislative session approvals to effectuate a constitutional amendment, but no popular ratification is required.

Another mechanism by which state constitutions are altered is through the ballot initiative process. Eighteen state constitutions provide some mechanism whereby the voters directly, without the participation of the legislature, may propose and adopt an amendment. Ballot initiative requirements among these states vary widely in their particulars. Indeed, in some states (e.g., Illinois, Massachusetts, Mississippi, and Oklahoma) the amendment process is rendered practically illusory by onerous procedural obstacles. Nevada, uniquely, requires amendments to be ratified at two general elections before taking effect.

Yet another method of state constitutional amendment is by commission referral. For instance, the Florida Taxation and Budget Reform Commission, established by Article XI of the Florida Constitution, convenes every twenty years to propose amendments for statewide ballot ratification. Eight such amendments were referred in 2008. New Mexico adopted a constitutional amendment in 1996 that created a process whereby proposed amendments are referred to the state legislature by a commission.

Finally, rather than merely providing means for amending their founding documents, forty-four states have adopted methods to replace their constitution entirely via constitutional convention. A number of states automatically place before their voters every ten, sixteen, or twenty years a general election ballot measure to call a constitutional convention. Other states permit only the legislature to initiate a constitutional convention, without requiring direct input from the voters. Still other states provide for the legislature to propose a constitutional convention by submitting the question to the voters through a ballot measure. Requirements vary concerning, for example, what percentage of the voting public must approve the measure, as well as what proportion of the legislature must vote in favor, or for how many consecutive legislative sessions, before the proposal to call a convention is placed on a ballot.

Most state constitutions have been amended much more frequently than the U.S. Constitution; indeed, many have even been completely replaced, sometimes more than once, by an entirely new foundational document. The frequency with which state constitutions are amended reflects both the comparative ease of the amendment process in most states, and the fact that many state constitutions serve as the locus for a much greater range of substantive law than does the U.S. Constitution. For instance, it is not uncommon for state constitutions to have provisions about public schools, natural resources, labor and unions, and rights to judicial remedies. As a result, state constitutions tend to be substantially longer than the U.S. Constitution.

Collectively, the fifty state constitutions and the U.S. Constitution give rise to a complex system of dual sovereignty, in which Congress is supreme in its power to legislate in certain enumerated areas (as established by the Supremacy Clause, U.S. Const. art. VI, cl. 2), but must leave the regulation of many other areas to the states. As a result of this dual sovereignty, substantial variation often exists in how state governments choose to handle specific issues within their purview, such as the legalization of marijuana, how to fund public education, or whether to impose the death penalty for certain crimes. Indeed, this variation is the key ingredient for states to be able to experiment with novel solutions to the challenges of governance, serving as the "laboratories" of democracy, as Justice Brandeis famously put it. *See New State Ice Co. v. Liebmann*, 285 U.S. 262, 311 (1932). These state policies are established primarily by state legislatures, but in certain states may also result from the popular initiative processes of direct democracy (described briefly in Chapter 5.E below).

3. LOCAL GOVERNMENTS

A brief word is also in order about the source of local government power in the United States. Although local legislative and regulatory bodies are responsible for the creation of important portions of American law, they are not a third level of sovereign government authority. Instead, throughout the United States, local governments (as well as various special improvement districts, utility districts, and the like) are creatures of the state in which they exist.

As required by state law, municipalities may need to adopt a charter in order to incorporate or otherwise be recognized, but this is not an act of an independent sovereign. Rather, it is an act dependent on the state, which chooses to bestow a portion of the state's authority upon a locality provided it has complied with state-imposed requirements. Counties, meanwhile, are typically established by the state legislature and given the ability to control specified matters of governance through county commissions or councils.

Many states grant "home rule" authority to cities and towns, giving these municipalities additional freedom from state legislative control of certain local affairs. But the precise manner in which municipalities exercise governmental power—the role of the city council, town manager, mayor, and other officials or entities—is either established in the state constitution or subject to the control of the state legislature, even if the legislature allows localities to make certain choices between various forms of governance.

B. FROM CONSTITUTIONS TO LEGISLATURES: LEGISLATIVE STRUCTURES AND LIMITATIONS

As described in section A above, the state and federal constitutions are the supreme law within their respective spheres at the state or federal level. Other sources of law—statutes, regulations, judicial orders, executive orders, local ordinances—all derive their authority from these constitutions. These constitutions, in turn, impose important structural features and substantive limits upon the subordinate powers of federal and state lawmaking.

1. CONSTITUTIONAL STRUCTURES OF CONGRESS

In establishing Congress as the source of federal lawmaking authority, the very first provision of the U.S. Constitution provides: "All legislative Powers herein granted shall be vested in a Congress of the United States, which shall consist of a Senate and a House of Representatives." U.S. Const. art. I, sec. 1. The remainder of Article I of the Constitution then goes on to specify a number of fundamental requirements that shape the structure of Congress and its two chambers.

One essential characteristic of Congress established by the Constitution is the representational nature of the two chambers. As a result of the Great Compromise, by constitutional design the Senate has always consisted of two Senators from each state, regardless of a state's population, thus giving residents of small states disproportionate influence. From twenty-six members at its founding, the Senate has grown to one hundred members today, each serving for six years at a time. Meanwhile, although state legislatures initially appointed their state's two U.S. Senators, since the adoption of the Seventeenth Amendment in 1913, the people of each state have directly elected their Senators. Senators are elected "at large," meaning each Senator is understood to represent the state's entire population. Other constitutional provisions concerning the qualifications and elections of Senators, as well as of Representatives, are discussed in more detail in Chapter 3 below. Some additional considerations about the representational roles of elected legislators generally, both federal and state, including the scope of the one-person, one-vote requirements, are also discussed in Chapter 3.

Meanwhile, the House of Representatives is composed of Representatives apportioned among the states according to each state's population, with each state guaranteed at least one Representative, and all Representatives elected for two-year terms. Although the Constitution initially provided for a House consisting of 65 members, *see* U.S. Const. art. I, sec. 2, cl. 3, since 1913 the total number of

Representatives has been set by Congress at 435. *See* The Apportionment Act of 1911, Public Law 62–5. Today, every state with more than one Representative must subdivide the state into geographical districts of equal population, with each district electing its own member of the House of Representatives. *See Wesberry v. Sanders*, 376 U.S. 1 (1964). But dividing states into congressional districts is not a constitutional requirement, and in the early years, many states elected their Representatives at-large rather than by district. After 1967, Congress entirely prohibited at-large representation for states entitled to more than one Representative. The apportionment and districting processes are discussed in more detail in Chapter 3.

Another bedrock constitutional requirement is that before any measure can become a law, both the Senate and the House must be in complete agreement upon its text. U.S. Const. art. I, sec. 7, cl. 2. This "bicameralism" requirement usually requires that the two respective chambers negotiate and compromise, a process that sometimes can give rise to subsequent interpretive problems when statutes are being construed and implemented. Occasionally, however, the bicameral bargaining process can provide understanding and insight about the meaning of ambiguities in the resulting text. These topics are discussed in Chapters 5 and 10.

Article I of the Constitution also provides that before any measure can become a law, either the President also must approve its text, or else both Houses of Congress must each agree to the measure by a two-thirds supermajority to "override" a President's disapproval (or "veto") of the measure. U.S. Const. art. I, sec. 7, cl. 2. This requirement of Presidential "presentment" derives its name from the Article I provision requiring that Congress must *present* the measure to the President in order to trigger the President's responsibility to either approve or disapprove the measure. *Id.* Give-and-take occurring between Congress and the White House in the shadow of this presentment requirement also can sometimes be instructive in understanding statutory meaning.

The U.S. Constitution leaves to Congress most decisions about its internal legislative operations, including whether and how to use committees, what role to ascribe to political parties, when to limit legislative debate, and whether to keep a transcript of proceedings. The effect on the legislative process of these and other internal operating procedures, rules, and norms also is discussed in Chapter 5.

2. CONSTITUTIONAL STRUCTURES OF STATE LEGISLATURES

With the exception of Nebraska, all fifty states follow the federal model of establishing a bicameral legislature. Nebraska departs from this model by establishing a unicameral legislature, consisting of only one chamber. (The District of Columbia, along with the territories of Guam and the Virgin Islands, also have unicameral legislative assemblies). But unlike the federal model, in which members of the U.S. Senate from different states represent constituencies of very different population sizes, the one-person, one-vote requirement of *Reynolds v. Sims*, 377 U.S. 533 (1964), requires that all state legislators be elected from districts of approximately equal population (unless they are elected from multi-member rather than single-member districts, an option that ten state legislatures presently use for at least one of their two legislative chambers).

As specified in individual state constitutions, the number of members of each state's legislative bodies varies substantially from state to state, as does the relative size of the larger and smaller chambers of each bicameral legislature. At 49 members, the unicameral Nebraska Legislature is the smallest state legislature, although Alaska's 60-member bicameral legislature is composed of the yet-smaller 40-member House of Representatives and 20-member Senate. Meanwhile, the largest state legislature, with 424 members, is New Hampshire. The average size of the 49 bicameral state legislatures is 150 members.

Of more importance, however, is the ratio of representation, or in other words, the number of citizens that each legislator represents. This varies from just over 3000 residents per representative in the New Hampshire House of Representatives to over 465,000 residents per representative in California's lower house. The size of this ratio may affect the legislative process, to the extent that legislators who represent a smaller number of constituents may be more responsive to those individual constituents.

Also following the federal model, each state constitution provides that legislation cannot become law without either the approval of the state's Governor, or if that approval is not given, the subsequent approval of a legislative supermajority, the size of which is specified in the state constitution. But in a departure from the federal model, many states allow their governor to disapprove individual parts or "items" of a legislative measure, rather than limiting the executive veto to the entirety of a measure. This item veto (or "line-item veto") authority can have a substantial impact on the legislative dynamic between the executive and legislative branches, even in states that limit these partial vetoes to only the dollar amounts of individual items in legislative appropriations measures.

In most bicameral state legislatures, the members of one chamber, typically called the lower chamber, serve two-year terms, while the members of the other chamber, typically called the upper chamber, serve either two-year or four-year terms. State legislatures, like Congress, establish many of their own internal operating procedures, rules, and norms. However, many state constitutions also establish additional procedural requirements having no analog in the U.S. Constitution. These include, for example, requirements concerning the number of "readings" (or times that a legislature must make the measure its formal business) that a measure must receive before it can become law; requirements concerning the contents of a measure's official title; and single-subject requirements intended to prevent combining two or more unrelated measures into one bill in an effort to increase its support.

3. CONSTITUTIONAL LIMITS ON CONGRESSIONAL LEGISLATION

As previously mentioned, in order for Congress to enact any particular measure, the federal Constitution must grant Congress authority to legislate in that particular area. To enforce this general principle, the U.S. Supreme Court has the ultimate responsibility, once a case raising the issue is properly before it, to determine whether Congress has overreached its constitutional powers in any specific legislative enactment, and if so to invalidate the congressional action as unconstitutional. *See Marbury v. Madison*, 5 U.S. 137 (1803). Over the years, numerous Supreme Court decisions have helped to clarify the limits of Congress's legislative powers, both those enumerated and those implied.

Among the various powers of Congress specifically enumerated in Article I, section 8 of the Constitution, the authority to regulate interstate commerce and the power to tax have both been frequent subjects of Supreme Court decisions regarding the scope of congressional power. For instance, in *National Federation of Independent Business (NFIB) v. Sebelius*, 567 U.S. ___, 132 S. Ct. 2566 (2012), the Court held (by a 5–4 majority) that the individual mandate of the Patient Protection and Affordable Care Act of 2010—the requirement that every individual have health care insurance coverage—could not be justified as an exercise of Congress's power to regulate interstate commerce, despite the substantial impact of health care expenditures on the national economy. But in the same decision the Court also held (by a different 5–4 majority) that the individual mandate was justified as an exercise of Congress's power to tax because the mandate relied on imposing a fine (or tax) for noncompliance.

Many other cases have required the Court to determine the scope of Congress's implied power under the Constitution's "Necessary and Proper" clause, U.S. Const. art. I, sec. 8, cl. 18. This clause, also called the "Elastic Clause," grants Congress the authority "to make all Laws which shall be necessary and proper" for executing any of the other powers expressly given to Congress. In 1819, in the foundational case of *McCulloch v. Maryland*, 17 U.S. 316 (1819), the Court gave a generally broad ambit to this clause, unanimously holding that Congress had the implied power to incorporate a national bank in order to effectuate its enumerated powers "to lay and collect taxes; to borrow money; to regulate commerce; to declare and conduct a war; and to raise and support armies and navies." In 2012, however, the Court in *NFIB v. Sebelius* also rejected the Necessary and Proper Clause as a justification for the individual mandate of the Affordable Care Act.

Congress's legislative authority is further limited by the Constitution's explicit protections of individual rights, especially the protections contained in the Bill of Rights, which operate to disable congressional power where Congress might otherwise be empowered to act. For instance, the

Fifth Amendment prevents the government from taking private property for public use without just compensation, and more generally from depriving anyone of life, liberty, or property without due process of law; and the Eighth Amendment prohibits the imposition of cruel and unusual punishments or excessive bail. The language of the First Amendment contains the clearest textual limitation of Congress's legislative power, expressly providing that "**Congress shall make no law** respecting an establishment of religion, or prohibiting the free exercise thereof; or abridging the freedom of speech, or of the press; or the right of the people peaceably to assemble, and to petition the Government for a redress of grievances."

Here too, courts regularly play an essential role in enforcing limits on congressional power, reviewing specific legislative enactments to determine whether they impermissibly encroach upon protected liberties, and striking down those that do. Thus, congressional power is limited first by the language of the Constitution, and then by the existence of an independent judiciary, with the power of judicial review over congressional action to enforce these constitutional limits.

Another limitation on congressional power comes through the independence of the executive branch, most saliently the President's power to veto congressional enactments. Although a presidential veto typically is simply an expression of a policy disagreement, a veto (or even the threat of a veto) also can serve as an additional check on legislative overreach.

4. CONSTITUTIONAL LIMITS ON STATE LEGISLATION

Although it was not always the case, today state legislatures operate under certain limits that are similar to the limits under which Congress operates. At the same time, state legislatures also confront several types of limitations not applicable to Congress.

Until early in the twentieth century, the Bill of Rights was generally understood to limit only the federal government. Beginning in 1925, however, the Supreme Court in a series of cases began a process of selectively incorporating most of the Bill of Right's guarantees into the Fourteenth Amendment's requirement that states provide their citizens with due process and equal protection. As a result, states today must also ensure, for instance, that no state action violates the individual rights to freedom of speech, press, assembly, or religion protected by the First Amendment; deprives an individual of property without just compensation in violation of the Fifth Amendment; or imposes cruel or unusual punishment contrary to the Eighth Amendment.

In addition, even before the process of selective incorporation made most of the federal Bill of Rights applicable to the states, almost all states had in their constitutions their own versions of a bill of rights, which similarly protected citizens from government actions that might otherwise limit their individual freedoms. Moreover, in many states these provisions comprise the first article of the state constitution, taking a position of prominence in the constitutional firmament. These state bills of rights are often even more protective of individual liberties than is their federal counterpart. For instance, several states include a guarantee that citizens have a right to a judicial remedy for a legal wrong done to them.

Apart from the expansive scope of many state constitutions' bills of rights, the plenary nature of state legislative authority also provides reason to build additional limits on state legislative authority into many specific provisions of state constitutions, lest the state legislature have too much free rein to establish any policy it wishes. One feature that is almost universal, and which stands in contrast to federal congressional authority, is the requirement that state legislatures keep the state budget in balance. Another common feature is a constitutional mandate that the state legislature fund a system of public schools. And almost all states have at least one constitutional provision addressing the issue of natural resource management or the environment, ranging from general policy statements regarding environmental protection to specific prohibitions on particular types of fishing nets.

A limit that state legislatures often must confront that has no analog at the congressional level is the principle of federal supremacy. That is, if Congress has legislated in an area within its jurisdiction, a state legislature is precluded from adopting an overtly contravening rule. It further means, as a result of what is labeled the "preemption doctrine," that state legislatures sometimes may not even pass a complementary measure if congressional action in that area indicates that Congress intended to exclusively "occupy the field." *See, e.g., Fid. Fed. Sav. & Loan Ass'n v. de la Cuesta*, 458 U.S. 141 (1982).

Finally, the fact that most state governors wield some version of an item veto authority serves as a greater limit on state legislatures than does the federal system's all-or-nothing veto authority.

C. FROM LEGISLATURES TO AGENCIES: DELEGATION OF LAWMAKING AUTHORITY

So far, this chapter has considered how the power to make laws reposes first in the people, and then is given by them, through state and federal constitutions, to the people's representatives, constituted as legislatures. Legislatures then may use this power as they see fit, subject to various procedural and substantive limits, including those described briefly above. In turn, one choice that legislatures routinely make is to allocate elements of this lawmaking authority to executive branch departments and independent government agencies.

To better facilitate the implementation and execution of law, it has long been an accepted feature of American government for legislatures to create departments within the executive branch to administer government policies over specified subject matters. Indeed, in 1789, several of the First Congress's earliest and most important actions were to establish the Departments of State, War, and

Treasury. But today, the duties given to government departments and agencies routinely include more than the mere execution of law, and also comprehend the development of substantive regulations and the adjudication of disputes. Indeed, although Article I, section 1 of the U.S. Constitution appears to grant Congress exclusive federal legislative authority, Congress routinely delegates to federal departments and agencies the authority to promulgate regulations that clarify, extend, or otherwise fine-tune statutory law in areas overseen by the relevant department or agency.

At the federal level, a long doctrinal history has developed concerning the extent of permissible delegations of lawmaking authority from Congress to executive branch departments and independent agencies. Variably labeled either the "delegation doctrine" or the "nondelegation doctrine," this doctrine, discussed further in Chapter 6 below, holds that Congress cannot delegate its legislative powers to actors outside the legislative branch unless Congress establishes an "intelligible principle" to guide the delegate's exercise of the delegated authority. *See J.W. Hampton, Jr. & Co. v. United States*, 276 U.S. 394, 409 (1928). However, in practice this doctrine has not seriously limited Congress's power of delegation. As the Court observed a quarter century ago in *Mistretta v. United States*, 488 U.S. 361, 372–73 (1989):

> our jurisprudence has been driven by a practical understanding that in our increasingly complex society, replete with ever changing and more

> technical problems, Congress simply cannot do its job absent an ability to delegate power under broad general directives . . . . Accordingly, this Court has deemed it "constitutionally sufficient if Congress clearly delineates the general policy, the public agency which is to apply it, and the boundaries of this delegated authority."

State practice is consistent: state legislatures are allowed to share lawmaking authority with state agencies and departments for the purpose of filling in the gaps in more broadly stated statutory schemes. For instance, although the Wisconsin Supreme Court observed in the 1945 case of *Clintonville Transfer Line v. Public Service Commission*, 21 N.W.2d 5, 11 (Wisc. 1945), that "the power to declare whether or not there shall be a law, to determine the general policy to be achieved by the law, and to fix the limits within which the law shall operate is vested by our constitution in the legislature *and may not be delegated*," the court also explained that nonetheless "when the legislature has laid down the fundamentals of the law, it may delegate to administrative agencies such legislative powers as may be necessary to carry into effect the general legislative purpose." All states permit their state legislature to give agencies the authority to promulgate rules provided they are doing so in furtherance of a specific purpose or policy that the legislature has established.

In large part because Congress is able to delegate its lawmaking powers, Congress has repeatedly created specialized agencies with regulatory authority beyond the existing fifteen cabinet-level executive branch departments and their subsidiary offices. The now-defunct Interstate Commerce Commission, created in 1887 as part of the Interstate Commerce Act, is considered the federal government's first independent regulatory agency, but similar agencies proliferated in the twentieth century. Today, other prominent independent federal agencies include: the Central Intelligence Agency (CIA), the Environmental Protection Agency (EPA), the Federal Communications Commission (FCC), the Federal Energy Regulatory Commission (FERC), the Federal Reserve (the Fed), the National Aeronautics and Space Administration (NASA), the National Labor Relations Board (NLRB), and the Securities and Exchange Commission (SEC), to name only a few. These agencies, along with the cabinet departments, are an essential contributor to the contemporary body of federal law.

Typically, when federal agencies and departments promulgate regulations, they do so by engaging in a statutorily prescribed "notice and comment" rule-making process. This process, described in more detail below in Chapter 6, provides the public with an opportunity for input. It also provides lobbyists and interest group representatives a prime opportunity to shape the resulting policies. Many state agency rulemaking processes are analogous, although state agencies also may often have the power to promulgate regulations using different processes.

An essential component of a legislature's ability—and willingness—to delegate some portion of its lawmaking authority outside its halls is its ability to maintain a measure of oversight of the way that the delegated authority is used. Thus, as agencies have come to play a larger role in actually promulgating law and implementing policy, the processes of legislative oversight of agency behavior have also become increasingly important. These tools of legislative oversight also are discussed further in Chapter 6.

CHAPTER 2

THE NATURE OF DEMOCRATIC REPRESENTATION

WHAT'S IN THIS CHAPTER:

A. Conceptions of the Role of the Legislator
   1. *Legislators as Agents*
   2. *Legislators as Trustees*
   3. *Hybrid Conceptions of the Legislator's Role*
   4. *Legislators as Constituting a Collective Microcosm, a Portrait-in-Miniature*

B. Conceptions of the Role of the Legislature
   1. *Classical Liberal or Pluralist Conceptions*
   2. *Republican Conceptions*
   3. *Critical Theories*

C. Perspectives on the Operation of the Administrative State
   1. *Lawmaking Procedures as Hurdles to Overcome*
   2. *Government as the Locus of Interest Group Bargaining*
   3. *The Impact of Institutional Dynamics on Lawmaking*

As detailed in Chapter 1, the primary lawmaking institutions of contemporary American government consist of the United States Congress and the fifty state legislatures, substantially assisted by the regulatory agencies they have created. Thus, it is essential for twenty-first century attorneys to have a sophisticated understanding of the structure, function, and operation of these legislative and administrative institutions. The rest of this Part of the Nutshell is devoted to that understanding.

First, this chapter will describe several different ways of viewing the roles of our elected representatives, as well as of how we expect our representative institutions to function. Chapters 3 and 4 will then explore features of the electoral processes, campaign finance practices, lobbying mechanisms, and bribery prohibitions through which we select and influence the representatives who populate our legislative institutions. Chapter 5 then will review the formal processes of creating statutes, while Chapter 6 will discuss the administrative entities and regulatory processes that these legislative bodies have created to assist in lawmaking and law implementation.

A. CONCEPTIONS OF THE ROLE OF THE LEGISLATOR

The renowned British statesman Edmund Burke is deservedly famous for his *Speech to the Electors at Bristol*, upon their selecting him to represent them in Parliament in 1774, in which he articulated his view of the role of a Member of Parliament. He argued that the Member ought not to function as the agent or ambassador of those constituents who elected him, but instead ought to devote his reason to making independent decisions about how to serve the public interest: "Your representative owes you, not his industry only, but his judgment; and he betrays, instead of serving you, if he sacrifices it to your opinion." Burke's quote raises a critical issue in representational theory: Should political representatives act as agents of their constituents, doing all they can to effectuate their constituents' will and wishes? Or should representatives instead act as trustees for their constituents, seeking the constituents' best interests as the representatives understand them? Are these views mutually exclusive, or can they be harmonized? Or might representatives conceive of their roles in yet other ways, or be chosen for yet other purposes?

1. LEGISLATORS AS AGENTS

The view that elected representatives should function as the agents of their constituents—a view obviously of some currency in eighteenth century Britain when Burke, who went on to lose his next election, challenged it—also holds great favor in America today. Also sometimes called the "delegate" view, it is the conception that the role of a representative is to carry her constituents' wishes with her to the Capitol building or Statehouse, and once there to act in her constituents' stead by voting in the manner that the constituents themselves would vote were they present. In its most extreme form, this is a view that the function of a legislature is to aggregate the preferences of the public it serves by having legislators deliver the proxies of their constituents.

In terms of a pure democratic ideal of every citizen having an equal say in government and in the setting of public policy, this agency view of representative democracy has some inherent appeal. It also can be a deeply attractive notion to constituents choosing between political candidates at the ballot box. Indeed, candidates frequently campaign for votes on the basis that other politicians do not sufficiently respect the voters' political preferences, and that the candidate, if elected, will better honor the voters' wishes. As a result, a great deal of political polling and opinion research occurs in order to help candidates and legislators match their campaign commitments and voting records with constituent views, so that they can promote themselves as better "agents."

Of course, this is an oversimplification. It assumes that a majority of the constituents of a given legislator all share the same wishes, when in fact constituents typically hold a range of views, even on one issue. Political scientists therefore sometimes speak in terms of a constituency's "median" or "pivotal" voter. Although this too remains an oversimplification, in today's connected world it is becoming easier and easier for representatives to be aware not only of which voters will be the determinative ones (whether in the general election or in the increasingly critical primary elections), but also of the views or wishes of those voters.

A legislator who conceives of her legislative role in agency terms need not always vote in lock-step with what she understands to be the views of her constituents, however. Rather, the agent legislator might depart from her constituency if she in good faith believes that the views of her constituency (or, perhaps more precisely, of the "pivotal" voter in her constituency) would align with her legislative actions were her constituents in her shoes; that is, if the constituents were informed by the same information-gathering and negotiation processes in which the representative has participated on behalf of her constituents. On some more nuanced agency conceptions, therefore, the task of an agent legislator is not necessarily to do what she is told, but to honor what she assumes *would be* the fully informed preferences of her constituents, who are her principals. This description of the agent's task may seem to blur the role of an agent with the role of a trustee (discussed next), but the key distinction remains that agents are acting to effectuate what they understand to be their principals' fully informed preferences, while trustees are acting in what they themselves believe is in the best interests of their beneficiaries.

2. LEGISLATORS AS TRUSTEES

On the trusteeship model of representation, the legislator's role is not to determine how her principals would have behaved, even in light of the information-gathering and negotiation processes in which the legislator participates. Rather, it is to use the legislative process as a collective act of public deliberation about the common good, and then to draw upon the legislator's own wisdom and experience, combined with that of the legislator's colleagues, to make an independent decision about what either is in the constituents' best interests, or best serves the public at large. These two formulations of a trustee's duties are not necessarily the same thing—indeed, one open question is whether the trustee's foremost responsibility should be to the constituents, or instead to the greater public. But in either case, on a trusteeship model, the constituents are the beneficiaries of the legislator's work, not the principals who direct that work.

Following Burke, this conception has a rich tradition in American politics as well. For instance, James Madison, writing in the FEDERALIST PAPERS, argued that a chief advantage of representative democracy over pure democracy was that a representative democracy would:

> refine and enlarge the public views by passing them through the medium of a chosen body of citizens, whose wisdom may best discern the true interest of their country and whose patriotism and love of justice will be least likely to sacrifice it to temporary or partial considerations. Under such a regulation it may well happen that the public voice, pronounced by the representatives of the people, will be more consonant to the public good than if pronounced by the people themselves, convened for the purpose.

FEDERALIST 10.

More recently, John F. Kennedy, while serving as a U.S. Senator, similarly observed:

> It is difficult to accept [the] narrow view of the role of United States Senator—a view that assumes the people of Massachusetts sent me to Washington to serve merely as a seismograph to record shifts in popular opinion. . . . The voters selected us, in short, because they had confidence in our judgment and our ability to exercise that judgment from a position where we could determine what were their own best interests, as a part of the nation's interest. This may mean that we must on occasion lead, inform, correct and sometimes even ignore constituent opinion, if we are to exercise fully that judgment for which we were elected.

JOHN F. KENNEDY, PROFILES IN COURAGE 16 (1956).

Indeed, politicians who are too much like a seismograph—too responsive to public opinion, in exactly the way a legislator-as-agent might justifiably behave in response to the evolving views of their constituent principals—often are pilloried as opportunistic "flip-floppers" who lack their own judgment or convictions. Yet in today's politics, it understandably would be politically difficult for candidates to seek representative office primarily by touting their personal wisdom, or by flaunting their confidence that they understand the public interest better than do their constituents. Rather, it is next to impossible for politicians to ignore the repeated complaints that legislators (and thus legislatures) are out of touch with the wishes of the greater public, or to resist the popular appeals for legislators to be more responsive to the demands of their constituents.

A fundamental tension therefore exists between these two primary ways of conceptualizing the role of a legislator.

3. HYBRID CONCEPTIONS OF THE LEGISLATOR'S ROLE

The trustee-versus-agent dichotomy is a valuable tool for reflection about how we would like our legislative institutions to function, and about how we therefore might shape other electoral and structural features of these institutions to foster that function, as discussed further in Chapters 3 through 5 below. But both as a normative and a descriptive matter, this dichotomy presents a false choice about the role of elected representatives. Instead, several hybrid characterizations are also possible, and, in fact, most legislators behave in some fashion as both agent and trustee.

One idealized hybrid view imagines that, if the representatives are well-chosen and the society is well-informed, then the action that a legislator would take as an agent will align with the choice that the legislator would make as a trustee. Of course, were that the case, either conception of the role of an elected representative would be adequate to the task, and the explanatory value of the two distinctive conceptions would largely evaporate. In particular, there would be little reason to argue for the trustee role, which implicitly depends on the assumption that elected representatives will be more capable than the public-at-large at identifying the common good, an assumption that is inconsistent with the premise of the idealized view. But the real world clearly is not one in which representatives' judgments consistently align with constituent preferences.

Another possible hybrid model invites distinguishing among specific legislative issues, categorizing some as more appropriate for the agency model, and others as more appropriate for the trustee model. This is a view that fits with the notion that a few high-profile legislative issues will have sufficient public salience that legislators should respect and follow the resulting public opinion, while many other issues will not generate either any meaningful public discussion or any reliable measure of informed public opinion, and so should be left for legislators to address using their own best judgment, perhaps influenced by the judgment and advice of experts. This view also accords with the substantial delegation of lawmaking authority to agencies, where greater specialization and expert knowledge can be brought to bear on issues of public policy, as discussed in Chapter 6.

Indeed, on some versions of this view, the public should welcome the fact that it releases the public from the responsibility to have an informed opinion about each of the myriad issues that a modern legislature typically addresses. The range and complexity of issues coming before legislatures and agencies today argue for the view that, at least for many of these issues, the task of the legislator is not to determine what the fully-informed pivotal constituent would want, but rather to determine what in the legislator's own judgment is best, or when to delegate the development of specific rules and standards to the administrative state, with its yet greater expertise.

One potential framework for distinguishing among types of legislative issues is to consider the distribution of their costs and benefits. In a landmark study of the regulatory process, political scientist James Q. Wilson many decades ago suggested the two-by-two categorization depicted in Chart 1 on the next page. The horizontal dimension depicts the distribution of the costs of a legislative measure across a spectrum, from highly concentrated to widely dispersed. Meanwhile, the vertical dimension depicts the distribution of the benefits of a legislative measure across a similar spectrum.

When benefits or costs are concentrated, constituents affected thereby may be more likely to mobilize to seek to influence legislators, while similar behavior is less likely when benefits or costs are dispersed. Thus, although this matrix undoubtedly oversimplifies things, it suggests that the agency model of legislator behavior may be well suited to what the matrix identifies as Interest Group Politics (where legislative costs and benefits are both concentrated), while the trustee model may be a better fit for what the matrix calls Majoritarian Politics (where both costs and benefits are dispersed).

Chart 1—Categories of Legislative Activity

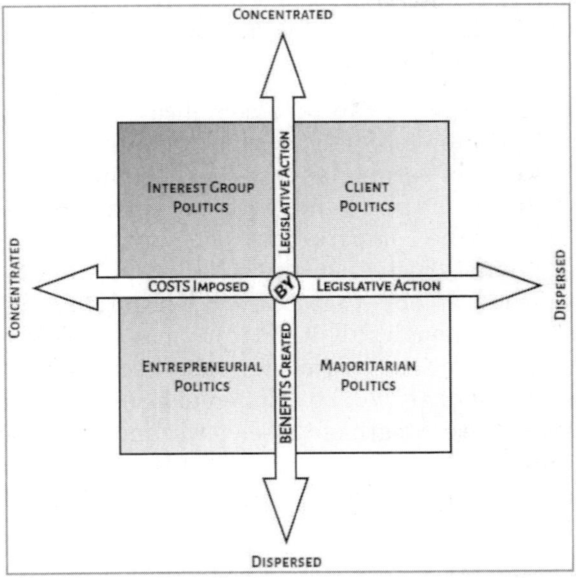

A third hybrid view recognizes the complexity not of the legislative agenda, but of legislators' motivations. On any given issue, each legislator is likely to have some mix of concerns about being responsive to constituent interests, and some desire to wisely promote the public interest. It bears noting that almost all elected representatives, despite their frequent caricature as primarily self-interested and ambitious, genuinely aspire to make a positive impact on matters of public policy and governance. Yet understandably they also worry about their own re-election, even if only out of their desire to continue to pursue their roles as public servants. They therefore work to protect their electoral prospects both by listening to the concerns of their constituents and by building a base of donors who will contribute campaign funds.

On this view, it can be a complicated calculation for a legislator to balance her genuine belief in the importance of serving as her constituents' agent or delegate, on the one hand, with her equally genuine belief in the importance of serving as her constituents' trustee, on the other hand. This third hybrid view accepts that for each legislative issue or action, a thoughtful legislator may make this calculation anew, even if subconsciously. The legislator not only will be attuned to her constituents' views, to the strength of those views, and to how well informed those views are, but also will remain focused on understanding and promoting the overall well-being of society.

A final, now vestigial, hybrid model might be identified with the structure of Congress prior to adoption of the Seventeenth Amendment in 1913. Before that amendment provided for the direct election of U.S. Senators, one might argue that Senators and Representatives were intended to have different kinds of electoral responsibilities. On this view, popularly elected Representatives would function more like agents of their constituents, while Senators appointed by their state legislatures would fulfill the role of trustees for the citizens of their states. The bicameral Congress thus would bring to bear both types of representation in establishing federal policy. But popular election of U.S. Senators has eliminated this hybrid model.

4. LEGISLATORS AS CONSTITUTING A COLLECTIVE MICROCOSM, A PORTRAIT-IN-MINIATURE

Other conceptions of representation depend neither on the trustee model nor the agent model. In particular, a descriptive model, championed in the founding generation most famously by John Adams, and still favored by some today, takes as its reference point the view that the representative body should be a descriptively accurate sampling of the public at large, a "portrait, in miniature." 4 THE WORKS OF JOHN ADAMS 205 (1850). Its claim is that legislative outcomes will be improved by populating the legislature with individuals whose demographic characteristics, taken collectively, closely match the characteristics of the society at large.

One difficulty, of course, is deciding just what characteristics are relevant to assessing a legislature's descriptive accuracy. Today, characteristics such as race, gender, income, age, sexual orientation, occupation, and religion would all be likely candidates. In some descriptive models, political party or ideology will be especially relevant. Yet John Adams' list surely would have been different, and there is no settled list of relevant characteristics (nor, if there were, of how to create an appropriate cross-section when any given legislator could represent multiple characteristics).

Nonetheless, the notion of creating a descriptively accurate representative institution has intrinsic appeal. A sense of its potential value underlies contemporary frustrations with gerrymandering, as well as concerns about the underrepresentation in legislatures of minority groups and women. It also lies behind other countries' practices of reserving certain numbers of legislative seats for representatives of specified groups (*see* Mala Htun, *Is Gender Like Ethnicity? The Political Representation of Identity Groups*, 2 PERSPECTIVES ON POLITICS 439 (2004)), or of using systems of proportional representation rather than winner-take-all elections (*see* Nicholas Stephanopoulos, *Our Electoral Exceptionalism*, 80 U. CHI. L. REV. 769 (2013)).

Moreover, even contemplating a descriptive model of the role of the legislator invites additional attention and insight into what it is that we expect our representatives to do when they "represent" us. It also invites us to think more carefully about how the structures of our election processes affect who become our representatives, and why our representative institutions have substantially less diversity than our overall population.

B. CONCEPTIONS OF THE ROLE OF THE LEGISLATURE

In addition to recognizing the preceding variations in the representational roles of a *legislator*, it also is helpful to consider two main conceptions of the institutional role of the *legislature* wherein legislators perform these roles. One main conception of the legislature derives from classical liberal theory (to be distinguished from today's common use of the term "liberal" to describe views on the left side of the political spectrum), and is somewhat akin to what is also often called pluralist theory. The other main conception derives from republican political theory (to be distinguished from contemporary Republican political views). In addition, since the later twentieth century, several critical theories also have invited attention to perceived shortcomings in the role and operation of representative institutions.

1. CLASSICAL LIBERAL OR PLURALIST CONCEPTIONS

Classical liberalism, often associated with John Locke, built upon ideas of natural rights to promote the ideals of individualism and liberty, particularly by protecting economic freedom and civil liberties, within certain limits. As applied to legislative politics, liberalism conceives of representative government as a system in which diverse, legitimate viewpoints are allowed to clash and compete for official recognition, within a framework that ensures the protection of minority rights against the threat of majority tyranny. The process is expected to give rise to a "marketplace of ideas" that rewards those legislative proposals that are able to garner more support, and in which factional or interest group bargaining is encouraged as a means of promoting equilibrium through compromise.

This liberal conception of the role of a legislature aligns more closely with the agency model of representatives (though not coextensively) than with the trustee model of representatives. Legislators-as-agents bring to the legislature their constituents' views of what government should do to protect and advance their individual interests and economic rights, and each legislator then must bargain and compromise with others in seeking the best outcomes for their respective groups of constituents. In the marketplace of ideas, legislators-as-agents also are free to support and adopt the ideas of other legislators, provided they conclude that were their constituents also participating in the marketplace, they would likewise be persuaded to do the same.

Because liberalism seeks to protect and promote individualism, it expects that a range of diverse interests will be represented and contested in the legislative arena. This view often is also labeled "pluralist," because it welcomes and responds to a multiplicity of positions. The legislative arena thereby functions as the forum for evaluating, refining, and choosing between these multiple positions.

At its heart, the pluralist conception is somewhat Madisonian in its acceptance of the presence in society of many narrow interests or factions. But Madison saw factions as tending to mischief, most famously in FEDERALIST 10, and defended representative government as a mechanism for controlling what would otherwise be the detrimental impacts of these factions. In contrast, many pluralists see factions or interest groups more favorably, as the most obvious way for citizens to become politically involved and to share political power. Pluralists therefore welcome many competing diverse interests into the legislative arena precisely to make the "marketplace" more robust, on the view that this is more likely to lead to socially desirable outcomes. *See, e.g.*, ROBERT A. DAHL, PLURALIST DEMOCRACY IN THE UNITED STATES: CONFLICT & CONSENT (1968).

But a classically liberal conception of the role of the legislature can also embrace the trustee model of legislators. For a trustee legislator, the question is how best to advance the liberal virtues of civil liberties and economic freedom. If legislators themselves have more wisdom or experience in these matters than their constituents, it would be in the constituents' best interests for the legislators, as trustees, to pursue these liberal ends even when their constituents desire otherwise. Constituent preferences may be inflamed by bias against certain minority rights, for instance, or may otherwise reflect some popular but misguided movement that in the long run will undermine liberal virtues. (Similar concerns may partially explain the Founders' decision to make the U.S. Constitution difficult to amend.) In these circumstances, rejecting the legislator-as-agent role and ignoring constituent views can be defended as advancing a liberal conception of the legislature.

2. REPUBLICAN CONCEPTIONS

Republican theory (again, "republican" with a small r, not to be confused with today's Republican

Party) focuses on the improved social benefits achievable through democratic institutions, and thus offers perhaps a more idealized or optimistic conception of representative government than does liberal theory. Tracing its ideas to ancient Greece, republican theory strives to promote a vision of the common good and to foster a commitment to civic virtue. It expects that legislators not only will eschew their own personal interests, but also will deliberate together about a common interest greater than can be achieved for or by their individual constituencies alone. Thus, deliberation itself is a civic act that can lead to the creation of better public policies.

This republican conception is also fundamentally Madisonian, but in a very different way than the liberal conception's focus on the abundance of diverse interest groups. Rather, in arguing for the supremacy of a republican form of government, Madison claimed that it would produce representatives with "enlightened views and virtuous sentiments" who could be "guardians of the public weal." FEDERALIST 59. As one twentieth-century scholar summarized this Madisonian view, a representative was to be "an independent man of republican virtue, tied to his constituents by duty, gratitude, and ambition and serving them with the affection of friends and the impartiality of judges." Robert J, Morgan, *Madison's Theory of Representation in the Tenth Federalist*, 36 J. POLITICS 852, 853 (1974).

The republican conception of the role of the legislature thus aligns more closely (though also not coextensively) with the representative-as-trustee conception of the role of the legislator. On the republican view, the legislature is a forum for acts of public deliberation. This deliberation occurs not primarily as a contest of ideas competing for acceptance or acclaim, but as a creative process in which solutions are forged in a cooperative effort to maximize the public interest or common weal. In undertaking that enterprise, legislators are expected to model civic virtue through self-sacrifice and avoidance of self-interest.

However, for Madison, the size and the scale of the new nation were critical to what he saw as Congress's ability to realize this vision of legislative deliberation. Indeed, he was often skeptical about the ability of state legislatures to replicate this vision. Nevertheless, his vision generally caught on, and today state legislatures are also routinely (if inaccurately) conceived of in republican terms.

In part, the continuing strength of the republican conception of legislatures reflects the influence of the "Legal Process" school of thought, developed in the mid-twentieth century largely by Harvard Law Professors Henry Hart & Albert Sacks. *See* HART AND SACKS' THE LEGAL PROCESS: BASIC PROBLEMS IN THE MAKING AND APPLICATION OF LAW (William N. Eskridge Jr. & Philip P. Frickey eds., 1994). Writing at a time when the administrative state was just blossoming into its modern complexity, Hart and Sacks argued that the function of elected representatives is to take part in a legislative process that is open, informed, and deliberative, in order to be able to enact rules or principles for the good of society. This focus on both the public good and the value of the deliberative process continues to echo in many descriptions of the legislature's role, as well as to shape various interpretive theories, as discussed in Chapter 8.

3. CRITICAL THEORIES

In contrast to the preceding accounts of the legislature, some observers have eschewed efforts to defend any normative conception of the legislative process, and instead have offered descriptive accounts that are deeply cynical or pessimistic. On these accounts, the institutions of representative democracy function to secure a privileged position and status for some subset of society, merely offering lip service to ideals of full democratic participation and class mobility for all citizens, while actually doing little to deliver on those ideals.

Some versions of these critical accounts of the legislative process took root in the thinking of a number of eminent legal scholars in the early twentieth century. Building on the work of late-nineteenth-century thinkers such as Oliver Wendell Holmes, these Legal Realists rejected what they saw as legal positivism's overly-formalistic or scientific attribution to the legal system of logic, order, and idealized free-market relations, and instead characterized law as consisting essentially of the raw exercise of judicial and political power. For the Legal Realists, both the economic marketplace and the marketplace of ideas operated as a melee of individuals, groups, and institutions struggling to create value for themselves through whatever levers of power they could bring to bear.

Critical perspectives intensified with the emergence of the Critical Legal Studies (CLS) movement in the late 1970s. Drawing primary strength from individuals recently involved in the civil rights and anti-war struggles, the CLS movement characterized the quest for political and legal dominance as slanted in favor of the particular social stratum of those already in power. CLS thinkers viewed the law not as a democratic creation applied in particular cases via impartial legal reasoning, but as the embodiment of a preexisting hegemony of privileged social elites, structured and deployed to preserve that social preeminence.

Different subsets of this view, such as Critical Race Studies and Critical Gender Studies, have focused on particular aspects of the perceived power imbalance. One aspiration of CLS scholarship is to bring to light previously unnoticed or ignored power dynamics in order to prompt scrutiny and correction in the open forum of public discourse, scrutiny that in theory could provoke counter-hegemonic ways of understanding and interpreting the meanings of legal text such as the statutes and regulations discussed in more detail in Part II. *See, e.g.*, *The Case of the Speluncean Explorers: Contemporary Proceedings*, 61 GEO. WASH. U. L. REV. 1754 (1993).

* * *

As these competing visions suggest, representative democracy is complex. Furthermore, the complexity of the interactions between the many competing interests can make the practice of politics quite different from its theory.

C. PERSPECTIVES ON THE OPERATION OF THE ADMINISTRATIVE STATE

In addition to the varying normative and descriptive conceptions of the role of the legislator discussed in section A above, and the varying normative and descriptive conceptions of the purpose and function of the legislature described in section B above, several descriptive perspectives on how legislatures and agencies actually operate can provide additional insight into the modern administrative state. This section summarizes three of these perspectives. They are by no means mutually incompatible; rather, each simply focuses on different characteristics of the legislative and regulatory processes. These characteristics include: (1) the many procedural steps that lawmaking must surmount; (2) the specific ways in which different interests negotiate and bargain in legislative and administrative settings, in light of these procedural obstacles; and (3) the relationships between the several distinctive institutions where this negotiation and bargaining occurs because of their role in some aspect of the lawmaking process.

1. LAWMAKING PROCEDURES AS HURDLES TO OVERCOME

One helpful perspective on the legislative and regulatory processes of both the federal and state governments is to consider the impact of the numerous required procedures that make it difficult to enact new laws and regulations. For instance, at the legislative level, these procedures include a legislature's internal rules concerning such matters as: how proposed legislation may be introduced; what authority legislative committees have to alter pending bills; when legislators may speak on a bill; how a legislative session can be delayed or manipulated; when and how voting occurs; and, in the U.S. Senate, the filibuster. These procedures also include the constitutional requirements of bicameralism and presentment, mentioned in Chapter 1 above. Agencies similarly have a set of often-complex requirements that govern their rulemaking procedures.

These required legislative procedures are discussed further in Chapter 5 below, while agency rulemaking procedures are described in Chapter 6 below. For now, it is sufficient to note that these requirements routinely function as obstacles or hurdles to the enactment of new laws and regulations. Recognition of this fact can highlight the many ways in which influence can be brought to bear on legislative and regulatory outcomes. In particular, these hurdles can have dramatic effects on how the lawmaking agendas are controlled and who controls them.

In addition, although these requirements can contribute to the problem of legislative gridlock or dysfunction, they also can have a salutary impact on the lawmaking process, depending on how they are used. It is worth considering here two justifications for the existence of these obstacles to lawmaking. One is tied to ideals of republican deliberation, the other to classical liberalism's preference for limited government.

From a republican perspective, the many procedural steps that can slow lawmaking to a crawl can be favorably viewed as mechanisms designed to ensure that the legislative process includes sufficient opportunities for meaningful deliberation. At least as a theoretical matter, each of these hurdles can function in quite different ways, thereby providing opportunities for various types of deliberation and input and reducing the ability of some narrow parochial interest to control the process. However, there is a rich empirical literature about how interest groups may, in practice, still be able to manipulate the complex legislative processes for their own benefit. Nonetheless, from a republican perspective, the complexity of the legislative process is often defended on the basis that absent its many hurdles, the risk is too great that legislatures will enact ill-considered laws or laws that fail to serve the greater good.

At the administrative agency level, hurdles in the processes of creating regulations (as will be discussed in Chapter 6) are also important. They not only may serve the same deliberation-enhancing purposes noted above, but also may provide safeguards against the misuse of delegated lawmaking authority. Thus, procedural constraints on administrative action in part respond to the fact that administrative officials, compared to legislators, have less democratic accountability for their duties. Additionally, a somewhat cumbersome rulemaking process arguably permits and even encourages greater consideration of the connection between proposed rules and authorizing statutes. If rulemaking processes were more streamlined, the argument runs, agencies might more readily undertake activities beyond their proper scope.

From a classical liberal perspective, in contrast, the value of legislative hurdles comes not by promoting deliberation, but instead by making it more difficult to pass new laws. Because liberalism anticipates that laws in general will tend to constrain liberty, it views with disfavor a legislative process that encourages or facilitates easy lawmaking. Instead, lawmaking should be cautious, requiring as many different actors as possible to agree to a new law, after multiple opportunities to contest its benefits.

From this perspective, legislative gridlock is not necessarily undesirable. Rather, it is an indication that sufficient consensus for new law does not exist. However, some empirical work has suggested that the procedural obstacles built into the legislative process can prevent legislators from acknowledging or even recognizing that a public consensus does exist, which the legislators themselves simply do not share. This disconnect between the public and the institutions of representative government is especially relevant to the legislator-as-agent view, as it reflects that elected representatives either are not honoring, or are actually unaware of, their constituents' preferences.

2. GOVERNMENT AS THE LOCUS OF INTEREST GROUP BARGAINING

A second perspective on the processes of representative government focuses on the wide array of interest groups that are active in legislative bargaining and agency rulemaking. In all fifty states and Congress, thousands of these interests have some formal recognition of their participation because of their status as registered lobbyists. Many other groups also take advantage of their First Amendment rights to petition government without registering as lobbyists.

Precisely because of the impact of these organized interests, a number of efforts to regulate their lobbying activities have occurred over the years, as discussed in greater depth in Chapter 4 below. For now, it is important to note that these interest groups can have enormous impact, partly because of the many hurdles that exist in the lawmaking process that give these groups additional opportunities to advance their position. Accordingly, an awareness of the various activities of these interest groups at critical stages of the process can often help reveal and clarify what is occurring in legislatures, as well as in agencies.

Several questions relevant to the interest group perspective include: what groups have formed, and why; who are their members; how do these groups gain access and create influence; how important is it that they be able to raise and spend money; and what interests are *not* well-represented, and why. Answers to these questions, even if incomplete or approximate, provide a vantage point for viewing the legislative process as a forum for these groups to interact with each other.

Attentiveness to interest group influence can be fruitful on either a republican or classical liberal conception of the legislature. On a republican conception, interest group participation bears careful study in order to determine the extent to which interest groups contribute to or undermine robust deliberation in promotion of the public good. Meanwhile, on a classical liberal conception, precisely because the clash of interest groups in a marketplace of ideas is a defining feature of the legislative process, interest group participation therefore bears close study in order to evaluate the extent to which this marketplace is operating fairly and efficiently.

From the interest group perspective, the legislature sometimes is seen as merely a forum in which the government facilitates deal-making between conflicting private interests. Once the bargaining is completed, the resulting legislation then can be understood as government's endorsement or ratification of whatever deal the parties have negotiated among themselves. Whether the public at large is well served on this view, however, may depend on whether a sufficiently representative and diverse range of interest groups has participated, and whether the process provided all groups an effective opportunity to voice their opinion.

In the latter twentieth century, Public Choice Theory appeared on the scene as another especially influential approach to the study of interest group influence on the legislative process. This often controversial theory examines legislative behavior from a market perspective, asking what are the incentives associated with various legislative proposals, or in other words what are the benefits and burdens that will accrue to those participating in the legislative process? Chart 1 (p. 45 above) again provides one schematic for categorizing the burdens and benefits of a range of legislative issues. Public Choice Theory views the legislative process as a political market, with interest groups demanding for themselves a good or service—namely a particular legislative action (or inaction)—which legislators in turn will supply based on their evaluation of what to them is their "best offer." The idea of the best offer is not necessarily an explicit quid-pro-quo arrangement, but instead is a prediction or assumption about the benefits that a legislator can expect to enjoy, particularly in the form of voter support and campaign contributions, depending on the legislator's choice of action.

Public Choice Theory then posits that, because legislators are motivated primarily by a desire to be re-elected, rather than by the public interest, they will evaluate their best offer in terms of which group(s) will most assist their re-election. Although re-election of course ultimately depends upon garnering the most votes, in the Public Choice model legislators determine what legislative positions or actions to take based on their assessment of the amount of campaign support—financial assistance in particular—that these positions are likely to generate.

3. THE IMPACT OF INSTITUTIONAL DYNAMICS ON LAWMAKING

A third perspective on the processes of representative government examines the relationships between at least five distinct institutions of American government, at both the federal and state levels, that play important and interdependent roles in the shaping of statutory law and its implementing regulations. These institutions include: (1) & (2) each of a legislature's two chambers (except in Nebraska, whose state legislature is unicameral); (3) the President or Governor, as head of the executive branch; (4) independent agencies or departments and agencies of the executive branch; and (5) the judicial branch. On occasion, multiple agencies can be involved in the same issue, or institutions at both the state and federal levels may sometimes be involved in a single issue (as, for example, when states had to decide whether to accept federal funds to expand their Medicaid programs under the Affordable Care Act, after the Supreme Court in *National Federation of Independent Business v. Sebelius*, 567 U.S. ___, 132 S. Ct. 2566 (2012), invalidated the provision of the Act that would have mandated this expansion). At the state level, in those states with a referendum or initiative process, the public at large can function as yet another institutional actor.

Though each of these institutional actors has an independent role to play, each also is keenly aware of how the other actors are likely to fulfill their respective roles. For instance, in the 2013 case of *Shelby County v. Holder*, 570 U.S. ___, 133 S. Ct. 1236 (2013), the U.S. Supreme Court struck down as outdated the provision in section 4 of the Voting Rights Act of 1964 that specified which state and local jurisdictions were required, under section 5 of the Act, to obtain federal pre-approval of any changes to their electoral processes. In doing so, the Court invited Congress to enact a new and up-to-date "coverage formula" to replace section 4. Yet the Court was acutely aware that the current Congress, for political reasons, was almost certainly not going to do so. By anticipating the congressional non-response, the Court therefore could expect that its decision would effectively nullify section 5 of the Act as well.

In contrast, when the Ohio Supreme Court repeatedly struck down Ohio's school funding statute, first in 1997, and again in 2000, the court not only invited but also expected the state legislature to enact a different school funding statute. *See DeRolph v. Ohio*, 78 Ohio St. 3d 193 (1997); *DeRolph v. Ohio*, 89 Ohio St. 3d 1 (2000). Yet in 2002, when the Ohio court remained unsatisfied with the state legislature's response and for the third time invalidated the school funding mechanism, it no longer truly expected a meaningful legislative response, even though it nominally invited the legislature to revisit the issue again. *See DeRolph v. Ohio*, 97 Ohio St. 3d 434 (2002). This time, because of an ensuing judicial election, the composition of the court was about to change, and the legislature could be expected effectively to ignore the court's decision in anticipation that the new court would no longer have a majority willing to continue what had become a divisive inter-branch conflict.

Courts are not the only institutions that may anticipate the reactions of other participants in the legislative process. In 2015, for example, President Obama at first insisted forcefully that he would veto any congressional measure that required his administration to seek congressional approval of the nuclear deal it was seeking to reach with Iran. But when a particular bill requiring such approval began to attract strong bipartisan support, the President retreated from the veto threat.

At first, the simple fact that independent democratic institutions can often be attentive to and even anticipate each other may seem neither surprising nor very interesting. Yet an understanding of these institutional dynamics can be especially important when examining how agencies respond to legislative authorization and direction, as well as in considering just what it is that Congress or a state legislature may have expected that an agency would do in furtherance of a legislative mandate. An appreciation of institutional dynamics also can have a meaningful effect in some judicial evaluations of questions of statutory interpretation.

Furthermore, these institutional dynamics also become more interesting under circumstances that suggest institutions are engaging in strategic behavior. Drawing on game theory, "positive political theorists" seek to develop and test models of precisely this type of strategic institutional behavior, and to determine both the background circumstances and the strategic choices that will give a particular institution the upper hand. But even without a formal political theory with which to analyze this conduct, it can be instructive to consider whether (and when) key institutions may be engaging in this behavior.

For instance, for years the Food and Drug Administration assumed that it lacked authority to regulate tobacco products, despite text in its authorizing statute that could easily be read to place nicotine within the scope of the FDA's jurisdiction over "drugs." Meanwhile, a strong tobacco lobby prevented Congress from amending the statute. But in 1996, with the support of President Clinton and sensing that the tobacco lobby, despite its power, would be unable to persuade Congress to override the action, the FDA decided to regulate cigarettes. In the ensuing legal battle, the Supreme Court invalidated the FDA's regulation, perhaps also sensing that Congress would be unable to muster the votes necessary to override the Court's decision by passing a new law to re-empower the FDA. *See FDA v. Brown & Williamson Tobacco Corp.*, 529 U.S. 120 (2000). And further demonstrating how an awareness of institutional dynamics can affect the modern administrative state, the Court's opinion invalidating the FDA's tobacco regulation relied heavily on the Court's own inferences concerning the long history of interactions between Congress and the FDA.

Issues like the one addressed in the tobacco case also raise important questions about institutional competence in the modern administrative state. What is it that government agencies are best suited to do? When is it that courts are well-positioned to override agency action? How much should the legislature be able to delegate to the experts who staff the agencies? Where are political pressures the greatest? Should political pressures be excluded from some stages of the process? Should they be taken into account in resolving interpretive issues? These and other questions deserve continuing reflection as part of the study of legislation and regulation.

CHAPTER 3

ELECTORAL STRUCTURES, OR HOW AMERICAN LEGISLATURES ARE POPULATED

Different theories of representation might counsel different methods of selecting legislative representatives. Were the primary object to be the creation of a descriptive microcosm of the society at large, then a selection mechanism closer to mandatory jury duty might work better than elections. Or a system of proportional representation, like that used in many other democracies, might be preferable to the single-member districts that dominate American legislatures. So the fact that all fifty state legislatures and Congress instead rely on winner-take-all elections in single-member districts to select their members therefore suggests something, at least implicitly, about the principal role that these representatives are expected to play.

Nevertheless, many details concerning how to structure legislative elections remain open for debate, depending in part on the underlying representational goals. This chapter considers a number of the essential legal rules and principles that determine who serves in the legislatures. These include some relatively fixed requirements, such as the eligibility criteria specified in the U.S. Constitution and state constitutions; evolving legal principles and political practices that determine how legislative district boundaries are drawn; and the frequently changing rules and principles of state law (as affected by an overlay of federal constitutional and statutory law) that determine how elections are conducted. The chapter concludes with a consideration of legislative term limits. Many of these topics also are discussed in much greater detail in DANIEL P. TOKAJI, ELECTION LAW IN A NUTSHELL (2d. ed. 2016).

A. QUALIFICATIONS TO SERVE AS LEGISLATORS

For Congress, the U.S. Constitution specifies a few basic eligibility requirements necessary to serve in either the Senate or the House, namely age, U.S. citizenship, and state residency. All state constitutions similarly specify some comparable eligibility requirements.

1. ELIGIBILITY TO SERVE IN CONGRESS

With respect to members of the U.S. House of Representatives, Article I, Section 2 of the U.S. Constitution provides that "No Person shall be a Representative who shall not have attained to the Age of twenty five Years, and been seven Years a Citizen of the United States, and who shall not, when elected, be an Inhabitant of that State in which he shall be chosen." Meanwhile, for members of the U.S. Senate, Article I, Section 3 provides that "No Person shall be a Senator who shall not have attained to the Age of thirty Years, and been nine Years a Citizen of the United States, and who shall not, when elected, be an Inhabitant of that State for which he shall be chosen."

These basic requirements are straightforward and rarely controversial. However, in the early years, three Senators served despite being under thirty years of age, beginning in 1806 with Henry Clay, whose age apparently went unnoticed. Much more recently, both Rush Holt in 1934 and Joseph Biden in 1972 were each elected to the U.S. Senate before age thirty, but each turned thirty before being sworn in.

More controversy has surrounded the question of whether additional eligibility requirements beyond age, citizenship, and state residency could be imposed on Members of Congress. For instance, on occasion states have contemplated requiring that a representative be a registered voter, or not be a convicted felon, or not have served previously in Congress for more than a limited number of years or terms. But the U.S. Supreme Court has construed the provisions of Sections 2 and 3 of Article I to be the exclusive requirements for service in Congress, rejecting the argument that the two constitutional provisions merely establish a threshold of minimum criteria, to which states might add their own additional requirements. For instance, this doctrinal understanding was the basis for the Supreme Court's invalidation of state efforts to prevent any one individual from serving more than a limited number of terms in Congress, discussed further in section D below. *See U.S. Term Limits v. Thornton*, 514 U.S. 779 (1995).

2. ELIGIBILITY TO SERVE IN STATE LEGISLATURES

Many state constitutions imitate the U.S. Constitution in requiring that their state legislators be of a specified age, be U.S. Citizens, and be state residents. However, some omit an age requirement, or replace it with a requirement that a state legislator be a registered voter, a condition that implicitly includes an age restriction. As an additional requirement, for which there is no parallel for members of Congress, most states further require that their state legislators reside in the district that each represents. Meanwhile, a number of states disqualify from state legislative service anyone convicted of a felony, or of some enumerated subset of state or federal crimes.

3. JUDGING MEMBERS' QUALIFICATIONS

When controversies do arise about legislators' eligibility to serve, it is typically the legislative institution itself that has the ultimate responsibility for determining the issue. Article I, Section 5 of the U.S. Constitution makes this clear with respect to Congress: "Each House shall be the Judge of the Elections, Returns, and Qualifications of its own Members . . . ." All state constitutions have an analogous provision. *See* MASON'S MANUAL OF LEGISLATIVE PROCEDURE, sec. 560, ¶¶ 3–4.

Over the years, legislatures have been forced to confront a variety of eligibility questions, occasionally concerning age or citizenship, but mostly concerning state residency. Questions have also arisen concerning whether legislatures can establish additional criteria for serving in a legislature, with courts consistently limiting the enforceable criteria to those specified in the U.S. Constitution or state constitutions. *See* MASON'S MANUAL, sec. 560, ¶ 5.

In one early twenty-first century case, a Kentucky state senator with homes in both Kentucky and

Indiana was seated by the state Senate, but then stripped of her seat when the state Supreme Court concluded that she was not a Kentucky resident. Arguably usurping the state legislature's responsibility to judge the qualifications of its own members, the state court held that the senator had not been eligible to be on the ballot in the first place, and hence that her election was void. *See Stephenson v. Woodward*, 182 S.W.3d 162 (Ky. 2005).

The most famous case concerning the eligibility of a member of Congress involved Congressman Adam Clayton Powell Jr., a long-time representative of Harlem embroiled in scandal in the 1960s. He was re-elected in 1968 despite the House having denied him his seat in the prior Congress, after a House investigation concerning his misuse of congressional funds. In *Powell v. McCormack*, 395 U.S. 486 (1969), the U.S. Supreme Court concluded that the House had lacked cause to exclude him from taking his seat (though in theory it could subsequently have expelled him completely, had it mustered the required two-thirds vote, as described in subsection 4.b below). The Court concluded that the only permissible bases for exclusion were failures to satisfy the age, citizenship, or residency requirements of the Qualifications Clause of Article I, requirements that Powell admittedly met. The Court invoked the principle that the public should have as much latitude as possible in determining their representatives, quoting Hamilton's expression "that the people should choose whom they please to govern them." 2 ELLIOT'S DEBATES 257. The Court reiterated this principle 25 years later when it invalidated state efforts to limit the number of terms that any one person could serve in Congress, concluding that these congressional term limits also unconstitutionally sought to add something else to the Qualifications Clause. *See U.S. Term Limits, Inc. v. Thornton*, 514 U.S. 779 (1995).

4. DISCIPLINE OF LEGISLATORS

As part of maintaining its desired representativeness, each legislature not only has the final authority to evaluate the elections and qualifications of its own members, but also has the responsibility to police its members, and when necessary to expel or otherwise discipline them.

a. Purpose of Legislative Discipline

Article I, Section 5 of the U.S. Constitution provides that each House of Congress may "punish its Members for disorderly Behaviour," and, upon the concurrence of two-thirds of its members, expel another member. Each chamber may proceed against its own members independently, without needing the concurrence of the other body. State legislatures have similar authority. On its face, this power to discipline individual legislators exists to maintain order, control, and decorum within the legislature. In addition, this power assists each legislative body to protect its institutional integrity, to foster civility among its members, and to promote public acceptance of its work.

The disciplinary power exists in addition to any criminal or civil proceedings that may be brought against an individual legislator for wrongdoing, and indeed is intended not primarily to punish individuals but to protect the legislative institution. However, in circumstances in which the legislative privilege, discussed in section A.10 of Chapter 5 below, may shield a legislator from civil or criminal punishment for legislative misconduct, the authority that each chamber has to discipline its own members may provide an appropriate alternative means for punishing such misconduct.

Each chamber is entitled to determine for itself what conduct amounts to "disorderly behavior" or is worthy of expulsion. Violations of civil or criminal law can certainly provide cause for legislative discipline, but so too can serious breaches of a chamber's own internal rules, privileges, or customs of decorum, as well as anything that brings discredit to the legislature. Indeed, even if not explicitly spelled out, some power to discipline, perhaps short of expulsion, would be inherent in a legislative body's authority to establish its own internal rules. *See* MASON'S MANUAL, sec. 562, ¶¶ 1–3.

b. Types of Legislative Discipline

Legislative discipline can take a variety of forms, from mild reprimands or modest fines, to stern censures and deprivations of legislative prerogatives, to expulsion from the body. Here too, each legislative chamber may determine for itself on a case-by-case basis, usually by simple majority except in the case of expulsion, what sanctions are appropriate for what misconduct. A legislative body often delegates the initial investigation of potential wrongdoing to its ethics or standards committee, which in some cases may issue its own letter of admonishment or other more informal statement of disapproval.

Expulsions from the legislature have been rare, and in Congress have been limited to circumstances of disloyalty or treason (all but one of them during the Civil War era), or of serious criminal offense. However, the threat of expulsion has often led members to resign, while other members facing potential expulsion have meanwhile lost their re-election bids. And although Congress has used its expulsion power only very cautiously, the Supreme Court has made clear that each House is free to expel a member for any conduct it deems "inconsistent with the trust and duty of a member," whether or not the conduct was "committed in his official character, [or] during the session of Congress, [or] at the seat of government." *In re Chapman*, 166 U.S. 661, 669–670 (1897). The most important limit on expulsions from Congress is that Article I, Section 5 requires a two-thirds vote, rather than a simple majority.

Short of expulsion, a legislative body is free to fashion other forms of discipline to suit its will. In Congress, "censure" typically involves adoption of a resolution disapproving a member's conduct, read aloud while the sanctioned member stands in "the well" (the central focal point) of the chamber. "Reprimand" is generally a lesser discipline, in which the resolution of disapproval is not read aloud. But either form of official criticism can cause personal or political embarrassment. Each may also be accompanied by the revocation of certain legislative privileges, including committee positions, seniority status, or leadership roles. Fines may also be imposed, but typically are reserved for when the underlying misconduct involved some financial impropriety or gain. Censures and reprimands, meanwhile, have often been imposed for breaches of decorum or obvious disrespect of other members of the legislature, as well as for a variety of financial improprieties or abuses of office.

For further examples and explanations of congressional discipline, see Jack Maskell, *Expulsion, Censure, Reprimand, and Fine: Legislative Discipline in the House of Representatives*, CRS Report for Congress (May 2, 2013); ANNE M. BUTLER & WENDY WOLFF, UNITED STATES SENATE ELECTION, EXPULSION, AND CENSURE CASES, 1793–1990. S. Doc. 103–33 (1995).

B. DRAWING (AND REDRAWING) LEGISLATIVE DISTRICTS

Most American legislators are elected to serve a specific geographic area, or district. Deciding how to construct these districts turns out to be one of the most critical steps in structuring the representative process. In all but about a half-dozen states, the state legislature controls the districting process, for both state legislative districts as well as for the state's congressional districts. Among critics, a frequent refrain is that these districting processes turn Hamilton's famous expression inside out, not allowing "the people [to] choose whom they please to govern them," but instead allowing elected representatives to choose whom it is they please to govern. The question of the extent to which this claim is true, including the few federal constraints on the redistricting process and related state efforts to refine the process, is the focus of this section.

1. THE GROWTH OF GERRYMANDERING

To some extent, the drawing of political district boundaries has always been subject to manipulation to advance the interests of a particular party or group. This so-called "gerrymandering" of districts was occurring well before Massachusetts Governor Elbridge Gerry, in 1812, approved the drawing of the salamander-like state senate district from which the term derives. For instance, in 1788, Virginia Governor Patrick Henry orchestrated the drawing of a district map that would force James Madison to run against James Monroe for a seat in Congress. *See* GEORGE A. BILLIAS, ELBRIDGE GERRY: FOUNDING FATHER AND REPUBLICAN STATESMAN 316–17 (1976).

Yet in the past fifty years in particular, the manipulation of legislative districts has exploded dramatically. This development can be traced primarily to two independent factors: the recognition of the constitutional principle of one-person, one-vote; and the technological progress that has facilitated both highly accurate predictions of political behavior and the fine-tuning of complex maps.

a. The Impact of the One-Person, One-Vote Requirement

Political districting practices underwent a seismic shift after 1962 as a result of the Supreme Court's decision in *Baker v. Carr*, 369 U.S. 186 (1962). Perhaps best known by most lawyers for its enunciation of the political question doctrine (describing when courts should decline to intervene in what are strictly "political" rather than "legal" questions), *Baker v. Carr* is also important for its holding that state decisions about how to draw legislative districts are not political questions, but are subject to federal court review, including Equal Protection scrutiny under the Fourteenth Amendment.

Two years later, in *Reynolds v. Sims*, 377 U.S. 533 (1964), the Court applied an Equal Protection analysis to require all state legislative districts within a given state to be drawn so as to contain substantially equal numbers of constituents (according to the most recent census). Prior to this decision, legislative districts were often organized along county lines or other natural boundaries, without regard to population size. But this practice inevitably meant that voters in urban districts with large populations were underrepresented compared to voters in sparsely populated rural districts. Indeed, in the Alabama state legislative districts under review in *Reynolds v. Sims*, the largest Senate district had 41 times the population of the smallest Senate district, vastly diluting the comparative voting strength of each individual voter in the larger district.

In *Reynolds*, the Court ruled that under the Equal Protection Clause, each person's vote had to have equal power in electing political leaders, a ruling that necessitated drawing state legislative districts with equal populations. The same year, the Court also held in *Wesberry v. Sanders*, 376 U.S. 1 (1964), that under Article I, Section 2, a similar one-person, one-vote principle applied to congressional districts. Accordingly, all congressional districts within a given state also must have equal populations, so that "as nearly as is practicable, one [person's] vote in a congressional election is to be worth as much as another's." *Id.* at 7–8.

As a result, after each decennial census since 1970, every state has had to redraw its state legislative districts, as well as its congressional districts, so that they contain roughly equal populations (as measured against demographic changes that have occurred since the previous census). The upshot, in addition to creating districts that conform to the one-person, one-vote principle, is an added opportunity for partisan manipulation in any state whose redistricting processes are controlled by elected officials or their appointees. Because population must be evenly divided, previous customs of keeping counties, communities, or even neighborhoods together now hold much less sway. Instead, the operative practice is to consider even the tiniest subdivisions of census tracts independently, and then arrange them together into whatever equally populated configurations will produce the politically most advantageous districts for those who control the mapmaking.

One question left unresolved by the *Baker v. Carr* line of cases is whether the population of legislative districts is properly measured in terms of (1) all residents of the district, (2) only U.S. citizens (a smaller class), or (3) only those eligible to vote (a yet smaller class). In other words, this is an issue of whether the one-person, one-vote principle is a principle of *representational equality* of some kind, or instead is one of *electoral equality*. In *Burns v. Richardson*, 384 U.S. 73 (1966), the Supreme Court allowed individual states to choose what type of measure to use for state legislative districts, as long as no significant gap existed between the various alternatives. Since then, most jurisdictions have used the representational equality measure of total resident population.

In 2016, the U.S. Supreme Court decided *Evenwel v. Abbott,* ___ U.S. ___, 136 S. Ct. 1120 (2016), a case that raised anew the question of whether the one-person, one-vote principle requires a particular type of population measure for state legislative districts. The plaintiffs argued that jurisprudential developments concerning the right to vote in the preceding fifty years now required states to employ the electoral equality measure of eligible voter population, rather than the representational equality measure of total population. Using an eligible-voter basis, rather than a total resident basis, would have enhanced the comparative voting strength of those districts with relatively fewer non-citizen residents than other districts, typically advantaging rural districts over urban districts (where noncitizens are concentrated). In an 8–0 opinion, however, the Supreme Court concluded that states retain the latitude to draw their legislative districts based on total population if they wish.

b. The Impact of Technology

The objective of producing the most politically advantageous districts for the party in power (or for incumbents) has been assisted by improvements in technology. Since the advent of the one-person, one-vote requirement in the 1960s, five decennial censuses, and thus five redistricting cycles, have occurred. With each decade, the individuals and institutions responsible for drawing the district maps have grown more sophisticated, relying on rapidly expanding amounts of data concerning political behavior, deploying increasingly powerful computers and software to analyze this data, and hiring more consultants to help program the software and predict the likely electoral results of a variety of possible maps. A process that once occurred laboriously, with pencils and a precinct map spread out across a table, now occurs mostly with sophisticated computer software, and with ample time and opportunity for tinkering to maximize partisan advantage.

In states that use a partisan redistricting process, there is little doubt that the resulting maps are exceptionally well-tuned for accomplishing their intended purposes. But there are several distinct purposes for which the maps may be drawn. The most obvious strategy is the partisan gerrymander, which seeks to maximize the number of districts likely to be won by the political party making the maps. Some element of strategic risk-taking inheres in this type of mapmaking, as the more districts a political party wishes to control, the more thinly it must distribute its supporters among these districts. And when supporters are spread thinly across more districts, the resulting districts become less safe, or in other words more vulnerable to a take-over by the opposing party as a result of even just a tiny change in party loyalties. The alternative—drawing more districts that are comfortably "safe"—can produce longer-term entrenchments, though only over a smaller proportion of the total districts. But in either case, it is substantially true that elected representatives (or their loyalists) are choosing their voters, rather than vice-versa.

A second purpose for which district boundaries can be drawn is to protect the electoral prospects of incumbent office holders. In these "bipartisan" or "sweetheart" gerrymanders, the incumbent representatives, or their proxies who control the redistricting process, create districts that are "safe" for existing members on both sides of the aisle, rather than just for one particular party. These districting plans are an even better example of the representatives choosing their voters, as the benefits of finely manipulating the district boundaries accrue not just to the party in power, but to many or most of the incumbent representatives.

A third purpose can be to group voters together in order to advantage or disadvantage those with certain demographic characteristics (other than political party *per se*). The only such characteristic that in fact receives much attention in contemporary districting practices is race or ethnicity. In the landmark case of *Gomillion v. Lightfoot*, 364 U.S. 339 (1960), the U.S. Supreme Court invalidated a local gerrymander consisting of a 28-sided map drawn deliberately to exclude almost all black voters from the city limits of Tuskegee, Alabama. The Court relied on the Fifteenth Amendment's guarantee that the right to vote shall not be abridged on account of race. Since then, a variety of cases, briefly discussed in the next section, have addressed when and how race can be a factor in drawing political boundaries.

2. FEDERAL CONSTITUTIONAL AND STATUTORY CONSTRAINTS

Since *Gomillion v. Lightfoot*, the Supreme Court has considered a number of cases concerning redistricting practices. These cases have variously raised issues under the Equal Protection Clause of the Fourteenth Amendment, under the Fifteenth Amendment, and under the Voting Rights Act. One set of cases concerns the use of race in drawing districts, while another set of cases concerns the use of party. These cases are only briefly summarized here; for a fuller treatment, see DANIEL P. TOKAJI, ELECTION LAW IN A NUTSHELL (2d. ed. 2016).

Other than the relatively weak legal constraints that emerge from these cases, and the one-person, one-vote requirement discussed above, almost no other federal law constrains the way in which political districts are drawn. The one additional federal requirement is the statute that requires congressional districts to be single-member districts. *See* 2 U.S.C. § 2c.

a. Limits on the Use of Race in Drawing Political Districts

The issue of the extent to which race can be a factor in drawing political districts must be understood not only in light of the Fourteenth Amendment's guarantee of equal protection and the Fifteenth Amendment's guarantee that voting rights will not be denied or abridged on account of race, but also in light of related provisions of sections 2 and 5 of the Voting Rights Act (VRA). Even in summary form, the history of the VRA offers an important example of the interplay between Congress and the Supreme Court, specifically with respect to the many redistricting measures to come before the Court under this statute.

As initially enacted in 1965, section 2 of the VRA prohibited any voting practice that denied or abridged voting rights "on account of race." This was a prohibition almost identical to that of the Fifteenth Amendment, and in *City of Mobile v. Bolden*, 446 U.S. 55 (1980), the Supreme Court held that, as with the Fifteenth Amendment, proof of an intent to discriminate on the basis of race was required to establish a violation of section 2. However, Congress quickly responded with a significant amendment to the Act, under which a voting practice that "*results* in the denial or abridgement" of voting rights, as measured by the "totality of circumstances," was a violation of section 2 of the Act. *See* Pub. L. No. 97–205, 96 Stat. 131 (1982) (emphasis added).

The new results-based standard of section 2 of the VRA was quickly invoked in cases claiming that the effect of a particular redistricting scheme was to "dilute" the voting strength of a group of minority voters. These were claims not that the weight of any particular voter's individual vote counted any less than any other voter's, but rather that a minority group's ability effectively to participate *as a group*, measured primarily in terms of its ability to elect candidates of its choice, was denied or abridged by the way in which members of that group of voters were distributed across districts.

In *Thornburg v. Gingles*, 478 U.S. 30 (1986), the Court specified three pre-conditions for a valid vote-dilution claim under section 2 of the Voting Rights Act:

(1) the minority group bringing the claim must be "sufficiently large and geographically compact to constitute a majority in a single-member district";

(2) the minority group must be "politically cohesive"; and

(3) the majority group must vote "sufficiently as a bloc to enable it . . . usually to defeat the minority's preferred candidate."

The issue in *Gingles* involved whether a multi-member or "at-large" representational scheme (in which voters are electing all the members of a representative body collectively, rather than being divided into districts) had the effect of diluting the ability of African-American voters to elect a representative of their choice. But the *Gingles* analysis also has been applied to challenges to single-member districting plans under section 2 of the VRA. *See, e.g., LULAC v. Perry*, 548 U.S. 399 (2006); *Johnson v. DeGrandy*, 512 U.S. 997 (1994).

Section 2 is not the only provision of the Voting Rights Act that has operated as an important constraint on the drawing of legislative districts. Until its neutralization in *Shelby County v. Holder*, 570 U.S. ___, 133 S. Ct. 2612 (2013), section 5 also had shaped many state redistricting practices. Section 5 requires certain covered jurisdictions, as specifically identified in section 4, to obtain advance approval or "pre-clearance" from either the U.S. Attorney General or the federal district court in Washington, D.C., before any new voting procedures—including new districting maps—can take effect. Section 5 provides that pre-clearance should be given only if the proposed new procedure "neither has the purpose nor will have the effect of denying or abridging the right to vote on account of race or color." This requirement is understood to mean that a new voting process or requirement must not put voters in a worse position than before the change.

Since the 1970 census, the Department of Justice has used this "non-retrogression" standard to review numerous redistricting plans of covered jurisdictions (which have usually preferred to seek pre-clearance from the Department of Justice rather than from federal district court). These covered jurisdictions are states and localities that Congress in 1965 deemed to have a history of voting discrimination and therefore required to bear the additional burden of obtaining federal pre-clearance. The result has been that redistricting plans in each of these covered jurisdictions often have had to take race into account—sometimes in response to a Department of Justice demand, other times to head off a potential Department of Justice objection—in order to ensure that the effect of a new map was not to dilute the voting strength of a minority group.

But the 2013 *Shelby County* decision held that the coverage formula of section 4, which specified the covered jurisdictions, was out-of-date, a ruling that effectively nullified the pre-clearance requirement of section 5. Unless and until Congress enacts an updated coverage formula, and justifies anew to the Court's satisfaction why the formula includes whatever jurisdictions it incorporates, section 5 no longer has any teeth. Nevertheless, an awareness of this section's history is essential to an understanding of an important line of Supreme Court cases concerning the permissible role of race in drawing political districts.

In the first several decades after *Gomillion* and the enactment of the Voting Rights Act of 1965, federal courts allowed states to consider racial composition when drawing political districts for the purpose of creating districts comprised of a majority of citizens belonging to an ethnic or racial minority group ("majority-minority districts"), or otherwise protecting the voting rights of these minorities. *See United Jewish Organizations, Inc. v. Carey*, 430 U.S. 144 (1977). But beginning with *Shaw v. Reno*, 509 U.S. 630 (1993), the Supreme Court became increasingly wary of redistricting done on the basis of race, even when done to avoid retrogression in compliance with VRA section 5.

Shaw and its progeny made clear that federal courts would review redistricting plans under a strict scrutiny standard if race had been the "predominant factor" in drawing the districts. Less clear was how to determine whether race was predominant if a redistricting plan had also been influenced by attention to other typical redistricting factors, such as partisan composition, contiguity, compactness, and existing political boundaries (as described further in subsection 3.a below). Also murky was what might amount to a "compelling state interest" sufficient to withstand strict scrutiny analysis. In *Bush v. Vera*, 517 U.S. 952 (1996), the Court made clear that compliance with a Department of Justice pre-clearance request under VRA section 5 was not necessarily a compelling state interest, although in certain circumstances it could amount to one.

The districting scheme at issue in *Shaw* went back to the U.S. Supreme Court four times. In the conclusion to the *Shaw* line of cases, the Court made explicit that redistricting plans in which race had been a consideration nonetheless would escape strict scrutiny as long as the state could show that political considerations, not race, had predominated. *See Easley v. Cromartie*, 532 U.S. 234 (2001). More recently, in *Alabama Legislative Black Caucus v. Alabama*, 575 U.S. ___, 135 S. Ct. 1257 (2015), the Court concluded that even where the non-retrogression requirement of the Voting Rights Act might provide a compelling state interest for making race a predominant consideration, it did not justify a "mechanical" comparison of the racial composition of the challenged districts.

Thus, as a matter of current federal law, which even the Supreme Court acknowledges is complicated, gerrymandering can take race into account as long as it is not the primary consideration, or it is justified by a compelling interest. Meanwhile, VRA section 5 no longer requires specified jurisdictions to pre-clear new district maps. But under VRA section 2, states still may not construct districts that have the effect of diluting the voting power of a minority racial group. However, determining when minority vote dilution occurs, as well as whether race has been the predominant consideration, remain complex questions that may not always permit easy judicial resolution.

b. Limits on the Use of Party in Drawing Political Districts

For very different reasons, the U.S. Supreme Court also has had a difficult time figuring out what to do with claims that partisan advantage has improperly affected the redistricting process. The difficulty here is the judicial line-drawing problem of determining how much partisan advantage is too much. As the Court wrote in an early case, "we have not . . . attempted the impossible task of extirpating politics from what are the essentially political processes of the sovereign States." *Gaffney v. Cummings*, 412 U.S. 735, 754 (1973). Thus, the Court has long accepted the idea that partisan considerations will inevitably play some role in any redistricting process controlled by partisan actors.

Nevertheless, on multiple occasions the Court has shown genuine concern about the potential for excessively partisan gerrymandering. In *Davis v. Bandemer*, 478 U.S. 109 (1986), a majority of the Court rejected the argument that all claims of partisan gerrymandering were nonjusticiable political questions. But the Court could not agree on what should be required to establish an Equal Protection claim of partisan gerrymandering. The four-justice plurality took the view that for such a claim to succeed, it needed to show both that the intent of the scheme was to disadvantage an identifiable political group, and that the effect was to "consistently degrade" that group's "influence on the political process as a whole."

Two decades later, a narrow majority of the Court in *Vieth v. Jubilerer*, 541 U.S. 267 (2004), again concluded that claims of partisan gerrymandering in theory could be justiciable, but still could not agree on a judicial standard by which to evaluate such claims. A four-justice plurality—Chief Justice Rehnquist and Justices Scalia, O'Connor, and Thomas—took the position that such claims were nonjusticiable political questions. Though not completely sanguine about the problem of partisan gerrymandering, their plurality opinion suggested that the remedy at least for gerrymandered congressional districts was for Congress to define appropriate redistricting processes, using its constitutional power to make rules for conducting congressional elections. *See* U.S. CONST. art. I, sec. 4. Four dissenters—Justices Stevens, Souter, Ginsberg, and Breyer—identified several different possible judicial tests of unconstitutional partisan gerrymandering, but could not agree on one. Finally, Justice Kennedy provided the swing vote, concurring that for the moment he could find no judicially manageable standard for adjudicating these claims, but leaving the door open to the possibility that "a standard might emerge" in a future case. While he observed that excessive partisanship in the drawing of districts could impermissibly "burden[ ] rights of fair and effective representation," he concluded that in the case before the Court, judicial determination of what was excessive risked assuming political rather than legal responsibility. As a result, the Court awaits either the articulation of an acceptable standard, or a change in its own view about the justiciability of claims of partisan gerrymandering.

Meanwhile, a 2016 three-judge district court decision invalidating Wisconsin's state legislative districts has now teed up a potential new case for the Supreme Court to consider. *See Whitford v. Gill*, ___

F. Supp. 2d. ___, 2016 WL 6837229 (W.D. Wisc. 2016). In *Whitford*, the lower court concluded that Wisconsin's 2011 redistricting plan unconstitutionally burdened the representational rights of Democratic voters. The court considered several categories of evidence about both the intent and the effect of the plan in concluding that it rendered the votes of Democratic voters substantially less effective than the votes of Republican voters.

Among other evidence of excessive partisanship in the districting process, the district court decision in *Whitford* relied on the concept of an "efficiency gap." The efficiency gap concept depends on comparing the number of each major party's "wasted" votes across all the districts in a redistricting plan. Wasted votes are the winning party's additional votes in excess of the losing party's total votes. The smaller the difference between each of the two major parties' total "wasted" votes, the more efficient the plan. If the result of a plan is that one party wastes substantially more votes than another party, the plan is inefficient. *See* Nicholas O. Stephanopoulos & Eric M. McGhee, *Partisan Gerrymandering and the Efficiency Gap*, 82 U. CHI. L. REV. 831 (2015).

It remains to be seen whether the Supreme Court will accept the lower court's conclusion in *Whitford* that although some degree of inefficiency and partisan advantage is inevitable, at some point the partisan burden becomes too great to tolerate. Meanwhile, many of those concerned about the impact of gerrymandering on our representative processes continue to focus their efforts on devising alternative methods for drawing legislative districts that constrain the opportunities for partisan manipulation at the state level.

3. STATE CONSTRAINTS ON REDISTRICTING PROCESSES

Although federal law provides relatively few constraints on the ability of states to gerrymander their congressional and state legislative districts, in many instances state law does impose some limits on how districts can be drawn, whether as a matter of state constitutional law or state statutory requirement. Additionally, in response to increasing public concern about the partisan manipulation of legislative districts, several states have taken the redistricting process entirely out of the hands of elected politicians or their appointees and developed alternative processes intended to reduce or eliminate partisanship; many other states continue to consider doing so.

a. Substantive Limits on Legislative Redistricting

Since the advent of the one-person, one-vote requirement, many states have adopted various substantive criteria to guide the way in which their legislative districts are drawn. In some states these criteria are merely hortatory "factors" that legislative mapmakers are urged to consider, but in other states these criteria impose obligations of varying degrees. In most states, the process remains that the state legislature draws the maps, subject to whatever limiting criteria have been adopted. But in other states these limiting criteria act in conjunction with procedural reforms that have taken the districting process out of the legislature's hands.

One factor that is an almost universal requirement is *contiguity*, or that each district be composed of physically adjacent territory. Exceptions usually are allowed for islands, and for districts with existing political subdivisions that are not contiguous (such as a city with an annexed portion physically separated from the rest of the city). The principle of contiguity is largely responsible for the distinctive and unusual shapes of many legislative districts today. In other words, but for an insistence on constructing each district out of contiguous territory, it would be much easier to create equally populated districts without contorted borders.

Another common districting factor is *compactness*, essentially a measure of how tightly concentrated the district's territory is around its central mass. Districts with long narrow spurs of territory stretching away from the center are less compact, while circles and squares are highly compact. One of several possible mathematical methods of assessing compactness is to compare the circumference of a district to its area; the smaller the circumference required to surround a given area, the more compact the district. Compactness is generally understood as a desirable characteristic of political districts, but often is sacrificed to other considerations.

In particular, political *competitiveness*, or producing districts that do not obviously favor one political party (or incumbent) is another potential redistricting factor often seen as desirable. However, competitiveness is a more contested criterion, in part because it frequently requires splitting apart communities that otherwise could serve as relatively compact districts into districts that are less compact, given demographic patterns that often see like-minded voters living near one another. For instance, demographic patterns frequently produce high concentrations of Democratic voters in urban areas, and less concentrated dispersions of Republican voters in suburban and rural areas. Because of this tendency towards partisan clustering, compact districts are therefore not always very competitive.

Representational fairness is a related yet distinct factor. Like competitiveness, it too requires measuring the partisan composition of legislative districts. But rather than seeking to balance the partisan composition of individual districts, it instead involves comparing a state's overall partisan composition with the resulting legislative districts. For instance, a state that casts 50% of its total votes in state legislative races for Republican candidates, and the other 50% of its votes for Democratic candidates, is not representationally fair if, because of how the districts are drawn, the resulting state legislature is 65% Democratic and 35% Republican (not an implausible result of partisan redistricting practices). Instead, representational fairness means that the partisan composition of the representative institution closely approximates the partisan composition of the voters who selected the representatives. (Lack of representational fairness is essentially what bothered the district court in *Whitford v. Gill*, discussed above.) Where representational fairness is an explicit redistricting goal, it too can require deviations from other redistricting considerations.

Of course, the opposite of a competitive district is a district that clearly favors a particular party (or incumbent). Though not usually a limiting factor in redistricting processes, the goal of creating partisan districts also can result in sacrificing compact districts. For instance, the Democratic voters of an urban area can be split apart, not in order to produce competitive districts by evenly balancing them with Republican voters in adjacent suburban and rural areas, but to overwhelm them with a larger number of suburban and rural voters, rendering them politically powerless. Or, depending on who controls the process, urban voters can instead be divided into non-compact districts not to render them powerless, but to spread their concentrated power more effectively across more districts.

Additional redistricting criteria include respecting existing *political boundaries*, respecting *geographical boundaries*, protecting *incumbents*, and protecting *communities of interest*. This last phrase lacks a universally accepted meaning, but when it is included as a redistricting criterion it generally means keeping together a group of citizens already in physical proximity who are defined by some shared cultural, political, social, or economic values and beliefs. Yet another potential criterion is to enhance the representational strength of some minority group, however defined.

Many of these potential redistricting factors do not provide bright lines for evaluating the desirability of a particular legislative map. Thus, questions arise not only of how to measure such factors as compactness or competitiveness or representational fairness, but also of how much compactness or competitiveness or representational fairness is needed. Moreover, answering this latter question also can require specifying a hierarchy of these criteria, including how much of one factor can be sacrificed for another. Many states that use these types of criteria to limit the opportunities for partisan gerrymandering have struggled with these questions.

b. Alternative Redistricting Procedures

Instead of, or in addition to, imposing substantive limits on what a redistricting map must look like, some states have attempted to limit the role of partisanship in legislative districting by creating an alternative procedure that removes the redistricting responsibility from state legislators or other political actors. A half-dozen states now assign the task of drawing congressional and state legislative districts to some form of independent commission, while a smattering of other states have formed advisory or other commissions that may reduce the amount of partisan influence on the redistricting process. For instance, as discussed below, Arizona and California are among the states with independent commissions, using very different models. Meanwhile, Iowa relies on its Legislative Services Agency to advise the legislature about the mapmaking process.

In 2015, some of these alternative state redistricting processes—specifically those adopted through a popular initiative—survived a legal challenge that they contravened the Constitution's Elections Clause, article I, section 4, clause 1. This clause provides that "The Times, Places and Manner of holding Elections for Senators and Representatives shall be prescribed in each State by the Legislature thereof; but the Congress may at any time by Law make or alter such Regulations." Opponents of these alternative redistricting processes argued that taking the redistricting authority away from the state legislature by popular initiative violated the Elections Clause because only a state's legislature can prescribe the process for drawing its congressional districts. But in a 5–4 decision, the U.S. Supreme Court read the phrase "by the Legislature thereof" broadly, holding that in a state with a popular initiative, the people themselves possess lawmaking power coextensive with that of the state legislature, and that their exercise of that power was thus equally legitimate. *Ariz. State Legis. v. Ariz. Indep. Redistricting Comm'n,* 576 U.S. ___, 135 S. Ct. 2652 (2015).

Arizona Independent Redistricting Commission. Ultimately at issue in the 2015 case was the survival of the redistricting mechanism that Arizona voters had adopted by popular initiative in 2000. That mechanism transferred the power to redraw Arizona's congressional districts, as well as its state legislative districts, from the state legislature to a five-member "independent redistricting commission." The five commissioners are drawn from a slate of 25 candidates nominated by the state appellate court appointment commission. From this slate of nominees, the majority leaders of the Arizona House and Senate appoint two members; the minority leaders of the Arizona House and Senate appoint two members; and these four members then choose an independent chairperson, who may not be affiliated with any of the political parties already represented on the commission.

Although the commission's work after the 2000 census was not without some controversy, its work after the 2010 census generated national attention. As Republicans criticized the emerging legislative maps, the Arizona Governor, with the concurrence of two-thirds of the state senate, sought to exercise her authority to remove the commission chair for "gross misconduct in office." The state supreme court rejected this action as unjustified, and the maps eventually became effective.

California Citizens Redistricting Commission. In 2008, California voters, also by popular initiative, created a more complicated mechanism to select a "citizens' commission" with authority to redistrict the two chambers of the state legislature after each census. In 2010, again by initiative, the state's voters assigned to this commission the additional responsibility of redrawing the state's congressional districts. In 2012, an initiative to repeal this commission failed.

The commission consists of fourteen members, selected through a process that begins by accepting applications from the general public. More than 30,000 individuals applied to be on the first commission. From among all applicants that meet specified criteria, a panel of state auditors then selects twenty republicans, twenty democrats, and twenty applicants of neither party and submits these candidates to the state legislature, which then winnows each pool to twelve candidates. The state auditor then randomly draws three republicans, three democrats, and two others, and these eight commissioners then select six more commissioners from the candidates remaining in the pools.

In drawing district boundaries, the commission must do its best to maintain the integrity of existing political boundaries and other communities of interest, and also to adopt compact districts. In order to adopt a map, a supermajority of at least three democrats, three republicans, and three other members of the commission must approve it. The commission's resulting maps are subject to the potential of a public referendum; if the public votes to disapprove a commission map, the California Supreme Court then will appoint a special panel to adopt a new map. After the commission adopted its first set of maps in 2011, a referendum to disapprove the state senate map qualified to be on the ballot in 2012, but a majority of the voters did not vote to disapprove the map.

Iowa Legislative Services Commission. Iowa offers a very different model, in which a nonpartisan commission plays an advisory role to the state legislature, which still retains ultimate authority to draw legislative districts. Since 1990, Iowa has tasked its Legislative Services Agency (LSA), a professional staff office of the state legislature, with the responsibility of preparing proposed maps of the state's congressional districts and state legislative districts after each census. The maps then go to the legislature for approval or disapproval. If the legislature disapproves, the LSA prepares a second set of maps, incorporating the legislature's feedback. The legislature can again only either approve or disapprove these maps. If it disapproves a second time, LSA prepares a third set of maps, which the state legislature then for the first time has the authority to approve *or modify*. However, since Iowa first began employing this process, the legislature has never reached the stage of rejecting all three LSA maps and substituting its own.

For more discussion of these and other examples of state redistricting processes, see Justin Leavitt, *A Citizen's Guide to Redistricting* (2010).

C. CONDUCTING LEGISLATIVE ELECTIONS

Achieving Hamilton's ideal "that the people should choose whom they please to govern them" also depends on having a voting process that makes this possible. Simply calling for an election for a specified office at a specified time is not sufficient. Instead, critical questions about the manner in which elections are conducted, including who can vote and how, must be addressed.

1. WHO VOTES?—TOWARDS UNIVERSAL SUFFRAGE

The U.S. Constitution provides that members of the United States Senate and the United States House of Representatives are to be chosen by the people of each state, and that those entitled to participate in this selection process in each state "shall have the Qualifications requisite for Electors of the most numerous Branch of the State Legislature." U.S. CONST. art. I sec. 2; U.S. Const. amend. XVII. Thus, who can participate in state legislative elections as well as congressional elections is largely a matter of state law. Several federal legal developments, however, have further affected who can vote.

In earlier eras, the right to vote in the United States was narrowly restricted. Indeed, at the time of the founding most states extended the franchise only to white men over age twenty-one who owned property. At other times, poll taxes and literacy tests have restricted the franchise. *See* ALEXANDER KEYSSAR, THE RIGHT TO VOTE (2d ed. 2009). But over the years most of these restrictions have been removed, first with the demise of property requirements, and then with the adoption of the Fifteenth, Nineteenth, Twenty-Fourth, and Twenty-Sixth Amendments to the U.S. Constitution, which now prohibit any voting exclusions based on race, sex, or failure to pay poll taxes, and lower the voting age to eighteen.

Today, the franchise extends to most adult citizens. The only exceptions to a policy of universal suffrage are that most states do not extend the franchise to incarcerated felons, and some states have at least nominal prohibitions that deny the franchise to incompetent persons (defined in various ways). Whether lifetime disenfranchisement is appropriate for convicted felons has been the subject of some debate in recent years, with the trend in favor of either restoring voting rights after the criminal sentence is served or eliminating felony disqualification entirely.

Although eligibility to vote is now almost universal, every state except North Dakota requires eligible voters to register to vote as a condition of exercising the franchise. (North Dakota allows its citizens to appear at the polls and vote without registering.) Several states allow registration to occur at the polls on Election Day simultaneously with voting, but in most states voter registration must occur in advance of Election Day. Since 1993, to increase the number of eligible voters who in fact register, the federal government has required states to offer a voter registration opportunity to any citizen who is applying for or renewing a driver's license. *See* National Voter Registration Act (NVRA), 42 U.S.C. §§ 1973gg et seq. (also known as the "Motor Voter Act").

The Help America Vote Act of 2002, Pub. L. 107–252, 116 Stat. 1666, expanded the NVRA by requiring many additional state agencies to provide citizens an opportunity to register to vote at the time those citizens receive other government services. To ease the voter registration process further, approximately three-quarters of all states have now adopted a system of on-line voter registration.

Nevertheless, the extent to which voter registration requirements continue to burden an eligible voter's opportunity to participate has been a topic of contemporary debate. Little reliable data exists concerning the number of otherwise eligible voters who do not vote because they have not satisfied their state's voter registration process, although recent turnout rates have generally been higher in states that permit voter registration to occur at the polls on Election Day. *See* Barry C. Burden, *et al.*, *Election Laws, Mobilization, and Turnout: The Unanticipated Consequences of Election Reform*, 58 AM. J. OF POL. SCI. 95, 95–109 (2014). Some voter advocates have called for more states to permit same-day registration, or for states to conduct an automatic voter registration process for citizens as they turn eighteen.

Meanwhile, states have also been working to coordinate with one another so that as the country's increasingly mobile electorate moves more frequently from jurisdiction to jurisdiction, voters are properly reregistered in their new home and removed from the voter rolls in their former jurisdiction. It would obviously be a violation of the one-person, one-vote principle for the same person to vote in congressional (or U.S. presidential) elections in two or more states in the same election. And while there is no necessary reason why a citizen with substantial ties to two states should not be eligible to vote for state legislators in each state, as a policy matter all states have insisted that potential voters establish a state of primary domicile, and vote only in that state's elections. The updating of voter registration lists therefore is an important task—and an ongoing burden—for state and local election officials.

Until 1972, one difficulty voters often encountered when moving from jurisdiction to jurisdiction were state requirements that voters have resided in the state for an extended period—typically one year—as a condition of registration. In *Dunn v. Blumstein*, 405 U.S. 330 (1972), the U.S. Supreme Court held that a one-year state residency requirement and a three-month county residency requirement were too long. Without specifying exactly how long is too long, the Court has looked favorably on a thirty-day residency requirement as a reasonable period, allowing time for states to handle administrative tasks associated with processing voter registration applications and preparing voter rolls.

One purpose of requiring voters to register, and for giving states a brief period of time before each election to process registration applications, is to confirm voter eligibility. Although demonstrated cases of voting by ineligible voters are rare, it remains important to assure the public of this. States with same-day registration (or without any registration at all) have established alternative mechanisms that, perhaps in light of their states' political culture and history, satisfy this concern. Proponents of same-day registration argue that it could be satisfactorily implemented everywhere in a manner that would address concerns about voting by ineligible voters.

Calls for various forms of voter identification at the polls are also defended as necessary to reduce the potential for voting by ineligible voters. In recent years, states have adopted a range of voter identification requirements, from more stringent rules that require voters to establish their identity and voting jurisdiction with a narrow category of acceptable government-issued photo ID documents, to less onerous requirements that allow voters to establish their identity using a broad range of documents, such as utility bills, bank statements, or paycheck stubs. Voter advocates note that the narrower voter identification requirements may impose a genuine burden on some populations, including the poor and the elderly, who are statistically less likely to have a required document, and who may have real difficulty, financial or otherwise, in obtaining one. In *Crawford v. Marion County Election Board*, 553 U.S. 181 (2008), the U.S. Supreme Court upheld what at the time was the nation's most stringent voter ID requirement, finding insufficient proof that the requirement would cause actual disenfranchisement or function in effect as a poll tax. Litigation remains possible, however, over whether some voter identification requirements, as applied, in fact result in disenfranchisement. Meanwhile, some advocates of universal voter registration also have called for the government to provide all voters with an acceptable voter identification card, at no direct cost to the voter.

2. GENERAL ELECTION PROCESSES

Outcomes of legislative elections can be shaped not only by who votes, but also by how they vote. Final election outcomes of course are determined by general elections, though primary elections play a central role in shaping or even determining these outcomes. This section will discuss a few general election considerations, and the next section will discuss some primary election considerations.

All members of the U.S. House of Representatives are elected to two-year terms, while U.S. Senators are elected to six-year terms, with one third of the Senators standing for election every two years. General elections for all members of Congress and most state legislatures are universally conducted on the first Tuesday after the first Monday in November of even calendar years. Federal statute specifies this day as Election Day for members of Congress. *See* 3 U.S.C. §§ 1, 7. Largely for reasons of efficiency, many states have also opted to conduct elections for their state legislatures on the same day, although a handful of states, including Louisiana, New Jersey, Mississippi, and Virginia, conduct these state elections in odd years.

In the country's early years, voting did not occur using the "Australian" or secret ballot. However, ballot secrecy became the norm in American elections almost a century and a half ago, at a time when almost all voting occurred in person on Election Day.

Today, as a result of dramatic increases in both absentee voting and early in-person voting, Election Day in fact is no longer the largely universal day for casting ballots that it once was. As of 2016, approximately one-third of all ballots cast in federal elections were cast before Election Day. Moreover, the proportion is already much higher in some states, and the trend is increasing. Meanwhile, several states (Washington, Oregon, and Colorado) now conduct their elections entirely by mail, sending ballots to all voters, who then can return their marked ballots either by mail or by dropping them off in person at designated collection points by the end of Election Day. But these alternative methods of voting often mean that ballot secrecy is no longer assured (just as does the increasingly popular practice of taking a photo of one's ballot in the voting booth).

These alternative methods of pre-Election Day voting also have forced candidates to adjust their campaign strategies. In part, these adjustments seek to take advantage of the early voting opportunities as a way to lock-in committed supporters and ensure their votes have been cast. Other adjustments recognize that the right moment for campaign efforts to peak is no longer clear, nor is how much campaign funding to save for use in the final days before Election Day. More detailed discussion of campaign financing matters is the special concern of Chapter 4.

For voters who rely on in-person voting on Election Day, polling places must be convenient and accessible. Long lines like those that have occasionally plagued certain polling places inevitably discourage some voters from participating. Long lines can result from misallocation of voting equipment, an insufficient number of voting locations, or equipment failures, among other common causes. When these problems are extreme, they can give rise to court orders to extend voting hours or provide alternative means of voting.

As a final concern, theoretical access to the polls is meaningless if voters are not aware of their correct polling location and precinct. Fortunately, when voters present themselves at an incorrect location, most poll workers are able to assist the voters to find the correct location. But on occasion these voters instead may be encouraged to cast a provisional ballot, which depending on state law may eventually be deemed invalid. Many other voters may be required to cast a provisional ballot not because of problems in determining the voter's correct precinct, but because of difficulty in verifying a voter's registration status. Analogous problems may infect the processing of absentee ballots, which must be matched with voter registration information. Problems in casting absentee, provisional, or regular ballots are often at issue in close or disputed elections.

3. PRIMARY ELECTION PROCESSES

Because American legislatures are constructed around single member districts using winner-take-all elections, most states narrow the general election field to only a few major candidates by allowing political parties to nominate only one candidate per office for the general election. Although in times past party leaders would choose their nominees in the fabled smoke-filled rooms, in most states today each major political party selects its general election candidate by holding a primary election. A few states continue to rely on party conventions or caucuses, if sometimes only to winnow the candidates who will appear on the primary ballot.

A critical decision concerning the structure of a partisan primary election is whether to limit the voters who can participate to only those who are registered as members of that party—a "closed" primary—or instead to allow any voter to participate whether or not the voter has an affiliation with the party sponsoring the primary election—an "open" primary. Open primaries generate "cross-over" voting, in which voters affiliated with one party participate in another party's primary, whether for strategic reasons or out of genuine support for a candidate of the other party. "Semi-closed" primaries allow unaffiliated voters, in addition to the party's own voters, to participate, but not voters affiliated with a party other than the one holding the primary election.

However, it is something of a misnomer today to speak of a political party as though it is the entity "holding" the primary election. Rather, the same public officials who conduct the general elections also conduct the primary elections, and do so according to rules and procedures determined as a matter of public law. Thus, even in states with closed primaries (and even more so in states with open primaries), primary elections have something of a hybrid quality as partly a private event, and partly a public function.

Political parties do get to make the decision whether to avail themselves of a state's election machinery for purposes of conducting primary elections. In only a few states today have the two dominant political parties decided not to do so and instead to rely at least partly on caucuses or conventions in lieu of primaries to nominate candidates. Minor parties do so more frequently.

Another notable exception is the "blanket" primary, a nonpartisan "top two" primary election, currently used in California, Louisiana, and Washington. In this election, all the candidates of any party who have qualified for the primary are pitted against each other on a single primary ballot. However, the election is held not for the purpose of identifying a single victor, but instead for narrowing the field to the top two candidates. These top two candidates, regardless of party, then face each other in the general election. Proponents of this design argue that it will lead to the election of more moderate representatives because it avoids the two major parties each pitting a more extreme candidate against each other in the general election. Opponents worry that it will reduce voter options, particularly by keeping minor parties off the general election ballot, while also increasing primary election costs.

Pre-Election Day voting has also complicated the scheduling of primary elections, which must occur sufficiently in advance to prepare general election ballots. Since 2010, federal law has required states to send general election ballots to overseas and military voters at least 45 days before Election Day, in order to provide ample time for what can be a protracted process of receiving, voting, and returning the ballot. *See* The Uniformed and Overseas Citizens Absentee Voting Act, Pub. L. No. 99–410, 100 Stat. 924 (1986), as amended by the Military and Overseas Voter Empowerment Act of 2010, Pub. L. No. 111–84, 123 Stat. 2190 (2009). As a result, a number of states had to abandon long-standing traditions of holding primary elections close to their general elections. To meet the 45-day requirement, it is now necessary to hold primary elections well in advance of Election Day.

4. FILLING LEGISLATIVE VACANCIES: APPOINTMENTS AND SPECIAL ELECTIONS

One other category of legislative election that merits brief mention is the special election, used to fill a vacancy that occurs in the middle of a legislative term. The U.S. Constitution provides that when vacancies occur in the representation of any state in the House of Representatives, "the Executive Authority [of the state] shall issue Writs of Election to fill such Vacancies." U.S. Const. art. I, sec. 2, cl. 4. The Constitution further provides that when vacancies occur in the representation of any state in the U.S. Senate, "the Executive Authority of such State shall issue Writs of Election to fill such vacancies: Provided, That the legislature of any State may empower the executive thereof to make temporary appointments until the people fill the vacancies by election as the legislature may direct." U.S. Constitution, amend. XVII.

Each state not only decides whether to empower its governor to appoint a Senator to fill a vacancy temporarily, but also establishes its own procedures for when and how the Governor may issue writs of election to fill congressional vacancies. Accordingly, when a congressional vacancy occurs, state law establishes how much discretion the Governor has in setting a special election. One consideration that often limits this discretion is the question of when to schedule special congressional elections, a matter complicated by the fact that such elections typically must include both a primary and a general election, sometimes during an already crowded calendar of other election events. States therefore often require that, where possible, special congressional elections occur in conjunction with some other regularly scheduled state or local election event.

The filling of vacancies in state legislative seats also varies by state. Some states permit the chamber of the state legislature in which the vacancy occurs to fill it until the next election. Other states permit the political party of the vacating occupant of the seat to fill the seat temporarily. Yet other states specify procedures for special elections. States also vary in how they deal with the death of a candidate in the period just before an election.

5. RESOLVING DISPUTED ELECTIONS

Occasionally, the results of an election are not immediately clear. Several processes then become critically important. These include election canvassing, recount, and contest processes overseen by the state, followed by congressional or state legislative processes undertaken in furtherance of each legislature's constitutional authority to be the final judge of the election of its own members.

a. State Processes

The modern American electorate is accustomed to same-day election results, and candidates likewise anticipate delivering their victory or concession speeches on Election Night. But results are never official until local and state election officials complete the *canvass*, a careful process of thorough review of the voting in every precinct.

The results of the official canvass are increasingly likely to differ from Election Night returns because of a combination of factors. In some jurisdictions, widespread absentee voting has increased the number of ballots whose eligibility is unresolved by Election Night, while in many states substantial quantities of provisional ballots also remain to be reviewed after Election Day. Meanwhile, some states have decided to accommodate military and overseas voters by allowing their ballots to continue to arrive for a few days after Election Day. In close races, all of these factors mean that Election Night outcomes may change during the canvass.

Administrative recount and judicial contest processes then provide opportunities for candidates to challenge election results. Each state has its own established recount procedures, typically providing for an automatic recount in a race within a specified narrow margin of victory, or allowing a candidate to request a recount if the candidate pays an administrative fee. However, the extent of automatic vote tabulation in today's election systems means that recount results rarely deviate much from canvass results.

A judicial contest may also result, challenging any number of possible aspects of how an election was conducted, but often without an obvious remedy if error or wrongdoing is established. Judicial reversal of election results is rare, though not unheard of. It typically requires proving that a number of votes greater than the margin of victory was improperly cast in favor of the official winner, or that a number of votes greater than the margin of victory was excluded from the count, such that the runner-up would have prevailed if these votes had been counted. These are difficult showings, especially given the use of secret balloting. But uncounted absentee or provisional ballots provide the potential for altering an election outcome, if the number of these ballots exceeds the margin of victory. Typically these ballots are preserved until their eligibility can be conclusively determined, and then those ballots originally excluded but subsequently deemed eligible are processed and added to the official count.

By far the best known recent example of a judicial contest of a legislative election is the 2008 U.S. Senate race in Minnesota. On Election Night, Republican incumbent Norm Coleman had a small lead over Democratic challenger Al Franken. Seven months later, the state supreme court affirmed a special tribunal's fact finding and legal conclusion that when all the eligible absentee ballots were included, Al Franken was the official winner by about 300 votes (or one-hundredth of one percent of the total votes cast). During those seven months, the candidates and their legal teams pursued a number of legal issues and theories in a complicated quest for additional votes. In the end, it was a testament to the strength of Minnesota's contest process that the result was generally accepted. *See* Edward B. Foley, *The Lake Wobegone Recount: Minnesota's Disputed 2008 U.S. Senate Election,* 10 ELEC. L. J. 1 (2011).

b. Legislative Review of Contested Elections

Had Senator Coleman not been willing to accede graciously to the Minnesota Supreme Court's determination of the outcome of the 2008 race, his remaining option would have been to ask the U.S. Senate to decide the matter. The same constitutional provision that gives Congress the final authority to determine the qualifications of its members also gives it the final authority to judge the elections of those members. *See* U.S. Const. art. I, sec. 5, cl. 1. All state legislatures have the same final authority, as noted above.

In the overwhelming number of legislative elections, this authority to judge the elections of a legislature's own members remains essentially dormant. (As a formality, however, this power is employed at the beginning of the legislative session, when the body ordinarily will accept the certificates of election of its new members as being in good order.) When an election contest does come before a legislature, the body will often await the conclusion of whatever state election recount and contest processes have been independently initiated before making its own decision about the election in question. The results of those processes then are part of the record before the legislature, but are not binding on it.

In the most important case addressing this authority, the U.S. Supreme Court held that the U.S. Senate's final authority to judge the elections of its own members did not divest a state of the authority to conduct its own recount. *See Roudebush v. Hartke*, 405 U.S. 15 (1972). The Court made clear, however, that the Senate's ultimate decision on the matter could be completely independent of the state proceedings.

D. LEGISLATIVE TERM LIMITS

Legislative term limits are a final consideration affecting how American legislatures are populated today. Fifteen states have state constitutional provisions that in some fashion limit how many terms an individual may serve in the state legislature. At the height of the term limits movement in the 1990s, twenty-one states had adopted these state legislative term limits, and some twenty-four states also had adopted provisions intending to limit how many terms their delegates to Congress could serve. But several states have subsequently repealed or invalidated their state legislative term limits, while as previously noted the U.S. Supreme Court found congressional term limits to be an unconstitutional attempt to impose an additional qualification on members of Congress beyond those specified in Article I. *See U.S. Term Limits, Inc. v. Thornton*, 514 U.S. 779 (1995).

1. THE JUSTIFICATION FOR LEGISLATIVE TERM LIMITS

Legislative term limits were a response to widespread dissatisfaction with representative government in the late twentieth century. Although proposed in various forms at earlier moments in U.S. history (and discussed and rejected at the time of the founding), the idea caught fire in the early 1990s as an antidote for a sclerotic political process. Then, as now, many legislators, particularly in Congress, were widely perceived as out-of-touch with their constituents and beholden to special interests, characteristics that seemed to grow the longer politicians remained in office. Popular support for term limits therefore derived partly from hostility towards entrenched politicians, and a collective desire among many citizens to "kick the bums out."

But there was an affirmative vision as well. Term limits aimed to promote "citizen legislators" who would set aside their regular careers for a brief period of public service, bringing greater diversity and more representativeness to the legislative process. It was also assumed that term-limited legislators would be less focused on their own reelection, and less influenced by the money in modern politics. Forced legislative turnover would make political campaigns more interesting and meaningful. And it was hoped that citizen legislators would, like Cincinnatus, return to their plows after their terms, and eschew becoming career politicians.

Opponents of legislative term limits feared that turning out so many experienced legislators would result in a substantial loss of institutional memory and expertise. Not only would this loss frustrate the ability of legislatures to function efficiently, but it also might shift the balance of power in legislative politics toward interest group representatives and executive branch officials, especially those whose longevity would give them disproportionate experience and institutional memory. Thus, at the core of the term limits movement was another contested vision about the role of representatives, with proponents idealizing the citizen legislator, for understandable reasons, and opponents idealizing legislators who could become experienced professionals, for a different set of understandable reasons.

Term limits measures were extremely popular among the general public, though not among elected representatives. The states that adopted legislative term limits between 1990 and 1995 were overwhelmingly those states with popular initiative processes that permit citizens to propose and adopt constitutional amendments or statutes directly (rather than through the legislature), as discussed more in Chapter 5. Perhaps ironically, the popularity of these measures was overwhelmingly driven by a desire to impact Congress, rather than state legislatures, yet the *Thornton* decision left Congress untouched by legislative term limits, leaving in place only those limits affecting state legislatures.

2. TYPES OF STATE LEGISLATIVE TERM LIMITS

Although twenty-one states adopted term limits for their state legislatures, six of these states eventually repealed or invalidated their measures. Five of these six states had adopted legislative term limits by statute, and in two of these five states—Idaho and Utah—the state legislatures subsequently repealed the provisions. In the other three states with statutory term limits—Massachusetts, Washington, and Wyoming—the state high courts invalidated their provisions as an unconstitutional imposition of additional legislator qualifications beyond those specified in their state constitutions (mirroring the U.S. Supreme Court's decision in *Thornton*). Sixteen other states adopted term limits by constitutional amendment, but in Oregon, the state supreme court invalidated the amendment because it had been adopted in violation of the Oregon constitution's requirement that proposed amendments contain only a single subject.

The remaining fifteen states with some form of legislative term limits vary in how their limits operate. Some states impose a lifetime ban on additional legislative service after a certain number of years. Other states merely temporarily ban a state legislator from additional service after a certain number of consecutive years, but permit subsequent legislative service after some specified interval out of office. Additional variations include the number of years allowed in office, and whether years in both of a bicameral legislature's two chambers count together.

Six states impose a lifetime ban. In California and Oklahoma, these bans limit legislators to twelve years of combined service in both houses of the state legislature. In Arkansas, the lifetime ban attaches after sixteen years of total service in both houses. In contrast, in Michigan, Missouri, and Nevada, separate lifetime limits are specified for each house of the state legislature. Michigan allows six years in the house and eight years in the senate, Missouri allows eight years in each chamber, and Nevada—with the longest limits of any state—allows twelve years in each chamber, or twenty-four years of total service. After reaching these limits, a legislator may not run again for these offices.

Nine states impose a consecutive-years ban. In these states, once a legislator has served a specified number of consecutive years, the legislator is ineligible for re-election until the legislator has sat out a specified period, typically a two-year legislative cycle. The consecutive-year clock then resets. In all consecutive-year states, the limits are specific to one house of the state legislature, allowing a term-limited member to move back and forth between the two chambers during the period of ineligibility.

Almost all consecutive-year states limit legislators to eight years in each chamber. These states are Arizona, Colorado, Florida, Maine, Montana, Ohio, and South Dakota. Eight consecutive years is also the limit in unicameral Nebraska. Louisiana imposes a twelve-year consecutive limit.

3. IMPACTS OF LEGISLATIVE TERM LIMITS

More than two decades after the term limits movement took hold, and more than a decade and a half since most of these measures began to displace veteran state legislators, many observers see few benefits (although some take a long view that it is still too early to have changed the political culture). Despite proponents' hopes that term limits would deplete the ranks of "career politicians," many state legislators remain interested in building careers in elected office, and simply have had to adjust their career paths to move more rapidly or frequently between positions, rather than being able to serve an extended career in the legislature. Furthermore, despite some proponents' hopes that term limits would curb state budgets by reducing the spending incentives of individual legislators, some studies have found a correlation between increases in state spending levels and the restrictiveness of states' term limit schemes. *See* H. Abbie Erler, *Legislative Term Limits and State Spending*, 133 PUBLIC CHOICE 479

(Dec. 2007). Meanwhile, as anticipated, affected legislatures have lost significant sources of institutional memory, in the process often strengthening the relative influence on the legislative process of executive branch officials and private lobbyists.

However, prospects of repealing legislative term limits outright appear remote, although some possibility exists that certain states might choose to lengthen their limits. Even legislators who were themselves elected in a term-limited environment often share the view that the length of the limits is too short, and that they are termed out just as they are beginning to hit their stride as a legislator. But despite legislative frustration with term limits and little evidence that their promised benefits are being realized, public support for the concept of term limits remains strong. Indeed, public support likely reflects some of the same sentiments that underlie the continuing calls for campaign finance regulation, discussed in the next chapter, namely, that elected officials are out of touch with regular people and instead are beholden to narrow, wealthy special interests.

CHAPTER 4

CAMPAIGN FINANCING, LOBBYING, AND BRIBERY: THE IMPACT OF MONEY IN POLITICS

The considerations in Chapter 3 of which citizens actually cast ballots, and in what aggregation with other voters, are not the only factors that determine who become our elected representatives. It also matters, of course, for whom each voter votes. A major influence on voter preferences is the ability of candidates and their supporters to get their message out. Today, that often means reaching potential voters through expensive media campaigns, as well as relying on paid consultants and political strategists to manage candidate image. At both the state and federal levels, modern legislative campaigns have become massively expensive undertakings. Although the 2016 presidential campaign of President Donald Trump may be a contrasting phenomenon, in which comparatively little expense generated substantial media attention and public interest, it is not at all clear that typical legislative candidates will be likely to replicate that success.

It has always been essential for American politicians to have sufficient resources to conduct effective campaigns. But the size and scale of the necessary resources have grown exponentially in recent generations, so that amassing campaign funds has become perhaps the central occupation of a successful state or federal legislator. In this environment, concerns understandably have increased about the potential influence on legislative outcomes of the tiny fraction of American society that provides the overwhelming majority of the financing for political campaigns. Yet just how much influence is inappropriate is a contested issue.

Meanwhile, corollary concerns also have grown about the influence of money not on election outcomes but on the choices that elected representatives make once in office (concerns that also appear to have fueled President Trump's appeal as an outsider not beholden to established interests). Today, many observers are deeply worried that those individuals and interest groups with the greatest financial resources are able to dominate or distort the First Amendment's cherished guarantee to all citizens of the right to petition their government, including by importuning their elected representatives. Understandably, as the practice of "lobbying" legislators has become a multi-billion dollar industry, efforts to monitor or regulate these influences have multiplied. But this too is a contested issue.

Finally, lobbying activities and campaign contributions have both occasionally raised concerns in the eyes of some observers that they amounted to disguised forms of bribery or influence peddling. Of course, outright bribery—the payment of money to a public official to purchase some specific performance of official duty—has always been illegal. But just how bribery and other anti-corruption measures operate today is also worth some exploration.

This chapter addresses these impacts of money in politics. It first considers the role of money in political campaigns, describing its essential character while reviewing various efforts over recent decades to control it. For purposes of the contemporary study of the legislative process, it is important to understand not only the current regulatory regime that affects campaign financing, but also something of the earlier debates and court battles that continue to shape this regime. The chapter then discusses lobbying and interest group influence, also addressing both the ways that money is brought to bear on the legislative process and the range of tools that have been employed to regulate it. The chapter concludes with a discussion of bribery law and related anti-corruption measures.

A. CAMPAIGN FINANCE REGULATION

This section considers various attempts to regulate the influence of money in political campaigns. It first offers a few thoughts on the skyrocketing costs of political campaigns, before summarizing some competing arguments about the value of regulating campaign expenditures. The bulk of this section then focuses on the current state of campaign finance regulation, a state of affairs that has resulted largely from the complex interplay between legislative measures designed to reduce political corruption, on the one hand, and the U.S. Supreme Court's review of the constitutionality of those measures, on the other. Meanwhile, this remains an evolving area. For additional treatment of these topics, see DANIEL P. TOKAJI, ELECTION LAW IN A NUTSHELL (2d ed. 2016).

1. THE ROLE OF MONEY IN LEGISLATIVE RACES

Money has always factored into legislative campaigns, though in different ways. In his 1758 campaign for a seat in the Virginia House of Burgesses, a young George Washington is reported to have spent $195 of his own money to participate in the then-common (though nominally illegal) practice of buying drinks for voters, a corrupt practice by today's standards. Meanwhile, in elections whose outcomes were controlled by political machines or effectively settled in smoke-filled rooms, money also inevitably played a central role, but often in terms of deals between party bosses, more than in funding individual campaigns to persuade voters.

Modern political campaigns are much more candidate-centered than the party-centered races of times past. Today, the overwhelming use of money in legislative races is to produce and distribute political advertisements for individual candidates, using television, radio, and a rapidly increasing array of social and other media. With each election cycle, as pressures mount to outpace what occurred in the previous cycle, the costs of securing sufficient airtime alone have skyrocketed. This is especially true for races in districts encompassing multiple media markets. These costs only grow higher as a rapidly proliferating number of independent groups also increasingly compete to purchase airtime for advertising in support of or opposition to specific candidates.

In addition to advertising costs, modern candidate-centered campaigns also must bear the expense of the increasingly sophisticated campaign apparatus, including paid political advisors, media consultants, pollsters, and organizers. Here too, the costs snowball with each new campaign cycle, as campaigns identify new ways to seek to outpace their competition. One result is that many candidates find it increasingly difficult to be their own person, as they feel hemmed in by strategic advice for which they often have paid a tidy sum.

2. WHY REGULATE CAMPAIGN FINANCING?

Concerns about the influence of money in political campaigns partake of two fundamentally different strands. One strand essentially worries that in excess, campaign contributions amount to a form of influence buying, even bribery. From the standpoint of contemporary efforts to regulate the American campaign finance landscape within the limits that the First Amendment's guarantee of freedom of political speech has been construed to impose, concern over this form of government corruption is by far the most important strand.

The other strand worries that the outsized influence that money now plays in political campaigns distorts the ability of average Americans to participate in the political process. But for over forty years, the U.S. Supreme Court has interpreted the First Amendment's protection of political speech to protect candidates' and their supporters' ability to spend unlimited amounts of money for campaign purposes regardless of its potential to distort the playing field or drown out other voices. *See Buckley v. Valeo*, 424 U.S. 1 (1976). Concerns about the potential distorting effects of money in politics therefore have had to be addressed through voluntary mechanisms, such as public financing programs that supply eligible candidates with equal funding.

Several other concerns also are often invoked in support of campaign finance regulations. These include freeing candidates and legislators to spend less time raising money and more time legislating and studying issues; promoting more competitive elections; and informing the electorate about candidates' supporters and sources of funding.

With the exception of the anti-corruption rationale, these various justifications for campaign finance regulation tend to have the deepest resonance for those who view the legislature primarily as an institution that should be devoted to promoting the public good, as discussed in Chapter 2. For those who view the legislature primarily as a forum for choosing between competing private interests, it may matter less whether a wealthy interest group has a stronger influence on policy choices, whether a legislator must spend substantial time currying favor with potential donors, or whether political campaigns generate meaningful public discussion of issues.

Meanwhile, opponents of campaign finance regulation argue that any limits on political spending infringe on both protected individual liberty and protected rights of political association. They also argue that limits on political contributions are themselves largely responsible for the exorbitant amount of time that candidates must spend fundraising, because candidates can no longer raise the necessary funds from relatively few large donors. In turn, they also argue that limits on contributors' ability to support their favored candidates directly are the primary cause of the rapidly increasing proportion of political spending that now occurs by independent groups and individuals, acting outside the control of actual candidates. Another thread argues that typical campaign finance regulations (which after all are enacted by legislators themselves) in fact function as incumbent protection measures that make it more difficult for challengers to oust sitting legislators. Finally, they note the "hydraulic" quality of money in politics: like water flowing downhill, those with resources will always find ways to deploy them to influence public policy, regardless of any particular measures intended to limit them.

3. SPECIFIC EFFORTS TO REGULATE CAMPAIGN FINANCING

For many of the preceding reasons, the ever-expanding role that money has come to play in American political campaigns has understandably generated increasing public pressure to do something about it. As early as the 1890s and 1900s, some states were experimenting with campaign finance reform measures, including imposing limits on how much money a campaign could spend, or providing public financing for campaign costs. But most of these early Progressive Era measures had either been declared unconstitutional by state courts or repealed by 1910.

Meanwhile, in 1907 Congress responded to concerns that corporations had unduly influenced the 1904 presidential race by enacting the Tillman Act, 34 Stat. 864 (1907), which prohibited corporations from making any monetary contributions to candidates for federal office. Provisions of the Taft-Hartley Act, 61 Stat. 159 (1947), similarly prohibited labor unions from making contributions to federal candidates, and also prohibited both corporations and unions from spending any funds from their general treasuries on federal elections. This prohibition led to the creation of separate funds, in the form of early political action committees, which were funded by donations from individual corporate executives and employees and union members. But enforcement of these federal prohibitions remained weak until Congress became increasingly involved in regulating campaign finance in the late 1960s and early 1970s, in response to the rise of expensive television-centered campaigns, increasing distrust of government, and the Watergate scandal.

In turn, the increased congressional activity led to a series of significant Supreme Court decisions interpreting the First Amendment to limit federal and state power to regulate campaign spending, beginning with *Buckley v. Valeo*, 424 U.S. 1 (1976), and extending through *Citizens United v. Federal Election Commission*, 558 U.S. 310 (2010). The *Citizens United* decision established that unions and corporations could spend their own funds without limit on *independent* political activities, or in other words on political activities not coordinated with any particular candidate's campaign. An understanding of the *Citizens United* decision, which in turn requires some knowledge of the statutory landscape and major court decisions that preceded it, is crucial to understanding the modern campaign finance landscape.

a. The Federal Election Campaign Act

In 1971, Congress enacted the Federal Election Campaign Act ("FECA"), a consolidation of previous campaign finance laws. Although FECA reflected growing concern about spiraling campaign costs, it was still a relatively weak measure. Almost immediately thereafter, alarm about the discovery of the role that a small number of very large donors played in raising $60 million for the 1972 presidential campaign of Richard Nixon, and the misuses of some of those funds, prompted Congress to enact the Federal Election Campaign Act Amendments of 1974. The now much stronger amended Act, codified at 2 U.S.C. § 431 *et. seq.*, then became the focus of the landmark 1976 *Buckley* decision, a case that continues to dominate the constitutional jurisprudence of campaign finance regulation.

In simplified terms, the amended FECA had four primary elements: (1) limits on *contributions* that any one donor could make to a candidate's campaign; (2) limits on campaign *expenditures* that any one candidate or supporter could make during a campaign; (3) requirements that political contributions and expenditures be publicly *disclosed*; and (4) a mechanism for *public financing* of the U.S. presidential election. The constitutionality under the First Amendment of each of these elements was tested in *Buckley*.

Contribution limits. As amended in 1974, FECA limited to $1000 the amount of money any one individual (and most groups) could contribute per election to a given candidate for federal office (or to the candidate's campaign committee). For purposes of this contribution limit, a primary election was treated as separate from the ensuing general election, a distinction that permitted total contributions to a given candidate of up to $2000 per election cycle. FECA also imposed a $25,000 aggregate limit on how much any one individual could contribute in a given calendar year to all candidates for federal office. These dollar limits were not indexed for inflation.

Expenditure limits. Other provisions of FECA imposed limits on how much each candidate for a federal office (or the candidate's campaign committee) could spend per election, with limits that varied depending on the federal office sought (House seat, Senate seat, or President). A separate provision limited how much a candidate could spend from personal or family funds. In addition, a third FECA provision limited to $1000 how much any individual (and most groups, with a critical exemption for media organizations) could spend, not including contributions to a candidate or committee, during a calendar year on political activities "relative to a clearly identified candidate" for federal office.

Disclosure requirements. FECA required candidates for federal office (and their committees) to report to the Federal Election Commission the names of all donors who contributed more than $100 to their campaigns. Candidates (and committees) also were required to report to the FEC all of their campaign expenditures over $100, while individuals and groups, other than candidates and their committees, who spent more than $100 (not including contributions to a candidate or committee) also were required to report their expenditures to the FEC. The FEC then was required to make these reports publicly available.

Public financing of U.S. presidential race. FECA also created a mechanism to provide each major party's presidential candidate with $20 million (indexed for inflation) in campaign funds for the general election, and lesser amounts for minor party candidates, provided the candidate (and the candidate's campaign committee) agreed not to raise or spend additional amounts. A companion provision provided public funds for the primary elections, based on a matching formula. Although the existence of a public financing mechanism for the presidential race is not directly relevant to congressional and state legislative races, the Supreme Court's subsequent approval of this public financing mechanism is relevant to understanding the set of tools currently available for regulating campaign financing.

Creation of Federal Election Commission. In addition to the four preceding categories of substantive campaign finance regulations, FECA also established the Federal Election Commission as a new independent federal agency. The FEC's mission was to administer the public financing system, manage the disclosure processes, and enforce FECA's contribution and expenditure limits. Although the Commission's original structure, which relied on Congress to appoint the commissioners, was deemed unconstitutional on separation of powers grounds in *Buckley v. Valeo*, Congress quickly amended the statute to reconfigure the Commission along constitutional lines (providing for their appointment by the President, with the Senate's advice and consent).

b. *Buckley v. Valeo*

As soon as the 1974 FECA amendments were signed into law, a diverse group of plaintiffs from across the political spectrum challenged the constitutionality of a number of provisions of the act. Led by Republican Senator James Buckley and Democratic Senator Eugene McCarthy, and motivated in substantial part by concerns that the act would make it harder for political outsiders, including third-party candidates, to challenge incumbents, the lawsuit took particular aim at the contribution and expenditure limits. In the first round, the U.S. Court of Appeals for the District of Columbia Circuit, sitting *en banc*, upheld almost all of the challenged provisions, including the contribution and expenditure limits. But on appeal, the U.S. Supreme Court reached a different result. In a set of opinions covering well over two hundred pages, the Court in *Buckley v. Valeo*, 424 U.S. 1 (1976), upheld the public financing system, the disclosure requirements, and the contribution limits, but struck down the expenditure limits. The result was both a dramatic reconfiguration of FECA's statutory scheme, and the development of a central canon of First Amendment jurisprudence that continues to govern the analysis of campaign finance regulation today.

In particular, the Court in *Buckley* rejected the argument that political expenditure and contribution limits were regulations of conduct, rather than speech. Because the Court analyzed these regulations in terms of their impact on political speech, they were subject to what the Court in *Buckley* called "exacting scrutiny" under the First Amendment. This scrutiny required the Court to balance the government's asserted justification for the regulations against the degree to which they infringed upon the free speech rights of citizens.

The Court agreed that reducing political corruption or the appearance of political corruption was a legitimate government interest. But the Court rejected the government's assertion of an independent interest in promoting greater equality in political contests: "[T]he concept that government may restrict the speech of some elements of society in order to enhance the relative voice of others is wholly foreign to the First Amendment." *Id.* at 48. This understanding of the freedom of speech continues as a central canon that informs all constitutional analysis of campaign finance regulations.

In balancing individuals' free speech rights with the government's legitimate anti-corruption interest, the Court found important differences between contribution limits and expenditure limits, on both sides of the scale. With respect to the infringements on the First Amendment rights of citizens, the Court found that reasonable limitations on the amount an individual could contribute to a candidate would not detract from the symbolically important act of making a donation. In contrast, the Court found that limitations on candidate or independent expenditures would directly impair communication with the public and "necessarily reduc[e] the quantity of expression." Meanwhile, with respect to the government's interests, the Court found that the anti-corruption rationale of preventing large contributions to candidates from corruptly influencing (or appearing to corruptly influence) those candidates was much stronger than the claim that large political expenditures made independently of particular candidates would corrupt (or appear to corrupt) those candidates. The result was that FECA's expenditure limits were struck down, given their relatively weak anticorruption justification and their more substantial infringement on political speech, while FECA's contribution limits were upheld, given the Court's view that direct contributions had a greater potential for *quid pro quo* corruption of elected representatives while caps on the amounts of allowable contributions to candidates would not substantially reduce contributors' political speech rights.

Separately, the Court upheld the public funding scheme for presidential elections, which conditioned the receipt of public campaign funds on a candidate's *voluntary* acceptance of a specified expenditure limit. The main challenge to the public funding scheme was its differential treatment of minor party candidates, but the Court concluded that Congress had a legitimate interest in distinguishing long-shot candidacies. That Congress could condition the receipt of what at the time was a generous amount of public funding ($20 million) on an agreement to limit one's First Amendment rights was not seriously disputed.

Against another First Amendment challenge, the *Buckley* decision also upheld the requirements that candidates and their campaigns disclose their contributors. Again applying "exacting scrutiny" to balance the First Amendment interests with the government justifications, the Court accepted that this disclosure infringed upon free speech rights, but found that the government had three "sufficiently important" interests to justify the infringement. Specifically, the Court agreed that disclosure: (1) would collect information relevant to the enforcement of contribution limits, (2) would help inform the public about the sources and uses of campaign funds, and (3) could reduce the potential for corruption by exposing large donors.

The decision also considered whether the disclosure requirement for any expenditure made "for the purpose of" influencing an election was unconstitutionally vague. By construing this disclosure requirement to apply only to expenditures "used for communications that expressly advocate the election or defeat of a clearly identified candidate," *id.* at 80, the Court also upheld this requirement. The Court left room for as-applied challenges to disclosure requirements if parties could demonstrate that disclosure would subject them to harassment or reprisal.

Though not clear in the complex *Buckley* opinion, subsequent Supreme Court jurisprudence has established that the analytical framework for judicial review of limits on campaign *expenditures* will be strict scrutiny, meaning that the limit must be "narrowly tailored" to achieve a "compelling government interest." Limits on campaign *contributions*, meanwhile, are reviewed under a somewhat less demanding "heightened scrutiny" standard, which requires that the limits be "closely drawn" to accomplish a "sufficiently important interest." *See Nixon v. Shrink Missouri Government PAC*, 528 U.S. 377, 388 (2000). These same levels of scrutiny are used to evaluate the constitutionality of state campaign finance regulations. Since *Buckley*, outright expenditure limits have never been upheld, while most contribution limits have been. However, in recent years the Court has found some contribution limits to be set too low, on the grounds that they effectively limit a challenger's ability to mount a successful campaign. *See, e.g., Randall v. Sorrell*, 548 U.S. 230 (2006).

Given the fundamental difference in treatment between contributions and expenditures, it is important to be able to place various uses of political funds into the appropriate category. A quintessential demonstration of this necessity is to consider the difference between giving a sum of money to a candidate's campaign committee, on the one hand, and spending that same sum of money to purchase media advertising on behalf of the candidate. The former use is clearly a contribution, and therefore is subject to limitation. But for purposes of First

Amendment analysis, whether the latter use also amounts to a contribution, or instead amounts to an expenditure, not subject to any limits, will depend on whether it is made independently of the candidate. If the media advertising is purchased *in coordination* with the candidate, federal law requires that it be treated as the functional equivalent of a contribution. Otherwise, it would be entirely too easy to circumvent the contribution limits upheld in *Buckley*.

One significant development in the decades after *Buckley* was the proliferation of thousands of political action committees, or PACs. The prototypical PAC is what FECA calls a "multicandidate political committee." These are political committees (not including political parties) that receive contributions from more than fifty donors and in turn contribute their funds to at least five federal candidates. Under FECA, political committees also are subject to contribution limits and disclosure requirements. But PACs have proliferated in part because the limits on how much one person can contribute to a PAC are higher than the limits on contributions to candidates. Donors who have maxed out their ability to contribute to individual candidates can give additional amounts to like-minded PACs, which in turn provide an important source of both direct and indirect funding for candidates. Some PACs are affiliated with corporations or unions, and can take contributions only from associated employees or members, while others are unaffiliated and can accept contributions from all donors.

By upholding contribution limits while invalidating expenditure limits, the *Buckley* decision dramatically altered the impact of the Federal Election Campaign Act. As one commentator observed, "contribution limits . . . made raising money harder, but the lack of spending caps maintained the system's voracious need for money. . . . Inadvertently, the *Buckley* opinion took a congressional program designed to minimize the impact of wealth on campaigns and turned it into an engine for the glorification of money." Burt Neuborne, *Campaign Finance Reform and the Constitution: A Critical Look at* Buckley v. Valeo, *The Brennan Center for Justice Campaign Finance Reform Series*, at 18 (1998). In the ensuing four decades, campaign finance reformers have struggled to overcome the resulting disequilibrium between raising and spending campaign funds. For a more recent account of the *Buckley* case and its continuing impact, see Richard L. Hasen, *The Nine Lives of* Buckley v. Valeo, *in* ELECTION LAW STORIES (Eugene Mazo & Joshua Douglas eds., 2016).

c. The Bipartisan Campaign Reform Act of 2002

Congress's other major effort to adjust federal campaign finance regulations came in 2002 with the passage of the Bipartisan Campaign Reform Act (BCRA), or what is also sometimes called the McCain-Feingold law (in honor of the two Senators who were the measure's bipartisan sponsors). Although pressure to amend FECA had been building for years, another scandal—this time involving the Enron Corporation—helped to propel both houses of Congress to impose new requirements, again adopted as amendments to the Federal Election Campaign Act. These requirements were intended to address many of the ways in which campaign finance practices had evolved since *Buckley*.

One obvious need was to update the contribution limits, which the 1974 amendments had not indexed for inflation. BCRA doubled to $2000 per election the amount that individuals could contribute to a specific candidate and indexed this limit for inflation. BCRA similarly sought to update other contribution limits, raising from $25,000 to $37,500 (and also indexing this limit for inflation) the aggregate limit that one individual could contribute to all federal candidates in each two-year federal election cycle. The Supreme Court struck down this aggregate limit by a 5–4 vote in *McCutcheon v. Federal Election Commission*, ___ U.S. ___, 134 S. Ct. 1434 (2014), on the basis that the aggregate limit infringed on individuals' First Amendment rights to freedom of political speech. In addition, for candidates facing self-financed opponents who invest more than $350,000 of their own money into their campaign, BCRA would have tripled the contribution limits, but the Supreme Court, also by a 5–4 vote, invalidated this "millionaire amendment" in *Davis v. Federal Election Commission*, 554 U.S. 724 (2008). The Court's opinion concluded that the First Amendment precluded treating individual candidates differently and disadvantaging candidates for spending their own money in a particular way.

More significantly, BCRA also sought to respond to concerns about the impact of "soft money" on elections. Though not a term in the law, "soft money" is used to describe money raised and spent for campaign purposes outside the purview of campaign finance regulation. In the 1980s and 1990s, political parties in particular became increasingly adept at raising large sums for grassroots activities, such as voter registration and get-out-the-vote drives, which had obvious benefit to their party's candidates but did not amount to a regulated "contribution" to the candidate. Soft money also became widely used to fund "issue ads," which by deliberate design did not expressly advocate the election or defeat of an identified candidate, and thereby escaped the FECA disclosure requirement that survived *Buckley*, but which nevertheless often functioned as campaign advertising.

BCRA sought to address soft money in several ways. First, the act prohibited the national committee of a political party from raising, soliciting, or spending any soft money; in other words, the national party committees were now allowed to raise and spend only those amounts that FECA authorized. The act also prohibited candidates for federal office from soliciting any funds other than "hard money" (money raised within FECA's contribution limits), except on behalf of nonprofit groups engaged in voter registration and get-out-the-vote drives.

In addition, BCRA imposed several new constraints on the funding of "electioneering communications," a type of advertising that the act defined as one that refers to a clearly identified candidate and airs within sixty days of a general election or thirty days of a primary election in a sufficiently large media market. This definition was designed to overcome the *Buckley* decision's protection of ostensible issue ads that did not expressly advocate the election or defeat of an identifiable candidate. Under BCRA, political parties could spend only hard money on electioneering communications; unions and most corporations (those other than nonprofit corporations organized for ideological purposes) were no longer able to fund these ads directly with general treasury funds, and instead could only use funds from their affiliated political action committees; and individuals and organizations that spent over $10,000 to fund electioneering communications were required to disclose the sources of all contributions over $1,000.

d. *McConnell v. Federal Election Commission*

Enactment of the Bipartisan Campaign Reform Act produced an immediate legal challenge. Led by Senator Mitch McConnell, almost eighty groups and individuals argued that most of the Act's key provisions violated the free speech clause of the First Amendment. After an intermediate stop in the lower court, these consolidated challenges produced another Supreme Court decision whose combined opinions totaled well over two hundred pages. *McConnell v. Federal Election Commission*, 540 U.S. 93 (2003). To the satisfaction of campaign finance reformers, the *McConnell* decision upheld almost all of the challenged BCRA provisions, while adding some new thinking to First Amendment jurisprudence. This satisfaction was to be relatively short-lived, however.

With respect to BCRA's limitations on raising and spending soft money, the Court analyzed the First Amendment challenges using heightened (rather than strict) scrutiny. On the basis of an extensive evidentiary record, the majority found that congressional concern with corruption was sufficient to justify these limits. In particular, the decision cited evidence that soft money contributions appeared to have shaped the congressional agenda on multiple occasions, and that "corporate interests had given substantial donations to gain access to high-level government officials." *Id.* at 150. Justice Kennedy dissented strongly from this rationale, observing that "favoritism and influence are not . . . avoidable in representative politics," and arguing that it was a dramatic expansion of a traditional definition of corruption to claim that it included gaining access to legislators. *Id.* at 297.

The *McConnell* decision also upheld BCRA's provisions concerning electioneering communications. With respect to the required disclosures of the sources of funding for these ads, the majority was strongly sympathetic to the claim that robust public debate could not flourish behind a veil of secrecy, although it preserved the possibility of an as-applied challenge if a disclosure requirement resulted in harassment or reprisal in the future. With respect to the prohibition against corporations and unions paying for electioneering communications using their general treasury funds, rather than segregated political action committee money, the Court sustained the measure's effort to limit " 'the corrosive and distorting effects of immense aggregations of wealth that are accumulated with the help of the corporate form and that have little or no correlation to the public support's for the corporation's political ideas.' " *Id.* at 205, quoting *Austin v. Michigan Chamber of Commerce*, 494 U.S. 652 (1990). *Austin* and *McConnell* are the only occasions when the Court has employed an equality-based rationale to uphold a campaign finance measure. In dissent, Justice Scalia argued that citizens who choose the corporate form to "pool their financial resources . . . for purposes of economic enterprise" are entitled to full First Amendment protection to use that corporate form to advance their political views. *Id.* at 258.

The *McConnell* majority had predicted that "[m]oney, like water, will always find an outlet." In the wake of the *McConnell* decision, another type of political group, organized under section 527 of the Internal Revenue Code, developed new prominence. BCRA's effort to clamp down on soft money, upheld in *McConnell*, brought to light the existence of these so-called "527" organizations. Section 527 provides a tax exemption for groups organized primarily for the purpose of influencing the election of public officials (527s in turn are distinguishable from "social welfare" organizations exempt under section 501(c)(4) of the Internal Revenue Code, which may engage in political activities only if such activities are not their primary purpose). To the extent that these 527s do not amount to political committees subject to FECA (not all 527s are FECA political committees, even though political committees normally are 527s), and do not directly contribute to federal candidates' campaigns, they arguably can raise and spend soft money. The pressure that mounted on the IRS to clamp down on what many saw as abuse of the section 527 exemption ultimately led to a 2013 scandal (whose aftermath continued for several years) surrounding what appeared to be the IRS's disproportionate scrutiny of 527s having conservative-sounding names.

e. *Citizens United v. Federal Election Commission*

Apart from the rise of 527s, campaign finance reformers faced a deeper challenge to their reform agenda in the form of the changing composition of the U.S. Supreme Court. In 2007, now under the leadership of Chief Justice John Roberts and with Justice Alito having replaced Justice O'Connor, the Court upheld an as-applied challenge to BCRA's electioneering communication requirements. *See Federal Election Commission v. Wisconsin Right to Life, Inc. (WRTL)*, 551 U.S. 449 (2007). The *WRTL* decision effectively allowed corporations and unions to air electioneering communications freely, notwithstanding the BCRA prohibition, except for ads that were "susceptible of no reasonable interpretation other than as an appeal for a vote for or against a specific candidate." *Id.* at 451. This was a narrow standard, harking back to the *Buckley* limitation on "express advocacy," which would allow corporations and unions to evade BCRA readily. But *WRTL* was only a precursor to the full-scale assault on the electioneering communications provisions—and on the existing campaign finance jurisprudence generally—that was to occur in *Citizens United v. Federal Elections Commission*, 558 U.S. 310 (2010).

The *Citizens United* case deeply divided the Roberts Court. Initially, it raised another as-applied challenge to the now-substantially narrowed BCRA prohibition on direct corporate funding of electioneering communications. The subject of the case was a 2008 Video-on-Demand documentary named "Hillary: The Movie," which admittedly was susceptible of no reasonable interpretation other than as an appeal to vote against Hillary Clinton during the 2008 Presidential campaign. But the Court used the case to reconsider the facial validity of the electioneering communications provision. Applying strict scrutiny, the *Citizens United* decision overruled *Austin* and part of *McConnell* to hold that under the First Amendment, corporations (and by implication, unions as well) have the same unlimited rights as individuals to engage in independent political activities, and therefore cannot be prohibited from funding electioneering communications or other forms of political advertising from their general treasury funds.

In practical terms, this was only a modest extension of the *WRTL* decision, which already had made it possible for corporations and unions that desired to do so to air most forms of political ads.

Nevertheless, *Citizens United* has been widely described as opening the floodgates to corporate influence on elections, even though *WRTL* had already done most of the work. Moreover, *Citizens United* is often mischaracterized as having allowed corporations (and unions) to contribute funds from their general treasury *to candidates*, when in fact the FECA prohibition on corporate and union contributions to candidates and their campaign committees remains firmly in place.

What *Citizens United* did do, in fact, was change the jurisprudence of campaign finance regulation. In particular, the five-justice majority opinion explicitly adopted a narrow definition of corruption that was limited to *quid pro quo* deals between candidates and their supporters. On this view, the purchasing of "influence and access" through campaign financing activities is not corrupting, and therefore "independent expenditures do not lead to, or create the appearance of, quid pro quo corruption." *Id.* at 360. This was a sweeping generalization that implicitly struck at the heart of all efforts to constrain independent expenditures.

The fallout was swift. Later in 2010, the United States Court of Appeals for the D.C. Circuit relied on this new jurisprudence to hold that FECA's contribution limits could not constitutionally be applied to contributions received by political committees that engaged exclusively in independent expenditures. *Speechnow.org v. Federal Election Commission*, 599 F.3d 686 (D.C. Cir. 2010). The result has been an explosion in these "independent expenditure only" committees, more commonly called "Super PACs." Unlike PACs, which can contribute funds directly to candidates and their committees but are limited in how they raise money, Super PACs can raise funds without limitations, but may not contribute those funds directly to candidates or their committees. In recent elections, many of these Super PACs have been established for the sole purpose of supporting one specific candidate, as they are free to do provided they do not coordinate their activities with that candidate.

A final note about the *Citizens United* decision: Eight members of the Court made clear that they would support at least some form of disclosure regime to inform the public about the sources of funds for political advertising and other activities. Although Congress initially took steps to develop a more comprehensive disclosure regime, particularly in the form of the proposed DISCLOSE Act, it has not been able to enact anything, and opposition has mounted against additional federal campaign spending disclosure requirements. Meanwhile, as Super PACs have proliferated in the absence of better disclosure, by some estimates as much as half of today's independent political expenditures may be undisclosed. This shadow spending is now often labeled "Dark Money."

For a fuller account of the *Citizens United* decision and its impact, see Heather K. Gerken & Erica Newland, *Three Tales of* Citizens United, *in* ELECTION LAW STORIES (Eugene Mazo & Joshua Douglas, eds., 2016); DANIEL P. TOKAJI & RENATA

E.B. STRAUSE, THE NEW SOFT MONEY: OUTSIDE SPENDING IN CONGRESSIONAL ELECTIONS (2014). Meanwhile, Chart 2 on the next two pages provides a chronological overview of the federal campaign finance landscape from the early twentieth century to today.

f. State Laws Regulating Campaign Financing

The Supreme Court's First Amendment jurisprudence applies equally to state governments, defining the limits of permissible federal and state government regulation of campaign finance practices. Yet state regulation of political campaigns has hardly moved in lockstep with congressional efforts to regulate federal campaigns. Instead, state campaign finance regulation today is characterized by a variety of approaches, including some states or municipalities that have imposed relatively low campaign contribution limits; a few states or municipalities that have adopted methods for substantial public funding of certain political campaigns; and some states that impose no limits at all on the amounts of permitted campaign contributions.

For instance, Montana limits individual campaign contributions to candidates for state legislative seats to $170 per election, while Ohio's limit is $12,532. But twelve states impose no limits at all on individual contributions, and six of these twelve states also allow corporations to make unlimited contributions to state races. Meanwhile, twenty-two states completely prohibit corporations from making

Chart 2—Chronological Overview of Federal Campaign Finance Law

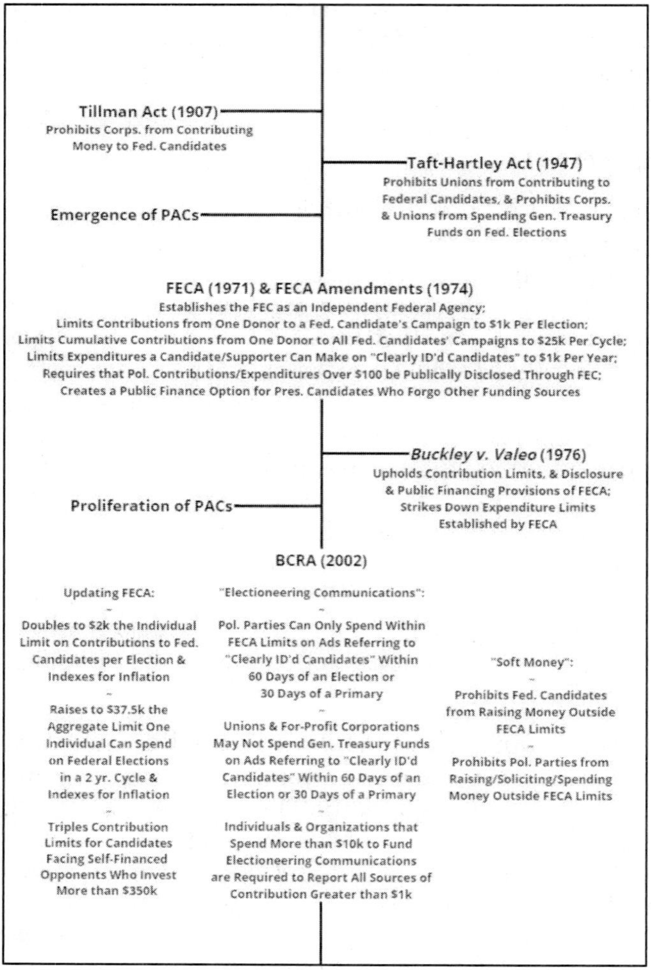

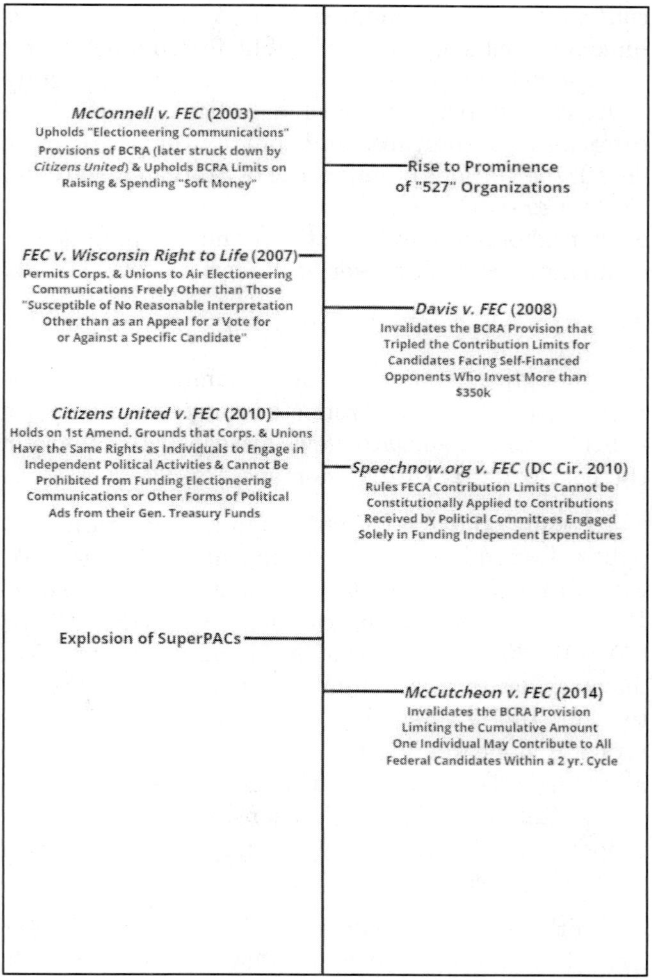
McConnell v. FEC (2003)
Upholds "Electioneering Communications" Provisions of BCRA (later struck down by Citizens United) & Upholds BCRA Limits on Raising & Spending "Soft Money"
Rise to Prominence of "527" Organizations
FEC v. Wisconsin Right to Life (2007)
Permits Corps. & Unions to Air Electioneering Communications Freely Other than Those "Susceptible of No Reasonable Interpretation Other than as an Appeal for a Vote for or Against a Specific Candidate"
Davis v. FEC (2008)
Invalidates the BCRA Provision that Tripled the Contribution Limits for Candidates Facing Self-Financed Opponents Who Invest More than $350k
Citizens United v. FEC (2010)
Holds on 1st Amend. Grounds that Corps. & Unions Have the Same Rights as Individuals to Engage in Independent Political Activities & Cannot Be Prohibited from Funding Electioneering Communications or Other Forms of Political Ads from their Gen. Treasury Funds
Speechnow.org v. FEC (DC Cir. 2010)
Rules FECA Contribution Limits Cannot be Constitutionally Applied to Contributions Received by Political Committees Engaged Solely in Funding Independent Expenditures
Explosion of SuperPACs
McCutcheon v. FEC (2014)
Invalidates the BCRA Provision Limiting the Cumulative Amount One Individual May Contribute to All Federal Candidates Within a 2 yr. Cycle

contributions to candidates. Only a handful of states have adopted some form of public funding option for state legislative races. All states, however, require that candidates for elected office report their campaign expenditures and contributions. For more detail, see National Conference of State Legislatures, *State Campaign Finance Laws: An Overview*, at www.ncsl.org/research/elections-and-campaigns/campaign-finance-an-overview.aspx.

4. THE CONTEMPORARY DEBATE

Although debates about campaign finance regulation have always reflected competing visions of politics, these disparate views are especially sharp in the post-*Citizens United* moment.

To some, the recent reduction of constraints on political spending was welcome and overdue. *See, e.g.*, JOHN SAMPLES, THE FALLACY OF CAMPAIGN FINANCE REFORM (2006); BRADLEY A. SMITH, UNFREE SPEECH (2001). It is seen as opening the political marketplace to more outsiders, providing an antidote to the tight rein that incumbent officeholders typically have kept on their offices. It also is seen as allowing better promotion of a wider range of political views. Relatedly, it also is seen as recognizing the proper scope of the First Amendment's protection of political speech.

To others, the same deregulation is alarming. *See, e.g.*, RICHARD HASEN, PLUTOCRATS UNITED (2016); ROBERT C. POST, CITIZENS DIVIDED (2014); LAWRENCE LESSIG, REPUBLIC, LOST (2012). It is seen as the triumph of greed over government, permitting a tiny fraction of society to have vastly disproportionate influence on public policy because of—and in service to—their immense wealth. It also is seen as drowning out the voices of those with fewer resources, and creating a political environment antithetical to a conception of the Free Speech Clause as designed to promote a fair playing field for all citizens (a conception that the Supreme Court has rejected). On this view, a fundamental concern is that money is increasingly able to buy election outcomes.

Empirically, these two divergent views are able to cite to conflicting evidence. Supporters of campaign finance deregulation point to figures suggesting that since *Citizens United*, corporations have been responsible for only a small fraction of total campaign spending. To show that money does not ensure electoral success, they also point to the failure of huge Super PACs to achieve their electoral objectives in the 2016 presidential primaries. In reply, promoters of campaign finance regulation argue that elections are complex, and that money remains critically important, perhaps even more so in legislative races than in presidential politics. They also point to how cynical and disenfranchised much of the electorate feels because of the way in which wealth appears to influence the political process, and observe that the amount of independent spending increased between the 2008 election and the 2012 election, and continued to rise in 2016. The groups and individuals who are spending these funds surely must think they are thereby getting something of value.

One unanswered question is the extent to which social media and other tools of modern communication will alter the dynamics of political campaigns, and what that will mean to the role of money in politics. In *Citizens United*, the Court noted the rapid evolution of the means of communicating political messages. Previously, the exemption for media organizations from prohibitions on corporate political spending may have been an obvious nod to the Freedom of the Press Clause in the First Amendment. But in an era of widespread blogging and a variety of other new media, it is becoming increasingly difficult to distinguish between exempt and non-exempt media activities. The Court in *Citizens United* was attentive to the ease and low-cost with which political messages can now be streamed over the Internet. It bears watching how campaign practices develop, and what those developments may mean to how candidates and their supporters raise and spend political funds.

B. LOBBYING AND ITS REGULATION

Money has the potential to influence not only how our elected representatives are chosen, but also how they behave in office. As early as seventeenth-century England, members of the public would frequent the hallways and lobbies of Parliament outside the chamber of the House of Commons in an effort to gain an audience with their representatives. Thus apparently was born the verb "to lobby," meaning to seek to persuade or influence government officials in the performance of their public duties. Of course, lobbying can occur not only in legislative anterooms, but also wherever and whenever interested parties can obtain access to government officials—restaurants, country clubs, home districts, conferences, by telephone or letter, and so on. (Indeed, the actual chambers of legislative bodies typically are private spaces, to which the public is not admitted, except into the observation galleries).

In the United States, the right to petition government for the redress of grievances is one of the cherished rights protected by the First Amendment. This right recognizes that public input is critical to the legislative process, whether that process is conceived in classical liberal/pluralist terms, or classical republican/legal process terms (see Chapter 2). And interest groups from across the spectrum are perhaps the most important forces influencing U.S. politics today. But in popular parlance, the term "lobbying" often is used not to describe a process of healthy public input concerning governmental policy, but to describe concerns that a form of privileged access, available only to moneyed interests and perceived by many as antithetical to norms of democratic equality, is corrupting or distorting the policy debate. This is not a universal view, however, as many pluralists will defend the rights of groups or individuals to use their resources—financial or otherwise—to make the strongest case they can to government officials.

As this section describes, during the twentieth century, concerns about corruption and distortion repeatedly led to legislative efforts, at both the state and federal levels, to regulate the lobbying process.

These efforts have intensified as the lobbying industry has expanded and become more sophisticated, and as many of the interest groups most active in lobbying activities also have become central players in campaign activities. But resistance to these efforts also has grown, insisting that any regulation must balance concerns about corruption and distortion with the First Amendment right to petition government, a right that extends both to individuals and to organizations.

1. DIRECT AND INDIRECT LOBBYING

Today, the term lobbying almost always is used to describe efforts by an organized group, not just a single individual, to influence government officials, particularly legislators and agency officials. At the outset, it is worth distinguishing between two methods for seeking to persuade or influence legislators and other officials: "direct" and "indirect" lobbying.

Direct lobbying refers to efforts to communicate a group's position or interests by having a group representative, or "lobbyist," meet, speak with, or write to government officials and their key staff members. This direct communication between an interest group and governmental actors may occur either at public hearings or in private meetings or correspondence. Direct lobbying also often includes making campaign contributions.

Indirect lobbying refers to interest group efforts to cultivate broad public support for a group's position, and then to turn that support into grassroots pressure on legislators or agencies. Increasingly, what may superficially appear to be spontaneous popular support for (or opposition to) a particular legislative or agency measure may in fact reflect an organized campaign by an interest group to arouse the participation of citizens-at-large (or at least of the interest group's own members, in the case of large membership-based organizations like the Sierra Club or the National Rifle Association). Groups cultivate popular support through mass mailings, mass emailings, and media campaigns, which often incorporate explicit requests for the public to contact government officials, especially their legislators.

2. EARLY EFFORTS TO REGULATE LOBBYING: THE FEDERAL REGULATION OF LOBBYING ACT OF 1946

Until the New Deal dramatically expanded the reach of the federal government, interest groups tended to focus more on what was happening in state legislatures, where matters of economic policy typically were shaped. Exceptions of course existed, for instance involving Gilded Age matters of tariffs or railroad rates, when lobbyists turned their attention to Congress. But whether in Congress or in state legislatures, lobbying practices were often connected with corruption and scandal, so that by the early twentieth century state lobbying had become one target of Progressive Era reforms.

Some members of Congress took up the reform mantle in the 1930s, largely in response to accounts—particularly political scientist Elmer

Schattschneider's famous study *Politics, Pressures and the Tariff: A Study of Free Private Enterprise in Pressure Politics, as Shown in the 1929–1930 Revision of the Tariff* (1935)—that business lobbyists had secretly dominated the congressional debate over the Smoot-Hawley Tariff. Proposed reforms were intended primarily to bring public accountability and disclosure to lobbying activities, not to limit the activities themselves. The reform effort languished for a decade, however, until Congress enacted The Federal Regulation of Lobbying Act of 1946 (FRLA), 60 Stat. 839.

The FRLA was a measure directed primarily at disclosure of federal lobbying activities. The Act provided that violations were punishable with fines and imprisonment. But in establishing what those violations were, the Act was not a model of legislative clarity. Enacted as but one minor part of a broader Legislative Reorganization Act (60 Stat. 812 (1946), a measure that had drawn much more attention to its other provisions), and pieced together from various measures that had been considered over the previous ten years, the FRLA gave rise to several crucial interpretative issues.

The U.S. Supreme Court resolved these issues in *United States v. Harriss*, 347 U.S. 612 (1954). In order to avoid problems of both constitutional vagueness and potential infringement upon the First Amendment, the Court essentially rewrote the FRLA, rendering it toothless in the eyes of most observers. In particular, and despite ample reason to think that Congress had intended otherwise, the

Court held that the disclosure requirements applied only to those who had raised outside money specifically to lobby, and did not apply to groups spending their own funds. The Court further held that all sections of the Act applied only to "lobbying in its commonly accepted sense," by which the Court meant *direct* communications with members of Congress. *Id.* at 620. Indirect lobbying therefore was not covered, nor was communication with legislative staffers other than members.

Thereafter, the Department of Justice rarely sought to enforce the FRLA, although some groups and individuals continued to register with Congress under the Act. Forty years would pass before Congress undertook another serious effort to establish a meaningful disclosure regime for federal lobbying.

3. THE BURGEONING OF AN INDUSTRY

Meanwhile, during the second half of the twentieth century, lobbying as an industry exploded, at both the state and federal levels. By one analysis, by the beginning of the 21st century some 12,000 registered lobbyists were spending over $1.5 billion in reported federal lobbying expenditures, compared to an estimated $10.3 million in 1950 (itself an aberrationally large year). By 2015, that figure had more than doubled to over $3.2 billion. *See* OpenSecrets.org, *Lobbying Database*, at http://www.opensecrets.org/lobby/. Lobbying expenses at the state levels also have experienced dramatic growth in recent years.

A variety of factors have contributed to this development. In part, lobbying activity has increased because of the growth in the scope and complexity of government regulation and activity itself, which provides more and more businesses and other groups with greater and greater motivation to influence government policy. In addition, lobbying, like campaign financing, tends to become more expensive each cycle, as participants must defend against the activities of competing participants, who all seek to outperform the previous round. Lobbying activities also have grown in tandem with the increased participation of interest groups in political campaigns. Meanwhile, the practice of earmarking, or specifying a particular recipient of a portion of a federal appropriation, which had its heyday at the end of the twentieth century and in the first decade of the twenty-first century, provided additional incentives for businesses and industries to hire lobbyists to compete for government benefits.

But perhaps as important as any of these factors is that corporate America has simply become increasingly convinced of, and eager to capitalize on, the potential value of a large and well-managed lobbying operation. For many large corporations, this involves a team of both in-house lobbyists and hired government relations firms, whose activities often involve collectively monitoring hundreds of different proposed legislative and administrative actions, first identifying and then working to control the most important opportunities and risks. For many corporate clients, lobbyists' most valuable contributions can be defensive efforts to prevent the enactment of an undesirable piece of legislation, capitalizing on the many "vetogates" described in Chapter 5 to defend against new regulations.

The importance of lobbying to most American corporations is evidenced by the fact that they spend substantially more resources on lobbying than on efforts to influence elections. By some accounts, in recent years corporations have favored spending on congressional lobbying over elections by five (or more) to one, even after *Citizens United. See, e.g.*, Robert J. Shapiro & Douglas Dawson, *Corporate Political Spending: Why the New Critics Are Wrong* 11 (2012). Lobbying by nonprofit organizations, although it accounts for only a small percentage of total federal lobbying, also has been increasing rapidly in recent decades.

By the end of the 20th century, the growth of the number of professional lobbyists, and of the amount of money flowing into the legislative and regulatory processes as a result, had given rise to increasing calls for Congress to regulate the lobbying industry further (see subsection 4 next). Meanwhile, states were employing their own regimes to regulate the lobbying process, in two broad categories. One category of state regulations requires only that groups and individuals engaged in lobbying, however a state chooses to define it, register with the state and disclose certain details concerning their lobbying activities and expenditures. A second category of state regulations not only requires registration and disclosure, but also imposes limits on who may engage in lobbying, or when lobbyists may participate in campaign financing efforts. For instance, some states prohibit lobbyists from contributing to legislative campaign funds while the legislature is in session, or even from contributing to campaigns at all. Other states have "revolving door" measures that prohibit former state legislators from conducting any lobbying activities within one or two years of when their legislative terms ended. (In at least one case, however, a lower federal court has found it unconstitutional to preclude former state legislators from engaging in *uncompensated* lobbying. *See Brinkman v. Budish*, 692 F. Supp. 2d 855 (S.D. Ohio 2010)).

4. THE FEDERAL LOBBYING DISCLOSURE ACT OF 1995

By the early 1990s, increasing public concern over the impact of professional lobbyists prompted Congress to begin working on a new law to regulate federal lobbying, focused on promoting greater transparency concerning the influence of lobbying on policy. These efforts eventually replaced the Federal Regulation of Lobbying Act of 1946 with the Federal Lobbying Disclosure Act of 1995 (FLDA), 109 Stat. 691. Although initially drafted to regulate both direct and indirect lobbying, substantial First Amendment opposition arose to the attempt to require disclosure of indirect lobbying activities, and those provisions were dropped from the enacted measure. The FLDA then was amended in 2007 by provisions of the Honest Leadership and Open Government Act ("HLOGA"), 121 Stat. 735, passed partly in response to lobbying scandals involving lobbyist Jack

Abramoff and Congressman Bob Ney, among others. In addition to strengthening certain provisions of the FLDA, the HLOGA imposed or strengthened constraints intended to control the "revolving door" of politics, primarily by prohibiting former members of Congress, as well as former congressional staffers, from taking positions as paid lobbyists for one or two years after leaving their government posts. The proportion of former members who take lucrative positions as government relations specialists has skyrocketed over the past few decades.

Today the FLDA, as amended, remains the primary mechanism for regulating congressional and federal agency lobbying. The FLDA is substantially more detailed than the 1946 Act, with elaborate definitions that specify its scope with precision, but which often require careful analysis to apply. At its core is its definition of a lobbyist as "any individual who is employed or retained by a client for financial or other compensation for services that include more than one lobbying contact," with an exception for an individual whose "lobbying activities" amount to less than 20% of the individual's work for the client. Separate provisions define "lobbying contact" quite broadly to include any oral or written communications with members of Congress and their staff, as well as with executive branch officials, "with regard to" federal legislation and regulation, except for a lengthy list of communications that are specifically exempted as not amounting to a lobbying contact. (These exceptions include, for instance, testimony at a hearing, or a simple request for a meeting, if the request does not include an attempt to influence a covered official.) Another provision defines "lobbying activities" to include preparations in support of lobbying contacts.

Individuals who meet the definition of lobbyist must register with the Senate and the House of Representatives, either individually or through the organization that employs them. They also must file quarterly disclosure reports. As a result, substantially more information about federal lobbying is now publicly available. Not only has the number of registered lobbyists increased (from about 6,000 under the old FRLA just before passage of the FLDA, to double that number today), but each of these registrants must disclose many details about their lobbying activities.

In particular, the quarterly reports must disclose, in rough terms, the legislative or regulatory issues for which the lobbyists engaged in lobbying activities; on whose behalf; the executive agencies or chambers of Congress they have contacted about these issues; and the approximate dollar amounts (above certain thresholds) expended or received in connection with these lobbying activities. These reports are then publicly available from the Clerks of the U.S. Senate and House of Representatives over the Internet. Lobbyists also must file semiannual reports of their campaign contributions. Violations of the Act are subject to both civil and criminal penalties. Annual reports by the Government Accountability Office suggest both that there is a high degree of compliance with the Act, and that the Department of Justice has increased its enforcement activity in recent years.

The Sunlight Foundation, a national nonpartisan government watchdog organization, is another source that collects data about lobbying.

Passage of the FLDA did not bring about an end to perceived lobbying abuses, however (and certainly not to occasional scandals resulting from undeniably corrupt influences of money in politics, such as bribery, discussed further below). Indeed, according to some analyses, the added requirements of the HLOGA may be driving an increase in the amount of "shadow" lobbying, in which former government officials find ways to sell their expertise without having to register as lobbyists. Furthermore, in the eyes of many reformers the available information remains incomplete. Perceived deficiencies, among others, include the Act's lack of any requirements to identify the extent to which lobbyists engage in grassroots (indirect) lobbying; the fact that lobbyists are not required to disclose the individuals, offices, or committees that they contact; and the exception from the Act's coverage for individuals who spend less than 20% of their work hours lobbying. *See* American Bar Association Task Force on Federal Lobbying Laws, *Lobbying Law in the Spotlight: Challenges and Proposed Improvements*, 63 ADMIN. L. REV. 419 (2011).

On the other hand, many lobbyists subject to the FLDA believe that even without any additional disclosure requirements, the Act already burdens their First Amendment rights. In one judicial challenge, the National Association of Manufacturers argued unsuccessfully that the requirement that a registrant disclose information about any organization that contributed more than $5,000 to support its lobbying activities infringed on its associational rights and chilled its members' political activities. After applying a strict scrutiny analysis, the appellate court upheld the FLDA, concluding that the required disclosure was narrowly tailored to meet the government's compelling interest in informing the public of the interests behind associations active in the political process, including "stealth coalitions." *Nat'l Association of Manufacturers v. Taylor*, 582 F.3d 1, 17 (D.C. Cir. 2009).

5. CONTEMPORARY LOBBYING PRACTICE

The rise in the number of former legislators and other government employees working as paid lobbyists is only one illustration that, with each election cycle, efforts to influence the legislative and regulatory processes of all levels of government grow increasingly sophisticated. Naturally, they also grow more expensive. Given the hydraulic quality of money in politics, which can be observed in the lobbying arena as well as in the campaign finance arena, reformers are often one step behind.

It is this cost factor, not the existence of lobbying per se, that most troubles many observers of contemporary politics. From the perspective of most republican theorists, as well as some (though by no means all) pluralist theorists, policy debates are unhealthily skewed when some voices are effectively drowned out by those voices that have been amplified to overpowering levels, often persistently, by sophisticated lobbying. This concern is not new: Professor Schattschneider wrote in 1960 that "the flaw in the pluralist heaven is that the heavenly chorus sings with a strong upper-class accent." ELMER E. SCHATTSCHNEIDER, THE SEMISOVEREIGN PEOPLE: A REALIST'S VIEW OF DEMOCRACY IN AMERICA 35 (1960). Since Schattschneider wrote, the accent has only grown stronger.

Nevertheless, some interest groups of relatively modest means, such as Common Cause, or the Natural Resources Defense Council, also manage to lobby quite effectively. Sometimes they do so through aggressive fundraising to support their cause. Other times they do so by simply making the more compelling case. Most often they do so through true grassroots organizing.

To most legislators and agency officials, the most effective lobbyists are those who are able to make clear and persuasive presentations of accurate information. Legislators, of course, are especially interested in careful analysis of how the issues of the day will impact potential voters, as well as in the question of which interest groups will support or oppose their reelection. Meanwhile, agency regulators may be interested in the public impact of various proposals, for purposes of maintaining both public and legislative support for their agency. Yet at the same time, they often are more likely to have a deeper understanding of the concerns of—and therefore more sympathy (sometimes subconscious) towards—the industry or business community that they are regulating. Inevitably, those who lobby repeatedly have an advantage when it comes to reaching key legislative and agency personnel, providing another reason for the general public to feel disempowered about their own ability to influence their elected representatives.

C. OTHER ANTI-CORRUPTION MEASURES

Regardless of one's views about the potential distorting effects of money in the lobbying and campaign financing realms, or about whether legislators should function as agents or as trustees, constituents expect legislators not to sell their authority or influence for personal gain. Unfortunately, in almost every era, temptations to profit from their position have proven too great for some legislators to resist. A number of restrictions seek to minimize these occurrences, including criminal prohibitions against bribery and unlawful gratuities, as well as conflict of interest provisions and ethics rules.

1. BRIBERY AND UNLAWFUL GRATUITY PROHIBITIONS

All states and the federal government in some fashion make it a crime for elected officials to accept or solicit bribes for their work. At common law, "bribery" amounted to giving, offering, or receiving something of value in order to influence the performance of a public officer's duties—the prototypical *quid pro quo*. *See, e.g.*, *People ex rel. Dickinson v. Van De Carr*, 87 App. Div. 386 (N.Y. App. Div. 1903). But what amounts to a prohibited "thing of value" is not very clear. Must it involve a personal benefit to the public official, or is a political benefit also proscribed? For instance, in the *Van De Carr* case, at issue was whether bargaining between local-level executive and legislative branch officials concerning the performance of their respective duties involved bribery. A New York City alderman and the head of the city's street cleaning department apparently agreed that if the alderman would help provide increased public funding for the department, the department would be able and willing to rehire a specific employee. Not clear from the facts of the case is whether the named employee was a friend or relative of the alderman, so that his rehiring might be of personal value to the alderman, or merely a constituent whom the alderman was seeking to help. (The state court found the allegations sufficient to uphold bringing a criminal charge against the alderman.)

Today the same difficulties persist in determining when legislative bargaining moves from political horse-trading to bribery. Indeed, this may sometimes depend on whether legislators are viewed primarily as agents or as trustees. If they are viewed as agents, then giving or receiving campaign contributions and other forms of political support might be natural and appropriate ways to influence the performance of a legislator's duties. But if legislators are viewed as trustees, then even campaign contributions might be problematic if they are not completely unconnected to any efforts to affect a legislator's performance of specific duties.

At the federal level, the main prohibition on bribery is found in 18 U.S.C. § 201, a provision that prohibits both bribery and making or receiving "unlawful gratuities." With respect to bribery, this provision provides for criminal punishment of up to fifteen years in prison for anyone who:

> (1) directly or indirectly, corruptly gives, offers, or promises anything of value to any public official . . . with intent— (A) to influence any official act; . . . [or]
>
> (2) being a public official . . . , directly or indirectly, corruptly demands, seeks, receives, accepts, or agrees to receive or accept anything of value personally or for any other person or entity, in return for: (A) being influenced in the performance of any official act; . . . .

One essential element of this federal bribery offense is that the offer, acceptance, or agreement concerning an exchange of a thing of value must be "corruptly" made. In contrast, the "unlawful gratuities" subsection of 18 U.S.C. § 201 establishes a separate crime, punishable by up to two years in prison, for giving or receiving anything of value "for or because of any official act," without any requirement that the gift be given or received "corruptly," and also without requiring that it be given or received with the intent to influence an official act.

No settled understanding exists about the meaning of "corruptly" as used in this statute with respect to the crime of bribery. The U.S. Department of Justice's Criminal Resource Manual (written primarily for the guidance of U.S. Attorneys) explains that it means to act "with a bad or evil purpose," but this definition also leaves much to interpretation, again depending at least partly on one's theory of the role of elected representatives. Historically, prosecutors reserved bribery prosecutions for politicians who were receiving personal benefits, not campaign contributions, unless a direct *quid pro quo* existed that conditioned a campaign contribution on the performance of a specific official act. Otherwise, prosecutors and courts recognized that campaign contributions, in the words of the Criminal Resource Manual, "are almost always given and received with a generalized expectation of currying favor with the candidate benefitting therefrom."

Another difficult question arising out of the statutory definition of bribery is what amounts to an "official act." The U.S. Supreme Court recently confronted this issue in *McDonnell v. United States*, ___ U.S. ___, 136 S. Ct. 2355 (2016), a major case involving the appeal of the federal criminal convictions of former Virginia Governor Bob McDonnell and his wife. At issue were whether the Governor's acts of "setting up a meeting, hosting an event, or calling another official" constituted an "official act" within the meaning of 18 U.S.C. § 201 (as well as under the Hobbs Act and the Honest Services Fraud statute, which formed the basis of the prosecution but were stipulated to use the term "official act" identically with the bribery statute). A unanimous court said "No": under the bribery laws, an official act "must involve a formal exercise of governmental power . . . . [T]he public official must make a decision or take an action on [a] question, matter, cause, suit, proceeding, or controversy" for which the public official has official responsibility. Otherwise, the Court worried, almost anything a public official accepts, "from a campaign contribution to lunch," could lead to criminal culpability for "nearly anything a public official does—from arranging a meeting to inviting a guest to an event." *Id.* at 2372.

The *McDonnell* decision was in many ways a natural coda to the Supreme Court's 1999 decision in *United States v. Sun Diamond Growers of California*, 526 U.S. 398 (1999), a case involving an unlawful gratuities prosecution of a trade association for gifts and favors it bestowed on President Clinton's Secretary of Agriculture. There, another unanimous Court similarly concluded that a defendant could not be convicted of violating the unlawful gratuities provisions of 18 U.S.C. § 201 unless the prosecution could establish that the gifts were given "for or because of" a specific official act, and not simply because of the recipient's official position.

The *Sun Diamond* and *McDonnell* decisions also are of a piece with the *Citizens United* decision, which described acceptingly, if not approvingly, the possibility that political spending might disproportionately enhance certain individuals' access to the levers of government power. (In the words of Justice Kennedy's majority opinion in

Citizens United: "Ingratiation and access, in any event, are not corruption." 558 U.S. at 360.) These decisions all seem to share an underlying presumption that politics appropriately (or inevitably) involves some degree of interested parties seeking to curry favor with their representatives. These are activities that in the Court's view do not, without more, amount to corruption, at least of a kind that can be legally actionable without running afoul of the First Amendment's protection of political speech and citizens' rights to pressure their government.

2. CONFLICT OF INTEREST RULES AND ETHICS MEASURES

Notwithstanding the relatively narrow scope of criminally actionable political corruption, politicians themselves have often been sufficiently concerned about other potential corrupting influences (and about even the appearance that corrupting influences are at play) to impose other restrictions on their own conduct. These measures are all directed at reducing temptations for legislators to act in their own self-interest, rather than on behalf of their constituents and the broader public. They also are closely related to efforts to regulate lobbying, discussed above.

At the congressional level, concerns about corruption, often in response to political scandals, have given rise to a steadily evolving set of statutes and ethics rules that affect how Members of Congress behave. These measures have included the Ethics in

Government Act of 1978, the Ethics Reform Act of 1989, and the Honest Leadership and Open Government Act of 2007, in addition to detailed internal rules typically reenacted with each new Congress, as well as the Federal Lobbying Disclosure Act discussed above. Specific restrictions that Congress has adopted include limits on outside income; bans on honoraria; prohibitions on accepting most gifts or trips from anyone with business before Congress; and restrictions on lobbying the federal government after leaving office. Congress also has adopted rules that prohibit Members from using their official position "to introduce or aid the progress or passage of legislation, a principal purpose of which is to further only [the Member's] pecuniary interest." Senate Rule XXXVII(4); *see* House Rule XXIII(3). In support of these measures, Congress also requires its Members to file regular public financial disclosure reports, which can help the public to identify whether a Member has a conflict of interest.

Many state legislatures have similar rules intended to reduce corrupt deliberation, including explicit requirements in most states that legislators recuse themselves from legislative activity with respect to any measure for which they have a potential conflict of interest. The Supreme Court recently upheld one such recusal requirement against a First Amendment challenge in *Nevada Commission on Ethics v. Carrigan*, 564 U.S. 117 (2011).

CHAPTER 5

INSIDE THE LEGISLATURE, OR HOW A BILL BECOMES A LAW

"Laws, like sausages, cease to inspire respect in proportion as we know how they are made."

— John Godfrey Saxe, 1869

Some version of this aphorism, often wrongly attributed to nineteenth century German Chancellor Otto von Bismarck, is frequently invoked to disparage how legislatures function, and sometimes even to discourage paying attention to them. Yet many aspects of the legislative process are worthy of respect, notwithstanding the ample presence of concomitant elements of distortion and dysfunction. Furthermore, all aspects of the process are deserving of close study, especially by lawyers, whose professional lives revolve so heavily around the work and work product of legislatures.

The bulk of this chapter is a synopsis of the legislative process, from bill introduction through presentment to the President or Governor. In addition to providing an abbreviated summary of the classic process through which an idea for legislation becomes a law, the synopsis stresses the most critical steps, which have the potential to offer the greatest insight into matters of statutory interpretation. It also acknowledges that in recent years many major pieces of federal legislation have not followed the classic process. The remaining sections of the chapter then separately identify some important differences between congressional procedures and many state legislative processes; offer some special considerations concerning budget matters; provide a short overview of the structure and function of a typical statute, in terms of its organization and primary components; and address the distinctive features of direct democracy that complement the legislative processes of many states. For fuller treatments of congressional and state legislative processes, see WALTER J. OLESZEK, *ET AL.*, CONGRESSIONAL PROCEDURES AND THE POLICY PROCESS (10th ed. 2016); BARBARA SINCLAIR, UNORTHODOX LAWMAKING: NEW LEGISLATIVE PROCESSES IN THE U.S. CONGRESS (1997); PEVERILL SQUIRE & GARY MONCRIEF, STATE LEGISLATURES TODAY: POLITICS UNDER THE DOMES (2d ed. 2015); JACK DAVIES, LEGISLATIVE LAW AND PROCESS IN A NUTSHELL (3d ed. 2007).

A. HOW A BILL BECOMES A LAW: FROM INTRODUCTION TO PUBLICATION

The process by which a legislative idea becomes an enacted statute usually—though not always—plays out over at least several months, and often years. But once a specific bill is formally introduced, it must be completed within the constitutionally defined term of the legislature (two years for each Congress, and also for many state legislatures) or the proposal will die and must be reintroduced from scratch in the next legislature. Outlined below are the key elements of this process (with the caveat that the growing dysfunctionality of politics under divided government at the federal level has prompted increasing departures from this traditional process; it remains to be seen whether the return of one-party control of Congress and the Presidency with the arrival of the Trump administration in 2017 will produce something of a return to traditional lawmaking). For convenience and clarity, this synopsis focuses primarily on congressional procedures, although most of its principles also apply to state legislatures.

One overarching point about the legislative process is that executive agencies are heavily involved in many of the steps in this process, contributing their expertise to individual legislative proposals in several different ways. Of course, one form of agency or executive branch participation in the lawmaking process is when an agency (or the President or Governor) promotes its own legislative agenda, finding a legislator to sponsor a bill on the agency's (or President's or Governor's) behalf. In addition to this frequent form of agency participation in the legislative process, agencies also often play an instrumental role by helping to refine a bill as it works its way through various stages of the process. Agencies may make these contributions publicly, as when agency personnel testify at legislative hearings or submit other kinds of evidence to legislative committees. Perhaps more influentially, agencies also may participate in the legislative process confidentially, providing what at the federal level is often called "technical drafting assistance." This is a relatively understudied aspect of the lawmaking process, which sometimes can take the form of truly "technical" advice, but often instead involves the agency sharing substantive views about the desirability of particular measures. *See* Christopher J. Walker, *Legislating in the Shadows,* 165 U. PENN. L. REV. ___ (forthcoming 2017).

For many legislative proposals, any of several steps in the process can prove to be insurmountable obstacles or "vetogates," which may prevent the proposal from ever becoming law. Understanding these obstacles and how proponents strive to avoid or overcome them can be valuable for purposes of resolving interpretive issues in statutory text, the focus of Part II below. Likewise, an awareness of the substantial amount of agency participation in the legislative process also can be relevant to the interpretive enterprise.

1. EXTERNAL RULES, INTERNAL RULES, AND NORMS

As a threshold matter, it is helpful to have some familiarity with the body of rules and norms that governs the activities of a legislature. Each legislative chamber sets most of its own procedural rules, subject to several general procedural requirements imposed upon on the lawmaking process from outside the legislature.

At the federal level, the U.S. Constitution imposes on the two houses of Congress only a few constraints on their lawmaking processes. In addition to the bicameralism requirement of Article I, Section 7 (providing that both houses must agree on the same text before a measure can become law), these few external requirements include: that a majority of members must be present to constitute a quorum sufficient to conduct any official business; that neither house may adjourn for more than three days without the consent of the other house; and that each house "Must keep a Journal of its Proceedings." U.S. CONST. art. I, sec. 5. Beyond that, the Constitution provides that "Each House may determine the Rules of its Proceedings," *id.*, as well as that each House "shall chuse" [sic] its officers, other than the

President of the Senate, who is to be the Vice-President of the United States, art. I, secs. 2 & 3.

At least implicit in the structure of Congress and state legislatures is that the concurrence of a simple majority of the members present is both necessary and sufficient, not only in choosing the officers of a legislative body, but also in agreeing to any other pending motion or matter of business, unless some supermajority is otherwise specified for particular matters. In the U.S. Constitution, this default decision rule is suggested, for instance, by explicit exceptions requiring "the Concurrence of two thirds of the Members present" for the Senate to convict on charges of impeachment, art. I, sec. 3, cl. 6, and also requiring the same supermajority for the Senate to ratify a treaty, art. II, sec. 2, cl. 2.

The Journal that Article I requires Congress to keep is not the relatively familiar Congressional Record. The Congressional Record instead is a transcript of the proceedings on the floor of both the U.S. House and Senate, which Congress since 1873 has independently opted, but is not required, to keep. (It was preceded by the Annals of Congress, the Register of Debates, and the Congressional Globe, a series of less comprehensive records). Meanwhile, the Journal of each house is a short but official summary account of the business conducted in that chamber, including records of the votes on pending legislation.

State constitutions occasionally impose additional requirements on the functioning of state legislatures. For instance, some state constitutions require that a measure address only one subject, or that a bill's title accurately describe what the measure will do. Other state constitutions require that state legislation operate uniformly throughout the state, thus precluding legislation that expressly targets a specific business or locality. In addition to these requirements that address the substance of a bill's text, many state constitutions impose requirements that address purely procedural matters, such as requiring three "readings" of a bill (on different days, ostensibly to promote greater collective deliberation, though actual reading of the full text is usually waived) before a vote; specifying mandatory time periods between a bill's introduction and a vote thereon; and imposing moratoriums on any substantial alterations of the purpose of a bill between introduction and enactment. But sometimes these constitutionally imposed procedural requirements are construed as not judicially enforceable (or not ordinarily enforceable), and instead subject only to internal enforcement by the legislature itself.

The internal rules, which typically are adopted (or re-adopted) as the first official act undertaken at the opening of each congress or legislature, then specify a host of additional requirements to govern the legislative process. These requirements include specifying the order of business, setting the schedule of the legislative session, assigning the power to appoint committees, and imposing specific rules regarding attendance and voting requirements for all members, among many others. Most legislatures today opt to do much of their work in committees, and the internal rules also define the committees' scope and operations. Great variation exists across the states in the level of specificity of their procedures.

ROBERTS' RULES OF ORDER is probably the best-known set of these legislative rules, but it is not the set of rules used in most state legislatures nor in Congress. Instead, MASON'S MANUAL OF LEGISLATIVE PROCEDURE, as modified to fit each state, is the dominant rulebook in most state legislatures (used in 70 of the 99 state legislative chambers). Meanwhile, the U.S. Senate publishes its own set of rules as the SENATE MANUAL, and the corresponding publication in the U.S. House of Representatives is entitled THE CONSTITUTION, JEFFERSON'S MANUAL, AND RULES OF THE HOUSE OF REPRESENTATIVES.

Not only are the requirements of these rules wholly within the control of the legislature, but the enforcement of these rules is also a matter entirely internal to the legislature. In other words, violations of these rules do not give rise to enforceable obligations elsewhere. Instead, enforcement generally occurs by a member of the legislature raising a point of order or an objection. For instance, a U.S. Senator could object to the consideration of a measure because it includes a substantive, non-technical/non-clerical amendment proposed by a committee on a matter outside that committee's jurisdiction, in violation of Senate rule XV, § 5. But if no one in the Senate raises this objection and the measure eventually is enacted into law, the procedural defect that occurred during the measure's Senate consideration cannot be used to challenge or invalidate the law. Expressed in more general terms, courts will not look beyond Congress's own attestation that a measure was duly enacted. *See Field v. Clark*, 143 U.S. 649 (1892). Most states have their own versions of this "enrolled bill" doctrine. *See, e.g., Consumer Party of Pa. v. Commonwealth*, 507 A.2d 323, 331–333 (Pa. 1986).

In the first instance, responsibility for ruling on a point of order usually rests with the body's parliamentarian, an unelected staff member appointed by the legislative leadership whose job is to interpret and apply the internal rules. However, the parliamentarian's decisions and interpretations are always subject to being overruled (or sustained) by the will of the body.

In addition to being governed by the many formal rules, both internal and constitutional, most legislative chambers also are deeply influenced by a set of norms that have developed over time. These include whether and how to appoint a parliamentarian, and what other officers and staff assistants to appoint or hire. They also include: various seniority norms, under which Members who have been serving in the legislature the longest are given favored positions or leadership roles, or are looked to for guidance; the creation and use of a variety of "caucuses" or subsets of Members, organized not only around political parties (the House Republican Conference, for instance) but also around ideology or subject area (the Blue Dog Coalition or the Congressional Bike Caucus, for instance), or racial or ethnic groups (the Legislative Black Caucus, for instance); and the manner in which the majority and minority parties organize themselves, establish their legislative agendas, and control their members.

Legislative norms also can include understandings concerning how committees will operate (for instance, when to issue published committee reports, or how to select witnesses to appear at hearings); the ways in which legislators communicate with each other (for instance, through "Dear Colleague" letters); and expectations surrounding the identification and addition of co-sponsors for legislative measures. Expectations concerning how lobbyists share information with legislators may also be part of the institutional culture, or norms, of a legislature, and may be constrained by lobbying regulations and ethics rules (as discussed in Chapter 4).

2. BILL INTRODUCTION AND COMMITTEE REFERRAL

Only duly recognized members of a legislature (as described in Chapter 3) have the privilege of introducing a legislative proposal to their respective legislative chamber. When a new proposal is introduced, it becomes a "bill" and is given a bill number, usually chronologically in numerical order starting at "1" with the first measure in each congress or legislature. Each chamber assigns its own bill numbers, in Congress using a prefix of "S." or "H.R." to distinguish Senate bills from House bills.

Individual members can be motivated to introduce a bill for many different reasons. Often legislators will be motivated to introduce a new law or law reform proposal by their own personal experience, by a constituent confronting an issue, or on the basis of staff advice. Legislative leaders may introduce a measure on behalf of an entire party caucus, endorsing it as part of the party's broader legislative agenda. Legislators also will often work closely with lobbyists in introducing measures that are supported (and often even drafted) by particular interest groups. And it is obviously important for a President or a Governor to have allies in the legislature who can introduce measures at the chief executive's request. State budget bills routinely begin with a courtesy introduction of the Governor's proposed budget.

After a bill is formally introduced in a particular house of the legislature, internal rules generally provide for a number of steps before it can be voted on, and indeed often even before it can be the topic of debate before the full chamber. Typically, the next step is for the parliamentarian of the chamber to refer the bill to a particular legislative committee. Legislative committees are usually constituted by subject areas, again entirely as a matter of internal process or custom. In Congress, some of these committees' subject areas include: Aging; Agriculture; Appropriations; Armed Services; Energy and Commerce; Foreign Affairs; Health, Education, Labor, and Pensions; Homeland Security; Judiciary; Small Business; and Veterans' Affairs. Bills then are also classified by subject, in order to match them with the most appropriate committee. In Congress, for example, when a measure covers subjects within the ambit of more than one committee, the "weight of the bill" test may be used to determine the appropriate committee assignment according to the bill's "predominant subject." Alternatively, a bill implicating multiple subjects may receive referrals to multiple committees. Committees in turn often have authority to organize subcommittees, with each subcommittee having some further substantive specialization.

It is important to note that reliance on committees is not a constitutional requirement, but instead is the legislature's deliberate delegation of its legislative workload to a trusted subsidiary body. Occasionally—and perhaps more frequently during periods of intense partisanship and legislative dysfunction—legislative leaders, rather than letting a measure be referred to a committee, may keep it before the entire body (as happened, for instance, in the U.S. Senate's consideration of the House version of the Civil Rights Act of 1964, and the U.S. House's consideration of the Senate version of the Patient Protection and Affordable Care Act of 2010). But the expertise cultivated in various subject-matter committees and subcommittees continues to enhance the efficiency and sophistication with which bills are considered.

3. COMMITTEE CONSIDERATION

The committee stage is critical to the traditional legislative process. In part this is because most bills "die" in committee, as can be seen by comparing the number of measures referred to committees in any given legislature to the number of measures reported out of committees. Not only is the committee phase crucial because most legislative proposals fail to survive the committee "gatekeeping" process, but also because, even for those that do survive, it is where the vast majority of substantive changes (amendments) are considered.

By internal rules, committees are led by a chair, typically appointed by the majority leader of the legislative chamber. The leader of the chamber also appoints the remaining members of each committee, drawing members of the minority party from the recommendations of the minority leadership, and in rough proportion to the parties' overall numbers in the full chamber. Thus, political control over a legislative chamber also brings with it control of all committees. In many legislatures, the position of committee chair typically goes to the committee member of the majority party with the most seniority, although this usually is a mere institutional norm. The committee members of the minority party also will have a minority leader on the committee, often called the "ranking member," who also is typically the most senior of the minority party members. Because of the gatekeeping role of committees and subcommittees, these chairs exercise enormous power.

Committees and subcommittees perform two primary and related functions in connection with the bills referred to them. First, they conduct hearings on the bill; and second, they "mark-up," or debate and amend the bill. When committees delegate consideration of a bill to a subcommittee, the subcommittee eventually must return the bill to the parent committee, rather than to the full chamber. As a result, hearings and mark-ups may occur at both the subcommittee and committee levels.

Hearings are an opportunity for committees (and subcommittees) to seek advice and input about the bill from a variety of knowledgeable experts and affected individuals. Although most witnesses appear voluntarily, Congressional committees, as well as some state legislative committees, have explicit authority, as necessary, to issue subpoenas to compel witnesses to appear and testify. These witnesses may testify in support of or in opposition to a bill, or they may simply provide information for the committee members to consider in deciding whether to support, amend, or oppose the bill.

Most committee hearings are public events, attended by representatives of interested parties, perhaps a few media organizations, and some members of the general public. On occasion, a hearing for a high-profile bill will draw a large crowd and many media representatives, but many committee hearings are subdued affairs. Representatives of concerned interest groups are a consistent presence at almost all hearings. As public events, hearings can also provide opportunities for legislators to "grandstand" to some degree, as they declare their own views, justify their positions, or seek to undermine opposing views.

A committee's (or subcommittee's) mark-up sessions are also typically public events. During mark-up, committees use their subject matter expertise, as informed by the information gathered through the hearings process, to recommend changes to the bill as it was originally introduced. Changes are suggested through proposed amendments, which must then be approved by a majority vote of the committee. Often, however, a committee will informally agree to a whole host of changes to a bill, and then formally adopt all of these changes en masse by agreeing to an "amendment in the nature of a substitute," which replaces the original bill with a wholly new measure.

After the conclusion of all the hearings and mark-up sessions, legislative committees have a third primary responsibility, discussed in the next subsection: to report back to the full body about the committee's work on a specific piece of legislation. When a subcommittee has finished its work, it returns the measure to the parent committee, perhaps with a draft committee report for the committee to decide whether to adopt and send on to the full chamber. Occasionally (and with increasing frequency), several congressional committees will collaborate in preparing a piece of "omnibus" legislation that combines the work of these multiple committees into one bill for full chamber consideration as a whole.

4. COMMITTEE REPORTS

When a committee is done considering a particular measure, it reports the measure to the full chamber. In Congress, the action of reporting a measure is almost always accompanied by a published document—the committee's formal Report. This document typically contains the full text of the bill, as amended by the committee; summarizes the bill; and presents the committee's views on the measure. The report also will often present accompanying views of dissenting members of the committee. As described in Chapter 10 below, committee reports are often used as aids in interpreting ambiguous provisions.

Many state legislative committees do not have a rule (or custom or practice) of preparing a published report to accompany bills sent back to the full legislature. Instead, the committee "report" consists of the procedural step of informing the leadership that the committee has completed its hearings and mark-up and is ready to reintroduce the measure, as amended in the committee, to the full chamber. Usually this step comes with the committee's endorsement of the measure, although occasionally a committee will report a measure "without recommendation."

Committee reports play a crucial role in the life of a bill. In Congress, the written committee reports are required, by internal rule, to be available to all members "at least 48-hours before" the time when the Senate plans to take up or debate the measure, and three calendar days prior to consideration in the House. *See* Senate Rule XXVIII, § 10(a)(1); House Rule XIII, § 4(a)(1). These requirements serve not only to provide members with advance notice of the upcoming agenda, but also to give them time to consider the merits of the bill as amended by the committee, in light of the committee's careful evaluation. Furthermore, for some legislative proposals, committee reports can be a more accessible and efficient means for legislators to understand how a proposed law would operate than reading the full text of the proposed measure. Finally, legislators often will rely on members of their staff to digest these committee reports, especially in areas of less interest or familiarity to the legislator, and then to brief the legislator on the merits of the bill. In the life of a busy legislator, this staff role can be an especially critical one.

5. GETTING A MEASURE TO THE FLOOR

Committees perform a significant "gatekeeping" function in winnowing down the number of measures that receive full consideration by a legislative chamber, but committee approval is no guarantee that a measure will reach the floor to receive the formal attention of the full chamber. Before a measure can become the pending business of a legislative chamber, it must be placed on the calendar (or one of several calendars) of that chamber. The leaders of the majority party in each chamber control the calendar and thus have substantial influence in setting the agenda of measures that the full chamber will take up.

For instance, in recent Congresses, the Speaker of the U.S. House of Representatives has followed an internal norm ("the Hastert Rule") of not bringing a measure to the floor unless it appears that a majority of the Members of the controlling party supports the measure. The House Rules Committee also can often prevent a measure from reaching the floor simply by refusing to adopt a "rule" to govern how floor debate concerning the measure will occur. Though procedural devices exist to circumvent some of this foot-dragging, use of these devices is unusual under congressional norms.

In the U.S. Senate, meanwhile, bringing a measure to the floor for consideration typically requires adoption of a "motion to proceed." Under the Senate's internal rules, both this motion and the underlying legislative proposal are subject to a potential "filibuster," in which opponents of a measure take advantage of the Senate's norm of permitting unlimited debate to keep the motion to proceed pending indefinitely. Ending a filibuster (or a threatened filibuster) takes the agreement of a three-fifths supermajority, or sixty Senators in today's 100-member Senate.

6. FLOOR DEBATE AND VOTING

The most visible stage of the legislative process is the "floor debate," or in other words the formal consideration that a measure receives in a particular legislative chamber by the full membership of that chamber. But in the typical congressional case, not much of interest actually occurs here. Instead, floor debate often takes place with very few members present in the almost empty chamber, and is mostly a dramatic show that precedes the official vote on a bill. Those substantive developments that do occur at this relatively late stage, primarily in terms of amendments, are usually highly scripted or noncontroversial. Floor debate in state legislatures can be somewhat more influential and often occurs in front of a full audience, as a result of both its importance and strict attendance rules.

In both Congress and state legislatures, legislative leaders will not allow a measure they support to become the official business of the legislative chamber until they are confident that the measure has sufficient votes to pass. Conversely, if it is a high-profile measure to which they are opposed, they may work to hurry it to a floor vote if they are confident it will fail, in order to exhibit that the measure lacked sufficient support. As a result, the "debate" that occurs at this stage often is primarily an opportunity for both proponents and opponents publicly to make their best case, justifying their position to both their constituents and the broader public, but not primarily to persuade their colleagues to support their position. In Congress, it also is an opportunity for members to have these statements of position published as part of the Congressional Record, a practice with the potential to influence subsequent interpretation of an enacted law, as discussed below in Chapter 10.

In the U.S. House of Representatives, floor debate is usually structured by a rule (promulgated by the House Rules Committee) crafted specifically for each measure that specifies how much total time will be spent debating the measure, how that time will be divided (including for how many minutes any one member may speak about the measure), and how many amendments may be offered. In the U.S. Senate, internal rules establish a default floor process that permits unlimited debate, although by internal rule this default may be altered by a three-fifths supermajority vote (sixty votes) to limit or close debate. The Senate's right of unlimited debate on occasion gives rise to a filibuster, a strategic effort to kill a measure by debating it incessantly until its proponents are forced to withdraw it, unless the measure can draw the support of a three-fifths supermajority. In recent decades, it is often the mere threat of a filibuster that achieves this end.

Once a measure has become the official business of a legislative body, debate concerning proposed amendments to the measure (sometimes with a little more member attendance) often consumes as much time as debate over the merits of the underlying proposal itself. Usually the outcome of these amendment attempts is a foregone conclusion, with some doomed to fail, and others anticipated to succeed. In either case their discussion can bring into relief what the bill would do with and without the amendment, again providing arguments of potential relevance to the interpretive problems discussed in Part II. Individual legislatures have internal rules governing whether or when amendments must be "germane" to the measure they are amending.

Floor amendments can be both strategically important and politically important. As a strategic matter, amendments may be essential to garnering sufficient support to ensure passage of the underlying measure. Amendments also may be offered in an attempt to weaken the underlying measure, or occasionally even with the hope that adoption of the amendment will amount to a "poison pill" that dooms the underlying measure, perhaps by fracturing whatever coalition had been prepared to support it, or by complicating its implementation. As a political matter, amendments may be offered in order for legislators to go on record with a more detailed or nuanced demonstration of their position than would be possible by a simple vote up or down on the underlying measure.

At some point, consideration of amendments ceases and debate on the underlying bill (as amended) begins. Here, committee leaders and sponsors of the measure usually take a lead role in promoting the measure. Because of their familiarity with the bill, their representations about its meaning and impact may be given great weight by colleagues who are unfamiliar with the bill. Opponents also have an opportunity to characterize the problems and weaknesses of the measure; their arguments are occasionally viewed as potentially more exaggerated, hyperbolic, or untrustworthy than supporters' arguments.

Once the time for debate on the bill has expired, or if a motion to proceed to the vote (often termed a motion "to call the question" or "to order the previous question") succeeds, members then vote on the measure. The results of this vote, often termed the vote on "final passage," are recorded in the Journal of the chamber, the official record of its actions.

7. THE SECOND BODY—BICAMERALISM IN ACTION

A measure that has succeeded in one house then must complete the same process again in the other house (except in unicameral Nebraska). Sometimes members of each body will introduce identical or similar measures in both houses at approximately the same time, and let each house proceed to consider the measures in due course. Eventually, one measure will be allowed to function as the primary measure, if only because it is the first one to have passed the chamber where it originated. This first chamber then formally notifies the other of its action and transmits the bill to the other chamber for consideration. At that point, the second house will put the measure through essentially the same process, beginning with referral to the appropriate committee; then committee hearings, mark-up, and reporting to the floor; followed by floor debate, amendment, and voting.

The second house has the full right to refuse to consider the measure at any stage, including holding it up in committee; to consider it and vote against it; or to amend it and pass it as amended. But unless the second house passes the measure exactly as it was received from the first house, the bicameralism requirement has not been met. At that point, if changes have been made, the measure may be shunted back to the originating chamber, where more work is then required.

8. CONFERENCE COMMITTEES

As just indicated, what often emerges from the second body is no longer the same measure that went in. In the typical case, either the two houses of the legislature then must work together to iron out the differences between the two versions that have each passed only one house, or one of the houses must acquiesce to the version that the other has passed. The two houses are equal in this regard, with neither having a superior position, either by dint of having passed the first version of the measure, or because of any difference between the "upper" and "lower" houses of the legislature.

Differences are usually ironed out by appointing a "conference committee," consisting of members of both chambers appointed by their leaders specifically for the one-time purpose of resolving differences between the two versions of a particular bill. For instance, the conference committee formed for a prison bill will be different from the conference committee for a hydraulic fracturing bill. Conference committee members are chosen based on their position as leaders in their respective chamber, or their substantive expertise concerning the specific measure at issue (often, though not necessarily, including members who have already helped handle the measure in committee, before it passed their chamber).

The role of the conference committee is to get supporters of the two versions to come to an agreement on one common measure. To that end, internal rules in Congress specifically prohibit a conference committee from taking up new matters or revisiting elements already common to both chambers' versions of the measure. But enforcement of this limitation is also entirely an internal matter, and conference committees may take up matters outside their jurisdiction if they are prepared to take the risk that some member of either chamber will raise an objection when the conference committee version is subsequently presented.

Assuming a conference committee is able to develop a compromise measure that it anticipates will be acceptable to both chambers, the conference committee then prepares its own written committee report to explain its work and support its recommendations. This report, including the full text of the proposed compromise measure, is then submitted to and voted on by both houses. If both houses agree to it, the bicameralism requirement of Article I is satisfied. If either chamber fails to agree to the conference report, it is back to the drawing board.

It also is possible for a conference committee to entirely fail to produce a conference agreement, or to conclude that one of the two measures with which it began should simply be reconsidered by the second house.

Once a measure has passed both houses, it is "enrolled." This means that an official version is prepared and certified by the chamber in which it originated, then signed by the presiding officers of each chamber (in Congress, the Speaker of the House and the President Pro Tempore of the Senate). The enrolled bill then is presented to the President or Governor for approval or disapproval (veto).

9. PRESENTMENT TO THE PRESIDENT OR GOVERNOR

Again, as part of the checks and balances built into a system of separated governmental powers, once a legislative measure has satisfied the bicameralism requirement, it cannot become law without its presentment to the head of the executive branch for approval or veto. If the measure is then vetoed, it can only become law if the legislature, after an opportunity to consider the chief executive's reasons for disapproving it, then passes it by a specified supermajority vote notwithstanding the veto.

The presentment requirement provides the President or Governor more than just an opportunity to veto a measure, however. It also can serve as a moment for another necessary actor in the lawmaking process—and the only individual actor personally necessary—to reflect upon and articulate an understanding of the intended purpose and effect of the measure, and to consider whether the text of the measure is adequate to effectuate that purpose. While on occasion this opportunity may devolve into mere "grandstanding," it also can serve as a reference point, both for understanding how the lawmaking process works generally as well as for understanding the specific measure approved or vetoed.

As discussed in Chapter 10 below, deriving interpretive guidance from a chief executive's statements upon signing a measure into law is not without some controversy. Also controversial are attempts at this stage by the chief executive to amend the enactment implicitly, for instance by purporting to condition approval of the measure on a claim that the measure can only be read in a narrow, or broad, or particular way, and would not have received the executive's approval were it to be read otherwise. Meanwhile, veto messages can be particularly instructive when they shape a subsequent legislative measure intended to respond to or accommodate the executive's reasons for disapproval.

In the federal system, once the President signs a measure, it is immediately effective, unless the measure by its own terms provides for a subsequent effective date. The Office of the Federal Register then publishes each new law as a "slip law," which can also be accessed electronically through the website of the Government Printing Office. The new law also will eventually be included in the United States Statutes at Large, a volume of "session laws," comprising all of the measures enacted into law during that same session of Congress.

If the President instead disapproves (vetoes) a measure, the measure is returned, along with the President's veto message, to the House of Congress that originated the measure. There Congress can begin considering whether to enact the measure into law notwithstanding the President's veto. Both Houses must approve the measure by a two-thirds supermajority in order to enact the measure into law over the President's objections. If both houses obtain the required supermajority, the Office of the Federal Register then publishes the "slip law" version of the new law.

In about half the states, measures signed by the Governor ordinarily are not immediately effective. Instead, these measures must wait a specified period (usually ninety days) in order to provide the state's voters their own opportunity to disapprove the measure using the popular referendum process (discussed further in section E below). In an emergency, the state legislature can avoid the referendum process and make a measure immediately effective upon the Governor's approval by passing a measure by a specified supermajority. In state systems, official publication of measures enacted into law then is typically the responsibility of the Office of the Secretary of State, first as slip laws, then later as session laws.

10. FOSTERING ROBUST DELIBERATION: LEGISLATIVE PRIVILEGE

This chapter's description of the legislative process concludes with an overview of the "legislative privilege," a topic of great importance to a legislature's ability to engage in robust, thoughtful deliberation in the public interest at all stages of the process. The legislative privilege is a long-standing protection of the independence of the legislative branch of government that shields legislators against harassment or intimidation by the other branches concerning the legislators' performance of their legislative work. However, this is a protection that occasionally complicates the enforcement of bribery laws and other external efforts to regulate legislative deliberations.

The Framers of the U.S. Constitution enshrined in Article I the principle that legislators should be formally accountable for how they perform their legislative work only at the voting booth or within their legislative body. They did so by adopting in the Constitution's "Speech or Debate Clause" a form of the English parliamentary privilege. This Clause assures Members of Congress that "for any Speech or Debate in either House, they shall not be questioned in any other Place." U.S. Const. art. I, § 6, cl. 1. Almost all states constitutions contain an analogous protection for their state legislators, and the few remaining states recognize a legislative privilege as a matter of common law.

At the federal level, the central elements of this legislative privilege (which occasionally also goes by the name of "legislative immunity") are well settled. It precludes both (1) imposing legal liability on legislators for how they legislate (a protypical "immunity"), as well as (2) efforts to compel them to explain their legislative activities (a protypical "privilege"). It applies only to activities that are "an integral part of the deliberative and communicative processes by which Members participate" in considering matters within the constitutional jurisdiction of their chamber, *Gravel v. United States*, 408 U.S. 606, 625 (1972), and does not extend to the full range of a Member's official activities and duties (such as constituent services, guest appearances, and administrative responsibilities, among other functions outside the scope of the Speech or Debate Clause). But where the privilege applies, it is an absolute rather than a qualified privilege, meaning it is not subject to a balancing of interests. It applies both to Members of Congress as well as to their staff, at least on those occasions when staff are assisting the Member with essential legislative activities.

The Supreme Court has described the fundamental purpose of the legislative privilege as "to prevent intimidation of legislators by the Executive and accountability before a possibly hostile judiciary." *Gravel*, 408 U.S. at 617. But it also has been understood as necessary to protect legislators against the burdens of defending themselves in civil or criminal matters, as well as against the burdens of responding to discovery requests in lawsuits in which the legislator is not a party. In this last regard, the protection of the Speech or Debate Clause against being "questioned" in any place other than Congress also has regularly been applied to a Member's legislative documents, as well as to personal testimony. The legislative privilege thus provides Members of Congress with both an evidentiary and testimonial privilege, as well as an immunity against suit.

In providing Members of Congress liability immunity for the performance of their legislative duties, the Speech or Debate Clause does not preclude the prosecution of a Member for violation of the federal bribery statute (discussed above). It does, however, make these prosecutions more difficult. In

United States v. Helstoski, 442 U.S. 477, 488 (1979), the Supreme Court candidly acknowledged this, noting that "the Speech or Debate Clause was designed to preclude prosecution of Members for legislative acts," even when those acts amount to the commission of a crime, in order "to preserve the constitutional structure of separate, coequal, and independent branches of government." As a result, the Court prohibited introducing evidence of the performance of a protected legislative act.

However, the Court has distinguished between prosecuting a Member for undertaking a legislative act in furtherance of a bribe—a prosecution the Clause prohibits—and prosecuting a Member for making a *promise* to undertake a legislative act in furtherance of a bribe. The Court has concluded that a promise to take a legislative act is not itself a protected legislative act, and therefore that the act of promising to do something official as part of a corrupt exchange for a prohibited thing of value can be prosecuted without running afoul of the Speech or Debate Clause. The difficulty for prosecutors, of course, is that proving the existence of the promise will in many cases be much harder than it would instead have been to establish the existence of a corrupt bargain by introducing the performance of the legislative act itself, had the legislative privilege not prohibited doing so.

The broad contours of the legislative privilege, and its purpose of ensuring that legislators can conduct their legislative debates and deliberations without fear of liability or harassment, are relatively well-settled. Nevertheless, many subsidiary issues occasionally arise at both the state and federal levels, including questions at the margins about whether something is protected legislative activity, as well as questions about what kinds of executive branch investigatory activities unconstitutionally infringe upon the independence of the legislative branch. Meanwhile, state courts are under no obligation to construe their analogous state provisions in lockstep with the federal jurisprudence, and indeed they have not, occasionally declining to extend the privilege to staff, or refusing to apply it to protect testimony or documents. On the other hand, at least one state court has construed its legislative privilege more broadly to protect legislators for their statements to the press about legislative activities, *see Abercrombie v. McClung*, 525 P.2d 594 (Haw. 1974), a coverage that the U.S. Supreme Court's Speech or Debate Clause jurisprudence does not make available to members of Congress, *see Hutchinson v. Proxmire*, 443 U.S. 111 (1979).

B. DISTINCTIVE FEATURES OF STATE LEGISLATURES

In addition to the simple truth that each legislature sets its own internal rules, and therefore that important variations may exist between Congress and state legislatures, as well as among individual state legislatures, several additional features distinguish the functioning of state legislatures. Nebraska is even more distinct in that it has only one legislative chamber, affectionately dubbed "the unicam." However, the remaining forty-nine states, like Congress, are bicameral.

Many state legislatures are considered part-time legislatures. These legislatures typically meet for only a constitutionally specified portion of each year (or each two-year cycle). In some states this period is as short as only six weeks each year. State legislators in these states are allowed to retain whatever other occupation or position they have, and to take leave from those commitments as necessary to fulfill their legislative service. A part-time legislator may be more likely to encounter conflicts of interest, but also may remain more in touch with the concerns and views of non-politicians.

Part-time legislatures typically operate with minimal staff support. Moreover, even full-time state legislatures often function with substantially less staff support than does Congress. Legislatures with limited staff make legislators more directly responsible for their own work, on the one hand, but also reduce the amount of work that each legislator can accomplish effectively. Compared to Congress, state legislative staffing is thinnest in committee staff and personal office staff, as most state legislatures today have a permanent professional staff office to perform nonpartisan research, bill drafting, and other support services.

Many states have a constitutional rule that requires each bill to treat only a single subject. Intended to require legislatures to consider each policy proposal on its own merits, rather than allowing legislators to package unrelated measures together to obtain majority support ("log-rolling"), these single-subject rules can present some interpretive problems of their own. One threshold interpretive issue is whether enforcement of a single-subject rule is the exclusive domain of the legislature, like an internal rule, or whether the rule instead gives rise to a judicially enforceable requirement. State courts have often struggled with this question, but in recent years have shown increased willingness to occasionally invalidate a piece of legislation on this ground. *See, e.g., C.C. Dillon Co. v. City of Eureka*, 12 S.W.3d 322 (Mo. 2000). In any case, determining just what is a single legislative subject can be problematic.

Hearings often have a very different flavor in state legislatures. This may be partly because witnesses at congressional hearings are usually tightly controlled, with testimony admitted only from individuals called by committee members, whereas many state legislatures regularly allow opportunities for any member of the public to testify on proposed measures. In addition, many state legislatures do not keep transcripts of committee hearings, and also may not prepare written committee reports, in part because they have little in the way of committee staff to support the drafting of such reports.

State legislative floor debates can also be quite different. While it remains true that floor debates are primarily an opportunity to make a public statement about one's position, rather than to sway one's legislative colleagues, it is more common in state legislatures for floor debate to generate actual deliberation and dialogue. This may be partly because of mandatory attendance requirements in many states, or the lack of a filibuster or other analogous practice. Perhaps the fact that many state legislatures do not keep an official transcript of these proceedings, akin to the Congressional Record, is another influence (although archived video coverage of floor proceedings and committee meetings is growing increasingly common).

At the Presentment stage, the legislative process of most states differs from the federal process because the state constitution gives the Governor line-item veto authority. This authority allows the Governor not only to disapprove or veto an entire bill presented for approval, but also to specifically reject discrete items within a single bill. In most states, this item veto authority is limited to items of an appropriations bill, although a few states allow their governors broader authority to disapprove parts of any bill presented for approval. Gubernatorial item veto authority can dramatically change the budget process. Indeed, at the federal level Presidents have long and repeatedly sought similar authority. Congress's effort to grant such authority in the Line Item Veto Act of 1996 was found unconstitutional in *Clinton v. City of New York*, 524 U.S. 417 (1998).

Finally, in a number of states, the legislative process differs from the federal legislative process because of the availability of mechanisms of direct democracy, discussed further in section E below.

C. BUDGET AND APPROPRIATIONS MEASURES

Perhaps the most fundamental legislative responsibility is to decide how to spend public money, or in other words to decide for what purposes to appropriate government funds. Most state legislatures exercise this "power of the purse" through the enactment of a state budget bill, which controls the uses to which public revenue will be directed. Although Congress also may adopt a federal budget resolution, Congress formally controls and directs the uses of federal funds through a set of appropriations acts, which in turn are constrained by a separate set of spending authorization acts. The congressional budget resolution, meanwhile, is in reality only a nonbinding statement of principle and priorities, not a necessary component of the federal spending process. Indeed, in recent years political difficulties have sometimes entirely prevented Congress from adopting the annual budget resolution.

Several factors influence how legislatures perform the critical function of appropriating government funds. First, before government can spend money, it must be able to raise or borrow it. At the federal level, the Constitution provides that all bills for raising revenue must originate in the House of Representatives. U.S. Const. art. I, sec. 7, cl. 1. The Founders included this "Origination Clause" in order to ensure that the branch of the federal legislature closest to the people controlled the government's purse strings. The Origination Clause (or Revenue

Clause) has been construed to pertain only to general tax measures, and not to preclude the Senate from originating bills having an incidental effect of raising revenue.

The federal government also may (and does) borrow money to fund its expenses. By statute, Congress has established a limit on the cumulative amount of debt the federal government may accumulate. But the limit does not operate as much of a constraint, as Congress routinely raises the debt limit in order to prevent the federal government from defaulting on its obligations. Other budgetary rules seek to control the size of the annual deficit in the federal government's fiscal year operating budget, or to require that any new federal spending be tied to a source of funds. These constraints can substantially limit congressional activity in a wide variety of areas.

In order for a federal government department or agency to spend money, Congress first must authorize the expenditure, usually through enactment of an *authorization* measure. But authorization alone is not sufficient, as the department or agency also must have funds at its disposal. The separate *appropriations* acts are the vehicles through which Congress actually makes funds available for specific purposes. It is not uncommon for a particular federal program to have authority to spend more money than Congress has made available to it through an appropriation.

One additional critical element of how Congress decides to spend federal funds is the "Reconciliation" process. Reconciliation has proven critical because it can provide a means of circumventing a Senate filibuster, allowing legislation to pass with a simple majority rather than super-majority vote. Developed entirely as a matter of the internal rules by which Congress has chosen to structure its deliberations, the Reconciliation process was intended to help Congress align ("reconcile") spending and revenue raising measures with the annual congressional budget resolution. The budget resolution typically includes an instruction to certain committees to achieve certain budget effects through development of a Reconciliation bill. The Reconciliation bill is limited in the content it can contain but receives expedited consideration under a privileged status that limits the terms of its debate and precludes the possibility of a Senate filibuster. The parliamentary details governing exactly what can be in the Reconciliation bill and how the Reconciliation process can be used are complex, but it has increasingly become the means of accomplishing significant non-budgetary goals, for instance enacting parts of the Patient Protection and Affordable Care Act of 2010.

Some state constitutions, like the U.S. Constitution, also provide that revenue measures must originate in the lower chamber of the legislature. But far more important than this constraint is that 49 states (excluding Vermont) have some sort of balanced budget requirement that precludes deficit spending, at least with respect to the state's operating budget. (Many of these states are permitted to incur debt for purposes of capital projects, such as constructing roads or buildings, financed by specific bonding legislation.) Some states, like Congress, appropriate operating funds on an annual basis, while other states use a biennial budget cycle. Appropriating only those funds that will be available during the budget cycle, without any possibility of deficit spending, is a complex task, and may necessitate mid-year budget corrections or adjustments when actual revenues fall short of estimates.

D. STRUCTURE AND ORGANIZATION OF TYPICAL STATUTES

Familiarity with the structure of a typical statute can help in reading it. Across all states and Congress, there are some similar components to statutes. The most common elements of a basic statute are: its title (and often a separate short title as well); some combination of preamble, statement of purpose, or background legislative findings; a separate section of definitions pertinent to the substance of the act; the substantive body of the act (sometimes dividing those substantive law provisions that are of a permanent nature from those substantive law provisions that are temporary); a separate section, as appropriate, containing penalties and other enforcement mechanisms connected with violations of the act; and matters of housekeeping and of conforming the act to existing law.

However, when a bill amends provisions of existing law, it may take on a different appearance. Many states require that an amendment not just contain instructions for how to alter the pre-existing law (for example, "in section 208, replace $10,000 with $20,000"), but instead show the full text of the preexisting section, with the old language stricken and new language highlighted (for example, "No individual may contribute more than ~~$10,000~~ $20,000 each election to any campaign committee.") This can make it easier to understand the impact of proposed amendments from the face of the bill, but also can complicate the appearance and length of the bill, especially when the amendments have any degree of complexity. In Congress, the practice is that amendments to existing law contain only the instructions for changing the text of previous enactments.

Statutes are not the same as codes. The term "code" is used to refer to a subset of a particular jurisdiction's enacted law that is organized by subject matter for ease of reference. For instance, all of the Ohio legislature's permanent enactments most relevant to motor vehicle use, regardless of their date of enactment, are gathered into the Motor Vehicle *title* of the Ohio Revised Code, and then organized by subtopic within that title. But not every enacted statute becomes a part of a code, and even those statutes that are codified may be divided into different parts for purposes of codification, so that some sections of the statute appear in one title of a code, and other sections appear in other titles of the code. Typically, laws that are expected to be of permanent or continuing effect will be codified, while temporary laws—including most short-term appropriations measures, for instance—will not.

Without the organizational framework of a code, the legislature's work product might amount to a vast sequence of acts or "slip laws" eventually bound in volumes in chronological order. This is precisely what "session laws" are, a designation that includes the volumes of federal law called Statutes at Large. A jurisdiction's session law volumes contain the official text of the law. Session laws also can be interesting for historical purposes, but they can be unwieldy for finding the governing law concerning a particular topic. Nevertheless, a jurisdiction's slip laws or session laws may be the only places to go to find uncodified law.

E. DIRECT DEMOCRACY

Regardless of one's theory of representation, representative democracy depends, by definition, on an institution—the legislature—to mediate the political will of the citizens and convert it into the text of enacted law. But many states have chosen to maintain mechanisms of unmediated or direct democracy alongside their representative institutions. These mechanisms, which include the direct initiative, the indirect initiative, the popular referendum, and the legislative referendum, allow a state's voters to have a direct influence over the content of the state's statutes, rather than having to depend for their influence solely on the opportunity to vote in legislative elections. In some states, another form of direct democracy includes the recall, which permits the voters to remove an elected official from office prior to the end of the official's regular term of office.

In particular, in fourteen states the direct initiative allows a group of petitioners to put the text of a proposed statute before the state's voters for their approval or disapproval at a regular election, and eighteen states allow voters similarly to initiate a constitutional amendment. The number of petitioners required to put the initiated proposal before the electorate at large varies with each state, as do requirements that petitioners must be geographically representative—requirements that may make initiative processes extremely difficult to accomplish. Meanwhile, in nine states (including two states with a direct initiative process as well) the indirect initiative allows a group of petitioners to compel the state legislature to consider a specific statutory proposal, while providing an opportunity for the voters themselves to consider the same proposal at an upcoming election if the legislature fails to act.

The legislative referendum allows the legislature to refer a specific statutory proposal to the state's voters for their consideration, letting their wishes as expressed at the voting booth, rather than the legislature's vote, determine whether the proposal becomes law. The popular referendum, on the other hand, allows the electorate at large to review a measure already enacted by the state legislature but not yet effective. If the electorate at large disapproves the legislature's enactment, the measure cannot take effect and is functionally nullified. The popular referendum, like the initiative, requires a specified number of signatories on a referendum petition, often with geographic distribution requirements, in order to place the issue before the electorate at large.

All of these mechanisms allow the voters a kind of check on the operation of the legislature, enabling citizens to act when legislators are unwilling or unable to do so, for whatever reason. For instance, state legislative term limits, as discussed in Chapter 3.D, were overwhelmingly the product of popular initiatives, given that many incumbent state legislators were themselves reluctant to support limiting their terms. Among other examples, initiative processes have also been used to restructure the processes by which legislative districts are drawn, or to impose tax limitations (perhaps most famously California's Proposition 13 in 1978).

Most states' methods of direct democracy trace to the Progressive Era and its efforts to make government more popularly accountable. But in recent decades the mechanisms of direct democracy have often been captured by well-financed interest groups, who may have a much easier time than grass-roots reformers collecting the requisite signatures, given the Supreme Court's decision in 1988 that under the First Amendment states could not prohibit initiative proponents from paying signature gatherers. *See Meyer v. Grant*, 486 U.S. 414 (1988). As a result, the processes of direct democracy have themselves become the focus of renewed attention and reform efforts. For instance, in an effort to reduce the degree to which outside interest groups could affect local policies, Colorado adopted several measures that regulated various aspects of the signature-gathering process for initiated statutes. In *Buckley v. American Constitutional Law Foundation*, 525 U.S. 182 (1999), the U.S. Supreme Court found unconstitutional several of these requirements, including that signature gatherers be Colorado voters, and that they wear name tags.

The existence in many states of direct democracy options provides an opportunity for continuing evaluation of the relative strengths and weaknesses of representative democracy. Important questions continue to be whether the mediated lawmaking that occurs in legislatures offers greater protection of minority interests from majority tyranny than direct democracy, and when and to what extent legislative deliberation helps to produce laws that are more carefully tailored to the complexities of contemporary American society than popular initiatives. Of course, concerns about legislative gridlock and other dysfunctions also continue to raise significant questions about the effectiveness of representative institutions.

CHAPTER 6

INSIDE THE ADMINISTRATIVE STATE: THE AUTHORITY AND OPERATION OF GOVERNMENT AGENCIES

WHAT'S IN THIS CHAPTER:

At both the federal and state levels, the twentieth century saw a dramatic increase in the extent to which government agencies not only implement but also shape and influence government policy. More particularly, in addition to performing an array of executive branch functions, these administrative agencies also partake of significant legislative and judicial functions. Indeed, today these agencies are responsible for vast amounts of both rule creation and conflict adjudication, and have become by far the dominant forum for interactions between citizens and their government. A basic understanding of their organization, role, and function therefore is essential.

At bottom, administrative agencies are a reflection that Congress, the President, and the federal courts (as well as the analogous institutional actors at the state levels) need assistance. To meet the challenges of governing an increasingly complex society, Congress has relied upon those with expertise in a particular field to develop and enforce regulations having a much finer grain than the broadly focused statutes that Congress is well-suited to enact. The New Deal Era saw a marked increase in the responsibilities of federal agencies, though their growth continued throughout much of the twentieth century. Meanwhile, Congress also has tasked these same experts to resolve numerous controversies related to their areas of expertise, subject to court review.

A. AGENCIES ARE SUBJECT TO SUBSTANTIAL LEGISLATIVE CONTROL

Although most government agencies are typically thought of as part of the executive branch of government (or as part of an extra-constitutional "fourth branch" of government), they nonetheless are usually creations of the legislative branch. Even in the states, most of whose constitutions establish multiple elected executive branch offices in addition to the Governor, such as State Treasurer or State Attorney General, it remains for the state legislature to specify the contours of the various departments that these officials will direct. Legislatures, in short, decide what responsibilities to assign to administrative agencies (subject of course to potential veto by the President or Governor), as well as what authority to give them to fulfill those responsibilities. Executive branch departments and agencies also depend upon the legislative branch for appropriations to fund—and direct—their operations.

1. FEDERAL AGENCIES ARE CREATURES OF STATUTE

At the federal level, Article II of the U.S. Constitution vests "The executive Power" in the President of the United States. As specified in Article II, this power includes the power to oversee "each of the executive Departments," to appoint "Officers of the United States, whose Appointments . . . shall be established by law," and to "Commission all the Officers of the United States." Yet Congress in the first instance must establish these executive departments, none of which are established by the Constitution. Congress also must specify those Officers within each department whose appointments are to be made by the President (whether unilaterally or with the advice and consent of the Senate), as well as those other executive branch positions that may be filled not by the President but by "the Heads of Departments."

In 1789, three of the First Congress's early legislative acts were the creation of the first three federal departments: the Department of Foreign Affairs (later that same year renamed the Department of State), the Department of War (what we today call the Department of Defense), and the Department of Treasury. Through enabling statutes, Congress gave each of these departments a specific charge, and provided that each was to be led by a Secretary, who was to be appointed by the President with the advice and consent of the Senate. The first Congress also established the position of Attorney General of the United States, but did so without creating a department for that official to lead.

As the country grew in size and complexity or confronted new challenges, Congress from time to time created other executive branch departments or reorganized existing federal departments. For instance, in 1870 Congress established the Department of Justice, and placed the Attorney General at its head. In 1979, Congress divided the Department of Health, Education, and Welfare into a reconfigured Department of Health and Human Services and a freestanding Department of Education. After the terrorist attacks of September 11, 2001, Congress created a new Department of Homeland Security, consolidating under one head an array of functions that previously had been scattered across many other departments and agencies.

Today, the federal government contains fifteen executive branch departments, each created by Congress and each led by a Secretary who is appointed by the President, with the advice and consent of the Senate, pursuant to article II, section 2 of the Constitution. Each of these department heads reports directly to the President and also serves as a member of the President's Cabinet. In furtherance of the President's constitutional responsibility to "take Care that the Laws be faithfully executed," U.S. Const. art. II, sec. 3, the President retains significant control over these departments, mainly through the authority to remove at will any of the department heads.

In addition to these fifteen departments, scores of other agencies—such as the Central Intelligence Agency, the Environmental Protection Agency, and the National Science Foundation—now also are part of the federal bureaucracy. Many of these bureaucratic offices are "independent" agencies, which differ from the departments and other executive agencies primarily in that Congress has opted to make them independent of direct presidential control. Instead, these agencies are typically led by a set of bipartisan commissioners, appointed by the President for staggered terms independent of the duration of any one presidential administration. The heads of these independent agencies are not removable by the President except for good cause (such as incapacity, neglect of duty, or malfeasance in office). The now-defunct Interstate Commerce Commission, established in 1887 primarily to regulate railroad rates (and disestablished in 1995), is usually identified as the first of the independent federal regulatory agencies.

A series of Supreme Court decisions has shaped the understanding of the relationship between the President and the officers of the various federal government departments and agencies. In *Myers v. United States*, 272 U.S. 52 (1926), a divided Court concluded that an inherent component of the President's constitutional responsibility to execute the laws was a unilateral power to remove those executive branch officials—in this case, a local postmaster—who no longer had the President's trust or support. Although the congressional statute creating the positions of postmasters had conditioned both their appointment *and their removal* on the advice and consent of the Senate, the Court held that conditioning the President's removal power on Senate consent was unconstitutional. As the Court explained, the President's ability to execute the laws depended on the assistance of subordinates who would act under his direction; it therefore was "essential" that the President have the "power of removing those for whom he cannot continue to be responsible." *Id.* at 117.

However, shortly thereafter, the Supreme Court in *Humphrey's Executor v. United States*, 295 U.S. 602 (1935), limited the scope of its *Myers* decision by distinguishing independent federal agencies from government departments under presidential control. Although the President's removal power remained "exclusive and illimitable" with respect to officials in the prototypical "units in the executive department," the Court explained that Congress was free to create agencies not subject to presidential direction or control, including agencies—in this case, the Federal Trade Commission (FTC)—whose Commissioners were not removable at will by the President. Part of the Court's reasoning was the recognition that Congress had given the FTC "duties" of a legislative and judicial character, not just executive duties, as a result of which the Court concluded that the FTC "cannot in any proper sense be characterized as an arm or an eye of the executive." *Id.* at 627–28.

Although the holding of *Humphrey's Executor* pertained only to whether the President had removal power over the commissioner of an independent agency, the decision also was important for the wide latitude it granted Congress to decide how to structure government agencies. The Court characterized the Federal Trade Commission "as an agency of the legislative and judicial departments," rather than of the executive department, because Congress had assigned to it "legislative and judicial powers." The Court made clear that Congress had the power, as it deemed fit, to create administrative bodies "free from executive control," in furtherance of whatever legitimate policy or purpose Congress intended the agency to pursue.

Today, however, independent agencies like the FTC are not generally classified as agencies of the legislative or judicial branches. Rather, it is common to speak of these independent agencies as still part of the executive branch, despite the facts that Congress often gives these agencies (as well as the prototypical executive branch departments) quasi-legislative or quasi-judicial responsibilities, and that the agencies are largely insulated from presidential control because of the job security that Congress has given the agencies' leaders. Alternatively, the independent federal agencies are sometimes referred to as the "fourth branch" of government, reflecting the reality that these agencies do not fit cleanly into the typical tripartite separation of powers. Meanwhile, both the legislative branch and the judicial branch also each now have a handful of their own "agencies" (such as the Congressional Budget Office and the Government Accountability Office, in the legislative branch, and the Judicial Conference of the United States and the U.S. Sentencing Commission, in the judicial branch) that perform important functions to assist their respective branches. These legislative and judicial branch agencies are not usually included in the category of independent agencies.

A few other examples of independent agencies within the federal government include the National Labor Relations Board, the Securities and Exchange Commission, the Federal Election Commission, and the Federal Reserve. But in the eyes of many scholars of federal bureaucracy, agency "independence" is not an all-or-nothing characteristic. Rather, the degree of agency "independence" may be a function of several congressionally specified factors, including not only the protection of agency heads against removal at will, but also such other criteria as requirements of bipartisan leadership, terms of office of the agency leaders, the nature of the agency's adjudicative responsibilities, and how the agency is funded.

Thus, consistent with *Humphrey's Executor*, Congress has substantial control over how it structures administrative agencies, including over the factors that determine a given agency's degree of independence. Congressional flexibility is not unlimited, however. For example, in *Buckley v. Valeo*, 424 U.S. 1 (1976), the Supreme Court invalidated Congress' first attempt to establish the Federal Election Commission (FEC) because Congress had reserved to itself the power to appoint two of the Commission's eight members. The Court held that because of their duties, FEC Commissioners were "Officers" of the United States and therefore could be appointed only by the President, in conformity with Article II, Section 2 of the Constitution. (In response, Congress restructured the Commission so that all commissioners were appointed by the President, with the Senate's advice and consent.)

A decade later, the Supreme Court in *Bowsher v. Synar*, 478 U.S. 714, 726 (1986), held that "Congress cannot reserve for itself the power of removal of an officer charged with the execution of laws" (other than through the use of its impeachment power). At issue was the Comptroller General's role in executing the Balanced Budget and Emergency Deficit Control Act of 1985 by preparing program-by-program budget reductions sufficient to achieve specified spending targets, which the Act mandated the President to follow. The Comptroller General was the head of what was then called the General Accounting Office (now the Government Accountability Office), a legislative branch agency. The Court explained: "To permit the execution of laws to be vested in an officer answerable only to Congress would, in practical terms, reserve in Congress control over the execution of laws." This would be an untenable "usurpation of Executive Branch functions." In response to the Court's decision, Congress once again was able to restructure the statutory scheme with relative ease (by moving the responsibility to oversee the budget reduction targets from the Comptroller General, within the legislative branch, to the White House Office of Management and Budget, within the executive branch) to preserve the Balanced Budget Act's underlying substantive ends. *See also Free Enterprise Fund v. Public Company Accounting Oversight Board*, 561 U.S. 477 (2010) (holding method for removing members of Public Company Accounting Oversight Board unconstitutional).

2. STATE AGENCIES ALSO ARE LARGELY CREATURES OF STATUTE

State administrative agencies also are largely creatures of state statutes, although the landscape surrounding state agencies and departments often differs somewhat from that of the federal system. Perhaps most significantly, many state constitutions expressly create several executive branch officers, in addition to the Governor, each of them separately elected. For instance, forty-three states elect their state Attorney General, while thirty-eight states elect the state Treasurer and the Secretary of State. Many other examples of independently elected state officials exist, including Insurance, Banking, or Public Utility Commissioners, heads of the Department or Board of Education, and Chief

Election Officials. These elected state officers do not report to the state governor, and may take positions at odds with other elected state officials. Nevertheless, they too are highly dependent on their respective state legislature to set the terms of their authority and to fund their activities.

3. DELEGATION OF AUTHORITY TO ADMINISTRATIVE AGENCIES

Just as important as the leadership structure of an administrative agency is the legislature's choice of what authority and duties to assign to the agency. An entire judicial doctrine—***the nondelegation doctrine***—has developed around the question of what legislatures may empower agencies to do without violating the separation of powers. Primarily, this involves the question of how much lawmaking authority the legislative branch can share with the executive branch.

As observed at the outset of this chapter, legislatures may find it advantageous to leave to a body of experts—an agency—the development of more detailed regulations in a specific area of law, be it tax law, environmental law, energy law, or election law. Arguably, these agencies can develop detailed legal requirements much more efficiently than could Congress or a state legislature. On the other hand, as described in Chapter 2 above, efficiency is not necessarily a virtue for the lawmaking process, and many inefficiencies or hurdles in the legislative process are often defended as helping produce better laws in the long run. In large measure, the nondelegation doctrine addresses to what extent these legislative hurdles can be constitutionally circumvented by delegating lawmaking authority to agencies.

Although delegations of regulatory power have occurred since the First Congress, the Supreme Court has repeatedly noted that "congress cannot delegate *legislative* power" to the executive branch. *E.g.*, *Marshall Field & Co. v. Clark*, 143 U.S. 649, 692 (1892) (emphasis added). The question, then, is what amounts to a delegation of *legislative* power. The canonical answer to this question, and the most frequently invoked statement of the nondelegation doctrine, is found in *J.W. Hampton, Jr. & Co. v. United States*, 276 U.S. 394, 409 (1928): "If Congress shall lay down by legislative act an intelligible principle to which the person or body authorized to [take regulatory activity] is directed to conform, such legislative action is not a forbidden delegation of legislative power."

But what is an "intelligible principle"? In the federal system, a litany of cases suggests that almost anything can be an "intelligible principle" and that the nondelegation doctrine therefore appears to have little direct bite (although as will be discussed below in Chapter 12, when a statute leaves the extent of delegated authority ambiguous, the application of a "nondelegation canon" of interpretation often may limit the scope of the delegation). In only two cases, both involving the same statute and both in 1935 during the height of the Supreme Court's rejection of New Deal legislation, has the Court held that

Congress unconstitutionally delegated legislative power to the executive branch: In *Panama Refining Co. v. Ryan*, 293 U.S. 388 (1935), and again in *A.L.A. Schechter Poultry Corp. v. United States*, 295 U.S. 495 (1935), the Court struck down provisions of President Roosevelt's National Industrial Recovery Act (NIRA) as unconstitutional legislative delegations. At issue in *Schechter Poultry* was a provision authorizing the President to impose "codes of fair competition" on certain trades or industries. In reviewing a challenge to a resulting poultry code, the Court found this authority "virtually unfettered," notwithstanding NIRA's "statement of the general aims of rehabilitation, correction, and expansion described in section one." *Id.* at 541–42.

Yet beyond those two cases, the Supreme Court has always found an adequate "intelligible principle" in every nondelegation issue that it has addressed. As the Court explained in 1989, "our jurisprudence has been driven by a practical understanding that in our increasingly complex society . . . Congress simply cannot do its job absent an ability to delegate power." *Mistretta v. United States*, 488 U.S. 361, 372 (1989). Indeed, in the more recent case of *Whitman v. American Trucking Associations, Inc.*, 531 U.S. 457, 474–75 (2001), the Court seemed to suggest that it would be unlikely ever to "second-guess Congress regarding the permissible degree of policy judgment that can be left to those executing or applying the law." At issue was an air quality regulation that the EPA had promulgated pursuant to a provision of the Clean Air Act that instructed the EPA only to establish air quality standards that were "requisite to protect the public health." Although the Court of Appeals had held that this provision constituted an unconstitutional delegation for lack of an intelligible principle, a unanimous Supreme Court found the delegation to be constitutional.

For more about the nondelegation doctrine at the federal level, *see, e.g.*, Eric A. Posner & Adrian Vermeule, *Interring the Nondelegation Doctrine*, 69 U. CHI. L. REV. 1721 (2002); Cass R. Sunstein, *Nondelegation Canons*, 67 U. CHI. L. REV. 315 (2000); Jerry L. Mashaw, *Pro Delegation: Why Administrators Should Make Political Decisions*, 1 J.L. ECON. & ORG. 81 (1985).

In contrast, at the state level the nondelegation doctrine continues to have real teeth, at least in many states. By one account, some twenty states permit legislative delegations only if the legislature has provided specific and definite standards to guide the delegated authority, a formulation that courts in these states enforce with some strictness. *See* Jim Rossi, *Institutional Design and the Lingering Legacy of Antifederalist Separation of Powers Ideals in the States*, 52 VAND. L. REV. 1167, 1193–97 (1999). Another two-dozen states enforce a less strict but still meaningful version of the nondelegation doctrine, while only a handful of states appear willing to tolerate almost any delegation, as has become the federal pattern. *See id.* at 1191–93, 1197–1200; *see also* Gary J. Greco, *Survey, Standards or Safeguards: A Survey of the Delegation Doctrine in the States*, 8 ADMIN. L. J. AM. U. 567, 580–99 (1994).

4. LEGISLATIVE VETO OF AGENCY ACTION

For many years, Congress sought to retain some measure of control over agency uses of delegated lawmaking authority through the use of a "legislative veto," a procedure in which either House of Congress, acting by majority vote, could override a proposed agency action. The Supreme Court invalidated this veto mechanism in *INS v. Chadha*, 462 U.S. 919 (1983). The Court reasoned that the exercise of a legislative veto amounted to lawmaking by one house of Congress in contravention of the requirement in Article I of the U.S. Constitution that both houses and the President must agree in order for a measure to become law.

In place of the invalidated legislative veto mechanism, some congressional delegations of authority now contain a "report and wait" requirement. Under these requirements, an agency must report to Congress about its proposed use of delegated authority, and then wait a specified amount of time before implementing its proposal. In theory, this time delay provides Congress the opportunity to use the lawmaking process to seek to enact a new measure to override the agency proposal.

Meanwhile, other federal laws continue to call for agencies to obtain congressional committee approval before undertaking certain actions. Although under *Chadha* these requirements are not legally enforceable, most agencies adhere to them because of their desire to maintain good working relationships with Congress. For more on these dynamics, see Louis Fisher, *The Legislative Veto: Invalidated, It*

Survives, 56 L. & CONTEMP. PROBS. 273 (1993); *see also* Stephen Breyer, *The Legislative Veto After* Chadha, 72 GEO. L. J. 785 (1984).

Many states also have experimented with variations on a legislative veto mechanism. The *Chadha* decision, predicated as it was on the U.S. Constitution's Article I lawmaking requirements for Congress, did not directly affect the validity of these state legislative vetoes. Nevertheless, most states that have addressed the issue have chosen to adopt the *Chadha* reasoning, invalidating legislative vetoes of agency action if they do not comply with their particular state constitution's lawmaking requirements. But in a departure from the *Chadha* rule, at least three states (Idaho, Iowa, and New Jersey), either through court decision or explicit constitutional permission, allow a bicameral legislative veto, without gubernatorial presentment or approval. Other states with some version of a legislative veto mechanism have yet to address the question of whether it violates their state constitution.

5. FISCAL CONTROL OF AGENCIES

Congress and state legislatures also retain substantial control over the activities of government agencies through the "power of the purse." This fiscal control exists both through current limits on the purposes for which an agency is permitted to spend government funds, and by explicit or implied threats to withhold future agency funding after the fact, if the legislature perceives the agency as having misbehaved or if the agency engages in activities of which the legislature disapproves.

As noted in Chapter 5, at the federal level Congress must both *authorize* agencies to spend federal funds in pursuit of specified activities, and then separately *appropriate* actual dollars for the agencies to spend in doing so. At either stage, Congress in various ways may constrain the way in which an agency operates. For instance, when appropriating funds for an agency such as the Centers for Disease Control and Prevention, Congress may provide that "None of the funds made available for injury prevention and control at the Centers for Disease Control and Prevention may be used to advocate or promote gun control."

Because the federal appropriations process occurs annually, every year Congress has the opportunity to revisit the scope of each federal agency's permitted activities. In turn, each year every agency must submit to Congress a budget request, specifying the intended uses of the agency's desired level of funding. Congress has unfettered authority to decide how much funding to appropriate, as well as with how fine a grain—from a lump sum appropriation to a program-by-program funding allocation—to specify the permitted uses of the funding. Congress also may choose to attach "riders" to appropriations measures, which are specific statutory provisions that may impose additional substantive obligations or limits on an agency.

6. CONTROL OF AGENCIES THROUGH OTHER FORMS OF LEGISLATIVE OVERSIGHT

The appropriations process provides a crucial opportunity for legislative "oversight" of agency activity, but Congress and state legislatures also have other means of overseeing or supervising how government agencies behave. At any point, legislative committees may schedule hearings concerning a particular agency's operations, requiring key agency personnel to appear and answer questions, often under oath. Sometimes these oversight hearings occur in response to a particular controversy, but they may also occur as a matter of routine monitoring or audits. As part of the oversight process, legislators also may request (or demand through subpoena) agency documents, although agencies frequently seek to protect some of their internal information from disclosure on the basis of a legal privilege, such as "executive privilege" or "deliberative process privilege." Further, individual legislators may occasionally share concerns or ideas with agency leaders, always under the shadow of more formal oversight hearings, if warranted.

Legislative oversight has something of a mixed history, at least at the federal level. A number of high-profile congressional investigations have been incredibly important to ferreting out governmental misconduct, such as the Watergate hearings or the Iran-Contra hearings. At times, however, oversight investigations may be nothing more than raw attempts to gain partisan advantage. The House Un-American Activities Committee hearings and the

Senate McCarthy hearings of the 1950s, ostensibly intended to rid the government of Communists, were undoubtedly a low point of legislative oversight. In both of these series of hearings, Congress abused its oversight authority to embarrass and humiliate government employees and private citizens. By contrast, most agency oversight today is much more routine, seeking to understand the details of how an agency is pursuing its legislative charge.

B. TYPES OF ADMINISTRATIVE AUTHORITY

Agencies may undertake to fulfill their statutory mandates using an array of authority and tools, which often vary from agency to agency. In different contexts, these agency powers may be described using distinctive labels. Accordingly, a brief overview of some nomenclature is in order.

At the most basic level, agency authority can be divided among rulemaking (or quasi-legislative) powers, adjudicatory (or quasi-judicial) powers, and what are essentially executive or enforcement powers. For present purposes, agency rulemaking and adjudicatory powers are most interesting because they involve agencies in activities traditionally (if simplistically) understood to belong to other branches of government and these activities routinely call upon agencies to interpret and apply statutory language. Furthermore, distinguishing between rulemaking and adjudicatory powers can be crucial yet difficult.

Agency **rulemaking power** is the power to establish rules and regulations (terms used here interchangeably) of legal force, pursuant to a statutory directive that the more specific regulatory provisions are helping to operationalize. These agency rules have binding legal effect on all parties subject to the agency's jurisdiction. For instance, when the Clean Water Act authorizes the Environmental Protection Agency to develop water quality standards, the standards the agency promulgates have the same binding authority as if they were a provision in the legislation.

Although rulemaking power is undoubtedly **"lawmaking"** power, some observers have insisted on distinguishing it from **"legislative"** power, primarily for purposes of adhering to the nondelegation doctrine described above. For instance, writing for the majority in *Whitman v. American Trucking*, Justice Scalia insisted that the EPA's delegated rulemaking authority to promulgate national ambient air quality standards was constitutional because it was *not* "legislative power." 531 U.S. at 472. But in a concurring opinion, Justice Stevens took the contrasting view that it would be more accurate to describe the EPA's authority as "legislative power," although still constitutional because sufficiently constrained by an intelligible principle. *Id.* at 488–90.

Adding to the confusion, many courts and commentators frequently refer to binding agency regulations as **"legislative rules."** This label generally covers an agency's prototypical substantive regulations, as distinguished from an agency's **"interpretative rules"** or **"general policy statements."** Legislative rules are promulgated by an agency pursuant to authority to exercise lawmaking power, while interpretative rules clarify pre-existing legal obligations, and general policy statements provide notice of how an agency understands its authority or intends to conduct its operations. Legislative rules establish new legal obligations and carry the force of law, while interpretative rules and policy statements do not. Distinguishing between legislative rules and interpretive rules is not always easy, however. *See American Mining Congress v. Mine Safety & Health Administration*, 995 F.2d 1106 (D.C. Cir. 1993).

Moreover, numerous significant government activities now result from the issuance of interpretative rules, general policy statements, and other expressions of agency and executive branch positions, including presidential orders. For instance, President Obama launched his "Deferred Action for Childhood Arrivals" (DACA) immigration policy in 2012 through a policy memorandum that instructed immigration officials how to use their discretionary authority to defer removing certain undocumented immigrants who arrived in the U.S. as children. The Obama administration also repeatedly used agency policy statements or guidance memoranda to delay the effective date of portions of the Affordable Care Act. As discussed in subsection C.1 below, these non-legislative rules generally are not subject to the same procedural requirements, including an opportunity for public comment, that apply to legislative rules.

See Hudson v. Federal Aviation Administration, 192 F.3d 1031 (D.C. Cir. 1999).

Meanwhile, agencies use **adjudicatory power** to resolve specific controversies, typically concluding the adjudicatory process by issuing an agency "order." Although these orders, like rules, also have binding legal effect, by their terms they generally apply only to the parties to the particular adjudication, not more widely. Nevertheless, the involved parties can sometimes be quite broadly representative, and adjudicative orders, like court decisions, may set a precedent that will likely govern similar controversies. As a result, agencies often use adjudications to establish general policies.

For instance, in the foundational case of *Securities and Exchange Commission v. Chenery Corporation,* 332 U.S. 194, 207 (1947) *(Chenery II)*, the Supreme Court approved what it acknowledged was an "administrative order wherein a new principle is announced," over the objection that any such new principle should be treated as a rule that the agency could apply only prospectively. Although the Court suggested that when agencies are "filling in the interstices" of the statutes they are enforcing, they should use their rulemaking authority rather than their adjudicatory authority "as much as possible," the Court also said that agencies must have the flexibility to resolve unanticipated problems that arise in adjudicatory proceedings. The Supreme Court reaffirmed the same principle three decades later, holding in *National Labor Relations Board v. Bell Aerospace Company*, 416 U.S. 267 (1974), that the NLRB could use an adjudicatory proceeding rather than a rulemaking proceeding to determine that certain classes of workers were not "managerial employees" under the National Labor Relations Act.

C. PROCEDURAL CONSTRAINTS ON AGENCY OPERATIONS

The dramatic rise in the number of federal administrative agencies in the first half of the twentieth century and the accompanying increase in the substantive responsibilities that Congress delegated to these agencies understandably led to calls to constrain and regularize the way in which federal agencies used their various powers. During the New Deal era in particular, a trenchant criticism was that agencies acted with no uniform procedure, and often without much public input. The most significant response was the Administrative Procedure Act, enacted in 1946 after a decade of consideration. Today, most states have adopted their own analogous measures to regulate agency processes. Meanwhile, the Due Process Clause of the U.S. Constitution, applicable to both federal and state agency action, imposes an additional constraint on how agencies operate. Of course, Congress and state legislatures also may impose additional constraints on how individual agencies operate through statutes authorizing particular agency action.

1. THE ADMINISTRATIVE PROCEDURE ACT

The Administrative Procedure Act (APA), 5 U.S.C. §§ 500 et. seq., is often characterized as the "constitution" of federal administrative law because of the foundational way in which it defines the functioning and the limits of the authority of federal agencies. In the main, it specifies in significant detail certain processes (such as public comment opportunities and notification requirements) that all federal agencies must follow when promulgating various types of rules or adjudicating certain kinds of disputes. It also requires that federal agencies take a number of affirmative steps to keep the public informed of their work and it establishes processes for judicial review of agency action.

The APA broadly defines the term "agency," the entities to which the Act's provisions apply, as "each authority of the Government of the United States, whether or not it is within or subject to review by another agency." However, the APA expressly excludes Congress and the federal courts from its coverage, as well as the governments of U.S. territories and possessions. *See* 5 U.S.C. § 551(1). Additionally, the Supreme Court has held that the President is not an APA agency. *See Franklin v. Massachusetts*, 505 U.S. 788 (1992).

The APA divides agency actions into two broad categories: rulemaking proceedings, which produce agency rules; and adjudications, which produce agency orders. These categories reflect the potential for agencies to engage in both quasi-legislative action and quasi-judicial action. In turn, both rulemaking proceedings and adjudications can be either *formal*, involving more elaborate processes, or *informal*, giving the agency greater flexibility. Although the APA does not itself label its various processes as "formal" or "informal," its provisions specify how each type of agency action must occur.

For instance, APA section 553 (5 U.S.C. § 553) sets forth the rulemaking requirements for one category of *informal rulemaking*, a category that today is generally called **"notice and comment rulemaking."** This most-widely used rulemaking process requires an agency to provide public notice of a proposed rule through publication in the Federal Register of the substance of the proposed rule. The notice also must describe the agency's source of authority to promulgate the rule and the means by which interested parties may express their views upon the proposal. Typically, parties share those views by submitting written comments to the agency, although agencies on rare occasions may also allow oral presentations. Section 553 further requires that the agency incorporate into any resulting rules "a concise general statement of their basis and purpose."

Meanwhile, section 553 also acknowledges that sometimes an agency may be required to conduct a full-blown, trial-like proceeding, in which rules are "to be made on the record after opportunity for an agency hearing." This is *formal rulemaking*, and two separate APA provisions—5 U.S.C. §§ 556 & 557—provide detailed requirements for how agencies are to conduct these proceedings. A third section—5

U.S.C. § 3105—provides for the appointment of administrative law judges (ALJs) to preside at these formal proceedings. ALJs are a type of non-Article III federal judicial officer whose appointment the APA vests in each agency. But Supreme Court decisions have significantly limited the circumstances in which agencies must adhere to the formal hearing requirements of §§ 556 and 557. Most important, in *United States v. Florida East Coast Railway Co.*, 410 U.S. 224, 241 (1973), the Court concluded that agencies must follow the formal rulemaking process only when Congress has specifically required that the rulemaking proceeding occur "on the record after opportunity for an agency hearing." The Court held that a statutory requirement that rulemaking merely occur "after hearing" could be satisfied through the informal § 553 notice-and-comment process, or what is often called a "paper hearing."

Section 553 also contemplates other types of even more informal rulemaking. In particular, it provides that agencies may promulgate "interpretative rules" and "general statements of policy" without complying with even the notice-and-comment requirements of § 553. *See Perez v. Mortgage Bankers Ass'n*, 575 U.S. ___, 135 S. Ct. 1199 (2015). However, these statements of agency position still must comply with the requirement of APA § 552 (5 U.S.C. § 552) that all agency rules of general applicability be published in the Federal Register.

Turning from the processes of agency rulemaking to the processes of agency adjudication, here too the relevant APA provisions implicitly create a distinction between formal adjudications and informal adjudications. Section 554 of the APA (5 U.S.C. § 554) explains that agency adjudications of issues that are "required by statute to be determined on the record after opportunity for an agency hearing," like formal rulemaking issues, must follow the detailed hearing procedures of §§ 556 & 557, unless all parties to the adjudication are able to reach agreement "by consent." But the Court's 1973 decision in *Florida East Coast Railway* (which as described above concluded in the rulemaking context that a requirement of an agency "hearing" did not necessarily require the formal trial-type proceeding of §§ 556 & 557) also gave federal agencies the green light to develop and employ informal adjudicatory processes whenever a governing statute called only for adjudication "after hearing," rather than specifically calling for a hearing "on the record." The Court's subsequent decisions in *Vermont Yankee Nuclear Power Corp. v. Natural Resources Defense Council*, 435 U.S. 519 (1978) (involving rulemaking), and *Pension Benefit Guaranty Corp. v. LTV Corp.*, 496 U.S. 633 (1990) (involving adjudication), made clear that federal agencies have great discretion to choose how to conduct both rulemaking proceedings and adjudications, subject only to constitutional limits, the narrow construction of §§ 553 and 554, and any specific constraints Congress may have imposed through the agency's organic statute.

Today, many agency adjudications, like almost all agency rulemakings, are informal. Section 555 of the APA spells out certain procedural rights applicable even to informal adjudications, including the right to be represented by counsel, as well as rights to subpoena relevant witnesses, to obtain copies of records, and to receive notice and an explanation of resulting agency action. Formal adjudications are usually conducted by Administrative Law Judges, who function like hearing officers, assisting the agency in developing a factual record and making an initial or recommended decision. But the agency itself, which has final responsibility for the matter, is not required to follow or adopt the ALJ's decision.

One fundamental question that the APA leaves open is when an agency should proceed by rulemaking rather than by adjudication. As noted above, in 1947 the Supreme Court held that an agency was free to announce a generally applicable rule through an adjudicatory proceeding and need not promulgate such a rule through the rulemaking process. *See Chenery II,* 332 U.S. 194. The Court said that "the choice made between proceeding by general rule or by individual, ad hoc litigation is one that lies primarily in the informed discretion of the agency." *Id.* at 203. Although *Chenery II* did not involve the APA, the Court reiterated this principle in an APA case a quarter century later, though it admitted "there may be situations where [agency] reliance on adjudication would amount to an abuse of discretion." *National Labor Relations Board v. Bell Aerospace*, 416 U.S. at 294.

Finally, and critically, the APA specifies in great detail the manner in which federal courts are empowered to review agency action. Sections 701 through 706 govern the way in which "[a] person suffering legal wrong because of agency action . . . is entitled to judicial review thereof." In addition to establishing a presumption that agency actions are generally reviewable, *see Citizens to Preserve Overton Park v. Volpe*, 401 U.S. 402 (1971); *Abbott Laboratories v. Gardner*, 387 U.S. 136 (1967), these provisions specify the form and venue of appellate review, as well as the scope of review. Of particular import is the standard of § 706(2)(A), which provides that a reviewing court shall hold unlawful any agency action that is "arbitrary, capricious, an abuse of discretion, or otherwise not in accordance with law." Judicial review of agency action is discussed further in section D below.

2. STATE ANALOGS OF THE APA

At about the same time that Congress was developing the Administrative Procedure Act, the National Conference of Commissioners of Uniform State Laws (NCCUSL, also often called the Uniform Law Commission), with the encouragement of the American Bar Association, was developing its own Model State Administrative Procedure Act (MSAPA). Most state administrative procedure statutes trace their pedigrees to this 1946 model act, and its subsequent revisions, more than to the federal APA. However, the model state act was substantively quite like the federal APA, and indeed was developed almost in tandem with the APA. By 1981, when NCCUSL released a second revision of the MSAPA, more than half the states had adopted some version of either the original 1946 MSAPA or its 1961 revision. Other states that did not adopt some version of the full model state act at least adopted portions of the model act. In 2010, NCCUSL produced a third revision of the MSAPA. *See* www.uniformlaws.org.

3. DUE PROCESS CONSTRAINTS

In addition to statutory constraints on agency activities (exemplified most prominently by the Administrative Procedure Act), the Due Process Clause of the U.S. Constitution provides another procedural limit on the functioning of federal and state government agencies. Decades before enactment of the APA, the Supreme Court established that in the circumstances of a government agency's individualized determination of a party's legal rights or obligations, the party must have notice of the impending agency action and an opportunity to be heard by the agency. *See Londoner v. Denver*, 210 U.S. 373 (1908). But less than a decade later, the Court clarified that this principle did not apply in the circumstances of a generalized rulemaking, where it would be "impracticable that everyone should have a direct voice in [the rule's] adoption." *Bi-Metallic Investment Co. v. State Board of Education*, 239 U.S. 441, 445 (1915).

D. JUDICIAL REVIEW OF AGENCY ACTION

Implicit in the notion that the activities of government administrative agencies are constrained by both the U.S. Constitution and statutes such as the APA (and state analogs) is the promise of judicial review of agency action for conformance with these safeguards and constraints. As previously noted, the APA itself provides for judicial review of administrative activities in specific circumstances. In addition, the organic statutes that establish agencies often include their own provisions for judicial review, which may supersede the generic APA judicial review provisions but only if the congressional intent to do so is clear. *See Dickinson v. Zurko*, 527 U.S. 150 (1999). Meanwhile, general federal question jurisdiction and mandamus actions also may provide opportunities for federal courts to review agency action, as may agency enforcement proceedings brought against parties who have failed to adhere to an agency directive.

Judicial review of agency action raises difficult questions of when and to what degree courts should defer to agency expertise (which after all is a primary rationale for delegating substantial discretionary authority to agencies in the first place). Accordingly, over the years several distinct doctrines of judicial review have developed for a variety of agency rulemaking and adjudication contexts. The paragraphs below sketch the outlines of several of the most significant of these doctrines. Other topics beyond the scope of this Nutshell concerning judicial review of agency action include: the "exhaustion" requirement, which requires aggrieved parties to exhaust all avenues for relief within the administrative process before turning to courts for relief; related requirements that an agency action must be "final" before it is reviewable in court; the APA provision that judicial review is not available for agency actions "committed to agency discretion by law"; the presumption that an agency's refusal to act is not reviewable; and who has standing to seek judicial review of agency action. For more detail about these topics, see ERNEST GELLHORN & RONALD M. LEVIN, ADMINISTRATIVE LAW & PROCESS IN A NUTSHELL (5th ed. 2006).

In *Securities and Exchange Commission v. Chenery Corporation,* 318 U.S. 80 (1943) *(Chenery I)*, the U.S. Supreme Court established a fundamental premise of judicial review of agency action. In examining an SEC order rejecting a corporate reorganization plan, the Court concluded that an agency action could be sustained only on the basis that the agency had explicitly articulated at the time of its decision, and that the agency therefore must set forth its rationale with clarity. In other words, courts may not substitute their own basis for upholding an agency action if the agency's avowed basis is legally insufficient. Instead, reviewing courts either may remand for elaboration an agency action that lacks a clear rationale or may decide to invalidate an insufficiently justified agency action as "arbitrary and capricious" under the applicable judicial review provision of the APA (enacted shortly after the *Chenery I* decision).

"Arbitrary and capricious" behavior is one of several distinct categories of agency action that the APA specifies a reviewing court must invalidate. Specifically, section 706(2) of the APA requires a reviewing court to "hold unlawful and set aside" an agency action if the court determines that it falls into any one of six categories. These categories include "agency action, findings, and conclusions" that are:

> (A) arbitrary, capricious, an abuse of discretion, or otherwise not in accordance with law;
>
> (B) contrary to constitutional [law];
>
> (C) in excess of statutory [authority], or short of statutory right;
>
> (D) without observance of procedure required by law;
>
> (E) unsupported by substantial evidence in a case . . . reviewed on the record of an agency hearing . . . ; or
>
> (F) unwarranted by the facts to the extent that the facts are subject to trial de novo by the reviewing court.

Subsection (E) is applicable only to the narrow category of formal on-the-record agency proceedings conducted under APA sections 556 and 557 (or analogous proceedings), and subsection (F) is also a very limited exception involving a few circumstances that call for the reviewing court to conduct a trial de novo. Meanwhile, subsections (B), (C), and (D) straightforwardly give reviewing courts explicit charge to evaluate whether an agency has acted contrary to law. But subsection (A) provides potentially wide latitude for reviewing courts to second-guess agency action. It has not been easy for federal courts to determine just what this so-called "arbitrary and capricious review" (also often called "abuse of discretion review") should entail.

In *Vermont Yankee Nuclear Power Corp. v. Natural Resources Defense Council, Inc.*, 435 U.S. 519 (1978), the Supreme Court reviewed the process by which the Atomic Energy Commission had developed a rule concerning the reprocessing of spent nuclear fuel. The D.C. Circuit had overturned the rule as arbitrary and capricious on the basis that the rulemaking process was inadequate "to ventilate the issues" surrounding questions of nuclear safety. The Supreme Court reversed, concluding that as long as the agency had complied with the APA's statutorily prescribed rulemaking processes, it was beyond the reviewing court's authority to impose its own view of the desired procedures. More recently, the Court similarly upheld an agency's authority to revise its own interpretative rules through the same process it had followed in first issuing the interpretative rules, rather than needing to conduct a notice-and-comment process. *See Perez*, 575 U.S. ___, 135 S. Ct. 1199 (2015).

Vermont Yankee was initially perceived as signaling that the Supreme Court might be prepared to grant agencies quite a bit of deference. But only five years later, the Court in *Motor Vehicle Manufacturers Association v. State Farm Mutual Automobile Insurance Co.*, 463 U.S. 29 (1983), conducted a somewhat searching review of agency rulemaking proceedings before invalidating the resulting rule. At issue was the National Highway Traffic Safety Administration (NHTSA) rescission of the agency's previously established requirement that automobiles incorporate a passive safety restraint system. The Court first summarized the long history of NHTSA's consideration of a passive restraint requirement. Then, after explaining that the reviewing court "must 'consider whether the decision was based on a consideration of the relevant factors and whether there has been a clear error of judgment,'" *id.* at 43 (citing *Bowman Transp. v. Arkansas-Best Freight Systems*, 419 U.S. 281 (1974)), the Court concluded that NHTSA had abused its discretion. Central to the Court's conclusion was the NHTSA's failure to consider automatic airbags as an alternative to passive seatbelts once the agency concluded that passive seatbelts no longer would produce sufficient safety benefits. The Court's *State Farm* opinion reinforced the "hard look" doctrine, under which judicial review of agency decision-making required courts to take a hard look at whether the agency could justify its action as the result of "reasoned decisionmaking."

State Farm and *Vermont Yankee* are but two of many Supreme Court decisions addressing the meaning of arbitrary and capricious review under subsection (A) of APA section 706(2). Of course, what is at issue in these cases is an agency's use (or abuse) of its discretionary authority. Meanwhile, subsections (B) and (C) of section 706(2) suggest that reviewing courts might engage in *de novo* review of an agency's determination of questions of law. Yet even here, it turns out that agencies often have some discretion in how they construe the statutes that govern them, which may entitle agencies to some judicial deference even with respect to questions of law.

In 2015, however, the Supreme Court appeared to impose a new hurdle on certain agency rulemaking powers. At issue in *Michigan v. Environmental Protection Agency*, 576 U.S. ___, 135 S. Ct. 2699 (2015), was the Environmental Protection Agency's 2012 threshold regulation of power plant emissions of specified pollutants, under a statutory delegation of authority that empowered the agency to regulate these emissions if it determined that doing so was "appropriate and necessary." By a 5–4 vote, the Court held that the agency could not properly determine whether this regulation was appropriate and necessary unless it had considered the costs involved. The agency had argued that it need not consider costs in making the initial decision to regulate power plant emissions, and instead could consider costs during subsequent stages of a lengthy rulemaking process that would follow its initial decision to regulate. But Justice Scalia's majority opinion for the Court concluded that by ignoring costs even at the threshold stage, the agency had not considered all relevant factors nor engaged in "reasoned decisionmaking," as *State Farm* required.

It is too early to know the full impact in other contexts of a requirement that an agency consider regulatory costs from the outset, even when the original congressional delegation does not specifically require the agency to do so. But lower courts appear to be embracing this new hurdle, and it certainly could have widespread impact on a range of agency discretionary decisions.

Apart from questions of how an agency may use its discretionary authority, a distinct question involves how courts should oversee agency interpretations of ambiguous statutory provisions. Indeed, the issue in *Michigan v. EPA* itself arose over whether the agency had reasonably construed the governing statute's phrase "appropriate and necessary" as not requiring a consideration of costs. The Court concluded that this construction was unreasonable because it was not consistent with the sort of "reasoned decisionmaking" that the Court's earlier cases, including *State Farm*, said should be the hallmark of agency action.

Over the years, the Supreme Court has articulated a variety of context-dependent standards for how to review the validity of an agency's resolution of a question of statutory meaning. *See* William Eskridge Jr. & Lauren Baer, *The Continuum of Deference: Supreme Court Treatment of Agency Statutory Interpretations from* Chevron *to* Hamdan, 96 GEO. L. J. 1083 (2008). But the watershed Supreme Court case remains *Chevron U.S.A., Inc. v. Natural Resources Defense Council*, 467 U.S. 837 (1984), in which the Court established the principle that an agency's reasonable interpretation of a statute that it is charged with administering is entitled to judicial deference, unless Congress has clearly addressed the interpretive issue (in which case the congressional determination must govern). Yet even as *Chevron* has become the most widely cited Supreme Court administrative law opinion ever, the Court itself does not always follow it.

A more comprehensive explanation of *Chevron* deference and other deference regimes, as well as of the general problem of judicial deference to agency interpretations of ambiguous statutory language, is the subject of Chapter 12, the concluding chapter of Part II's treatment of the doctrines and tools of statutory interpretation.

PART 2

UNDERSTANDING STATUTES AND REGULATIONS

CHAPTER 7

THE CHALLENGE OF TEXTUAL INTERPRETATION

The first six chapters (Part I) of this Nutshell focused on the roles of legislatures and agencies in the American legal system, and the processes through which legislatures and agencies create law. The remaining six chapters (Part II) address the reality that, for many reasons, it is inevitable that the statutes and regulations that emerge from these lawmaking processes will often contain ambiguities that require interpretation. The primary focus of this second Part is on how these ambiguities in the law are resolved, and by whom. This chapter begins that effort with an overview of the necessity of legal interpretation and of the challenge this necessity poses.

A. THE BASIC PROBLEM OF MEANING AND INTERPRETATION

Though historically the law has not always been written, all modern legal systems depend on written, accessible statements of the law. In the common law tradition, that is why for centuries judicial decisions have been "reported" in published volumes, to which lawyers and citizens generally can refer for guidance and advice. In turn, part of being a lawyer then involves recognizing when the implications of the reported or recorded law are not clear, in which case the lawyer's role includes marshaling arguments for how to understand, construe, extend, and refine the law when it is applied to a new or unaddressed circumstance.

Furthermore, interpretive ambiguities are not confined to matters of judge-made or common law. Comparable challenges also routinely arise in determining textual meaning in statutes enacted by legislatures, as well as in regulations promulgated by agencies. Indeed, as the examples later in this chapter and throughout Part II reflect, statutes and regulations are replete with examples of interpretive ambiguities. In part, these ambiguities result because it is simply unrealistic to expect lawmakers always to craft language that covers all existing circumstances. Ambiguities also can arise when circumstances change or unanticipated developments happen; when a legislature deliberately uses vague or broad terms; or when drafting error or sloppiness occurs in the lawmaking process. As suggested in Chapters 2 and 5, legislatures are simply not structured to be nimble enough to resolve all of these ambiguities themselves (although agencies, as suggested in Chapter 6, are often better able to do so than legislatures). It therefore frequently falls to the courts to construe these provisions.

Of course, the problem of linguistic interpretation is not unique to law. In almost any context (except perhaps computer code), language is inherently incomplete, imperfect, and imprecise. In the late nineteenth century, Francis Lieber illustrated this point with a famous hypothetical, in which a household servant is directed to "fetch some soupmeat." By its terms, this directive leaves many questions unanswered, including what kind of soupmeat, what quantity, from where, how soon, with what funds, and at what price. But presumably a course of dealing between the household and the servant helps the servant fill in most if not all of these gaps in the meaning of the directive, at least in the normal case. And as Lieber pointed out, it would have been odd—perhaps even counterproductive, because it might have only compounded the potential for ambiguities in the interpretive process—for the directive to have specified the answers to all of those questions. *See* FRANCIS LIEBER, LEGAL AND POLITICAL HERMENEUTICS (1880).

Indeed, ordinary interpersonal communication routinely depends on the listener (or reader) making a host of assumptions, informed by context and usage, about the implication of the speaker's (or writer's) words. As Wittgenstein and other philosophers of language have argued, a speaker's words do not have intrinsic meaning, but instead are only linguistic signifiers that connect with a variety of social conventions to convey content. *See* LUDWIG WITTGENSTEIN, PHILOSOPHICAL INVESTIGATIONS (1953). These shared assumptions on which all communication depends also mean that in ordinary conversation, a directive like "fetch some soupmeat" can often be successfully reinterpreted when circumstances change (for instance if the regular butcher shop is closed or is out of soupmeat, or the number of expected dinner guests changes), without the need for a supplemental directive.

Because of these interpretive assumptions or conventions, a statement's literal meaning often gives way to another understanding, shared by both parties to the communication. This is obviously true for idiomatic expressions, such as "bite your tongue," "hit the hay," or "not in a million years," but it is also true for a range of ordinary statements. For example, "please take a picture" means one thing when standing at the edge of the Grand Canyon, and means something very different when helping an artist pack up framed photographs after a photography exhibit. Similarly, the imperative "we need to do this right away" could imply any of a variety of possible timelines, depending entirely on circumstance, though it also might be ambiguous. An understanding of context likewise may dramatically shape the answer one gives to the question, "Where are you from?" Thus, language scholars sometimes distinguish between semantic (or literal) meaning and pragmatic (or contextual) meaning. In the end, no matter how clear we may attempt to make our words, ordinary human communication requires, as Lieber put it, that we "trust at last to common sense and good faith."

But is the same approach relevant to the interpretation of law? Or does legal interpretation require its own set of tools? Unfortunately, interpreters of legal texts are not of one mind about how to solve interpretive problems in the law, and instead have injected different jurisprudential views of language and meaning into the pragmatic task of resolving textual ambiguity. Some examples of interpretive problems in legal text will help set the stage for an exploration of this fundamental difficulty.

B. THE NEED FOR TEXTUAL INTERPRETATION IN LAW

Statutes and regulations offer a trove of interpretive challenges. This section begins with a few representative examples, before offering a set of categories of causes or types of interpretive difficulty.

1. EXAMPLES OF INTERPRETIVE PROBLEMS IN THE LAW

A classic interpretive problem in the law is a municipal ordinance providing that "no vehicles are allowed in the park," a version of which debuted in a famous mid-twentieth century exchange between legal philosophers H.L.A. Hart and Lon Fuller. *See* H.L.A. Hart, *Positivism and the Separation of Law and Morals*, 71 HARV. L. REV. 593 (1958); Lon L. Fuller, *Positivism and Fidelity to Law: A Reply to Professor Hart*, 71 HARV. L. REV. 630 (1958). It is not hard to imagine a range of interpretive possibilities arising from this ordinance. For instance, it seems implausible that the ordinance should prohibit a baby stroller in the park, but why not? Is it because a stroller is not a vehicle? Or is it because the ordinance should apply only to motorized vehicles? If so, why is that, and how is the intended audience of this ordinance to know that? Or should the ordinance instead also prohibit bicycles and skateboards? Perhaps only bicycles and skateboards that are being ridden, as opposed to ones being walked or carried through the park? In winter, what about a sled or skis? How about a police cruiser driven by an officer on patrol? Or an army tank placed on a pedestal in the park as a war memorial?

Resolving these problems obviously depends at least in the first instance on interpreting the meaning of the term "vehicle." Does this term have a settled legal meaning? If it does, will knowing that meaning be enough to answer the question of whether the ordinance prohibits skis or a police cruiser? Or will "pragmatic" or contextual meaning also be relevant? What roles will "common sense and good faith" play in applying this ordinance?

In fact, the term "vehicle" has been a recurring source of interpretive challenge in the law. For instance, a 1930 British law required any "vehicle" on public roads to have pneumatic tires. In *Garner v. Burr*, 1 K.B. 31 (1951), the court concluded that for purposes of this statute "vehicle" included a chicken coop on wheels, towed by a tractor. Does this British precedent help us decide whether a baby stroller is a vehicle for purposes of our park ordinance?

Probably not. As in almost every case, the assignment of meaning to specific words like "vehicle" inevitably depends on an understanding of the context in which these words are used, often also including some sense of the purpose or intent behind their usage. In 1930, Britain required pneumatic tires apparently to reduce wear and tear on its roads. Although this context helps explain the court's decision in *Garner v. Burr*, it sheds little light on whether the same chicken coop on wheels, perhaps now being pushed like a handcart as a stage prop in an outdoor theater—let alone a baby stroller—would violate a rule of "no vehicles in the park."

Resolving this interpretive problem might depend on knowing more about how the legislature that enacted the measure understood the term "vehicle." Or it could be influenced by knowing whether the park ordinance was intended to protect the condition of the park's trails and paths, or to reduce air or noise pollution, or to improve safety, or to achieve some other goal. It might also be influenced by the interpreter's understanding of the general role in the community of the legislative body that passed the measure and of the relationship between that legislative body and the executive branch officers or agencies expected to enforce the measure. An understanding of the full context and purpose behind each statement of law, and of how various legal institutions operate and interact, thus can be helpful in assigning meaning to its words. (However, as described in more detail in Chapter 8, some legal interpreters are wary of interpretive strategies that draw upon anything other than the text, supplemented by various "canons" of interpretation, and reject seeking external clues about the underlying rationale for a measure.)

Interpretive issues can arise not just from problems of defining the scope of a key term like "vehicle," but also from problems of deciding what the key terms even are. To take another example, an Ohio municipal ordinance provides: "It shall be unlawful for any person . . . to park . . . upon any street . . . in the Village, any *motor vehicle camper*, trailer, farm implement and/or non-motorized vehicle for a continued period of twenty-four hours." *See West Jefferson v. Cammelleri*, 2015-Ohio-2463 (Ohio App. 2015) (emphasis added). Notice the absence of a comma within the phrase italicized above. The reviewing court construed this ordinance as punctuated, throwing out a citation against the owner of a pick-up truck, a simple "motor vehicle," because it was not a "motor vehicle camper." But might the Village council perhaps have intended for this ordinance to have prohibited "any motor vehicle, camper, trailer," etc., from parking for over twenty-four hours? Does it matter whether the council's omission of a comma between "motor vehicle" and "camper" was accidental? If the council deliberately omitted the comma, what exactly did the council mean by "motor vehicle camper"? Does the ordinance then not cover regular automobiles? And what (if anything) does the prohibition on parking a non-motorized vehicle for over twenty-four hours add to the context of this measure that might aid in understanding how to interpret the rest of the language?

In another classic example, legal philosopher Lon Fuller invited consideration of whether a hypothetical criminal statute that required the imposition of the death penalty against anyone found guilty of willfully taking another person's life applied to a fictitious group of cave explorers trapped for weeks by a cave-in. When it becomes clear to the group that none of them will survive otherwise, they agree to draw lots to determine which among them the others will kill to provide a source of sustenance until their rescue. In *The Case of the Speluncean Explorers*, 62 HARV. L. REV. 616 (1949), Fuller explores several possible interpretive rationales through which jurists (or others) might seek to answer the question of whether the surviving explorers are guilty of violating the hypothetical state's murder statute. Fuller's two primary protagonists, Judge Foster and Judge Keen, clash over whether the statute must be construed in light of its purpose, or instead must be applied faithfully according to its terms. Significantly, both approaches (which in essence respectively represent the "Purposivist" and "Textualist" approaches that dominate interpretive theory today, as described in Chapter 8) find their primary justification in a sense of loyalty and service to the legislative institution that enacted the statute.

Finally, to take a textually more complex but real interpretive problem, consider a 2015 Supreme Court decision involving Obamacare, the Patient Protection and Affordable Care Act. Provisions of this act provide that certain individuals who enroll in a qualifying health insurance plan "established by the state" are eligible for a federal tax credit to defray the cost of their health insurance premium. When a number of states opted not to establish a qualifying health plan, the federal government, pursuant to other provisions of the act, established its own plans that individuals could join. Opponents of the act then brought a legal challenge claiming that individuals who enrolled in plans established by the federal government were not eligible for the tax credit, arguing that the statute's words "established by the state" limited the tax credit to only those insurance plans established by one of the fifty states, not plans established by the federal government.

In *King v. Burwell*, 576 U.S. ___, 135 S. Ct. 2480 (2015), a divided Supreme Court rejected this challenge. The Court majority concluded that the phrase "established by the state" was ambiguous about whether it should be read narrowly to cover only actions of the fifty state governments. The majority then resolved this ambiguity in light of its understanding of the Affordable Care Act's overall statutory scheme, concluding that all government-sponsored health insurance plans were eligible for the tax credit. Three dissenters, led by Justice Scalia, argued that the critical phrase was entirely unambiguous in granting the tax credit only to state plans, not federal plans. This divide on the Court, reminiscent of the divide between Judge Foster and Judge Keen in Lon Fuller's *Speluncean Explorers*, is typical of many of the Supreme Court's recent disagreements about matters of statutory interpretation.

2. CATEGORIES OF COMMON INTERPRETIVE PROBLEMS

Examples of statutory and regulatory text that call for interpretation can be grouped into several main categories, which in specific instances may overlap: (1) incomplete or inapt definitions; (2) drafting errors, including "scrivener's" errors; (3) absurd results; (4) changed circumstances; (5) unanticipated consequences; and (6) conflicting provisions. These categories, organized by the source or cause of the interpretive difficulty, capture the kinds of problems that interpreters see again and again.

a. Incomplete or Inapt Definitions

The largest category of interpretive problems in statutes and regulations arises when the meaning of some textual term, such as "or other immoral purpose," is imperfectly specified or understood. The examples earlier in this chapter of legal rules involving the use of the term "vehicle" without providing any further definition of its meaning also fit this category. The interpreter is left to assign a meaning to this term for purposes of the statute or regulation in which it is used, relying on any number of the possible interpretive tools such as those discussed in Chapters 9 through 12. Notwithstanding these tools, however, some of those interpretive problems may be quite difficult to resolve.

Many other instances of this particular kind of interpretive problem involve a statute or regulation that includes a definition of a key term, yet still leaves ambiguity about how to apply that term in some specific case. For instance, the Americans with Disabilities Act prohibits employers from discriminating against employees on the basis of a disability, which the act defines as "a physical or mental impairment that substantially limits one or more of the major life activities . . . ." In *Sutton v. United Airlines*, 527 U.S. 471 (1999), the Supreme Court concluded that although a vision impairment, if it were uncorrected, might substantially limit a major life activity and therefore amount to a disability under the act, it nevertheless was not a disability under the act if the impairment was correctable with eyewear, even though the statute said nothing about correctable disabilities.

Or, to take an example with a more detailed yet still ultimately contestable definition of a key term, the Endangered Species Act makes it unlawful to "take" any endangered species of fish or wildlife and defines "take" to mean "to harass, harm, pursue, hunt, shoot, wound, kill, trap, capture, or collect, or to attempt to engage in any such conduct." The Secretary of the Interior, responsible for administering the Endangered Species Act, promulgated a regulation that in turn defined the term "harm" (as found in the statutory definition of "take") to include "significant habitat modification or degradation where it actually kills or injures wildlife . . . ." In an important case (discussed further in Chapter 9) concerning the adverse impact of the logging industry on the northern spotted owl and red-cockaded woodpecker, the Supreme Court considered whether the Secretary's regulation misconstrued the statutory definition of "take." *See Babbitt v. Sweet Home Chapter of Communities for a Greater Oregon*, 515 U.S. 687 (1995). It is not hard to see how Congress's effort to be thorough in defining the statutory term "take" nonetheless left room for debate about what "harm" meant, much as Francis Lieber had cautioned about the difficulties of trying to respond in advance to all the interpretive issues that might arise in connection with the instruction to "fetch some soupmeat."

b. Drafting Errors, Including "Scrivener's Errors"

A different kind of interpretive challenge arises when the legislative text appears to contain a drafting error. For instance, should the phrase "motor vehicle camper" in fact have read "motor vehicle, camper"? And if so, has the careless omission of a comma, potentially even by a scribe or secretary (a scrivener), given rise to a needless interpretive problem? Of course, one critical step in dealing with this interpretive category is deciding that in fact the problematic text is, simply, an error. What evidence of error might be relevant? In arguing for a fairly narrow ambit for correcting drafting errors in construing statutes, Justice Scalia argued that it should be "clear to the reader" that a scrivener's error has occurred, in which case it will also be "clear to the reader . . . what *the text* means." *See* Antonin Scalia & John F. Manning, *A Dialogue on Statutory and Constitutional Interpretation*, 80 GEO. WASH. L. REV. 1610, 1613 (2012). But not all drafting errors, even scrivener's errors, may always be so clear.

For instance, the Federal Land Policy and Management Act, which governs private rights to mineral claims on federal lands, requires that claimants file an annual notice of their continuing interest in the claim "prior to December 31" of each year. Should this language be construed to require that claimants file on or before December 30, or should it allow claimants to file prior to the close of business on December 31? In *United States v. Locke*, 471 U.S. 84 (1985), the Supreme Court divided on the issue. The dissenters believed the statutory deadline was simply an inartful attempt to require filing prior to the end of the calendar year, or in other words before the close of business on December 31, and that the ambiguity resulted because "Congress is too busy to do all its work as carefully as it should." *Id.* at 118 (Stevens, J., dissenting). In contrast, the Court majority concluded that Congress well could have intended to require filing on or before December 30, and that without evidence that the deadline was unmistakably a drafting error, the Court lacked the authority to rewrite the statutory deadline.

Sometimes drafting or scrivener's errors are as simple as omitting a comma, or neglecting to realize that the locution "prior to the end of the calendar year" is not the same thing as "prior to December 31" (although many commentators might not view this latter example as a true "scrivener's error" unless it was simply a mistake in transcription). Other times, even transcription errors can be more complicated, and much harder to identify. For example, in the case of *Shine v. Shine*, 802 F.2d 583 (1st Cir. 1986), an amendment to the federal bankruptcy laws emerged from a complicated set of congressional negotiations. The amendment provided that a debt "to a spouse, former spouse, or child of the debtor, for alimony to, maintenance for, or support of such spouse or child, *~~or under a property settlement~~* in connection with a separation agreement, divorce decree, *or property settlement agreement*" was not dischargeable in bankruptcy. Arguably, the interpretive problem the court faced in construing the amendment resulted from the fact that in an early draft of the amendment, the italicized phrase "or property settlement agreement" had not appeared where shown above but had appeared instead between the two asterisks above as the stricken (and slightly different) language "or under a property settlement." This language was subsequently deleted, perhaps inadvertently, and then restored but in the later and possibly mistaken location. This change in location may thereby have unintentionally converted all of the text after the asterisks into a modifier of all the text preceding the asterisks. But no clear evidence existed that this particular transcription error had occurred. Thus, at least hypothetically although not conclusively, this could be an example of a pure but complicated scrivener's error.

c. Absurd Results

Occasionally courts will decline to follow the literal language of a law because doing so would produce an "absurd" or unjust result. The idea that a statute should not be read to produce absurd or unjust results was a settled rule at least by the time of the famed British legal commentator William Blackstone. *See* 1 WILLIAM BLACKSTONE, COMMENTARIES 60 (Cooley ed., 1879). Sometimes the absurdity can be the result of a drafting error; sometimes it may flow from an inapt definition (or at least what becomes an inapt definition when applied to an unanticipated circumstance).

For instance, Blackstone (citing Pufendorf before him) related that the ancient Bolognian law "that whoever drew blood in the streets should be punished with utmost severity" was deemed inapplicable to a surgeon providing emergency care by drawing the blood of the victim of a seizure. In essence, this construction amounted to the simple triumph of common sense over literal text. Is this because the phrase "drew blood" was inapt or not adequately specified? Or did the provision imply some limiting connotation? Similarly, in *United States v. Kirby*, 74 U.S. 482 (1868), the Supreme Court invoked common sense in refusing to apply a federal criminal statute that prohibited the willful obstruction of "the passage of the mail, or of any driver or carrier" to a sheriff executing an arrest warrant upon a mail carrier charged with murder. The Court wrote that a statute's "[g]eneral terms should be so limited in their application as to not lead to injustice, oppression, or an absurd consequence." *Id.* at 486.

Unfortunately, the existence of absurdity is not always so clear and instead often can be a subjective determination. One interpreter's absurd or unjust application can be another interpreter's unavoidable construction of a legal text, as for instance in the Supreme Court's disagreement in *Tennessee Valley Authority v. Hill*, 437 U.S. 153 (1978) (discussed in more detail in subsection e), about whether the Endangered Species Act required the cessation of construction of a federally funded hydroelectric dam. One implication of this matter of perspective is that problems of statutory interpretation simply do not generate obvious answers, nor (as Chapter 8 will explore) is there even a settled methodology for resolving them.

d. Changed Circumstances

A different interpretive problem can arise when the text of a law must be applied to a circumstance that, because of changes in social conditions, the enacting lawmakers likely did not foresee. Consider two examples.

The first arises out of changing social norms and the advent of gay parenting. The New York adoption statute had long provided that upon the making of an adoption order, all parental rights and responsibilities of the natural (biological) parent(s) would cease. Meanwhile, by 1995, changes in New York legal doctrine permitted unmarried individuals and gay couples to adopt. The case of *In the Matter of Jacob*, 660 N.E.2d 397 (N.Y. 1995), then confronted the circumstance in which the gay partner of the biological mother of a child wished to become an adoptive parent. No legal barrier prevented this, except that the adoption statute, if applied according to its terms, would then require the natural mother (the partner of the adoptive mother) to lose all of her parental rights. The state high court, in a divided opinion, rejected this "Catch-22" and construed the problematic provision not to apply.

A second example involves the interpretation of the federal Communications Act of 1934, which authorizes the Federal Communications Commission to regulate the rates that communications companies—a category essentially limited to the Bell telephone companies when the act was passed—charge their customers and requires companies to file tariffs (schedules of their charges) with the Commission. The act also grants the Commission authority to "modify" the tariff-filing requirement. In the 1970s and early 1980s, technological and economic changes, clearly unforeseen in 1934, led to the judicially supervised breakup of the Bell telephone monopoly and the advent of a number of additional "non-dominant" providers of telecommunications service. The Commission decided that the economic competition between these non-dominant providers rendered the tariff-filing requirement superfluous as applied to them and "modified" the requirement by exempting them. In *MCI Telecommunications Corp. v. AT&T,* 512 U.S. 218 (1994), the Supreme Court concluded that the Commission had exceeded its authority because rather than just modify the requirement, the Commission instead had fundamentally changed it. In contrast, three dissenters argued that "the advent of competition" in the telecommunications industry was an unforeseen circumstance that "might legitimately call for different treatment." *Id.* at 240 (Stevens, J., dissenting).

In both of these examples, the courts addressing the statutory issue divided on whether the changed circumstances provided information or context relevant to the question of how to apply or construe the textual provision. This division is emblematic of the reality that many interpretive problems do not have universally accepted answers. Furthermore, as is often true, the divide also tracks the contemporary divide between Purposivists and Textualists (described in more detail in Chapter 8).

e. Unanticipated Consequences

In a similar vein, a statutory interpreter sometimes will need to apply a statute to a situation that, although not quite new or the result of changes in circumstance, nevertheless simply may not have been anticipated. This category often overlaps with the "absurd results" category.

For example, in *Tennessee Valley Authority v. Hill* (introduced in subsection c), the Supreme Court considered the impact of the Endangered Species Act of 1973 ("ESA") on the Tennessee Valley Authority's (TVA) construction of the Tellico Dam. The TVA had begun building the dam in 1967 as part of a decades-old congressional effort to enhance electric utility services in rural portions of the country. But completing the dam and filling its reservoir would destroy the habitat of a small fish called the snail darter, which in 1975 had been classified as endangered under the act. The TVA was a federal agency, and the act required all federal agencies to "insure that any action [of such agency] is not likely to jeopardize the continued existence of any endangered species."

On a strict application of the statutory language, the ESA would prohibit the TVA from completing the dam, despite the substantial investment already made. A majority of the Court concluded that the ESA permitted no exceptions: "Our individual appraisal of the wisdom or unwisdom of a particular course consciously selected by the Congress is to be put aside in the process of interpreting a statute," the Court explained. 437 U.S. at 194. But the dissenting opinion viewed this as an absurd result that would waste all the previously expended public funds and be inconsistent with Congress's repeated demonstrations of support for the dam, including the appropriation of funds for its construction both before and after enacting the ESA.

For other significant examples of judicial interpretation in light of consequences arguably not anticipated by the enacting Congress, see the discussions in Chapters 8 and 10 of the *Weber* and *Bob Jones* cases.

f. Conflicting Provisions

Occasionally, a statute will contain conflicting directives, or will conflict with another related statute. For instance, consider two of the state statutory provisions at issue in the Florida contest over the 2000 presidential election. After the Democratic Party requested a manual recount of several key Florida counties, a question arose about the time for completing these recounts. One provision of Florida law, enacted in 1951, provided that county election returns (results) not received by the Secretary of State by 5 p.m. on the seventh day after the election "shall be ignored." But another provision, enacted in 1989, provided that if a county's returns were not received by 5 p.m. on the seventh day after the election, the returns "may be ignored," and that county board members then were subject to fines for each day thereafter that their county's returns were late. These two provisions conflicted about whether the Secretary of State had discretion to accept returns after the deadline. For multiple reasons, the Florida Supreme Court concluded that the more recent statute governed the question and the Secretary of State therefore had the discretion to accept late returns. The court also concluded that in the circumstances of the 2000 election the Secretary of State had abused that discretion, acting unreasonably and unlawfully in not accepting late-arriving recount totals from two counties. *See Palm Beach County Canvassing Board v. Harris*, 772 So.2d

1220 (Fla. 2000), *vacated sub nom. Bush v. Palm Beach Canvassing Board*, 531 U.S. 70 (2000).

As another example, consider again the provision of the Endangered Species Act at issue in *Tennessee Valley Authority v. Hill*, which required all federal agencies to "insure that actions [of such agency] do not jeopardize the continued existence of [an] endangered species." Yet in 1975 and 1976, after Congress became aware that the snail darter had been listed as endangered and was threatened by the Tellico Dam, congressional budget and appropriations committees continued to approve the use of federal funds to complete the dam, directing in one committee report that the dam "be completed as promptly as possible." In 1976, Congress enacted a budget measure appropriating all the remaining funding the TVA had requested for the purpose of completing the dam. In the face of this conflict between the ESA and a more recent congressional appropriation (itself also fully law), the Court chose to enforce the ESA. But the dissent argued that the Congress that had enacted the ESA in 1973 not only had shown no awareness that the act might preclude the completion of the Tellico Dam, but also that the subsequent Congress's continuing appropriation of funds for the dam showed that Congress intended the ESA not to interfere with the dam. (In response to the Court's broad reading of the ESA, Congress amended the act to allow exceptions for projects like the Tellico Dam.)

* * *

Alternative ways certainly exist of classifying interpretive problems other than the categories described above. These categories are typical, however, and are intended to invite some reflection concerning the difficulties that lawmakers face in crafting written text so as to avoid interpretive difficulties. Occasionally, lawmakers may justifiably be faulted for sloppiness, but it is unrealistic to expect them to avoid all potential errors, and in any event, interpretive ambiguity frequently results from other causes. Recognizing that interpretive problems are inevitable is an important foundation for considering how to approach them.

C. WHAT THE LAW IS: ESSENTIAL ROLES OF COURTS, LEGISLATURES, AND AGENCIES

As the preceding examples begin to demonstrate, legal text can be rife with interpretative problems similar to those that affect other forms of communication. But problems of legal interpretation also present a special case. In a fundamental sense, the words of the law are themselves *the law*, and the ideal of the "rule of law" that we prize so highly is predicated in turn on the existence of these words. It is these words that give rise to enforceable rights and obligations, shared among all citizens. As Justice Scalia observed a quarter century ago in a famous law review article, ordinary citizens ought to be able to read the words of the law and to rely on their understanding of the words' ordinary meaning. *See* Antonin Scalia, *The Rule of Law as a Law of Rules*, 56 U. CHI. L. REV. 1175 (1989). Accordingly, even as we concede that the meaning of the written law will sometimes be ambiguous, we aspire for the law to be specified with sufficient clarity that it will consistently convey the same meaning to a variety of listeners or audiences.

Indeed, in an earlier era, most statutory interpreters presumed that legal text had an inherent or intrinsic meaning, which courts and other readers could and should find primarily through textual analysis. Today, however, legal interpreters all recognize that meaning is to some degree dependent on unstated assumptions shared between author and audience, or on pragmatic rather than semantic meaning. Thus, Lieber's notion of "common sense and good faith," an essential component of ordinary communication, also could play a valuable role in interpreting ambiguities in legal text.

Yet when the meaning of an authoritative statement of public law is at issue, with its power to determine rights, privileges, duties, and obligations, some may view common sense and good faith as improper or at least insufficient bases for an interpretive methodology. How, then, should ambiguities in legal text be resolved? Who should resolve them? What are the appropriate ways of identifying, and then drawing from, the shared assumptions upon which legal communication also depends? What should be the role of context? How much clarity of meaning can there be without an understanding of context? How should the context of a statute or regulation be understood and assessed?

How much attention should be placed on identifying the written law's underlying purpose? What sources can reliably establish this purpose?

Many of these and other aspects of interpretive methodology are the subject of the next chapter. As additional foundation for that discussion, this section will reflect briefly on what the "law" itself is and where it comes from, including both the role of courts as well as the place of statutes and regulations in American law. Although the general question "what is law?" is far too broad for this chapter to even begin to address well, a few thoughts will provide some relevant background. Some theory of "the law" and how it is created, even if it is entirely implicit, inevitably undergirds one's theory of textual interpretation (as does some theory of language, even if also implicit). For a full Nutshell treatment of what "law" is, see S. PRAKASH SINHA, JURISPRUDENCE: LEGAL PHILOSOPHY IN A NUTSHELL (1993); *see generally* H.L.A. HART, THE CONCEPT OF LAW (1961).

1. LEGAL FORMALISM AND LEGAL REALISM: EARLY ANSWERS

Chapter 1 described the hierarchy of American legislative and regulatory lawmaking authority. Not included in that discussion was the place in the American legal system of courts and the common law. Many jurisprudential theories focus heavily or entirely on the role of courts, sometimes even describing "law" simply as "what courts do." Moreover, that is the framework around which the case method of much of American legal education has been built. Yet any sophisticated understanding of law today also requires an understanding of how legislatures and agencies behave, as well as of the relationships among courts, legislatures, and agencies.

Of course, Justice Marshall famously said in *Marbury v. Madison*, 5 U.S. 137, 177 (1803), that it was emphatically the duty of the courts "to say what the law is." This pronouncement was not a truism about the judiciary's role in promulgating common law, but a claim about its authority to have the last word regarding the meaning of all legal text, including statutory and regulatory text. Frequently, many other types of people besides judges also take on the role of legal interpreters, including agency officials, lawyers, politicians, and citizens. But all must take cognizance that courts have the authority to be the final interpreters of the work of legislatures and agencies. Therefore anyone with an interest in understanding the meaning of legal texts should be attentive to how judges may ultimately assign a definitive interpretation to ambiguous language.

On the **Legal Formalist** account of law that dominated American jurisprudence at the beginning of the twentieth century, the role of courts was to "find" the law through the application of neutral principles. On this conception, the common law already existed, waiting to be discovered. In contrast, legislatures were viewed as institutions that could "make" law as a matter of pure political will (with state legislatures in particular even sometimes viewed as examples of "mob rule"). Typically, this account exalted courts as normatively superior because in their hands law was a deductive science involving the logical application of accepted rules and doctrines to the problems of social living and circumstance, while statutory lawmaking in the hands of a legislature was simply crass power politics. Statutes might be formally and hierarchically superior to common law, but in practice they might often be functionally inferior, diminished by social attitudes and a pejorative perception that legislative outputs reflected only the non-rational exercise of raw political power.

Formalists viewed courts as deductive not only in the ways in which they fostered the development of the common law, but also in the ways in which they interpreted and applied—arguably even refined—the crude statutory law. Under a Formalist account, the role of the court as the interpreter of legal text was to find the intrinsic meaning of that text. Hierarchical relationships among written constitutions, legislative statutes, and agency regulations, as described in Chapter 1, helped courts to identify and prioritize the application of these rules and principles.

Over the years, many challenged the Formalist view of how courts operate. They typically did so, however, without challenging the exalted position of the courts as the central institution in the American legal system. For instance, Justice Oliver Wendell Holmes once declared, in a speech that is often seen as the opening salvo of the **Legal Realism** movement of the first half of the twentieth century, that rather than being a deductive process, law was nothing more than a prediction of what the courts will do. *See* Oliver Wendell Holmes, *The Path of the Law*, 10 HARV. L. REV. 457 (1897). On Holmes' still court-centric view, the task of the lawyer was to understand, and exploit, the range of reasons or motivations that might sway the courts, but not to expect that this was a matter of simple deduction. Statutes were important primarily because of how they might figure in predictions of how courts would act. As Holmes' contemporary, John Chipman Gray, famously said: "legislative acts, statutes, are to be dealt with as sources of Law, and not as part of the Law itself." JOHN CHIPMAN GRAY, THE NATURE AND SOURCES OF THE LAW 119 (1909). On this view of the law, statutes remained functionally inferior to what judges did, even though what judges did was no longer merely deductive.

But while Holmes rejected the fiction that judges simply "found" the law deductively, he recognized that judges are not completely unconstrained or willful. Rather, judges develop a legal result by attending to an accepted set of precepts and by honoring the work of the legislatures, at least to some degree. Thus, even on his view of law as prediction, law was a prediction about how courts will use legal rules, principles, and philosophies in resolving the matters that come before them. Courts do not function without guidelines and constraints.

Nevertheless, Holmes' view was still a somewhat skeptical one, espousing the notion that courts, like legislatures, also "make" rather than "find" the law.

Specifically with respect to matters of statutory interpretation, the Legal Realists who followed Holmes similarly argued that courts were making rather than finding the law because a court often could have articulated several equally defensible arguments to support contrasting interpretive results, allowing the court to choose, rather than deduce, a particular outcome. This Realist view explicitly acknowledged the idea of judicial power and discretion. Ever since, the prospect of judicial willfulness has raised important questions of objectivity and subjectivity in law and judicial interpretation.

2. LEGAL PROCESS THEORY: A 20TH-CENTURY REPLY

By the mid-twentieth century, a number of other legal thinkers were pushing back against Holmes' and the Legal Realists' more skeptical views of law. So too was the rapid expansion of the administrative state, with its reliance on bureaucratic expertise. As part of what would become known as the **Legal Process** school, these thinkers argued that rather than being primarily a prediction of how courts will use their authority, law was a complex arrangement of obligations that depended, for their acceptance and validity, on being the output of legal institutions (courts, legislatures, and agencies) governed by a set of rational processes. These processes were public, accessible, deliberative, reasonable, and stable. They brought a form of coherence to the legal system, a system that depended on the institutional competence of distinctive bodies such as courts, legislatures, and agencies, each operating in their own spheres yet each dependent on the sound and often-collaborative operation of the other institutions.

In pushing back against the Legal Realists, the Legal Process thinkers certainly did not reassert the notion that the role of courts was to "find" the law. But they did argue, much more than Holmes, that the processes by which courts "make" law were regularized and carefully constrained. In particular, judicial law creation, they asserted, involved a "reasoned elaboration" of each issue before the court, premised on neutral principles generally applicable to any case. Legal Process thinkers also defended legislatures as worthy institutions in which the citizens' representatives pursued reasonable purposes through reasonable means in a process that permitted public observation and accountability. On this account, statutory law not only was still formally superior to common law, but also was now embraced as functionally superior as well. Each resulting statute was entitled to full respect not merely as a source of law but as part of the law itself.

Meanwhile, at both the federal and state levels, the twentieth century witnessed an explosion of lawmaking activity by legislatures and agencies, producing what has sometimes been called "The Age of the Statute." As a result, law today is a complex hybrid of legislative statutes, agency regulations, and common law, all subject to overarching constitutional rules and principles. Each of these various sources of law is enforced primarily by courts and agencies, who thereby also are inevitably responsible for interpreting the law (once the fiction is abandoned that their role is merely to find the law), but with a recognition of the legislature's superior authority to make the law.

3. LINGERING CONCERNS ABOUT WILLFULNESS IN INTERPRETATION: WHO IS TO SAY "WHAT THE LAW IS"?

In the hybrid state of law just described, the problem of potential judicial willfulness is, if anything, more acute than in Justice Holmes' day. Meanwhile, the related issue, introduced in Chapter 6, of how much lawmaking authority agencies may properly exercise, also remains a significant one. Thus, an essential concern is how to prevent or discourage excessive willfulness on the part of both courts and agencies, whose law "elaboration" role is significant but understood to be subservient to that of legislatures.

The Legal Process defense of the reasoned operations and individual competencies of courts, legislatures, and agencies can offer assistance in thinking about the nature of each of these lawmaking institution's responsibilities to "say what the law is." For instance, one important question is how the principle of *stare decisis* should operate to constrain a court once it has construed the meaning of a statute (or regulation). As a principle of judicial restraint, *stare decisis* is generally understood to have even stronger force with respect to precedents that have resolved questions of statutory meaning. The underlying rationale for this strong form of statutory *stare decisis*, predicated heavily on Legal Process ideas, is that once a court has clarified a textual ambiguity in the legislature's handiwork, the legislature is in the vastly superior institutional position to revise this meaning at some subsequent time, if it wishes. If the legislature does not do so, courts should not lightly second-guess that legislative inaction, even when the courts might no longer be persuaded by the reasoning of their original precedent.

An especially noteworthy example of this principle involves a series of three U.S. Supreme Court decisions about the application of the federal antitrust statute to Major League Baseball, culminating in *Flood v. Kuhn*, 407 U.S. 258 (1972). In 1922, at a time when the Court understood the scope of the Constitution's "interstate commerce" clause much more narrowly than it later would, the Court found professional baseball beyond the scope of the antitrust law. Three decades later, the court adhered to this precedent in a second case, even though both the scope of interstate commerce had expanded dramatically and the economics of Major League Baseball had become closely linked to interstate radio (and soon television) broadcasts. Two more decades on, having already once adhered to an otherwise outdated ruling, the Court found it even harder to abandon its statutory precedents exempting baseball from federal antitrust law, even though a number of more recent decisions involving other professional sports leagues had rejected the same reasoning and subjected these other leagues to antitrust laws. The Court thought that it was solely for Congress to upset whatever expectations might have come to attach to the fifty-year history of exempting baseball and to remedy "any inconsistency or illogic" that had thereby arisen. *Id.* at 284. This principle of statutory *stare decisis* thus embodies a judicial reluctance to intrude upon the legislature's perceived prerogatives because of its superior institutional ability to establish public policy.

A sense of the legislature's institutional competence may affect not only the notion of *stare decisis*, but also a sort of inverse question of to what extent courts should look to statutes (or regulations) to derive policy guidance to help refine the common law. A Legal Process approach suggests that, at least on occasion, courts might profitably take note of legislatively established policies as a basis for updating or filling-in gaps in the common law doctrines that are primarily the courts' responsibility. For instance, in *Moragne v. States Marine Lines, Inc.*, 398 U.S. 375 (1970), the Supreme Court confronted the issue of whether to overrule its own common law precedent that federal maritime law (a type of common law) did not permit recovery in tort for wrongful death. The Court looked to a series of statutory developments that had extended rights to recover in tort for wrongful death in several other contexts, and concluded that it should harmonize the maritime law to accord with these statutory developments: "It has always been the duty of the common-law court to perceive the impact of major legislative innovations and to interweave the new legislative policies with the inherited body of common-law principles . . . ." *Id.* at 392. The Legal Process school thus can encourage courts not only to respect but also to reflect the legislature's establishment of policy.

In addition, and more important than its influence on ideas about either *stare decisis* or incorporating legislative policy into common law, the Legal Process school can offer a set of principles to constrain the amount of willfulness with which courts and agencies might approach issues of statutory and regulatory interpretation generally. As a threshold matter, consider again the question of whether an interpreter *finds* the meaning of an ambiguous text, or *creates* it. Interpretive issues can be placed along a continuum between the easiest cases, where an interpreter might truly only need to find or "discover" the meaning of the term of a legal text, a task with relatively little room for willfulness, and the hardest cases, where in order to reach a decision it might be necessary for the interpreter willfully to "create" that meaning. Yet for many interpretive problems, the reality is that "it is extremely difficult to say in practice and in conceptualization just where discovery gives way to creation." KENT GREENAWALT, STATUTORY INTERPRETATION: 20 QUESTIONS 17–18 (1999); *see* REED DICKERSON, THE INTERPRETATION AND APPLICATION OF STATUTES 22–23 (1975).

For instance, consider a provision of the now-archaic White Slave Traffic Act that once criminalized the transportation of any woman in interstate commerce "for the purpose of prostitution or debauchery, or for any other immoral purpose."

How should an interpreter determine the meaning of the phrase "any other immoral purpose," as used in this provision? *See Caminetti v. United States*, 242 U.S. 470 (1917). Does that task involve *finding* the meaning implicit in the words chosen by the enacting Congress? Or does it involve *creating* the meaning, either on behalf of the enacting Congress or as an independent act, through subsequent application of various tools of legal interpretation?

Of central importance to thinking about this question is to ask what the interpreter's responsibility is to the legislature or agency, as the author of the text. Consciously or subconsciously, interpreters may conceive of their role in at least three distinct ways: as dutiful executors, as faithful agents, or as cooperative partners. Whichever role the interpreter assumes in turn will affect the amount of freedom that the interpreter feels in seeking to further the work of that author. These distinct roles deserve brief elaboration as points of reference for the discussion in ensuing chapters of the various interpretive theories or methodologies.

One model of the interpretive role is as a **"Dutiful Executor."** On this view, the interpreter's responsibility is to hew as closely as possible to the instructions given by the author, just as the executor of a will must seek to effectuate the precise wishes of a deceased testator. This view provides the interpreter little latitude, and to the extent that ambiguities arise in administering the author's wishes, the executor may be bound by (and perhaps therefore take comfort in) established default rules.

Chapters 8 and 9 will explore some theories and doctrines that rely heavily on a variety of such default rules, even though in the statutory interpretation context they may not be binding in the way that they are in the interpretation of wills.

A less constraining model is to view the interpreter as a **"Faithful Agent"** of the enacting legislature or promulgating agency. In this model, the role of the interpreter, as the agent, is to honor the principal's desires above all, including by exercising some discretion to adjust, as appropriate, the means of accomplishing them. Lieber's domestic servant likely would function this way in fetching soupmeat. A faithful agent model depends on the agent having a means of knowing or ascertaining the principal's desires. Chapters 8, 9, and 10 will explore some theories and doctrines of statutory interpretation that address the question of how to determine the enacting legislature's underlying desire or will, whether characterized as legislative intent or legislative purpose. But identifying this purpose often may be a difficult enterprise, and as a practical matter some interpretation also must occur when the agent cannot or does not know the principal's desires.

An even less constraining model is to view the interpreter as a **"Cooperative Partner"** of the legislature, working to effectuate the broader public good by building upon the policies embodied in the legislature's work and striving to make the overall body of the law as coherent and public-regarding as possible. This model is not unconstrained, as the aspiration of making the law "coherent" incorporates the notion that the interpreter cannot just ignore the statutory law; rather, statutory text must still provide a foundation and a tether for any such cooperative lawmaking. Chapters 8, 9, and 10 also will consider some theoretical and doctrinal perspectives relevant to statutory interpretation on something like a "Cooperative Partner" model.

The Cooperative Partner model of interpretation is in some respects closest to how government agencies (rather than courts) work to effectuate legislative policies, within general limits set by the legislature. But as discussed further in Chapters 11 and 12, all three of these models of the interpreter's role may have some validity in thinking about the many circumstances in which agencies construe and enforce statutory text, as well as the various ways in which courts construe and enforce agency regulations in addition to statutes.

* * *

Having considered the hybrid quality of law as the output of the legislative, executive, and judicial branches, and the critical interpretive and law-elaborating role that courts and agencies play, the remaining chapters of Part II now explore in greater depth the theories, doctrines, and tools of statutory interpretation of greatest potential relevance in addressing the kinds of interpretive problems introduced in this chapter.

CHAPTER 8

THEORIES OF STATUTORY INTERPRETATION

WHAT'S IN THIS CHAPTER:

A. Early Approaches to Problems of Statutory Interpretation

B. Intentionalism

C. Purposivism

D. Plain Meaning Interpretation: A Textualist Approach

E. (New) Textualism

F. Pragmatic and Dynamic Interpretation

Issues of statutory interpretation like those introduced in Chapter 7 have long abounded in the law. Over the years, courts, practitioners, and scholars have employed a variety of techniques and approaches to resolve these interpretive problems. These approaches have ebbed and flowed across a landscape marked with changing views about the respective roles of the courts and the legislatures in articulating what law is, as also described in Chapter 7. But especially during the twentieth century, as statutes grew in importance at both federal and state levels, several distinct interpretive theories flourished, generating increasingly widespread attention and commentary in the past several decades.

This chapter first provides a short historical overview of how courts in earlier eras addressed problems of statutory interpretation. Building on that history, it then summarizes six prominent theories of statutory interpretation that are most relevant today, namely Intentionalism, Purposivism, Plain Meaning Interpretation, Textualism, and Pragmatic and Dynamic Interpretation.

At the outset, it bears noting that the meaning of most statutes and regulations, as applied to most circumstances, is usually clear. For instance, when a state statute provides that public schools shall provide their pupils with 180 days of annual instruction, public school districts generally understand what this obligation requires as they go about setting their academic calendar. Or when federal law provides that a voter who appears at a polling place without a required form of identification must at least be allowed to cast a provisional ballot, the fundamental obligation that this law imposes on election workers and systems is clear. Yet even for the clearest of legal texts, circumstances may arise for which the meaning of the words is no longer obvious. It is primarily to the difficult cases that the theories and tools of interpretation in this and the following chapters are directed.

It also bears noting that, with respect to this small minority of occasions when the meaning of statutory text is contested, no one theory of interpretation is universally accepted. As Professors Henry Hart and Albert Sacks, two prominent scholars of statutory interpretation, famously said almost sixty years ago:

"Do not expect anybody's theory of statutory interpretation . . . to be an accurate statement of what courts actually do with statutes. The hard truth of the matter is that American courts have no intelligible, generally accepted, and consistently applied theory of statutory interpretation." HART AND SACKS' THE LEGAL PROCESS: BASIC PROBLEMS IN THE MAKING AND APPLICATION OF LAW 1169 (William N. Eskridge Jr. & Philip P. Frickey eds., 2006). Since that time, arguments about the major interpretive theories have often been pitched, but the basic point remains: courts continue to deploy various interpretive theories without much uniformity (indeed, often without explicit recognition of any theoretical framework).

A. EARLY APPROACHES TO PROBLEMS OF STATUTORY INTERPRETATION

From before the Founding, the most frequently invoked method for resolving ambiguities in statutory text was typically expressed in terms of finding and following the "legislative intent" behind the language in question. The same standard remains in widespread though not universal use today. But in practice, this simple touchstone permitted the courts, as the primary interpreters, to use a variety of methods to decide what the legislature that had enacted the provision had intended. These methods included: reading the full text of the statute, to consider how it held together as a whole; examining the immediate circumstances surrounding the measure's enactment, to identify evidence of the legislature's motive; considering the broader context of the times, in an effort to understand the problem or "mischief" at which the statute was directed; and applying any of numerous "canons of construction" (such as "*exceptions to a measure should be narrowly construed,*" or "*qualifying words should apply only to the last antecedent*"), which were understood, even if as benign fictions, to specify norms that would advance the will or intent of the enacting legislature.

Centuries earlier, in the initial years of the British parliamentary system, judges (who themselves were often also members of Parliament) conducted the interpretive task quite differently, functioning essentially as collaborators or partners with legislators. Parliament was not an independent branch of government and the idea of legislative supremacy had not yet taken root. In this era, statutes were hardly more constraining of judges than the common law. Indeed, courts could deploy their equitable powers to correct what they often saw as defects in the work-product of Parliament. (For a rich treatment of the history of both British and American courts in interpreting statutes, see WILLIAM D. POPKIN, STATUTES IN COURT (1999).)

Among the most famous of the early expositions of the judiciary's role in the interpretive enterprise is *Heydon's Case*, 76 Eng. Rep. 637 (1584). It identified four considerations relevant to the judicial construction of the meaning of an ambiguous statutory provision:

(1) the pre-existing common law;

(2) "the mischief and defect for which the common law did not provide";

(3) the remedy chosen by the legislature;

(4) "the true reason of the remedy."

This last consideration suggests an effort to understand the legislature's actual or "true" motive for its remedial requirement, though it also could invite attention to how the remedy might be expected specifically to address the defect. After listing these four considerations, *Heydon's Case* then described the court's role as construing the statute in order to "suppress the mischief, and advance the remedy . . . according to the true intent of the makers of the Act, *pro bono publico*."

The concluding phrase "for the public good" adds an interesting gloss to the interpretive enterprise, suggesting that interpretive problems should be resolved in a manner that promotes the public interest. On the one hand, this statement might be rather unremarkable. To the extent that the legislative process itself is often similarly described as a process by which elected representatives pursue the public interest (see Chapter 2), this coda to *Heydon's Case* might be just a final way of saying "honor the intent of the legislators *because* they have been acting for the public good." But the injunction *pro bono publico* is perhaps better understood as saying that the interpreters themselves, in their own judgment, should ensure the constructions they assign to ambiguous provisions are in the public interest. On this reading, *Heydon's Case* seems explicitly to give the interpreter some discretionary choice. The question of how to cabin the discretionary power or willfulness of the statutory interpreter, introduced in Chapter 7, looms large today over all theories of statutory interpretation. As explored further below, this concern has particular resonance in the contemporary debate between *Purposivists* and *Textualists*.

At the time of *Heydon's Case*, however, a different form of discretionary influence—a court's equitable powers—also sometimes played a role in the resolution of interpretive problems. When confronting an ambiguous statutory provision, courts up through the late eighteenth century might have used their equitable powers to do something quite distinct from advancing the intent of the legislature. Instead, they might have used the statutory ambiguity as an opportunity to achieve what they viewed as the fair, just, or *equitable* application of the statute. Indeed, in this earlier era, courts could rely on their own training, judgment, and authority to identify the "spirit" or "soul" of an enactment, in order to construe the textual meaning so as to advance their vision of the law. (For a history of the development of equitable interpretation, see POPKIN, *supra*, at 11–19; *see also* John F. Manning, *Textualism and the Equity of the Statute*, 101 COLUM. L. REV. 1 (2001).) In the courts, both common law cases and statutory cases therefore could be vehicles for judicial exposition and development of the law.

Yet by the time of the Founding, the supremacy of legislative enactments over the common law had already been clearly established, at least as a matter of theory. As a result, when these two sources of law have conflicting clear meanings, the statutory expression prevails. However, when the meaning of a statute is unclear, courts often have construed the statute in light of their reading of the surrounding law, to avoid or minimize any conflict. Thus, courts might refer to the common law in resolving a matter of statutory interpretation not only for its potential as a tool for understanding what defect the legislature was seeking to remedy, per *Heydon's Case*, but also to further the ideal of making only the most incremental changes in the overall body of the law, except when the enacting legislature has clearly intended a more dramatic change. Put another way, the legislature is often presumed to understand the existing common law and to intend its continuation unless its legislative enactment clearly shows otherwise. (This is an example of another of the many "canons" of interpretation, discussed in their own right in Chapter 9.)

By the later nineteenth century, the idea of courts deploying equitable powers had waned and observers of the problems of statutory interpretation were urging courts to show greater deference to the legislature. A number of treatises and legal commentaries of this Formalist era argued that statutory interpretation was reducible to a science, which when properly applied to a legal text would yield but one definitive meaning (as Chapter 7 noted). Still, where the meaning was not clear, courts frequently adhered to the interpretive canon that statutes in derogation of the common law were to be strictly or narrowly construed.

With the ascendance of the idea of legislative supremacy, one widely accepted interpretive theory was that the judiciary should fulfill its duty to effectuate the legislature's intent by following the ordinary or "plain" meaning of a statute's words. Indeed, a court was to do so even if it thought this reading of the words was "injudicious." *River Wear Commissioners v. Adamson*, [1877] App. Cas. 743 (H.L.). **Plain Meaning Interpretation** as a modern theory is discussed further in section D below. But as a historical matter, one well-known statement of this approach came from Lord Atkinson of the British of Lords, who said that where the language of a statute is plain, it must be enforced even if it is unjust, unwise, or produces "absurd or mischievous results." *Vacher & Sons Ltd. v. London Society of Compositors*, [1913] A.C. 107 (Eng.). This strict adherence to the literal meaning of the legislature's chosen text was defended on the basis that it was the most appropriate way to respect and honor the legislature's superior lawmaking authority.

This extreme defense of enforcing the plain language of a statute regardless of outcome was something of a pushback against a competing approach that invited interpreting courts to disregard the letter of the law in favor of its spirit when following the letter would produce an absurd or obviously unintended result. The most famous example of the deployment of this rule is the *Holy Trinity* case, decided by the U.S. Supreme Court in

1892. *Rector, Holy Trinity Church v. United States,* 143 U.S. 457 (1892). At issue in *Holy Trinity* was whether an 1885 congressional enactment forbidding any person or organization from encouraging or helping foreigners to immigrate to the U.S. "to perform labor or service of any kind" applied to a religious society that contracted with an Englishman to come to New York to serve as the society's pastor. The specific issue of statutory interpretation was whether working as a pastor amounted to "labor or service of any kind," within the meaning of the 1885 statute.

The Supreme Court conceded that the literal language of the act, because it covered labor or service "of any kind," would appear to include service as a religious minister. Under Lord Atkinson's view, described above, that concession surely would have meant that the religious society had violated the act (precisely as the lower court had concluded). But the Supreme Court decided otherwise: "we cannot think Congress *intended* to denounce with penalties a transaction like that in the present case" (emphasis added). The Court then wrote, in one of the most famous judicial statements related to the interpretive task: "It is a familiar rule, that a thing may be within the letter of a statute and yet not within the statute, because not within its spirit, nor within the intention of its makers." *Id.* at 459.

With this principle as its guide, the Court then explored the act's spirit. In something of a watershed moment for statutory interpretation, the Court did so in significant part by carefully reviewing the congressional committee reports, a source of information that in general courts had previously ignored. After reviewing these congressional committee reports and committee testimony, as well as the act's title, other provisions of the act, and the legal protections generally afforded to religious activities and observances, the Court concluded that Congress's intent in enacting the measure was only to prohibit the importation of "cheap unskilled labor," not to prohibit the importation of religious ministers. As for the mischief to which the statute was directed, the Court identified it as the disruption of the U.S. labor market caused by the importation of "an ignorant and servile class" of laborers paid low wages. From this perspective, the Court did not view ministers as within the ambit of the statute, even if within the ambit of its literal text.

The *Holy Trinity* case remains among the most widely cited cases in the field of statutory interpretation in part because of how clearly it juxtaposes the choice between enforcing a statute according to its literal terms or "plain meaning," and enforcing it according to its spirit or purpose. Although the Court seemed to conclude easily that the spirit of the act justified construing the prohibition more narrowly than would its letter, the Court's opinion acknowledged countervailing arguments. In particular, the act already had a section excluding certain categories of workers from its coverage, yet said nothing about excluding ministers or religious teachers. By implication, Congress's decision explicitly to exempt some categories of workers from what was otherwise a blanket prohibition on "labor or service of any kind" could have meant that Congress had thereby demonstrated its intention to cover every other kind of labor or service not explicitly exempted. Furthermore, it was not necessary for the Court to graft onto the act an additional exclusion for religious ministers in order for the act to serve its purpose of improving the labor market for American workers. Nonetheless, the Court in essence judicially amended the statute because it could not imagine Congress would have intended, as a side-effect of protecting the American work force, to also prohibit the free migration of ministers.

In reaching this result, the Court arguably was acting as what as noted in Chapter 7 is sometimes described as a "faithful agent" of the legislature, working to further the congressional purpose. Notably, by the time the Court decided the case, Congress had already amended the statute to exclude ministers from its coverage in future cases. To some, this congressional amendment confirmed that the Court was properly construing the statute. But to others, the congressional revision merely demonstrated that Congress, not the courts, always has both the responsibility and the opportunity to refine its work-product, and that the Court therefore had meddled where it did not belong. Of course, even had Congress not already amended the act, the Court likely could have anticipated that its *Holy Trinity* decision would provoke very little objection, in Congress or elsewhere (unless with respect to the theoretical question of whether the Court overstepped its role in departing from the plain language of the statute).

Searching for the "spirit" of the law as a means for resolving interpretive problems certainly could be consistent with being guided by legislative "intent"—in other words, what the enacting legislature intended the words of its statutory text to signify. But the idea of following the spirit of the law also seems to capture something larger, more akin to the "purpose" of the statute—in other words, the animating motive behind the legislation. As discussed in the following two sections, the interpretive methods of *Intentionalism* and *Purposivism* each build on the traditional notion of following the legislative intent, though they have distinguishable approaches.

B. INTENTIONALISM

Both Intentionalism and Purposivism are quite similar methods for construing ambiguous statutory language by seeking to understand and effectuate the will of the enacting legislature. In that respect, they are interpretive theories in which the interpreter's role could be described as being a *faithful agent* of the enacting legislature, seeking to complete the legislature's work. The principal difference between these two theories is the level of generality at which the legislative will is assessed. Intentionalism is attentive to the enacting legislature's specific intent with respect to the textual language at issue, while Purposivism focuses on the legislature's more general intent or purpose behind the measure. These two theories also have somewhat different philosophical groundings.

Intentionalism asks, “What did the enacting legislature believe (or intend) that the text of its statute would mean as applied to this interpretive problem?” The text of the measure itself is generally the most reliable evidence for ascertaining intent, whenever it sheds light on the question. But when the text does not supply an understanding of the intent, Intentionalist interpretation presumes (often counterfactually) that the enacting legislature nevertheless knew how it would have wanted its statute to apply to the interpretative problem and simply failed to use sufficiently clear language to that effect in the statutory text. Intentionalism then seeks to ascertain that intent through other evidence. It thus partakes of something of an “originalist” quality, inasmuch as its touchstone is identifying what the original authors of a measure meant, in order then to seek to implement that meaning faithfully.

Intentionalist interpretation can be used most successfully when the interpreter is able to identify a figurative “smoking gun” of some sort, which provides evidence that the enacting legislature both contemplated applying its statute to the issue at hand and also said something specific about how it should apply to that issue. In practice, however, it is often difficult to find a reliable smoking gun.

For instance, perhaps the minutes of the Village Council meeting at which the ordinance that prohibited the parking of a “motor vehicle camper” for over 24 hours (as introduced in Chapter 7) contain clear or repeated evidence of the Council's understanding that the parking prohibition would apply primarily to cars, as well as to trucks, campers, and a range of other vehicles. Such intent evidence might persuade a court to read the phrase "motor vehicle camper" as if it were two terms separated by a comma, and that the omission of the comma after "vehicle" is a pure scrivener's error (in contrast to the decision of the appellate court actually hearing this issue, which instead insisted on reading the provision precisely as written). But meeting minutes may not exist. Or if they do exist, they may not contain any indication of what the Council intended.

In theory, if not too much time has passed, one way of filling this evidentiary gap regarding the legislative intent behind a measure would be to interrogate the Council members or legislators themselves, after the interpretive issue has arisen, asking them what they had intended their words to mean in this specific case. But doing so would raise significant reliability problems. First, at least in many contexts there would be a risk that the legislators would not in fact even have had, or at least would not recall, a specific intent concerning the interpretive problem. Moreover, in the absence of an actual historical intent, some legislators nonetheless might claim (counterfactually though not necessarily deceitfully or maliciously) to know what the intent was. Other legislators, meanwhile, might disagree. (Indeed, as discussed further below, the idea of an institution having its own intent might be problematic.) Furthermore, such after-the-fact disagreement could arise even in circumstances in which the legislature may have had an actual historical intent. Finally, in any of these scenarios, ulterior motives might cause a legislator to claim falsely that the legislature did have a particular intent at the time of enactment, which in fact bears no relationship to what had actually been intended. Thus, the idea of obtaining first-person testimony after the interpretive problem arises is fraught with difficulty.

Instead, the Intentionalist therefore typically resorts to evidence produced at the time of enactment, principally in the form of several kinds of "legislative history" materials, discussed in greater detail in Chapter 10. These materials can include published committee reports and records of legislative debates, to name the kinds of materials usually seen as providing the most reliable evidence of specific legislative intent. These extrinsic materials will be more reliable the more they establish that they reflect a widespread or consensus view of the enacting legislature.

To understand how this historical investigation could play out, consider the celebrated case of *Nix v. Hedden*, 149 U.S. 304 (1893). The interpretive problem before the court was whether a tomato was a fruit or a vegetable, for purposes of a tariff statute that imposed high tariffs on vegetables but exempted fruits. As the Court noted, "Botanically speaking, tomatoes are the fruit of a vine . . . [b]ut in the common language . . . [they] are vegetables, which are . . . usually served at dinner . . . and not like fruits

. . . as dessert." *Id.* at 307. The Court thus recognized two different ways of defining or understanding the crucial statutory text: technical meanings and ordinary meanings. (In this case, the Court favored the ordinary meanings.)

To pick between these two meanings, an Intentionalist would focus on the legislature's will by asking something like, "Did the Congress that enacted this tariff intend for the measure to treat tomatoes as a type of fruit, or as a type of vegetable?" The interpreter might then choose to explore and examine a variety of sources of information to resolve this question. For instance, other provisions of the statute might say something that could shed light on whether Congress intended a botanical definition or a dinner table definition. Or legislators involved in the passage of the measure, during the course of its enactment, might have said something in a committee report or a legislative debate specifically about tomatoes or about the meaning of the terms "fruit" and "vegetable." Or perhaps during consideration of the measure participants in the legislative process other than Members of Congress might have behaved in ways that provided information potentially relevant to the question, for instance if trade groups active in the issue had assumed in testimony before a congressional committee that tomatoes were vegetables.

Yet even if the interpreter can find evidence in the legislative history that sheds light on the enacting legislature's intended meaning, that does not answer the normative question of whether it is appropriate for the interpreter to go about interpreting in this way. Some observers of the legislative process believe it is never (or rarely) appropriate to rely on legislative evidence outside the enacted text to determine the textual meaning. These "Textualists," to be discussed in more detail in section E below, object to searching for legislative intent evidence in legislative history materials outside the statute, in part because this evidence can easily be manipulated and may not be reliable or truly reflect the will of the legislature as a body.

In addition, Textualists and other critics of Intentionalism argue that the legislature as an institution may not have had *any* intent other than what it expressed in its enactment. Indeed, these critics point to the difficulty of identifying the intent of an institutional or corporate entity because an institution itself lacks a will or motive. Instead, it is composed of many individuals, each with their own wills and motives, which may have combined to cause the institution to adopt a particular position or course of conduct but will not always combine to produce a single collective intent. Professor Max Radin remains famous today for articulating this concern almost a century ago. *See* Max Radin, *Statutory Interpretation*, 43 HARV. L. REV. 863, 870–71 (1930). Furthermore, each of these individuals may have their own way of expressing their view of the collective intent of the entity and be unable to speak definitively for the collective. Just as no single legislator, acting alone, can bestow legal force on the enacted text, no single legislator's statement of an underlying intent should govern the interpretation of a piece of legislative text. Textualism therefore argues for an interpretive methodology independent of any attempt to find the legislative intent, except as it may have been collectively expressed by the institution in the statute itself.

Intentionalism nonetheless has many defenders, who observe that in other contexts the law routinely assumes that institutions and groups, though not strictly willful actors themselves, yet can be presumed to have an intent that motivates their actions. In interpreting private contracts, for instance, it is common to seek to understand the intent or purpose behind a provision to which a corporation or organization has agreed. The crucial interpretive question is what evidence will suffice to establish the intent of the institution. Similarly for legislatures, the question is whether certain forms of extra-textual evidence, alone or in combination with text and context, suffice to establish an underlying legislative intent. Chapter 10 discusses in more detail some of the principal sources of extrinsic evidence typically used to ascertain legislative intent and ways in which interpreters may assess the reliability of these sources.

In the absence of contemporaneous evidence of the enacting legislature's intent, and as an alternative to interrogating legislators after the fact about their intent, one instead could simply *imagine* asking the legislators what they had intended their words to mean, as Judge Learned Hand (in the twentieth century), and British commentator Edmund Plowden long before him (in the sixteenth century), had encouraged. *See* POPKIN *supra*, at 12. Some Intentionalist theories of statutory interpretation thus distinguish between "Specific" Intent and "Imagined" or "Reconstructed" Intent. *See* Roscoe Pound, *Spurious Interpretation*, 1907 COLUM. L. REV. 379. Imagined intent, however, obviously lacks any "smoking gun" evidence about what the enacting legislature meant and instead is a speculative reconstruction about what the legislature would have said about the interpretive problem, had it specifically addressed it.

For instance, in 1976 the question arose whether employment discrimination based on pregnancy amounted to a violation of Title VII of the Civil Rights Act of 1964, the text of which prohibited discrimination on the basis of "race, color, religion, sex, or national origin." *See General Electric Co. v. Gilbert*, 429 U.S. 125 (1976). An Intentionalist approach might imagine putting this specific question to the enacting Congress. In other words, would Congress in 1964 have said that discrimination on the basis of pregnancy was discrimination on the basis of sex, as prohibited in Title VII? It is not hard to imagine the enacting Congress giving a negative response to this question. But the Intentionalist interpreter may never be entirely sure of the answer to this or any other effort to imagine or reconstruct the intent.

In today's debates about theories of statutory interpretation, Intentionalism is often overshadowed by Purposivism. Nevertheless, Intentionalism still has plenty of adherents, especially in the state systems. For instance, New York has long followed a set of statutory interpretation guidelines that specifically invite its courts to be Intentionalist interpreters. These guidelines provide that "[t]he primary consideration of the courts" is to "give effect to the intention of the Legislature," first "from a literal reading of the act itself," and then "if the meaning is still not clear . . . from such facts [as may] legitimately reveal it." *See* N.Y. STAT. LAW § 92 (McKinney 2016). Minnesota has a statute providing that "[t]he object of all interpretation ... is to ascertain and effectuate the intention of the legislature," and to do so using a range of sources "[w]hen the words of a law are not explicit." MINN. STAT. 645.16 (2016). Many other state legislatures have codified a requirement that courts must construe their statutes so as to render them consistent with the "manifest intent of the legislature," although in these provisions the phrase "manifest intent" is sometimes a limiting phrase that describes only the intent that is evident from either the measure itself or the rest of the body of law, not necessarily through the analysis of legislative history. For more detailed discussion of Intentionalism in all of the fifty states, see Jacob Scott, *Codified Canons and the Common Law of Interpretation*, 98 GEO. L. J. 341 (2010); Abbe R. Gluck, *The States as Laboratories of Statutory Interpretation: Methodological Consensus and the New Modified Textualism,* 119 YALE L. J. 1750 (2010).

C. PURPOSIVISM

Purposivism, like Intentionalism, also looks beyond the literal meaning of the words of a law in an effort to understand the underlying legislative will. As distinguished from Intentionalism, however, Purposivism asks not, "What did the enacting legislature expect that the statute's words would mean as applied to this specific interpretive problem?," but instead, "What purpose did the enacting legislature expect that the statute would serve, and how might the statute's language be construed to serve that purpose in this instance?" Focusing on this question may not lead as directly to an answer as might Intentionalism in those cases in which the interpreter can find evidence of specific intent, but in cases in which there is little or no evidence of the legislature's specific intent, Purposivism may be a preferable way of furthering the legislative will.

Indeed, to some observers, the effort to identify the general "purpose" may be a more objective enterprise than trying to identify specific "intent" because purpose might often be more evident from just the text alone, taken as a whole, without reference to extrinsic sources of meaning. However, the interpretive theory that today is called "Purposivism" wholeheartedly embraces the use of extrinsic sources as well, not just the text, and therefore must be distinguished from a narrower use of text alone to identify the general purpose. Because of its reliance on legislative history materials, Purposivism draws all of the same critiques that Intentionalism does, including a concern about the difficulty of imputing a motive or purpose to an institution except through the institution's official actions (namely, the enactment of the statute), and a concern about the reliability of legislative history materials. Moreover, many critics worry that once extra-textual sources are part of the interpretive enterprise, the effort to identify a measure's general purpose may well be *less* objective than an effort to identify the legislature's specific intent, precisely because a variety of "purposes" may be found at different levels of abstraction, rather than being limited like Intentionalism by the particular interpretive problem that has arisen.

One of the more famous judicial statements of a Purposivist approach is from the Supreme Court's opinion in *United States v. American Trucking Associations, Inc.*, 310 U.S. 534, 543 (1940) (footnotes omitted):

> There is, of course, no more persuasive evidence of the purpose of a statute than the words by which the legislature undertook to give expression to its wishes. Often these words are sufficient, in and of themselves, to determine the purpose of the legislation. In such cases, we have followed their plain meaning. When that meaning has led to absurd or futile results, however, this Court has looked beyond the words to the purpose of the act. Frequently, however, even when the plain meaning did not produce absurd results but merely an unreasonable one "plainly at variance with the

policy of the legislation as a whole," this Court has followed that purpose, rather than the literal words. When aid to construction of the meaning of words, as used in the statute, is available, there certainly can be no "rule of law" which forbids its use, however clear the words may appear on "superficial examination."

As the *American Trucking* opinion suggests, American courts in the mid-twentieth century were departing from a strict plain meaning approach to statutory interpretation. In part, this likely reflected the growing influence of ideas that would shortly lead to the mid-century emergence of the "Legal Process" school of jurisprudence. Indeed, Purposivism is often equated with Legal Process interpretation, and while Purposivism had previously flourished on its own, today it certainly owes much of its contemporary theoretical basis to the Legal Process school.

As summarized in Chapter 7, the Legal Process school responded to the Legal Realists of the early twentieth century, who had somewhat skeptically described the law as not the result of a process of logical reasoning from premises to conclusions, but as what judges willfully chose to do in furtherance of certain social, political, or economic ends. In contrast, Legal Process thinkers argued that in the American system of law, both courts and legislatures were involved in a process of "reasoned elaboration" of the law, a process that deserved respect as having a discernible coherence and rationality.

Harvard law professors Henry Hart and Albert Sacks are credited with playing leading roles in the development of Legal Process theory, including developing their own rubric of the "Rudiments of Statutory Interpretation." This was a detailed and nuanced set of guidelines for courts to follow when interpreting a statute. Central to the Hart & Sacks Purposivist rubric were the following points, worth comparing to those in *Heydon's Case* described above in section A:

- courts should "[r]espect the position of the legislature as the chief policy-determining agency of society";
- courts should "[b]e mindful . . . that every statute is a part of the law" and should be part of "striving for even-handed justice";
- with these premises, courts should "[d]ecide what purpose ought to be attributed to the statute";
- courts should then interpret the statute "so as to carry out the purpose as best [they] can";
- except if doing so would require giving the words of a statute "a meaning they will not bear," or would violate a policy that certain types of laws (such as those establishing the boundaries of criminal conduct) must be clear on their face.

See HART & SACKS' THE LEGAL PROCESS, *supra*, at 1374.

As part of seeking to understand the legislature's purpose in enacting a measure, Hart & Sacks, in a pithy statement of a core tenet of the Legal Process school, called on the interpreter to "assume, unless the contrary unmistakably appears, that the legislature was made up of ***reasonable persons pursuing reasonable purposes reasonably.***" *Id.* at 1378 (emphasis added). Meanwhile, the interpreter was then likewise called upon to continue this same enterprise as a faithful agent of the legislature, reasonably furthering the legislature's reasonable purposes.

As applied to *Nix v. Hedden*, for instance, the Purposivist might ask, "Why did Congress impose high tariffs on vegetables, but entirely exempt fruits?" If the answer to this question was that the tariffs were intended to protect certain domestic agricultural producers, that answer might shed light on how to classify tomatoes for purposes of the tariff statute. Or if Congress instead was in fact attempting to distinguish between different geographic regions from which various agricultural products originated, that factor could influence how a Purposivist would construe the statute for purposes of classifying tomatoes.

A key question for Purposivism is what sources to consult in the effort to understand the enacting legislature's purpose. As with Intentionalism, the context of the enactment, including legislative documents (in addition to the statute itself) that appear to reflect the views of the legislators involved, will often play a central role. These "legislative history" materials (whose interpretive use again will be the focus of Chapter 10) can include official committee reports; committee hearing transcripts, testimony, and exhibits; records of legislative debates; and even correspondence between legislators and constituents, interest groups, or other legislators. Beyond legislative history materials, Purposivists may also explore the broader context of an enactment, with an eye to identifying the "mischief" to which it was directed or even perhaps to finding some broader values implicitly embodied in the measure.

To take a much more complicated example, Title VII of the Civil Rights Act of 1964 makes it unlawful for an employer to discriminate against employees because of race. In *United Steelworkers of America v. Weber*, 443 U.S. 193 (1979), the Supreme Court confronted the question of whether this prohibition precluded a private employer from following a voluntary affirmative action plan that provided preferences to its black employees in gaining admission to a company training program, arguably to reduce the employer's potential liability for the lingering effects of past discrimination against its black employees. Conceding that a literal reading of the act could preclude providing this preference to black employees, the Court majority, in an opinion by Justice Brennan, nonetheless found this literal reading of the act inconsistent with what it found to be Congress's purpose in enacting Title VII, namely to enhance the employment opportunities of the nation's black workers.

Yet, had it wished, the Court readily could have identified a different reasonable purpose behind Title VII, namely to rid the American work force of raceconscious decision-making. Justice Rehnquist's dissenting opinion made precisely this point, arguing that the Court majority substituted its own view of the underlying purpose or "spirit" of the act for what his dissenting opinion claimed was the enacting Congress's real purpose, namely to promote complete equality of opportunity throughout the workforce without any regard to race. Justice Rehnquist's dissenting opinion also provides a good example of Intentionalist interpretation, as it uses a variety of pieces of legislative history to argue that the Congress that enacted the Civil Rights Act of 1964 fully intended Title VII to prohibit any race-based distinctions in employment.

Of course, it is quite possible that the enacting Congress had both purposes equally in mind, seeking both to rid the work force of race-based distinctions and to improve the employment experiences and opportunities of black workers. The enacting Congress may not have seen these purposes as conflicting or perceived the way that in practice they might at times be at odds with each other. Purposivist interpreters thus may sometimes need to choose between two (or more) reasonable purposes.

The possibility that a Purposivist inquiry may identify multiple purposes is one reason, as noted earlier, that its critics see it as a potential vehicle for judicial willfulness. For instance, do the two quite distinct purposes of Title VII that the contrasting opinions of Justice Brennan and Justice Rehnquist identified in *Weber* simply reflect these jurists' own preferences, rather than congressional purpose? Hart

& Sacks explicitly acknowledged that a statute might have multiple purposes. In such a case, their interpretive guidance for identifying the most relevant purpose was for the court to imagine being in the position of the enacting legislature, with a *modus operandi* of "pursuing reasonable purposes reasonably," rather than of being influenced by "short-run currents of political expedience." HART & SACKS' THE LEGAL PROCESS, *supra*, at 1378. How akin is this guidance to the *Heydon's Case* instruction to construe ambiguities "*pro bono publico*"? Is this guidance enough to help a judicial interpreter fairly decide between conflicting purposes in a typical case?

On a related note, Purposivist interpretation also may be less constrained by the idea that textual meaning must not change over time. In particular, a Purposivist might well argue that while the original purpose of a measure does not change, the meaning that an interpreter gives to an ambiguous or broadly worded statutory phrase might well evolve in light of current conditions, in order to advance that purpose. Arguably, this is one way of understanding Justice Brennan's majority opinion in *Weber*, which discounted specific intent evidence that some members of the enacting Congress thought Title VII would prohibit all race-based distinctions in employment. (As discussed above, Justice Rehnquist's dissenting opinion's use of legislative history evidence of precisely that specific intent is a good example of Intentionalist interpretation.)

At the state level, state courts construing state legislation do not engage in Purposivist interpretation nearly as much as do their federal counterparts construing congressional legislation. (As noted at the end of section B, however, many states direct their courts to construe ambiguous statutes so as to further "legislative intent" or "legislative purpose," but only in a small number of these states does this instruction explicitly contemplate using whatever legislative history materials are available as part of determining the purpose). This divergence between the amount of Purposivist interpretation in state and federal courts at least partly reflects the fact that state legislatures historically have not produced much in the way of the kinds of legislative history materials upon which Purposivist interpretation typically depends (and which Congress has long prepared). But the historical lack of state legislative history materials is gradually changing, as more and more state legislatures have begun to prepare transcripts or to produce searchable video archives of their proceedings.

D. PLAIN MEANING INTERPRETATION: A TEXTUALIST APPROACH

In contrast to both Intentionalism and Purposivism, many interpreters in many eras have argued for the fundamental primacy of the text itself. As Oliver Wendell Holmes expressed it, "We do not inquire what the legislature meant; we ask only what the statute means." For generations of lawyers, this approach was typically described as interpretation according to the "plain meaning" of the text. Be mindful, however, that as a jurist Justice Holmes on occasion did rely on legislative history to decide "what the statute means," even to give it a meaning at odds with what others saw as its plain meaning. *See, e.g., Boston Sand & Gravel Co. v. United States*, 278 U.S. 41 (1928). As noted in section A above, Plain Meaning Interpretation has long been a rejoinder to an interpretive approach that places primacy not on the text but on legislative intent, determined through whatever means possible. As Justice Frankfurter once cautioned, interpreters should be careful not "to give point to the quip that only when legislative history is doubtful do you go the statute." Felix Frankfurter, *Some Reflections on the Reading of Statutes*, 1947 COLUM. L. REV. 527, 543. Plain Meaning interpretation is particularly critical of any intent-based approach that encourages creative usage—or even distortion—of the text in order to promote the perceived intent. E.g., *Christian Disposal, Inc. v. Village of Eolia*, 895 S.W.2d 632, 634 (Mo. Ct. App. 1995) (claiming "courts have not hesitated to hold that legislative intent will prevail over common meaning"). Meanwhile, some interpreters view a plain meaning approach as a narrow type of intentionalist theory, in which the text itself is the only (or by far the most reliable) evidence of the underlying legislative intent. *See American Trucking,* 310 U.S. at 543.

At its core, the Plain Meaning approach—often characterized as interpretation according to what is called the **Plain Meaning Rule**—reflects that sometimes an interpretive issue arises not because the meaning of a key statutory term is textually ambiguous, but because applying what appears to be a clear legal provision to a particular circumstance seems counterintuitive or otherwise contrary to what the lawmaker likely intended. Examples might include whether an ordinance prohibiting all vehicles in a public park applies to a construction vehicle bringing in playground equipment, or whether a prohibition against importing a foreign laborer precludes importing a religious pastor. But it is precisely to these circumstances that the Plain Meaning Rule is most obviously directed. However, the Rule also pertains to circumstances in which the literal text alone simply is not plain, providing that in a case of genuine ambiguity, the interpreter should work outward from the key text to related statutory provisions, then to the act as a whole, and eventually to a host of "intrinsic" interpretive aids (of the kind described in Chapter 9), in order to find the meaning that then should become "plain."

The Plain Meaning Rule provides that even when the result seems contrary to what the lawmaker presumably intended, the authority charged with interpreting the law should apply the law according to its plain meaning. As the Supreme Court wrote one hundred years ago, "if [the meaning of a law] is plain, . . . the sole function of the courts is to enforce it according to its terms." *Caminetti v. United States*, 242 U.S. 470, 485 (1917). Plain meaning interpretation views the interpreter as more of a dutiful executor than a faithful agent or cooperative partner of the legislature. Updating this idea almost a century later, Justice Thomas in 2003 called this a "seemingly obvious rule": "Unless Congress explicitly states otherwise, 'we construe a statutory term in accordance with its ordinary or natural meaning.' " *Barnhart v. Peabody Coal Co.*, 537 U.S. 149, 184 (Thomas, J., dissenting) (*quoting FDIC v. Meyer*, 510 U.S. 471, 476 (1994)).

Yet precisely how far to follow the Plain Meaning Rule is not universally accepted, even by the Supreme Court. A **strict version** of the rule, such as the version that Lord Atkinson articulated in 1913 (see p. 310), would insist on adhering to the text even when it produces a ridiculous outcome. But a competing rule against interpreting a law to produce absurd results might justify a more **"moderate" plain meaning** approach, which is willing to look for guidance outside the text when reliance on the text alone would lead to an absurd result or an interpretive stalemate. However, there is no obvious standard for determining when a plain meaning interpretation is "absurd," as arguably might be the case in not allowing a vehicle into the park to deliver playground equipment, but might less arguably be the case in refusing to allow the importation of a foreign pastor.

Legal interpreters also may differ in their willingness to apply the Plain Meaning Rule in the face of evidence that doing so would violate the intent or purpose behind the measure. The result is that the Plain Meaning Rule can be formulated and deployed in varying degrees. For instance, a **weak version** of the rule is that "absent clear evidence of a contrary legislative intention, a statute should be interpreted according to its plain language." *United States v. Apfelbaum*, 445 U.S. 115, 121 (1980). This version, in striking contrast to the formulations in *Caminetti* and *Myer* described above, explicitly invites the interpreter to look for evidence sufficient to depart from the plain meaning. This formulation typifies the approach of the majority opinion in *United Steelworkers of America v. Weber*, 443 U.S. 193 (1979), discussed above, which conceded that a literal application of the antidiscrimination provisions of Title VII of the Civil Rights Act might well invalidate a private employer's voluntary affirmative action plan. The opinion rejected this literal reading of the statute on the basis that it would thwart what the Court, after considering a variety of extrinsic sources of legislative history (of the types discussed in Chapter 10), concluded was Congress's underlying purpose: "the integration of blacks into the mainstream of American society," without disrupting private employers' traditional prerogatives any more than necessary.

Meanwhile, a **"soft" plain meaning** approach, while seeking to ground its interpretation solidly in the plain meaning of the text, is also open to using a range of additional interpretive tools, including extrinsic evidence of the kinds discussed in Chapter 10, to confirm or fine tune its understanding of just what the plain meaning is. For instance, in *Tennessee Valley Authority v. Hill*, 437 U.S. 153 (1978), introduced in Chapter 7, the Supreme Court relied on several arguments from legislative history materials to reinforce its conclusion that the plain meaning of the Endangered Species Act (specifically its provision that all federal agencies must ensure that their actions "do not jeopardize the continued existence" of an endangered species), draconian though it might be, was that the TVA could not complete the Tellico Dam. For another prototypical example of "soft" plain meaning interpretation, see *Griffin v. Oceanic Contractors, Inc.*, 458 U.S. 564 (1982).

In its typical formulation, the Plain Meaning Rule invites attention to what is often called the **"ordinary or natural meaning"** of the text at issue. For instance, in the famous case of *McBoyle v. United States*, 283 U.S. 25 (1931), the Court confronted the question of whether an airplane was a vehicle for purposes of the National Motor Vehicle Theft Act, which criminalized the interstate transportation of a stolen vehicle. Writing for the Court, Justice Holmes explained the statute's definition of a vehicle, namely "an automobile, automobile truck, automobile wagon, motor cycle, or any other self-propelled vehicle not designed for running on rails," called to mind the "everyday" or "popular" meaning of the term as "a thing moving on land," and should not be construed to include something that flies, even though an airplane could comfortably fit within the category of "any other self-propelled vehicle not designed for running on rails." The search for the ordinary, natural, or prototypical meaning of a law is a search for how the text itself will most naturally strike the typical reader.

But the focus on the ordinary or prototypical meaning gives rise to another issue about the application of the Rule, namely how to determine what meaning is the "plain" meaning. The ordinary meaning is often distinguishable from the **literal**

meaning of the text. If construed literally, the National Motor Vehicle Theft Act would have applied to a stolen airplane, but the Court in *McBoyle* thought a literal meaning was at odds with the plain or ordinary meaning. Nevertheless, one strict version of the plain meaning rule does call for the words of a statute to be construed literally. But a literal or **"strict" construction** approach to interpretation should not be confused with the prototypical or ordinary meaning approach.

Just what the natural or ordinary or even literal meaning of a term is may depend on context and audience. Indeed, depending on audience, determining the plain meaning sometimes may require understanding a term's technical or scientific or legal meaning. For instance, to the general public, the ordinary meaning of a term in the statute of wills may be different from the ordinary meaning of that same term to an estate lawyer. If the statute of wills is directed primarily to estate lawyers and probate courts, then perhaps it is this audience's ordinary reading of the term that should establish its plain meaning. Or a public health statute replete with scientific and medical terms concerning disease tracking and prevention may invite interpretation according to the "plain" or "ordinary" *technical* meaning of its terms, as understood by the medical and public health communities. Thus, the plain meaning rule occasionally can be applied with respect to the meaning that a particular intended audience would most naturally ascribe to the text, even if this is not the ordinary meaning for the average citizen.

An example of an interpretive disagreement over whether to give a statutory term its ordinary meaning or its legal meaning arose in *Moskal v. United States*, 498 U.S. 103 (1990). The federal statute at issue criminalized the knowing transportation in interstate commerce of "falsely made" securities, which included state motor vehicle titles. The Court majority applied this statute to vehicle titles that, because the vehicles' odometers had been physically rolled back, bore a false odometer reading. Justice Scalia, in dissent, argued the titles themselves had not been falsely made because at common law that phrase had an established legal meaning akin to fraudulently made or counterfeit, a characterization that was not true of these genuine vehicle titles even though the information on them was inaccurate. The majority relied on a broader, ordinary meaning of "falsely made" to apply that characterization to the titles in question because of the underlying fraud involved in the falsified odometers.

One increasingly frequent aid in applying the plain meaning rule is to turn to **dictionaries** as a source for understanding the text. Of course, an enacting legislature can always include its own definitions of critical statutory terms for purposes of a given measure, and many statutes have a separate section devoted to definitions. But absent these internal definitions (and sometimes even in spite of them, or to understand undefined terms contained within a statutory definition), courts, agencies, and other interpreters may choose to consult dictionaries, on the theory that dictionaries can help identify the ordinary or natural meaning of a term. Moreover, dictionary definitions can be used not only to develop an understanding of the ordinary meaning of a term, but also to identify technical, scientific, or legal definitions of a term, in contexts in which those specialized uses may be the more appropriate "plain" meanings.

For instance, the Court Interpreters Act provides that the costs that may be awarded to prevailing parties in federal court include the costs of "compensation of interpreters." In *Taniguchi v. Kan Pacific Saipan, Ltd.*, 566 U.S. ___, 132 S. Ct. 1997 (2012), the Supreme Court considered whether to construe this provision to include the costs of compensation of document translators. In concluding that the ordinary meaning of "interpreter" was limited to one who provides oral translation, not "those who translate writings," the Court surveyed more than a dozen dictionaries, focusing on the editions in print at the time Congress enacted the Court Interpreters Act. Three dissenters, relying on a few dictionary definitions of their own in support, would have defined "interpreters" more broadly to encompass document translators, and could find no reason to think the enacting Congress had intended not to cover written as well as oral translation services.

In fact, however, some recent empirical research suggests that legislative drafters rarely draft with dictionary definitions in mind. *See* Abbe R. Gluck & Lisa Schultz Bressman, *Statutory Interpretation from the Inside: An Empirical Study of Congressional*

Drafting, Delegation and the Canons, 65 STAN. L. REV. 901 (2013). But should this empirical claim matter to one's theory of interpretation, or should interpretation nonetheless presume that drafters ought to be familiar with dictionary definitions? Some interpreters have long worried that relying on dictionary definitions in interpreting ambiguous legal text can be misleading. Judge Learned Hand once cautioned against "mak[ing] a fortress out of the dictionary," and urged the interpreter instead to remain focused on understanding the statute's actual purpose. *See Cabell v. Markham*, 148 F.2d 737 (2d Cir. 1945). On the other hand, as Hart and Sacks observed, "reputable dictionaries" may provide more reliable and "impersonal" sources of understanding than the idiosyncratic meanings that a particular judge may assign to ambiguous text based on the judge's own personal experience. *See* HART & SACKS' THE LEGAL PROCESS, *supra*, at 1190.

Consider the interpretive issue arising out of a federal firearms statute, 18 U.S.C. § 924 (c)(1), which stiffens the otherwise applicable criminal penalties if a defendant "uses or carries" a firearm "during and in relation to any crime of violence or drug trafficking crime." In the terms of this statute, does bartering a handgun for illegal narcotics amount to the "use" of a firearm during and in relation to a drug trafficking crime? Once again, the Supreme Court divided over this interpretive issue, with the majority relying on a number of dictionary definitions of the prototypical meaning of the word "use" to confirm that trading a handgun for drugs amounted to the use of a firearm. In contrast, the dissent argued that in the phrase to "use a firearm," the word "use" had a contextualized meaning that implied using the firearm *as a weapon*. In essence, the dissent was arguing for a specialized or technical dictionary meaning of the term "use," rather than an ordinary meaning. *See Smith v. United States*, 508 U.S. 223 (1993). In a separate case a few years later, the Court similarly divided over how to interpret the meaning of the phrase "carries a firearm" in the same statute, when applied to defendants who had a gun in their trunk or glove box but not on their person. Assorted competing dictionary definitions, this time of "carry," again figured prominently in the case. *See Muscarello v. United States*, 524 U.S. 125 (1998).

Several of the opinions in *Muscarello* and *Smith* are characteristic of the interpretive approach generally known as "New Textualism" (or occasionally just "Textualism"), which in essence is a strong version of Plain Meaning Interpretation. The next section discusses New Textualism in its own right because of its importance to contemporary debate about the interpretation of legal text.

E. (NEW) TEXTUALISM

In the final two decades of the 20th century, a group of jurists and theorists, with the late Justice Scalia as its most visible member, developed and forcefully argued for a version of Plain Meaning interpretation that relies almost exclusively on the enacted text and eschews using any legislative history materials. This movement, sometimes called simply Textualism but more appropriately known as

New Textualism to distinguish it from earlier Plain Meaning or "textualist" approaches to interpretation, continues to have a profound influence on interpretive methodology today, even though it has never become the dominant interpretive approach. It has, however, dramatically reinvigorated the Plain Meaning doctrine, which in the eyes of many jurists and observers had become largely moribund at the federal level by the time of New Textualism's arrival in the 1980s. New Textualism also has reshaped the way most other interpreters structure their analyses, leading all theories of interpretation to focus substantial attention on the text itself and then to evaluate whatever extrinsic sources also may have interpretive value in light of the implications of the text.

Recall that Plain Meaning Interpretation, in its earlier formulations, was driven fundamentally by the rise of a positive view of legislative supremacy in the nineteenth century. Although New Textualism builds upon this same foundation, it also incorporates a strong negative view of the dangers of judicial willfulness in matters of interpretation. It accordingly seeks to limit the courts' interpretive discretion as much as possible and argues that an important way of doing so is to insist on adhering almost exclusively to the text and to reject the use of legislative history materials. New Textualism thus generally opposes both a "soft" version of Plain Meaning Interpretation (which as described above is willing to supplement the text with legislative history materials in a wide range of cases), as well as a "moderate" version (which as also previously described is willing to look beyond the text for clues to meaning in legislative history materials when following the text alone would lead to an absurd result or an interpretive impasse).

New Textualism's insistence that it is improper to resort to legislative history does not mean that it embraces the extreme version of the Plain Meaning Rule that Lord Atkinson championed a century ago, in which the interpreter must adhere to the text even when it produces absurd results. Rather, New Textualism insists only that the tools for resolving interpretive problems must not include looking to legislative history. When the text alone does not avoid the problems of an absurd result or an interpretive impasse, New Textualism typically resolves the problem by construing the text in light of the larger body of the law or by relying on other intrinsic "canons" of interpretation, as described further in Chapter 9. These canons are widely accepted interpretive guidelines or maxims that, much like dictionaries, can be used to help choose between interpretive possibilities. Nor does New Textualism amount to a form of "strict constructionism" that requires a hyperliteral reading of the text. Rather, it depends on identifying ordinary, "fair," and sensible readings of the text, through use of canons of construction and other intrinsic interpretive tools as necessary. Most contemporary Textualists (including Justice Scalia) reject being equated with Strict Constructionists.

One widely cited example of New Textualist interpretation is the majority opinion in *West*

Virginia University Hospitals, Inc. v. Casey, 499 U.S. 83 (1991). At issue was whether a litigant's costs for expert services could be part of "a reasonable attorney's fee" awarded to the prevailing party under 42 U.S.C. § 1988. Section 1988, like numerous "fee shifting" provisions, permits imposing on the losing party some of the winning party's costs of litigation. In arguing for a "yes" answer to whether these costs should include paying for experts who were essential to winning a civil case, the dissenters relied heavily upon legislative history, including language in a 1976 committee report that plaintiffs in federal civil rights actions should be able "to recover what it costs them to vindicate these rights in court." In addition to this suggestion of the purpose of the statute, the legislative history also described the measure as intended to counter the impact of a 1973 Supreme Court decision, which had said that the federal courts lacked authority to use their equitable powers to award either expert fees or attorney's fees to prevailing plaintiffs, as had been the frequent practice.

The majority of the Court, in an opinion authored by Justice Scalia, rejected this approach:

> The best evidence of [the statute's] purpose is the statutory text adopted by both Houses of Congress and submitted to the President. Where that contains a phrase that is unambiguous—that has a clearly accepted meaning in both legislative and judicial practice—we do not permit it to be expanded or contracted by statements of individual legislators or

committees during the course of the enactment process.

Id. at 98–99. Of course, crucial to this approach was the majority's determination that the critical statutory phrase—"a reasonable attorney's fee"—had an "unambiguous" meaning. Indeed, the majority opinion concluded that, as used in the statute, this phrase plainly did not include the costs of expert services, even though the text of the phrase considered alone arguably is not at all clear on this point.

Nevertheless, the majority found the meaning of the phrase to be clear by comparing the phrase to language Congress had used in a number of other similar measures. The opinion noted that in almost three-dozen other federal statutes, Congress had authorized courts to award the prevailing party both attorney's fees and expert witness fees, and that several other statutes authorized fees for expert services beyond appearing as a witness. Given the congressional inclusion of this element in other fee shifting measures, Congress's failure to mention expert costs specifically in section 1988 was fatal: "We think this statutory usage shows beyond question that attorney's fees and expert fees are distinct items of expense." *Id.* at 92. The fact that many of these other measures were enacted at close to the same time as section 1988 reinforced the Court's determination to read the phrase "attorney's fee" narrowly to exclude fees for expert services.

Justice Scalia's concurring opinion in *Green v. Bock Laundry Machine Co.*, 490 U.S. 504 (1989), offers another window into New Textualist interpretation. At issue was a Federal Rule of Evidence providing that "for the purpose of attacking the credibility of a witness, evidence that the witness has been convicted of a crime" is admissible only if either: (1) the crime involved dishonesty, or (2) the crime was a felony punishable by imprisonment for more than one year *and* "the probative value of admitting this evidence outweighs its prejudicial effect to the defendant." This last caveat requires a court to balance the prejudice "to the defendant" against the potential value to the trier of fact of receiving the evidence. The problem was that this rule, like the rest of the Federal Rules of Evidence, was to apply in both criminal and civil cases.

Balancing probative value against prejudicial impact *on the defendant* makes eminent sense in a criminal case, in which the parties are always the government against a criminal defendant. But it leads to nonsensical results in a civil case, in which the positioning of the parties as plaintiff and defendant often involves an accident of timing of who filed suit first. If the defendant in a civil case seeks to impeach a witness testifying on behalf of the plaintiff by introducing evidence of the witness's prior felony conviction, the defendant by definition would experience no prejudicial effect. Accordingly, by its terms the Rule would always permit introducing the evidence against a plaintiff's witness. Yet if the parties happened to be reversed, so that the party who seeks to introduce the evidence is denominated the plaintiff and wants to use the prior crimes evidence to impeach the defendant's witness, the Rule could result in the court concluding that the prejudice "to the defendant" requires the exclusion of the very same evidence that the court would have to admit if offered by the defendant.

Writing for the majority, Justice Stevens said: "No matter how plain the text of the Rule may be, we cannot accept an interpretation that would deny to a civil plaintiff the same right to impeach an adversary's testimony that it grants to a civil defendant"; indeed he noted that it might even be unconstitutional to do so. *Id.* at 510. The majority opinion then identified various ways of construing the rule to avoid this problem: reading it to protect against prejudice to *any party*, not just any defendant; against prejudice to any witness (rather than any party); or against prejudice to only any criminal defendant. The Court then examined in detail the legislative history with which this Rule was adopted, in order to conclude that the Rule's application should be limited to only defendants in criminal proceedings.

In his concurrence, Justice Scalia reached the same result, specifically rejecting as "absurd" the result of giving the word "defendant" its "literal" meaning. He then concluded that the Rule should therefore be limited to criminal cases, but he refused to be guided to this interpretation through legislative history. Instead, he argued simply that the word "defendant," as used in the Rule, was best understood to have impliedly meant only the "criminal defendant." He saw this reading as "most in accord with context and ordinary usage," as well as preferable to any alternative ways of reading the rule because they would require a greater departure from the actual text. He did, however, find it "entirely appropriate" to consult the legislative history for one discrete purpose: to confirm that indeed no Member of Congress had contemplated the absurd possibility that the Rule would apply to both criminal and civil defendants but not to civil plaintiffs. (Of course, another option that a textualist interpreter could have taken, rather than finding the Rule's plain meaning to be absurd and therefore choosing a less objectionable revision of the Rule, would have been to invalidate the Rule entirely on the basis that as written it was simply unconstitutional.)

Several points about New Textualism as an interpretive theory merit brief mention. One is that although New Textualism is radically different from Purposivism, it too grounds itself on a sense that the interpreter's role is to serve as a **faithful agent** of the enacting legislature or agency. But while Purposivism seeks to be a faithful agent of the legislature by identifying and furthering the legislative purpose, Textualism seeks to do so by dutifully honoring the legislative will exactly as expressed in the enacted text, taking the legislature's choice of words as the only legitimate and reliable evidence of what the legislature wants its agent to do. In this respect, a strain of Legal Process theory also undergirds New Textualism because it fully embraces the view of the legislative branch as institutionally competent to generate law through a coherent and rationale process.

Independently important for Textualism is the fact that the text is **legitimate**. Because only the enacted text is the law, all other sources of interpretive guidance are illegitimate for a Textualist interpreter. To allow illegitimate sources to alter the meaning contained in legal text would undermine the idea of legislative supremacy.

Of almost equal concern to New Textualists is their view that extrinsic sources of interpretive guidance are not **reliable**. The Textualists' repeated refrain, discussed in greater detail in Chapter 10, is that evidence of legislative purpose or intent found in committee reports, floor statements, and other legislative history materials cannot be trusted to express the view of a majority of legislators, but rather may reflect the results of strategic manipulation. In other words, because the full legislative body does not approve legislative history materials by a majority vote the way the legislature must approve the enacted text, individual legislators or even their staff members may be able to incorporate in speeches or legislative reports statements of intent that in fact do not reflect a broadly held view. Indeed, they may do so primarily or even exclusively for the purpose of seeding the historical record with statements that can be used later, when interpretive issues arise, rather than for the purpose of persuading or influencing their legislative colleagues during the enactment process. In contrast, enacted text is fully reliable.

Note, however, that even though New Textualism is profoundly critical of Purposivism's use of extra-textual evidence to identify legislative intent or purpose, a Textualist is not necessarily opposed to taking legislative purpose or intent into account. Instead, Textualists object only to the search for what they view as a subjective purpose and to relying on extrinsic evidence to ascertain that purpose. But reliance on objective purpose—the purpose apparent on the face of the statute—is acceptable.

Critics of New Textualism offer two fundamental critiques. One is that its formalist insistence on honoring only whatever legislative intent is apparent in the enacted text disserves and disrespects the legislative branch in any case in which the text alone lacks a sufficiently clear or plain meaning. In those cases, Purposivists and others insist that extrinsic sources of meaning at least deserve to be consulted, albeit with an awareness of their potential pitfalls. Only by thoughtfully considering in each specific case whether these materials provide reliable evidence of legislative purpose or intent can the interpreter truly function as a faithful agent of the enacting legislature; by not doing so Textualist interpretation often leads to results that are manifestly unjust. New Textualists respond that it is not the role of the interpreter to seek to accomplish what the legislature may have intended but simply failed to effectuate; the legislature, through new lawmaking, is free to correct any judicial or agency interpretation it finds unjust or with which it disagrees. Critics reply that the notion that legislatures can readily correct interpretations with which they disagree ignores the difficulties inherent in the legislative process and slights the complexities of the relationships between the various institutions of government.

Another criticism is that Textualism is vulnerable to the influence of the interpreter's personal preferences in those cases in which the statutory text lacks a sufficiently plain meaning. This argument claims that while a good-faith examination of legislative history materials operates to constrain an interpreter's freedom, Textualist interpretation leaves the interpreter with greater freedom to roam the many interpretive canons, various dictionaries, and whatever arguably related textual provisions the interpreter can find elsewhere in statutory law to justify whatever particular interpretive choice may happen to align most closely with the interpreter's own preferences, consciously or subconsciously. New Textualists counter that when an interpretive issue does not have a clear answer, Textualism's reliance on interpretive doctrines developed independently of any specific issue reduces the risks of importing judicial preferences into the interpretive enterprise, as compared to Purposivist interpretation, which often may provide the interpreter a host of competing extrinsic legislative history evidence from which to choose.

Yet Textualism, despite both its trenchant identification of several hazards of Purposivist interpretation, and its proffer of a conceptually simple alternative, has not become widely followed. It has, however, significantly altered the way in which interpretive problems are analyzed and argued. Much more than in the heyday of unconstrained Purposivism, today almost all litigants, jurists, and agency officials focus substantial attention on the enacted text before turning to extrinsic tools.

For instance, an example of what is sometimes called the "New Purposivism" or "Textually-Constrained Purposivism" is *General Dynamics Land Systems, Inc. v. Cline*, 540 U.S. 581 (2004). The interpretive issue involved the key provision of the Age Discrimination in Employment Act, which makes it unlawful for employers to "discriminate against any individual [between the ages of forty and sixty-five] with respect to [that individual's terms and conditions of employment] because of such individual's age." Textualists and Purposivists alike readily agreed that the statute prohibited employers from favoring younger workers over older workers. But the question in the case was whether the statute also prohibited favoring older workers over younger workers within the protected age range.

Textualists would easily answer yes to this question—as the dissenters did in this case—on the basis that the statutory language plainly prohibits any age-based distinctions in employment. Traditional Purposivists, meanwhile, would find abundant evidence in both the legislative history and the context of the measure's enactment that its spirit was concerned entirely with protecting older workers against more favorable treatment of younger workers, and that this spirit should trump the literal language. But in *Cline,* the majority's Purposivist opinion also analyzed at some length how the text itself was amenable to a narrower reading than its most natural plain meaning, in which "discriminate because of age" means only "discriminate because of one's relatively older age." The majority opinion then could argue that because this narrower textual meaning is most consistent with the ADEA's underlying spirit or purpose, the act should be construed to prohibit only discrimination against relatively older workers.

New Textualism deserves credit for this focus on textual meaning in what is still a heavily Purposivist landscape. Another recent example of this influence is *Zuni Public School District No. 89 v. Department of Education*, 550 U.S. 81 (2007). Although the Purposivist majority opinion in *Zuni* began with an analysis of the underlying purpose, rather than with an analysis of the statutory text, it nonetheless felt constrained to address in specific detail how the literal language of the measure could be read to square with what the opinion had already identified as the statute's underlying purpose. In dissent, Justice Scalia complained that the majority opinion had reinvigorated what he thought was the discredited spirit-trumps-letter approach of the *Holy Trinity* case, which he described as "that miraculous redeemer of lost causes." *Id.* at 116.

As the competing opinions in both *Zuni* and *Cline* reflect, debates about interpretive theory continue to rage, both within the academy as well as among judicial interpreters and the practicing bar. A must-read treatise of New Textualism is ANTONIN SCALIA & BRYAN A. GARNER, READING LAW: THE

INTERPRETATION OF LEGAL TEXTS (2012). For some Purposivist responses, see WILLIAM N. ESKRIDGE JR., INTERPRETING LAW: A PRIMER ON HOW TO READ STATUTES AND THE CONSTITUTION (2016); ROBERT A. KATZMANN, JUDGING STATUTES (2014).

F. PRAGMATIC AND DYNAMIC INTERPRETATION

Although the contemporary debate about interpretive theory has been dominated by Purposivists and New Textualists, two other categories of interpretive theory—Pragmatism and Dynamic Interpretation—require brief mention. Each of these closely related approaches are in important ways both practical (or pragmatic) and adaptable (or dynamic).

Pragmatism, as its name suggests, involves interpretation in light of a sense that other interpretive theories are not sufficiently attuned to certain practical realities of lawmaking and interpretation. These include the impossibility of legislatures' drafting statutes that make clear how they are to cover every possible application (and the necessity therefore of leaving many interpretive issues to the courts and agencies); the difficulty of legislatures' revising or updating existing statutes to reflect evolving legal concepts and changes in social conditions; and the institutional ability that courts in particular have to do justice while enhancing the overall coherence of American law. For instance, Judge Richard Posner, a leading pragmatist and a judge on the United States Court of Appeals for the

Seventh Circuit, describes the interpreter's role as to produce the best result through common sense and "practical reasoning."

Dynamic Interpretation similarly calls for a practical interpretive approach nimble enough to adapt a statutory text to accommodate new circumstances. Dynamic theory usually still takes the enacted text itself as the starting point, and also draws upon both the purpose(s) behind the statute and the context of its enactment as interpretive tools. But Dynamic Interpretation then adds an additional focus on subsequent changes in social conditions, including how the overall fabric of the law has itself continued to evolve since the time of the measure's enactment. Harking back to notions of the "equity of the statute," Dynamic Interpretation then encourages the interpreter to seek a reasonable construction of the statutory text in light of these changes, in a kind of clarification, extension, or even updating of the statute to keep it in tune with the times. Dynamic interpreters are operating much more as cooperative partners with the legislature than as its faithful agents. *See* WILLIAM N. ESKRIDGE JR., DYNAMIC STATUTORY INTERPRETATION (1994).

One version of a dynamic theory is Ronald Dworkin's description of interpretation as akin to writing a chain novel. This metaphor seeks to capture the notion that just as each sequential author who contributes a passage to the creation of a chain novel must take the previous material as given and seek to build upon it, the statutory interpreter likewise must be moored in the language of the statute and all those factors that have already helped give it meaning and content. Yet at the same time, the author's or interpreter's role is to continue building on that body of work as a "creative . . . partner" to deepen and enrich the evolving story or law in the most coherent way. *See* RONALD DWORKIN, LAW'S EMPIRE 313 (1986).

The story of the Supreme Court's acceptance of an employer's voluntary affirmative action plan in the *Weber* case, discussed above as an example of a purpose-based interpretation of Title VII, might alternatively be understood as an example of both a pragmatic and a dynamic reading of the statute. At least two significant changes that had occurred since the statute's enactment in 1964 might have prompted this dynamic reading: First, as a matter of social conditions, the problem of race-based discrimination in employment had turned out to be almost intractable, proving much harder to eliminate than the enacting Congress presumably had anticipated (or hoped). Second, as a matter of law, the Court had previously construed the statute to prohibit discrimination against either black *or white* employees (as well as employees of any other race), *see McDonald v. Santa Fe Trail Transportation Co.*, 427 U.S. 273 (1976), making it very difficult for an employer to rectify the continuing effects of past discrimination that already left the employer vulnerable to a Title VII lawsuit. In light of these new realities, the *Weber* Court arguably adopted a construction of Title VII less true to either the original intent or the original purpose of the enacting Congress and more in line with the Court's sense of the place of the statute in American law by 1979. Justice Blackmun's concurring opinion in the case is a particularly good example of this type of dynamic reasoning, in light of its explicit recognition of the unforeseen difficulties that the statute was now confronting.

A couple of state law examples of dynamic interpretation include *In the Matter of Jacob*, 660 N.E.2d 397 (N.Y. 1995) (introduced above in section B.2.d of Chapter 7, and discussed again below in section B.3 of Chapter 10), and *Commonwealth v. Maxwell*, 114 A. 825 (Pa. 1921). In *Maxwell*, the Pennsylvania Supreme Court confronted a statute that called for jurors to be selected from the list of the state's "qualified electors," or voters. At the time of the statute's adoption, women were not allowed to vote in Pennsylvania. The court held that the Nineteenth Amendment's extension of the franchise to women some years after adoption of the juror selection statute required that women also now be part of the potential jury pool. By contrast, at about the same time, high courts in Illinois and Massachusetts reached the opposite result, accepting the counter-argument that the legislatures responsible for enacting these jury selection statutes, in providing that jurors were to be drawn from the ranks of qualified electors, had thereby intended to limit the class of jurors to men; as a result, the subsequent inclusion of women in the class of qualified voters would not be transferred to the juror statutes. *See Commonwealth v. Welosky*, 177 N.E. 656 (Mass. 1931) (describing the adoption of the Nineteenth Amendment as "giving rise to radically diverse circumstances presumably not within the dominating purpose of those who framed and enacted" the juror selection statute); *People ex rel. Fyfe v. Barnett,* 150 N.E. 290 (Ill. 1925).

At their most abstract level, Dynamic and Pragmatic Interpretation might derive interpretive guidance from broad public norms, as part of promoting the overall coherence of the law generally. One example of this approach is the Supreme Court's decision in *Bob Jones University v. United States*, 461 U.S. 574 (1983). At issue was whether the federal income tax exemption available to educational organizations under section 501(c)(3) of the federal tax code could be conditioned upon not having a racially discriminatory admissions policy. Although this charitable exemption had long been available to educational organizations, in 1970 the I.R.S. began to impose a nondiscrimination requirement. The Court concluded that the purpose of the charitable exemption was to support organizations that "serve a public purpose," and that "there can no longer be any doubt that racial discrimination in education violates deeply and widely accepted views of elementary justice." *Id.* at 592. This was an explicit acknowledgement of the impact of social progress on an interpretive problem. The dissenting opinion concluded that in enacting section 501(c)(3), Congress had already made the judgment that an educational organization, without more, was in the public interest and thus merited the tax exemption; therefore the statute provided no basis for an extra-textual requirement that the organization also operate consistent with contemporary norms of public policy.

Obviously, as the dissenting opinion in *Bob Jones* suggests, the idea that the process of statutory interpretation could be a mechanism for updating a statute may strike many as counter to the idea of legislative supremacy at the foundation of both Textualism and Intentionalism. In particular, Textualists decry most forms of Pragmatic or Dynamic Interpretation as disrespectful of the legislature's superior authority to make the law. The result could be a type of judicial lawmaking that circumvents the many procedural hurdles deliberately built into the legislative process as safeguards. Meanwhile, the prospect of judicial updating of statutes also may introduce some unpredictability in the law, as affected parties may be less sure precisely what a law means, even as defenders of Dynamic or Pragmatic Interpretation argue that it allows courts to enhance the overall coherence of the law.

A very different form of pragmatic interpretation is to deploy certain elements of economic reasoning in the service of interpretative choice. Both Judge Posner, from a non-Textualist position, and his Seventh Circuit colleague Frank Easterbrook, from a Textualist position, have repeatedly exemplified how economic frameworks may affect interpretive choices. For instance, Judge Easterbrook has suggested that an interpreter might first identify whether a statute is best understood as a broad, public-interest measure, or instead as a narrow, "rent-seeking" measure. (This framing builds on the economic analysis of Public Choice Theory, discussed above in section C.2 of Chapter 2.) If the statute is more of a public-regarding measure, an interpretive effort to fill in gaps in the measure might also be broad, seeking to further its public purpose, as a faithful agent of the legislature. If the statute is closer to a private contract among competing groups, interpretive problems might be approached with more of the narrow lens of a dutiful executor, holding the rent-seekers to only whatever benefits are clearly within the terms of their legislative "bargain."

Additionally, while courts typically are prone to focus on the impact of their decisions on the parties before them, engaging in a kind of *ex post* reasoning about the law and what it means with respect to past conduct, economic reasoning may occasionally lead some judicial interpreters to think in more *ex ante* terms about the nature of the incentives that a given interpretive choice will create for future conduct and cases. The harshness of the result in a given case before the court matters less than whether the result will enhance the overall coherence of the law, particularly in terms of leading participants in the legislative process to be able to rely upon the outcome of that process.

An interesting example is the decision in *United States v. Marshall*, 908 F.2d 1312 (7th Cir. 1990), which concerned the criminal sentences applicable to the federal crime of distributing specified weights of "a mixture or substance containing a detectable amount" of LSD. Judge Easterbrook's majority opinion took a Textualist position that the statute's plain language required including the weight of the carrier medium as part of the "mixture or substance" containing the LSD, even if this led to harsh—even absurd—sentencing results (for instance, for a defendant distributing a single dose of LSD in a glass of orange juice). As can usually be said of Textualism generally, this approach sought to preserve public confidence in the work of Congress by enforcing its legislative bargain expressed in the text. In contrast, Judge Posner's dissenting opinion in the same case also sought to protect confidence in Congress, but by excluding the weight of the carrier medium so as to rationalize the sentencing scheme. He wrote that the courts' interpretive role was to "not make Congress's handiwork an embarrassment to the members of Congress and to us." *Id.* at 1338 (Posner, J., dissenting). Although Judge Posner's approach also would avoid a harsh result in the particular case, his primary concern, as was Judge Easterbrook's, was in the implications of the decision on a range of future possibilities.

* * *

As the major theories discussed in this chapter suggest, no method of legal Interpretation is immune from the criticism that it provides opportunities for judicial willfulness, in usurpation of the legislative role. Nor does any theory have an objective basis for claiming that it provides the best method for furthering the legislative will. Constraints such as text, context, and purpose may limit the interpreter's choices, but interpretation inevitably still requires some exercise of discretion. And some interpretive theories argue that interpreters ought to serve additional ends, such as enhancing the overall coherence of the law. The next two chapters look in greater depth at the specific tools that statutory interpreters use in applying these interpretive theories.

CHAPTER 9

CANONS OF CONSTRUCTION AND OTHER INTRINSIC TOOLS OF INTERPRETATION

WHAT'S IN THIS CHAPTER:

Whether one is a Textualist, a Purposivist, or almost any other kind of interpreter, the process of statutory and regulatory interpretation at least begins with a close reading of the words of the measure. As Justice Felix Frankfurter, while a professor at Harvard Law School, famously urged his students, the three critical interpretive steps are: "(1) Read the statute; (2) read the statute; (3) read the statute." *See* Henry J. Friendly, *Mr. Justice Frankfurter and the Reading of Statutes*, in BENCHMARKS 202 (1967); *cf.* Felix Frankfurter, *Some Reflections on the Reading of Statutes*, 1947 COLUM. L. REV. 527. While Purposivists may thereafter deploy a wide range of interpretive tools to refine their understanding of the meaning of the words, Textualists generally limit their tools of interpretation to rules and principles of intrinsic textual analysis. These intrinsic tools include linguistic and substantive maxims, or "canons of construction," for decoding the text itself without reference to any external evidence about the meaning of the particular words at issue. Yet a thorough familiarity with these intrinsic tools of interpretation is essential to any interpretive approach. Furthermore, while at the federal level most of these interpretive canons or maxims exist only as rules of thumb, many states have now codified a number of these canons as interpretive commands, at least with respect to how courts are to construe statutes. *See* Jacob Scott, *Codified Canons and the Common Law of Interpretation*, 98 GEO. L. J. 341 (2010).

This chapter begins with a discussion of three categories of "textual canons" of interpretation:

(1) linguistic (or semantic) canons; (2) grammar canons; and (3) the "Whole Act Rule" and its corollaries and variants. The chapter then describes half a dozen examples of substantive policy canons, which are canons of interpretation that embody substantive values, and which like textual canons can help justify particular interpretive choices without reference to any external interpretive aids. The chapter concludes with a few caveats about the use of these intrinsic interpretive tools.

A. TEXTUAL CANONS AS TOOLS OF INTERPRETATION

Interpretation of legal text generally begins with a reading of the words attuned to their plain meaning. Indeed, the Plain Meaning approach to legal interpretation, discussed in some detail in Chapter 8 as an interpretive theory, is also frequently characterized as a rule or canon of interpretation and included among the list of intrinsic tools of interpretation. For instance, see 2A SUTHERLAND STATUTES AND STATUTORY CONSTRUCTION §§ 46:1 & 47:27 (7th ed. 2014); REED DICKERSON, THE INTERPRETATION AND APPLICATION OF STATUTES 190 (1975).

As noted in Chapter 8, however, the plain meaning of a text may not always be the accepted interpretive touchstone, particularly when the result seems at odds with a sensible construction. In addition, the reality is that plenty of statutory provisions lack a plain meaning in some contexts, at least without additional attention to the linguistic structure and the relationship of the words of the provision at issue to each other and to other parts of the statute. Over the years, a number of canons of construction have developed concerning these linguistic relationships to help in refining one's understanding of what might otherwise be ambiguous legal text. These quite sensible, even intuitive, interpretive presumptions include linguistic maxims, grammar rules, and principles concerning how to read an ambiguous provision in light of the larger body of legal text to which it relates. Many of these canons of construction trace their origin to ancient languages and interpretive struggles. *See* Geoffrey P. Miller, *Pragmatics and the Maxims of Interpretation*, 1990 WIS. L. REV. 1179. Moreover, they continue to appear regularly in American jurisprudence. *See, e.g.*, James J. Brudney & Corey Ditslear, *Canons of Construction and the Elusive Quest for Neutral Reasoning*, 58 VAND. L. REV. 1 (2005).

1. LINGUISTIC CANONS: INTERPRETATION USING MAXIMS OF WORD MEANING AND ASSOCIATION

The primary linguistic canons are three maxims of word meaning and association, each often still known by its Latin name: (a) *noscitur a sociis*, (b) *ejusdem generis*, and (c) *expressio unius est exclusio alterius*. (In the United Kingdom, more than in the United States, many additional linguistic canons remain in use today, often also still known by their Latin names.) Although legislatures rarely draft with the names of these linguistic canons in mind, they often are consciously or subconsciously aware of the underlying intuitive logic of these canons. This can lead legislators to try to be exhaustive, only to find later they still omitted something unanticipated.

a. *Noscitur a sociis*

"[A word is] known by its associates." This maxim invites the interpreter to assign meaning to an ambiguous word or phrase in light of the company it keeps, namely the surrounding terms, especially if the word is part of a list.

For instance, a provision of the Sarbanes-Oxley Act of 2002 provides for criminal punishment for anyone who "knowingly alters, destroys, mutilates, conceals, covers up, falsifies, or makes a false entry in *any record, document, or tangible object* with the intent to impede, obstruct, or influence" any federal investigation (emphasis added). Note that this provision contains three distinct lists: a category of impermissible actions, a category of objects to which those actions could be directed, and a category of intents or motives for those actions. At issue in *Yates v. United States*, ___ U.S. ___, 135 S. Ct. 1074 (2015), was whether the middle list's term "tangible object" included a fishing boat's catch of undersized red grouper, which the ship's captain threw overboard despite federal authorities' instructions that he preserve them. Invoking the *noscitur* canon, the Supreme Court held that fish were not a tangible object within the meaning of this provision, explaining that, in context, the term "tangible object" is "appropriately read to refer, not to any tangible object, but specifically to the subset of tangible objects . . . used to record or preserve information," like records or documents. *Id.* at 1085. But four dissenters insisted, in "plain meaning" fashion, that "[a] 'tangible object' is an object that's tangible"; fish therefore were plainly included. *Id.* at 1091.

To take another example, the Endangered Species Act makes it unlawful for anyone to "take" any endangered species. In the *Sweet Home* case discussed previously in Chapter 7, at issue was the meaning of the term "harm," as used in the statute's definition of the term "take" to mean: "to harass, *harm*, pursue, hunt, shoot, wound, kill, trap, capture, or collect, or to attempt to engage in any such conduct" (emphasis added). The Secretary of the Interior had promulgated a regulation further specifying that "harm . . . means an act which actually kills or injures wildlife," including "significant habitat modification or degradation . . . ." Again the Court divided, this time with three dissenters invoking the *noscitur* canon to argue that "harm" should be understood, like the other words in the definition, to require affirmative conduct "directed immediately and intentionally against a particular animal," and not to include acts affecting protected wildlife "indirectly and by accident." *Sweet Home*, 515 U.S. at 718, 720. But the majority upheld the Secretary's much broader application of the term as a reasonable interpretation (relying on the principles of judicial review of agency interpretations discussed in Chapter 12).

b. *Ejusdem generis*

"Of the same class or kind." The point of this canon is that a broad or generic catch-all term, particularly at the end of a list of specific terms, should be understood as a catch-all for only the same kinds of things that have been more specifically identified by the associated terms. In a sense, this maxim is a variant of the *noscitur* canon, which suggests that the meaning of an ambiguous word can be determined by the surrounding words.

For instance, the *ejusdem* canon also understandably played a role in the *Yates* case, given that the phrase "other tangible object" was construed to function there as a catch-all to cover the class of things that the more specific terms "document" and "record" exemplified. The Court described the purpose of the *ejusdem* canon as "to ensure that a general word will not render specific words meaningless," noting that construing "other tangible object" broadly to mean any tangible object would render pointless the act's inclusion of the terms "record" and "document." 135 S. Ct. at 1087. The general class that these specific terms exemplified was things that preserve information.

A second example is a state statute that required a plaintiff to file a bond in connection with any civil action against "any sheriff, constable, peace officer, state road officer, or *any other person charged with the duty of enforcement of the criminal laws* of this state . . . ." In *Heathman v. Giles*, 374 P.2d 839 (Utah 1962), the state Supreme Court decided that this statute did not apply to an action against a prosecutor or deputy prosecutors, but was limited to actions against a class of "badge-wearing officers . . . in the front line of law enforcement . . . charged with . . . seeking out persons suspected of crime; and of making arrests . . . ." The court further explained that prosecutors, "although 'charged with the duty of enforcement of the criminal laws,' are officers of such a significantly different character" as to fall outside the meaning of the statute's catch-all phrase. *Id.* at 840; *but see Ali v. Federal Bureau of Prisons*, 552 U.S. 214 (2008) (construing "any officer of customs or excise or any other law enforcement officer" to cover all law enforcement officers, including prison officials, not just officers involved in enforcing customs and excise laws).

One more example involves the Federal Arbitration Act of 1926, which excluded from its coverage "contracts of employment of seamen, railroad employees, or any other class of workers engaged in foreign or interstate commerce." Although standing alone, the phrase "any other class of workers engaged in foreign or interstate commerce" is quite broad, potentially excluding all employment contracts from the arbitration act's coverage, the *ejusdem* canon would suggest that, as used in this act, the phrase should be limited to workers like seamen or railroad employees. The Supreme Court adopted this narrow reading in *Circuit City Stores, Inc. v. Adams*, 532 U.S. 105 (2001), thus excluding from the Federal Arbitration Act's coverage only contracts of transportation workers, and not of the retail sales employee who also wanted to be excluded from the act's coverage.

c. *Expressio unius est exclusio alterius*

"The expression of one thing implies the exclusion of other things (not expressed)." This maxim is typically deployed when a statute contains a list of items or terms, identifying with some specificity when or to what the statute should apply, and the omission from that list of some other possible item or term suggests that the statute does not apply to it.

For example, the Resource Conservation and Recovery Act permits private suits against anyone "who has contributed [to the] handling, storage, treatment, transportation, or disposal of any solid waste [that] may present an imminent and substantial endangerment to health or the environment." The act in turn defines "disposal" as "the *discharge, deposit, injection, dumping, spilling, leaking, or placing* of any solid waste . . . into or on any land or water so that such solid waste . . . may enter the environment or be emitted into the air or discharged into any waters . . . " (emphasis added). Relying on the *expressio unius* canon, the Ninth Circuit concluded that two railroad companies had not violated the act's prohibition against disposal of solid waste by emitting diesel particulates directly into the air, because "emitting" into the air was not included among the defined ways that prohibited solid waste disposal could occur. Even though the definition did make reference to the possible subsequent emission into the air of a solid waste after its disposal "into or on any land or water," the definition first required that disposal itself involve one of seven specified types of conduct, which did not include emitting solid waste into the air. *See Center for Community Action v. BNSF Ry. Co.*, 764 F.3d 1019 (9th Cir. 2014).

In an earlier case, the Supreme Court considered the Warsaw Convention in light of the *expressio* canon. The Convention has several provisions that limit the liability of commercial airlines for loss of baggage or cargo but waive the liability limits if the carrier has not provided the customer with adequate notice of these limits. The Convention also has another provision that limits the airlines' liability for passenger injury or death but does not waive the limit in the absence of adequate notice to the passenger. In *Chan v. Korean Air Lines*, 490 U.S. 122 (1989), the Court invoked the *expressio* canon to conclude that airlines that had not provided passengers with notice of the liability limits for injury or death were still entitled to the protections of these limits because the Convention had expressly provided in other contexts that lack of notice would mean the waiver of the liability limits, but said nothing about waiving the liability limits for lack of notice in this context.

As one more example, in the *Holy Trinity* case discussed in Chapter 8, the *expressio* canon could have supported the opposite result. The statute at issue, which prohibited contracts to import foreigners to perform "labor or service of any kind," contained a set of exceptions that expressly excluded from its coverage "professional actors, lecturers, or singers, [or] personal or domestic servants." Under the *expressio unius* canon, because pastors and ministers were not included in this list of very specific types of labor or service, that could have implied that pastors and ministers were not meant to be among the exceptions (and therefore were intended to be covered by the act). Of course, that the Court did not use this canon to reach the opposite result confirms that the canons are merely a source of interpretive guidance, not binding interpretive methods.

On many occasions some word of inclusion is deliberately used only to identify examples of a common set of items to which a statute applies, rather than to exhaust the list of possible members of the set. The most obvious such usage is the phrase "including but not limited to," when it precedes a list of covered items. But sometimes the word "including" alone is used to introduce the list, and other comparable phrases such as "for instance" or "for example" may be used to identify representative items within a set without intending to exclude other items not specified. For instance, in *United States v. Phillip Morris U.S.A. Inc.*, 566 F.3d 1095, 1110–16 (D.C. Cir. 2009), the District of Columbia Circuit construed language in the RICO statute (the Racketeer Influenced and Corrupt Organizations Act) providing that " 'enterprise' includes any individual, partnership, corporation, association, or other legal entity, and any union or group of individuals associated in fact although not a legal entity." The court rejected the argument that the list of included entities was exclusive. Even without the use of introductory terms like "including" or "for example," sometimes a list may only be illustrative.

Thus, interpreters must be cautious in their deployment of these linguistic canons. As indicated by the number of occasions when the Supreme Court itself has divided on the appropriateness of using one or more of these canons, there is no accepted criterion for determining when a particular canon fits a textual problem. Instead, even the choice to use a canon is contextual. As Justice Souter wrote in 2003 specifically about the *expressio* canon, "[the canon] does not apply to every statutory listing or grouping; it has force only when the items expressed are members of an 'associated group or series,' justifying the inference that items not mentioned were excluded by deliberate choice, not inadvertence." *Barnhardt v. Peabody Coal Co.*, 537 U.S. 149, 168 (2003). With respect to canons more generally, Justice Scalia has observed (jointly with his co-author Bryan Garner) that canons should not be used thoughtlessly, but must be deployed in light of context: "The skill of sound construction lies in assessing the clarity and weight of each clue and deciding where the balance lies." SCALIA & GARNER, *supra*, at 59.

2. GRAMMAR CANONS

Grammar canons are another class of interpretive textual canons. These are rules of English grammar that arguably have special force in legal writing, precisely in order to reduce ambiguity. Some of these rules themselves have evolved over time, and they also are not necessarily universally embraced in the same form. Even where they are widely followed or accepted, they are only presumptions, not hard-and-fast requirements.

a. The Punctuation Canon

For generations, the rule in English law was that the punctuation of a statute could not be used to resolve (or create!) ambiguity. This was because in an earlier era, marks of punctuation typically were added to the written law after the fact by clerks or recorders, rather than being added by Parliament itself during the process of enactment.

In contrast, as Sutherland's famous statutory interpretation treatise explains, "The better rule is that punctuation is part of an act and courts may consider punctuation to interpret an act but not to create doubt or to distort or defeat legislative intent." 2A SUTHERLAND STATUTES AND STATUTORY CONSTRUCTION § 47.15 (7th ed. 2014). (Until the 2014 release of the 7th edition, the Sutherland treatise had provided that in the United States statutes are typically "read as punctuated unless there is some reason to do otherwise." 2A SUTHERLAND STATUTES AND STATUTORY CONSTRUCTION § 47.15 (6th ed. 2000).) Commas can often be especially significant in determining meaning, helping to establish how words and phrases relate to each other, as for instance in distinguishing the phrase "motor vehicle trailer" from the phrase "motor vehicle, trailer." Semicolons likewise can be especially helpful. Yet where punctuation seems problematic, the punctuation rule can easily give way to judicial adjustment of punctuation under the theory of a scrivener's error.

b. The Last Antecedent

A second grammatical canon, which for its proper application may often depend in turn upon the proper use of serial commas, is the rule of the last antecedent. This rule provides that words of limitation, qualification, or clarification that follow and relate back to a set of terms or clauses should be understood to modify only the most immediately preceding antecedent to which they can sensibly apply, unless punctuation, context, or "other indicia of meaning," *Barnhart v. Thomas*, 540 U.S. 20, 26 (2003), clearly suggest otherwise. Determining when to apply this canon is not always easy, however.

For instance, 18 U.S.C. § 2252(b)(2) prescribes a tougher criminal sentence for a defendant convicted on federal child pornography charges if the defendant already has a previous state law conviction "relating to aggravated sexual abuse, sexual abuse, or abusive sexual conduct *involving a minor or ward*" (emphasis added). Should the qualifying language "involving a minor or ward" be understood to limit only the state law crime of abusive sexual conduct? Or should it apply to all three of the possible kinds of state law crimes listed? How would the interpretive dilemma have differed if a comma followed the phrase "abusive sexual conduct"? Without that comma, the rule of the last antecedent would support applying the limiting phrase to only the final category of state law crime. In a 6–2 opinion, the Supreme Court followed this approach in *Lockhart v. United States*, 136 S. Ct. 958 (2016). But the dissenters thought this a patent misuse of the last antecedent rule (as well as contrary to clear legislative history about congressional intent) and invoked a contrary maxim that " '[w]hen there is a straightforward, parallel construction that involves all nouns or verbs in a series,' a modifier at the end of the list 'normally applies to the entire series' " (quoting SCALIA & GARNER, *supra*, at 147).

c. May Versus Shall

A more straightforward maxim is that mandatory words ordinarily should be given a mandatory meaning, while hortatory or precatory words should not. Yet on occasion, "may" has been construed to carry a mandatory meaning. *See In re Cartmell's Estate*, 138 A.2d 588 (Vt. 1958). Meanwhile, sometimes the extent to which "shall" is mandatory may also be at issue. For instance, in *Barnhart v. Peabody Coal Co.*, 537 U.S. 149 (2003), the Supreme Court considered how to construe a statute providing that the Commissioner of Social Security "shall, before October 1, 1993," assign specific companies the responsibility for funding the retirement benefits for all eligible coal industry retirees. The Commissioner had missed this deadline, and three dissenters argued that this failure meant the Commissioner could no longer make the assignments. But the majority opinion concluded that to deprive the Commissioner of jurisdiction for failing to meet the deadline would frustrate Congress's purpose and upheld assignments that the Commissioner had made after the deadline.

The usually significant difference between "may" and "shall" also figured importantly in one of the central legal issues surrounding the 2000 presidential election in Florida. As noted in section B.2.f of Chapter 7 above, Florida law had two conflicting provisions, one of which told the Secretary of State that county election totals arriving after the statutory canvassing deadline "shall be ignored," and another providing that late-arriving canvass totals "may be ignored," with specified fines for each day that a county's returns were late. The Florida Supreme Court concluded that the permissive provision controlled the result because (1) it was more recently enacted; (2) it was more specific; and (3) it made better sense of the overall statutory scheme. *See Palm Beach County Canvassing Board v. Harris*, 772 So.2d 1220 (Fla.), *vacated sub nom. Bush v. Palm Beach Canvassing Board*, 531 U.S. 70 (2000).

d. And Versus Or

As a matter of English grammar, "and" is conjunctive and "or" is disjunctive. Unfortunately, these terms can be used ambiguously. As a result, one formulation of a relevant canon is that "terms connected by a disjunctive [should] be given separate meanings, unless the context dictates otherwise." *Reiter v. Sonotone Corp.*, 442 U.S. 330, 339 (1979). But "or" can be read to mean "and" when to do otherwise would frustrate legislative intent. *See De Sylva v. Ballantine*, 351 U.S. 570 (1956).

e. Plural Versus Singular Nouns; Gendered Pronouns

In theory, a drafter's choice to use a plural noun or pronoun might be cause for distinguishing its meaning from a singular construction, and the use of a gendered pronoun to exclude the opposite gender. For instance, in *People v. Rodriguez*, 290 P.3d 1143 (2012), the Supreme Court of California construed a state criminal statute that targeted the activities of street gangs. Elements of the offense included that the alleged perpetrator (1) participates in a street gang, and (2) "willfully promotes, furthers, or assists in any felonious criminal conduct by members of that gang." The court concluded that the statute's plural term "members" precluded convicting a gang-member who acted alone; multiple gang "members" had to participate.

However, unless the specific context shows otherwise, the plural is generally understood to include the singular, and vice-versa; gendered pronouns similarly are usually construed to be all-embracing. Indeed, as a matter of federal law, these rules of construction are codified in section 1 of Title 1 of the United States Code: "In determining the meaning of any Act of Congress, unless the context indicates otherwise—words importing the singular include and apply to several persons, parties, or things; words importing the plural include the singular; words importing the masculine gender include the feminine as well . . . ." 1 U.S.C. § 1. Most states have analogous interpretive directions in their codes (and similar directions are found in the United

Kingdom under the Interpretation Act of 1889). Meanwhile, 1 U.S.C. § 1 further provides that in federal statutes, "the words 'person' and 'whoever' include corporations, companies, associations, firms, partnerships, societies, and joint stock companies, as well as individuals."

3. THE WHOLE ACT RULE AND ITS COROLLARIES

A final text-based canon is the Whole Act Rule. This canon sensibly encourages the interpreter to be attentive not only to the way that the specific term in question interacts with the immediately surrounding words, but also how it fits with the entire act of which it is a part. In its simplest form, this rule is helpful because sometimes the same term is used in multiple places within a statute, and assigning a meaning to the term that can be used consistently in every place in the act in which the term appears may resolve an interpretive ambiguity that otherwise would remain in just an isolated usage of the term in a particular portion of an act. Even when the term in question is not used elsewhere in the act, occasionally the interpretive difficulty can be resolved by considering how the various interpretive possibilities will affect the functioning of other parts of the act.

Implicit in the Whole Act Rule are the assumptions that a statute both should function as a coherent whole and is drafted as a coherent whole. The many corollaries of the Whole Act Rule discussed below also are based on this idea of coherence. Legislatures, however, often cobble together several distinct parts, purposes, or ideas into one act, without always having time or opportunity to ensure consistency or integration among the many constituent pieces (a practice that has become a recurring hallmark of today's era of increasingly "unorthodox" lawmaking). Nevertheless, the rest of an act is the most immediate source of context for understanding the meaning of a provision at issue, and it is eminently sensible to construe individual components of an act in order to enhance the act's overall coherence. Indeed, Justice Scalia liked to argue that courts should use textual canons like the Whole Act Rule if only to encourage legislatures to write their statutes more carefully and with greater coherence. *See* SCALIA & GARNER, *supra*, at 51.

The Supreme Court's treatment of the interpretive problem at issue in *Babbitt v. Sweet Home Chapter of Communities for a Greater Oregon*, 515 U.S. 687 (1995), included several distinct uses of the Whole Act Rule. Pursuant to the Endangered Species Act ("ESA"), the Secretary of the Interior had promulgated a regulation prohibiting "significant habitat modification or degradation where it actually kills or injures [endangered or threatened] wildlife." The question before the Court was whether this regulation went beyond the statutory provision that made it unlawful to "take" any endangered or threatened species, in light of the statute's definition of "take" to mean "to harass, harm, pursue, hunt, shoot, wound, kill, trap, capture, or collect." Plaintiffs who were opposed to the Secretary's regulation argued that the statutory definition of "take" encompassed only "direct applications of force against protected species." Had the Secretary's regulation added an additional type of prohibited conduct beyond what Congress had prohibited by statute?

Writing for the majority, Justice Stevens relied on three Whole Act points to affirm the Secretary's regulation: (1) the word "harm" in the definition of "take" would be superfluous if it encompassed only direct impact, and not also indirect impact in a way that the other words in the definition of "take" did not; (2) the broad sweep of the ESA's other provisions, and the overall coverage of the act as compared to its predecessor statutes, supported a "comprehensive" construction of the definition of "take"; and (3) an amendment of the act authorized the Secretary to permit "incidental" takings of protected species, thus implying that Congress understood the act could apply to incidental or indirect takings. (Justice Stevens' opinion for the Court did not actually construe the statute directly, but instead concluded that the Secretary's construction of the statute was a reasonable one to which the Court would defer, according to the principles of agency deference that will be described in Chapter 12.)

Dissenting, Justice Scalia relied on three different Whole Act Rule arguments to support his view that the Secretary's regulation was impermissible: (1) the penalty provisions of the ESA made little sense when applied to the types of indirect impact on protected species covered by the regulation; (2) using the regulation's expansive definition of "harm" would not fit well with many other uses of the defined term "take" elsewhere in the Act; and (3) the broader structure of the ESA included separate provisions that already charged federal agencies with avoiding destruction or adverse modification of protected species' habitat on federal lands, a requirement that the Secretary's regulation would render superfluous, and that by implication suggested Congress had not meant to reach habitat modification on private lands.

As the *Sweet Home* opinions demonstrate, the Whole Act Rule actually is a set of multiple related ideas about how to read a statute holistically. The Rule's corollaries include:

a. The Rule Against Surplusage

This rule, which again is only a rule of thumb and not a hard and fast requirement, suggests that each unique word or phrase in a statute ought to be construed to add meaning, and not just to repeat a meaning adequately covered by other terms. Thus, Justice Stevens construed "harm" to mean something more than already covered by the other nine actions in the ESA's definition of "take," while Justice Scalia argued that if "harm" could be construed to include indirect impact through habitat modification, it would render superfluous a separate provision focused precisely on that conduct by the federal government. Of course, the problem with this rule is that legislators not only have no obligation to follow this rule in drafting their enactments, but also frequently depart from it. In drafting legislative measures, overkill is typical and legislators routinely include redundancies and surplusage to be sure that all bases are covered.

b. The Rule of Consistent Usage and Meaningful Variation

The point of this corollary of the Whole Act Rule idea is that a term repeated in multiple places within a statute ought to be presumed to have a consistent meaning throughout, while in contrast a different term used where the same term might have fit should therefore be understood to reflect the drafters' deliberate choice to convey a different meaning. Justice Scalia used this corollary in *Sweet Home* in decrying the difficulty of applying the Secretary's definition of "harm" in other places where the ESA employed the term "take."

c. Titles and Headings

The Whole Act Rule also invites legal interpreters to look at titles and section headings, common parts of most legislative enactments and regulations today, for clues about meaning. For instance, in *Almendarez-Torres v. United States*, 523 U.S. 224 (1998), the Supreme Court relied upon a section heading's title of "criminal penalties" to help determine that the section did not define a separate crime but only specified punishments. The general rule here is that while headings and titles may be considered, they should not trump the text itself. *See Intel Corp. v. Advanced Micro Devices, Inc.*, 542 U.S. 241 (2004). Furthermore, in a number of enactments dating back over a hundred years, Congress has instructed interpreters not to consider certain titles and headings, although courts routinely do so anyway.

d. Preambles, Legislative Findings, and Statements of Purpose

Similarly, in modern legislatures, it has become increasingly typical to include some background for an act in the statute itself, at least in major pieces of legislation. While historically "preambles" and "whereas" clauses were seen as preceding the enacted text, it has become common for similar statements of background and purpose to be incorporated as components of the duly enacted law itself, even if taken alone these provisions typically do not create or impose new legal obligations. Either explicitly or implicitly, these components may explain something about the enacting legislature's intent or in other ways provide the context for the measure. And because they are fully "law," interpreters may see these sources of context and legislative intent as more reliable than legislative history.

For instance, in *Sutton v. United Airlines*, 527 U.S. 471 (1999), the Supreme Court relied on the preamble to the Americans with Disabilities Act ("ADA") to conclude that myopia was not a protected disability under the ADA. The act's preamble had specified that some 43 million Americans were affected with a disability and therefore would be the beneficiaries of the act. The number of Americans Congress identified in the preamble as disabled was significant because had Congress considered myopia to be a disability for which the ADA offered protections, the number of disabled Americans in the preamble would have been much greater.

e. Provisos and Exceptions

Another Whole Act Rule corollary is that provisos and exceptions in an act ought to be narrowly construed. The idea behind this corollary is to keep the exception from swallowing the rule by construing ambiguous exceptions to do less rather than more. *See Commissioner v. Clark*, 489 U.S. 726, 739 (1989) (construing an exception to favorable capital gains tax treatment narrowly "in order to preserve the primary operation of the provision").

f. The Whole Code Rule

The Whole Act Rule also partakes of a variant known as the "Whole Code Rule." This corollary seeks to assign meaning to an ambiguous term by construing it not only to accord with the rest of the enactment of which it is a part, but also with other similar or related laws. A prime example is *West Virginia University Hospitals v. Casey*, 499 U.S. 83 (1991), discussed above in Chapter 8. There, the Supreme Court decided that the phrase "a reasonable attorney's fee," used in a statute that permitted a prevailing party to seek reimbursement from the losing party for their legal costs, did not include expenses for expert services. Crucial to the decision was the Court's view that attorney's fees and the costs of expert services were distinct items of litigation expenses, based on a review of provisions in many other statutes that explicitly permitted reimbursement for expert services as a separate item from attorney's fees.

A related maxim is the ***in pari materia*** canon, a Latin phrase meaning "upon the same or like matter," which provides that statutes dealing with similar material should be construed similarly. This canon is discussed in more detail in Chapter 10.

B. SUBSTANTIVE CANONS AS TOOLS OF INTERPRETATION

In contrast to the linguistic and textual canons discussed in subsections A.1, A.2, and A.3 above, which at least on their face appear to be policy neutral (and are often defended as such, although as discussed in subsection C.3 below there may be reason to be skeptical, or at least cautious, about this claim), a number of interpretive canons explicitly embody some substantive preference about the law. This section introduces a half-dozen of the best known of these substantive policy canons; the Appendix lists a number of other examples. A key question with respect to each of these canons is whether its substantive preference operates merely as a "tie-breaker" when no better basis exists for choosing between possible interpretations, as a mild presumption to be followed unless the interpreter finds sufficient evidence of contrary legislative intent, or as a heavy presumption unless the legislature has stated a contrary intent in clear and unmistakable terms.

1. THE RULE OF LENITY

One ancient canon, with roots in medieval England, is that a law imposing a penalty should be narrowly construed. Known as the Rule of Lenity, this canon is most applicable to criminal statutes, and invites courts to interpret statutory ambiguities in favor of the defendant. For instance, Justice Holmes' opinion in *McBoyle* (see pp. 336–337) invoked the Rule of Lenity in declining to include an airplane within the National Motor Vehicle Theft Act's definition of vehicle. He explained that penal statutes should give the public fair notice of exactly what conduct will be penalized, something that an ambiguous provision simply does not do. The dissenting justices in *Muscarello* (see p. 341) also referenced the Rule of Lenity to support their conclusion that the phrase "carries a gun" should be interpreted narrowly to require that the gun be carried "on or about one's person."

In *United States v. Bass*, 404 U.S. 336 (1971), the Supreme Court considered the meaning of a statute that imposed criminal penalties on any convicted felon who "receives, possesses, or transports in commerce or affecting commerce . . . any firearm . . . ." Although the rule of the last antecedent would have argued for applying the "in commerce or affecting commerce" limitation to only the conduct of transporting a firearm, the Court relied upon the Rule of Lenity to apply this limitation also to the conduct of receiving or possessing a firearm.

But as the dissenters in *Muscarello* discovered, the Rule of Lenity is not consistently favored or followed.

Indeed, it has been falling out of favor in recent decades. For instance, it was not followed in *Moskal v. United States*, 498 U.S. 103 (1990) (see pp. 338), to avoid treating vehicle titles with erroneous odometer readings as "falsely made" securities. At one time, more than two-thirds of the states had codified some version of the Rule of Lenity, but most of those states eventually repealed their version of this rule, often in favor of a non-substantive canon that instructs courts to construe penal statutes "according to their terms to promote justice."

Although the Rule of Lenity is typically applicable to criminal statutes, it will occasionally figure in civil contexts as well, when what is at issue is some form of civil penalty. An interesting and important wrinkle concerning its application is whether to use it as a heavy presumption, favoring the defendant whenever there is ambiguity in a penal measure, or just as a tie-breaker, when all other sources of clarifying textual ambiguity leave the issue unresolved. Examples of both kinds of uses abound.

2. THE CONSTITUTIONAL AVOIDANCE CANON

Another substantive canon is that statutory provisions should be construed to avoid giving rise to a serious constitutional question. In other words, if two (or more) interpretations of a measure are possible, but one interpretation might place the constitutionality of the underlying measure genuinely at issue, the interpreter should choose an available interpretation that would not raise the constitutional issue: "[I]f a serious doubt of constitutionality is raised, it is a cardinal principle that this Court will first ascertain whether a construction of the statute is fairly possible by which the question may be avoided." *Ashwander v. Tennessee Valley Authority*, 297 U.S. 288, 348 (1936) (Brandeis, J., concurring). At one time, the constitutional avoidance canon took a narrower form, providing only that an interpretation that would actually make a measure unconstitutional should be avoided if any other interpretation was fairly possible. But today, the canon is used to avoid even needing to resolve a serious question about a law's constitutionality.

A well-known example of the use of this canon is the U.S. Supreme Court's decision in *National Labor Relations Board v. Catholic Bishop of Chicago*, 440 U.S. 490 (1979). At issue was a provision in the National Labor Relations Act that gave the National Labor Relations Board jurisdiction over "employers" with respect to matters of collective bargaining between employers and their employees. The Catholic Bishop of Chicago argued that it would be an unconstitutional encroachment on freedom of religion for the NLRB to assert jurisdiction over the terms and conditions of employment of the teachers and other employees of the Catholic high schools in Chicago. But rather than determining if in fact a constitutional violation would occur (as, for instance, if the NLRB had jurisdiction over questions about teacher control of curriculum), the Court instead concluded that the NLRA should be construed not to confer NLRB jurisdiction over Catholic schools, to avoid raising the constitutional question.

However, the statute itself was not at all ambiguous. The Court conceded that the NLRA defined the NLRB's jurisdiction "in very broad terms," covering employers generally while listing eight specific exceptions, not including parochial schools. Nevertheless, the Court said that absent Congress's "clear expression of an affirmative intention" to cover church-operated schools, it would not read the NLRA in a way that "presents a significant risk" of a constitutional problem. When the Court majority thus carved parochial schools out of the NLRA's definition of "employer," the dissenters argued that this was not interpretation or construction, but judicial amendment of the statute. The dissent disagreed with this deployment of the avoidance canon, citing *International Association of Machinists v. Street*, 367 U.S. 740 (1961), to argue that the proper formulation of the canon requires that the interpretation that avoids raising a constitutional question must be a "fairly possible" one, reasonable in light of the language and history of the statute.

The avoidance canon often comes in for some criticism. One criticism is that it permits the judiciary to issue stealth advisory opinions about the constitutionality of various measures. At the same time, because its use typically means a court has not resolved the underlying constitutionality, the canon deprives the legislature of the opportunity to learn the true limits of its constitutional power. A third criticism is that at least in some instances, the result of a court's relying on the canon will be to expand the degree to which a constitutional provision constrains the legislature's authority beyond what the provision would require if squarely interpreted, thus limiting a measure's scope to less than the full scope of the legislature's constitutional power.

3. THE "NEW FEDERALISM" CANONS—RULES THAT DISCOURAGE INTRUSIONS ON STATE SOVEREIGNTY

An entire group of substantive canons operate to protect specific constitutional values even when the interpretive issue is not likely to raise any concern about possible unconstitutionality. Among the most widely employed of such canons are those that protect state government sovereignty from federal encroachment unless Congress has clearly stated in the enactment that it intended to infringe on state authority. These are often collectively called the "New Federalism" canons, reflecting their relatively recent creation or reinvigoration during the 1980s and 1990s, when the U.S. Supreme Court repeatedly articulated various ways of narrowly construing the reach of federal statutes to promote America's system of dual sovereignty.

The New Federalism canons include a canon against abrogating a state's eleventh amendment immunity absent a clear textual statement, *see Atascadero State Hospital v. Scanlon*, 473 U.S. 234 (1985); a canon requiring that Congress must clearly state in the statute any conditions it imposes on federal funding of state programs, *see Pennhurst State School & Hospital v. Halderman*, 451 U.S. 1 (1981); and a canon that a federal statute should not be read to abrogate state sovereign immunity unless its text clearly allows doing so, *see Seminole Tribe of Florida v. Florida*, 517 U.S. 44 (1996).

But perhaps the best known of the New Federalism canons is the canon against construing a federal statute to interfere with traditional state government prerogatives absent the statute's clear statement to this effect. This version of a New Federalism canon traces to *Gregory v. Ashcroft*, 501 U.S. 452 (1991). At issue was whether the Age Discrimination in Employment Act (ADEA) protected state court judges in Missouri against a mandatory retirement provision of the Missouri Constitution. By its terms, the ADEA prohibits covered employers from imposing a mandatory retirement age on covered employees. State governments are covered employers under the ADEA, but the ADEA excluded "appointees on the policymaking level" from the category of "covered employees." The interpretive issue before the U.S. Supreme Court was whether Missouri's state court judges were "appointees on the policymaking level."

A range of interpretive tools could have been brought to bear on this question. But the Court instead relied on a historical and political account of the nature of America's system of dual sovereignty to explain that construing the ADEA to limit how a state structures its government would intrude on "the most fundamental sort" of decision "at the heart of representative government" through which "a State defines itself as a sovereign." The Court decided that this area of sovereignty "traditionally regulated by the States" should be protected from federal interference unless it was clear that Congress intended to "upset the usual constitutional balance of federal and state powers." In applying this New Federalism canon, the Court wrote: "We will not read the ADEA to cover state judges unless Congress has made it clear that judges are *included* . . . . [I]t must be plain to anyone reading the Act that it covers judges." Unable to find that degree of clarity, the Court concluded that the ADEA did not apply to Missouri's judges to protect them from the state's mandatory retirement age. *Id.* at 460–67.

A more recent application of this canon is *Bond v. United States*, ___ U.S. ___, 134 S. Ct. 2077 (2014). The case involved a criminal prosecution arising from what the Supreme Court called an "amateur attempt by a jilted wife to injure her husband's lover," specifically by spreading toxic chemicals on surfaces that the lover would be likely to touch, hoping to cause a rash. The perpetrator was charged with violating a provision of the Chemical Weapons Convention Implementation Act, enacted as its title suggests to implement an international treaty, which the U.S. ratified in 1997. A provision of the act prohibits the use of "any chemical weapon," which the act defines as a "toxic chemical . . . except where intended for a purpose not prohibited by [the act]. The act defines "a purpose not prohibited by [the act]" as "any peaceful purpose related to" industry, agriculture, medicine, research, and the like.

The defendant brought both statutory and constitutional challenges against her conditional guilty plea. Justices Scalia, Thomas, and Alito thought it "utterly clear" that the statute's terms covered her conduct, but would have found the statute unconstitutional as beyond Congress's treaty power. But a majority of the Court concluded that the statute did not make sufficiently clear that the defendant's tawdry and mundane criminal act amounted to the kind of use of chemical weapons that the act prohibited. This conclusion was driven in significant part by a concern that if what the defendant had done was covered by the act, it would "fundamentally upset the Constitution's balance between national and local power." *Id.* at 2093. Absent a clear statement that Congress intended to upset this relationship, the Court majority refused to extend the statute to cover a kind of criminal conduct that traditionally was the province of state law, observing that "the global need to prevent chemical warfare does not require the Federal Government to reach into the kitchen cupboard."

4. PRESUMPTION AGAINST PREEMPTION OF STATE LAW

Another federalism-based canon, but a more long-standing and less restrictive one, is the presumption that a federal statute does not preempt state law. As articulated in 1947 in *Rice v. Santa Fe Elevator Corporation*, 331 U.S. 218, 230 (1947), "the historic police powers of the States were not to be superseded by [a congressional statute in a field of law that the States have traditionally occupied] unless that was the clear and manifest purpose of Congress." Unlike the New Federalism canons, which in their typical formulation can only be overcome by a clear statement in the text of the statute itself, the presumption against federal preemption can be overcome by evidence outside the statute of congressional purpose or intent to preempt state law, including evidence of an actual conflict between federal and state law, *see, e.g., Geier v. American Honda Motor Co., Inc.*, 529 U.S. 861 (2000), or evidence that Congress intended its enactment to "occupy the field," *see, e.g., Fid. Fed. Sav. & Loan Ass'n v. de la Cuesta*, 458 U.S. 141 (1982).

5. STATUTES IN DEROGATION OF THE COMMON LAW ARE TO BE NARROWLY OR STRICTLY CONSTRUED

An even more long-standing canon, reflecting the functional supremacy of the common law in an earlier era, as discussed in Chapter 8, is the Derogation Canon: Statutes in derogation of the common law are to be narrowly construed. In other words, the legislature's output should be interpreted so as to change the underlying common law as little as possible. For instance, in *Norfolk Southern Railway Co. v. Sorrell*, 549 U.S. 158 (2007), a negligence action brought under the Federal Employers' Liability Act (FELA), the Supreme Court held that common-law principles of causation survived FELA's enactment because the text of the act did not expressly reject those common-law principles.

6. REMEDIAL MEASURES ARE TO BE BROADLY CONSTRUED

A final substantive canon, which can often run directly counter to the Derogation Canon, is the Remedial Canon: a remedial statute should be construed broadly to effectuate its public-regarding purposes. For its proper application, this canon obviously depends on classifying a particular statute as "remedial," a task fraught with subjectivity. This canon also does not by its own terms identify what amounts to a broad construction. But in determining what makes for a remedial statute, it may be worth recalling the discussion in Chapter 2 of the difference between statutes that are the result of narrow interest group bargaining in a legislature, on the one hand, and statutes that reflect a more thorough republican deliberation about what will best promote the public interest.

Because of its indeterminacy and over-inclusivity, today the Remedial Canon is widely derided. But its underlying principle has occasionally featured in important cases. For instance, in *Griggs v. Duke Power Co.*, 401 U.S. 424 (1971), the Supreme Court concluded that an employer had violated Title VII of the Civil Rights Act by relying on an ability test that operated to disadvantage minority workers, even though there was no evidence that the employer had intended to discriminate. The statutory text at issue included a provision that made it unlawful for an employer to "adversely affect" an individual's employment opportunities "because of such individual's race," which on a broad reading could prohibit actions with a discriminatory impact even without discriminatory intent. But a separate provision nonetheless allowed an employer to use a "professionally developed ability test" as long as the test was "not designed, intended or used to discriminate because of race." A narrow reading of this provision would suggest that an employer must have had a discriminatory purpose or intent in order to violate the act.

Focusing on what it saw as the underlying remedial purpose of Title VII to "remove barriers that have operated in the past to favor [white employees]," the Court construed the act broadly to also cover employment practices "neutral on their face, and even neutral in terms of intent, . . . if they operate to 'freeze' the status quo of prior discriminatory practices." *Id.* at 430. This was a significant departure from the plain meaning of the statute, in service of its perceived remedial purpose.

C. SOME CONCERNS ABOUT CANONS—DETERMINING THEIR PROPER SCOPE AND APPLICATION

Canons have an obvious appeal because of both their simplicity and their independence from any particular interpretive issue. But they are not always as clear or helpful as they may seem at first. Three main concerns have arisen about the use of canons: (1) they require a fair amount of judgment concerning when to deploy a given one; (2) if structured as binding requirements, they may entrench upon the judicial function; and (3) they may not be as neutral as they claim or appear to be, at least in their application.

1. KARL LLEWELLYN'S "THRUST AND PARRY"

As suggested above by the tension between the Remedial Canon and the Derogation Canon, an interpreter often faces a choice between two or more competing canons. Legal Realist Karl Llewellyn illustrated this point straightforwardly in a famous 1950 law review article describing what has become known as Llewellyn's "Thrust and Parry" of dueling canons. Over the course of 6 pages, Llewellyn identified almost thirty pairs of competing canons, such as "words are to be interpreted according to the proper grammatical effect of their arrangement" versus "rules of grammar will be disregarded where strict adherence would defeat purpose"; or "if language is plain and unambiguous it must be given effect" versus "not when literal interpretation would lead to absurd or mischievous consequences or thwart manifest purpose." Karl Llewellyn, *Remarks on the Theory of Appellate Decision and the Rules or Canons About How Statutes Are to be Construed*, 3 VAND. L. REV. 395, 401–06 (1950).

To many Legal Realists like Llewellyn, the point of this juxtaposition of competing canons was to show that because judges and other interpreters might simply pick whichever canon served their preconceived notion of how to interpret the text, canons therefore might not actually provide a neutral basis for interpretation. But many Legal Process thinkers have countered that canons can still be matched to circumstance, and that at least in many instances, the choice between two competing canons may come down to a question of fit, with some amount of objective rationality supporting the choice of which canon best responds to a given interpretive problem. Furthermore, it is often the case that several canons can be brought to bear collectively on an interpretive problem, mutually reinforcing each other. Nonetheless, Llewellyn's argument introduces a strong note of caution about the use of interpretive canons.

For a contemporary look at examples of two or more competing interpretive canons at use in opposing interpretive arguments, see Anita S. Krishnakumar, *Dueling Canons*, 65 DUKE L. J. 909 (2016).

2. INTERPRETIVE DIRECTIONS IN STATUTES

As just noted, an interpreter who might otherwise struggle to choose between competing maxims may sometimes find that context can help identify the most appropriate canon(s). Another way that interpreters might be guided in their choice of which canon(s) to apply is when statutes themselves specify the enacting legislature's interpretive expectations. Perhaps the most common such direction is when a statute says something like "[t]he provisions of this title shall be liberally construed to effectuate its remedial purposes," as Congress provided in enacting the Racketeer Influenced and Corrupt Organizations

Act of 1970. *See* PUB. L. NO. 91–452, § 904(a), 84 Stat. 941, 947 (1970).

Alternatively, separately codified rules of interpretation may offer guidance or direction. For instance, as a matter of federal law, Congress has provided some minimal guidance, including that the singular usage includes the plural and that male pronouns should be read to include both genders. *See* 1 U.S.C. § 1. Many more examples of codified interpretive directions exist as a matter of state law, including states that have codified the Plain Meaning Rule, states that have codified the presumption of consistent usage, and even states that have codified a presumption that the legislature intends its statutes to be "reasonable," to name only a few of various state interpretive directions. *See* Jacob Scott, *supra*; Abbe R. Gluck, *supra*. Some states also have codified that legislative history (to be discussed in detail in the next chapter) may be used to construe an ambiguous statute.

An important issue related to the enactment into law of interpretive directions or canons is whether these legislative instructions to courts encroach upon the judicial function. That is, do they amount to the legislature telling the judiciary how to do its job? Obviously, courts have the last word, and so may with impunity ignore these directions if they feel that they constrain the courts' ability to determine the appropriate interpretive methodology. At the same time, these directions do amount to law and plainly establish the legislature's intent concerning interpretive difficulties. It is hard to imagine these kinds of directions not having at least some impact at the margin on how a court will approach a problem of statutory construction.

3. CANONS AS "NEUTRAL" TOOLS—OR NOT

Interpretive canons are attractive in part because they are seen as either neutral, in the case of the linguistic and grammatical canons, or as expressing widely accepted policy preferences divorced from a particular interpretive problem, in the case of the substantive canons. In theory they thereby may give the interpreter some protection against being accused of interpretation based on personal preference or ideology (about which briefly more below). Meanwhile, canons have experienced something of a resurgence in the past two decades because of the impact of the New Textualist school of interpretation, which often requires additional sources of interpretative direction other than the extrinsic tools.

But with the resurgence of canons of interpretation also has come increased attention to whether the textual canons in fact are neutral, or just how appropriate the substantive canons' policy preferences are. Justice Scalia often expressed skepticism about the value of the substantive policy canons, precisely because their embodiment of a substantive position made them the equivalent of "dice-loading rules." In this respect, he contrasted substantive canons with textual canons, which he viewed as neutral. Later, however, he appeared to become more open to the value of at least a few of the substantive canons, including the constitutional avoidance canon and the rule of lenity. *See* SCALIA & GARNER, *supra*, at 249, 299–301.

Others, meanwhile, have challenged the assertion that any of the canons can be deployed neutrally. For instance, one study found that in the past half-century, liberal Supreme Court Justices were more likely to use canons to justify liberal outcomes, and conservative Supreme Court Justices were more likely to use canons to justify conservative outcomes. The same study also found that in close cases, conservative Justices used canons to reach conservative results, when liberal justices argued that legislative history favored reaching liberal results. The researchers concluded that canons are often used for ideological ends, even if subconsciously. *See* James J. Brudney & Corey Ditslear, *Canons of Construction and the Elusive Quest for Neutral Reasoning*, 58 VAND. L. REV. 1 (2005); *see also* James J. Brudney: *Canon Shortfalls and the Virtues of Political Branch Interpretive Assets*, 98 CAL. L. REV. 1199 (2010).

CHAPTER 10

LEGISLATIVE HISTORY AND OTHER EXTRINSIC TOOLS OF INTERPRETATION

The "intrinsic" tools of interpretation described in Chapter 9 provide interpretive assistance based on generally applicable textual, linguistic, and substantive canons of construction, applied to the enacted text alone. In contrast, a set of "extrinsic" tools of interpretation offer help in understanding the meaning of legal text through reference to various extra-textual materials directly connected to the specific text at issue. These extrinsic tools also are sometimes "canonized," in which case they are often collectively referred to as the "reference" canons. (However, the label "canons" is more commonly used to identify the intrinsic tools of Chapter 9). Today, the extrinsic tools are almost always deployed in combination with at least some of the intrinsic tools, not in place of them.

This chapter describes the major categories of extrinsic tools of interpretation. These include: (1) the relationship between the specific text at issue and any relevant **common law** principles; (2) the relationship between the specific text at issue and **other statutes or regulations**: and (3) interpretive guidance that may be available through the study and analysis of the **legislative and statutory history** of the text at issue. A given measure's legislative history may include a variety of types of evidence of its meaning, from official reports of legislative committees to remarks of individual legislators to presidential or gubernatorial signing statements to testimony at hearings. This chapter reviews each of these types of legislative history materials, with a focus on the importance of assessing their reliability in individual cases. Although the notion of "extrinsic" tools (or aids) of interpretation is a long-standing one (dating at least to the early decades of the twentieth century), it is worth noting that in an earlier era, courts generally viewed recourse to legislative history as neither helpful nor appropriate in resolving textual ambiguity. For a brief summary of these earlier judicial attitudes towards legislative history, see SCALIA & GARNER, *supra*, at 369–90.

A. INTERPRETATION BASED ON COMMON LAW

The common law contributes to the interpretive enterprise in at least three distinguishable ways. First, it will sometimes be helpful for the interpreter to understand the related common law in order to recognize the gap that the statutory or regulatory text is filling. Placing the enacted text in the context of its relationship to pre-existing law is akin to using the "mischief" rule identified in Chapter 8. Second, the common law may also be helpful when lawmakers have used words with established common law meanings, to the extent that understanding those common law meanings may aid in construing the statutory text. (Note, however, that this deployment of the common law may run counter to the preceding type, as sometimes reference to common law definitions may reinforce existing doctrine, rather than allowing statutory measures to fill in gaps in the common law.) Third, applying common law principles may itself provide an aid in construing an ambiguous provision.

1. STATUTES AS REMEDYING COMMON LAW DEFECTS

If the statutory text seeks to remedy a defect in the existing common law, then understanding the common law background can help in understanding the purpose behind the statute, which in turn can shape the interpretive task. As an example of referring to the common law to supply an understanding of the mischief to which a statute is directed, consider the admiralty case of *Isbrandtsen Company v. Johnson*, 343 U.S. 779 (1952). At common law, maritime employers liable to their employees for unpaid wages were entitled to deduct or set-off damages for the employees' alleged derelictions of duty. But in *Isbrandtsen*, the Supreme Court concluded that because Congress had intended "to change the general maritime law so as to improve the lot of seamen," federal statutory law now preempted what would have been the employer's common-law deductions. The Court acknowledged the interpretive rule that "[s]tatutes which invade the common law . . . are to be read with a presumption favoring the retention of long-established and familiar principles" (a version of the **derogation canon**, summarized in Chapter 9, that statutes in derogation of the common law are to be narrowly construed) but observed that this rule did not govern "when a statutory purpose to the contrary is evident." The Court saw federal maritime legislation as designed to depart from the common law, "emphasiz[ing] that such legislation is largely remedial and calls for liberal interpretation in favor of the seamen." *Id.* at 782–83.

Of course, this is an example of the tension described in Chapter 9 between the **derogation canon** and the **remedial canon**. Furthermore, the presumption that a statute should be construed to remedy a defect in the common law, even if only very narrowly, is just a presumption, and may not always hold true. Sometimes a legislative measure is intended merely to codify, clarify, and render more stable or permanent common law principles already in place, not to expand upon them or correct a shortcoming. Thus, as with so many interpretive challenges, deciding when particular interpretive tools and analyses are appropriate is itself usually an exercise in judgment.

2. STATUTES AS ADOPTING COMMON LAW DEFINITIONS

Sometimes statutes will use a term with an established common law meaning. As an example, consider *Buckhannon Board & Care Home, Inc. v. West Virginia Dep't of Health and Human Resources*, 532 U.S. 598 (2001). At issue was how to construe the statutory term "prevailing party," under provisions of both the Americans with Disabilities Act and the Fair Housing Amendments Act that provided for the award of attorneys' fees to a prevailing party. The Supreme Court followed common law doctrine to conclude that to be a prevailing party, a party must have prevailed formally in the outcome of a legal proceeding; securing a legislative change that rendered moot the underlying legal proceeding was not sufficient. *See also People ex rel Dickinson v. Van de Carr*, 84 N.Y.S. 461 (1903) (construing state bribery statute in light of "what was embraced in [the term 'bribery'] at common law").

3. COMMON LAW PRINCIPLES AS AN AID TO RESOLVING AMBIGUITY

On occasion, an interpreter may apply common law doctrine to resolve textual ambiguity. For instance, consider *Smith v. Wade*, 461 U.S. 30 (1983). At issue was whether a state prison inmate injured at the hands of other inmates could obtain both compensatory *and punitive* damages against prison officials, under 42 U.S.C. § 1983, if their conduct in failing to protect him was in reckless disregard of his safety. Section 1983 provides a federal cause of action—specifically a kind of tort liability—against state actors who deprive an individual of federal rights. The Supreme Court explained that in determining how to apply section 1983, it often recurred to principles of common law tort liability, particularly those in place in 1871 when section 1983 was enacted. In this case, the question was whether at common law punitive damages were available in tort only on a showing of actual malicious intent or could be imposed for reckless conduct alone. However, the majority opinion and one dissenting opinion reached opposite conclusions about what to make of the common law tort principles that existed in 1871.

Sometimes interpreters may look not to the common law in existence at the time of a measure's enactment, but to the law at the time of the interpretation. For instance, in another section 1983 case, the Supreme Court decided that common-law liability immunity for prosecutors that was not even recognized until a quarter century after 1871 nevertheless was available in actions brought under section 1983 in the later twentieth century. *See Imbler v. Pachtman*, 424 U.S. 409 (1976). Likewise, in an important state law example, the California Supreme Court updated a statutory provision of its tort law so that it embraced the common law doctrine of comparative negligence, even though the same provision had long earlier been construed instead to codify the quite different common law tort rule of contributory negligence. *See Li v. Yellow Cab of California*, 532 P.2d 1226 (Cal. 1975).

B. INTERPRETATION BASED ON OTHER STATUTES

Much as common law understandings or principles may shed light on an interpretive problem in a statute or regulation, so too may the purposes, policies, or principles enshrined in other statutes or regulations occasionally provide interpretive assistance. Likewise, a definition included in one statute may prove helpful when the same term is used without definition in another similar statute. Often the key interpretive issue is whether the referenced text is sufficiently related to the text in need of interpretation.

1. "BORROWED" AND "MODELED" STATUTES

One way in which other statutes may influence an interpretive problem is the "borrowed" or "modeled" statute rule. When a legislature adopts language from another statute, the presumption is that the legislature intends the new statute to receive the same construction that the copied statute has received. Statutory copying can occur not only when Congress or a state legislature adopts language from its own prior handiwork, but also when a legislature adopts a measure from another jurisdiction, as frequently occurs when state legislatures borrow ideas from other states or Congress. (Indeed, some commentators use the "borrowed statute" label to refer only to cross-jurisdiction borrowing, and the "modeled statute" label to refer to copying some components of an earlier statute within the same jurisdiction.)

For instance, in *Menard v. Alaska*, 578 P.2d 966 (Alaska 1978), the Alaska supreme court looked to Oregon jurisprudence to construe the meaning of the term "assault" in a provision of the Alaska criminal law that the Alaska legislature had borrowed from Oregon. The court explained that "statutes are presumed to have been adopted with the interpretations which had been placed upon them, prior to their Alaska enactment, by the highest court of the states from which they were borrowed." But state courts interpreting a provision of their own state law derived from another state's law may feel much less constrained to adopt the other state's interpretive approaches to that measure, absent a persuasive interpretation by the other state's highest court and fairly clear evidence that the adopting state's legislature knew and approved of that interpretation. *See Zerbe v. Alaska*, 583 P.2d 845

(Alaska 1978); *see also Smith v. Bayer Corp.*, 564 U.S. 299, (2011) (discussing potential interpretive variations between Federal Rule of Civil Procedure 23 and identically worded state rule).

As an example of Congress's borrowing or "modeling" its own handiwork, consider *Lorillard v. Pons*, 434 U.S. 575 (1978). There, the Supreme Court assumed that when Congress enacted the Age Discrimination in Employment Act (ADEA) and included in it enforcement provisions that tracked the enforcement provisions of the Fair Labor Standards Act (FLSA), Congress meant for the ADEA's enforcement provisions to have the same meaning and interpretation as the enforcement provisions it borrowed from the FLSA.

2. STATUTES "*IN PARI MATERIA*"

Closely related to the borrowed or modeled statute rule is the *in pari materia* canon. This Latin phrase, which translates as "upon the same or like matter," encourages interpreters to interpret similar or related statutes consistently. Many commentators classify *Lorillard v. Pons*, above, as an example of the use of this canon, though its enforcement provisions involved essentially the wholesale adoption of the statutory text on which it was modeled.

Before going further, a bit of reflection is in order concerning the classification of the *in pari materia* canon. In some lexicons of statutory interpretation, *in pari materia* is considered an intrinsic canon, applicable either as an (obvious) explanation for why two parallel provisions of a single statute should be construed holistically under the Whole Act Rule (described in Chapter 9), or as a similar (if not quite as obvious) explanation for why two analogous or comparable provisions in different statutes should be construed in light of each other, now as an instantiation of the Whole Code Rule (also described in Chapter 9). But in other lexicons, *in pari materia* is treated as an extrinsic interpretive tool for reasoning from one statute to another. These lexicons classify it as an extrinsic tool because the focus is on how a settled meaning in some other statute can help resolve an interpretive problem in an ambiguous statute. It is fair to note, however, that on this basis the Whole Code Rule, typically deemed a corollary of the Whole Act Rule, could in its entirety instead be classified as an extrinsic tool of interpretation.

Indeed, an excellent example of the deployment of the *in pari materia* canon is *West Virginia University Hospitals v. Casey*, 499 U.S. 83 (1991), also discussed in Chapter 9 as one of the best examples of the Whole Code Rule. At issue was whether the costs for expert services necessary in preparing a complex Medicaid reimbursement case for trial could be included in the award to the prevailing party of "a reasonable attorney's fee" under 42 U.S.C. § 1988. The Supreme Court relied on dozens of similar federal statutes that provided not only for the award of attorney's fees, but also for the award of other costs of litigation, including expert witness fees, to establish that the omission from section 1988 of any mention of expert fees meant that those costs were not allowable under section 1988. In contrast, the dissenting opinion argued that there was no rational reason to exclude witness fees from the costs allowable under section 1988, when so many other comparable federal statutes included them.

In *Cartledge v. Miller*, 457 F. Supp. 1146 (S.D.N.Y. 1978), a federal district court construed provisions of the recently enacted Employee Retirement Income Security Act of 1974 (ERISA) in light of similar provisions of the Social Security Act, the Veterans Benefits Act, the Railway Retirement Act, and the Bankruptcy Act. At issue was whether ERISA's proscription against the assignment or alienation of an employee's pension benefits precluded garnishing the pension benefits to enforce court support orders for the employee's wife and children. Although the court concluded that "[t]he debates and reports on ERISA furnish little or no direction" about whether Congress intended ERISA to supersede "the ancient family law right of maintenance and support," the court found in the exemption sections of the other named federal statutes "a general congressional intent not to preclude enforcement of family support obligations." Relying heavily on these other statutes, the court read a similar exemption into ERISA's non-assignment provision. *Id.* at 1155.

3. COHERENCE WITH OTHER LAW

Other statutes also can be used to enhance the overall coherence of the law, sometimes in fairly dramatic ways. In its more straightforward deployment, this also is arguably an application of the Whole Code Rule, as for instance when the Supreme Court in *Casey* construed the scope of the phrase "reasonable attorney's fee" through reference to congressional usage of the same term in a number of other statutes. Similarly, in *FDA v. Brown & Williamson Tobacco Corp.*, 529 U.S. 120 (2000) (also discussed in Chapter 12), in which at issue was the FDA's asserted authority to regulate tobacco products, the Court relied on a half-dozen other federal statutes to reject the FDA's asserted authority. The other statutes required disclosure of information about the health effects of tobacco products but did not ban them, an approach the Court saw as incompatible with the FDA's claim of jurisdiction over tobacco products.

A more dramatic example of promoting coherence in the law is the New York high court's consideration of the impact of several statutory changes to the state adoption law in *In the Matter of Jacob*, 660 N.E.2d 397 (N.Y. 1995), a case discussed previously in Chapters 7 & 8. As a result of these changes, single adults were permitted to adopt, regardless of their sexual orientation, and gay couples were also able to adopt. But another statutory provision required the termination of the parental rights of the biological parents upon the conclusion of an adoption proceeding for an adoptive parent who was not married to the child's biological parent. In two companion cases involving adoption petitions by the cohabitating but unmarried partners of the biological mothers of the children being adopted, the court acknowledged that by its terms, the statutory framework created a Catch-22 that would allow the cohabiting partners to adopt only if the biological mother's parental rights were then terminated. In light of more recent changes in other elements of adoption law, the court found a latent ambiguity in the termination requirement and concluded that the requirement should not apply to the adoptions at issue.

4. PRESUMPTION AGAINST IMPLIED REPEALS

Finally, one more interpretive aid often included among the extrinsic tools involving other statutes is the presumption against implied repeals. This canon assumes (often counter-factually) that the legislature is aware of the entire body of enacted law, and therefore that the legislature usually will specifically state when it means for a new measure to repeal or overrule a preexisting measure. Absent a clear statement to this effect, the interpretive presumption is against construing the newer measure in a way that would undermine the older measure, unless the new measure produces an irreconcilable conflict with the older one.

Morton v. Mancari, 417 U.S. 535 (1974), is a famous example of the application of this rule. For at least 140 years, the federal government had afforded Native Americans an employment preference for positions in the Bureau of Indian Affairs (BIA) and related services, and this preference had been enacted into federal law in the Indian Reorganization Act of 1934. But after Congress enacted the Equal Employment Opportunity Act of 1972, which called generally for all federal personnel actions to "be made free from any discrimination based on race, color, religion, sex, or national origin," other employees of the BIA challenged these preferences. However, in light of the long-established federal policy, the Supreme Court refused to construe the non-discrimination provision of the 1972 act as impliedly repealing the preference in the 1934 Indian Reorganization Act. The Court called it "a prototypical case where an adjudication of repeal by implication is not appropriate," observing that both statutes could continue largely to co-exist. *Id.* at 550.

By contrast, as an example of an irreconcilable conflict, two Nevada statutes imposed penalties for selling certain controlled substances. The earlier statute classified violations as felonies; the later statute classified the same violations as misdemeanors. In *Washington v. Nevada*, 30 P.3d 1134 (Nev. 2001), the state supreme court concluded that the later statute had implicitly repealed the earlier one. Arguably, *In the Matter of Jacob*, discussed in the preceding subsection, also presents a case of an implied partial repeal, as the decision invalidated the statute that would have terminated the parental rights of the biological parent in the context of an adoption by the partner of the biological parent.

A set of related principles are that when two statutes do conflict, a more specific measure will control a more general measure, and the more recently enacted measure will control an earlier measure. The first of these principles sometimes calls for a somewhat subjective analysis of whether one measure is more specific than another. The second principle appears to run counter to the rule against implied repeals, as it leads to the later statute overriding the earlier one. However, this principle is simply an exception to the implied repeal rule in the case of an irreconcilable conflict. And once again, these principles are only guidelines, subject to consideration of whether they fit a particular problem.

An example involving both of these principles is *Palm Beach County Canvassing Board v. Harris*, 772 So.2d 1220 (Fla.), *vacated sub nom. Bush v. Palm Beach Canvassing Board*, 531 U.S. 70 (2000), a case discussed previously in Chapters 7 and 9. The Florida Supreme Court confronted two conflicting provisions of the state election law, one enacted in 1951 that said the Secretary of State "shall" ignore a county's certified election returns if they arrive after the statutory deadline, and another enacted in 1989 that said the Secretary of State "may" ignore such returns. The court concluded the Secretary of State had discretion to ignore late returns but was not required to do so, given not only that the permissive measure was more recently enacted, but also that it was more specific, by including a graduated system for imposing fines on county boards whose returns were late.

C. INTERPRETATION BASED ON LEGISLATIVE HISTORY

Using the common law and other statutes as aids in interpretation is widely accepted under most interpretive theories, even if just as a variation on the "Whole Code Rule" discussed in Chapter 9. In contrast, the use of what is typically called the "legislative history" of the text in question is more contested. Almost by definition, most Textualists, as discussed in Chapter 8, will rarely rely on these extrinsic tools. Rather, the use of a measure's legislative history is largely the province of Purposivist and Intentionalist interpreters, precisely because these interpreters find these extrinsic tools to be a valuable means of discerning and understanding the purpose or intent behind an ambiguous provision.

1. TYPES OF "LEGISLATIVE" AND "STATUTORY" HISTORY

In the United States, the phrase "legislative history" has acquired a term-of-art status, referring to specific kinds of materials produced as part of a legislature's consideration of a particular measure. These materials typically include different versions of the measure that the legislature considered at various points; committee reports about these versions; proposed amendments to the measure; legislative branch and executive branch staff analyses; testimony at committee hearings; statements of individual legislators concerning the measure, whether offered on the floor of the legislative chamber during debate, or in letters to other legislators, or as press releases concerning the measure; executive branch messages about the measure; and press accounts. For a relatively comprehensive listing of a score of specific types of legislative history, see OTTO J. HETZEL, MICHAEL

LIBONATI, & ROBERT WILLIAMS, LEGISLATIVE LAW & PROCESS 438 (2d ed. 1993).

"Legislative history" of this sort should be distinguished from "statutory history." Occasionally, the latter term is used much more narrowly, to describe only the way in which the enacted text itself, through amendment, may have changed over time. On the other hand, the same "statutory history" phrase also is occasionally used much more broadly, to describe the entire context of a measure, including not only the range of legislative history materials generated by the enacting legislature, but also the broader circumstances surrounding a measure's enactment. An often-studied example of the way in which the circumstances surrounding an enactment can provide valuable "statutory" history or context is *Leo Sheep Co. v. United States*, 440 U.S. 668 (1979). There, the Supreme Court relied on an exposition of the exploration of the American West and the coming of the transcontinental railroad to help determine whether a railroad land grant act adopted contemporaneously with those historical moments included an implied easement. The Court concluded that an implied easement was inconsistent with "the open range" of the enacting era.

More recently, in construing an ambiguous provision of the Patient Protection and Affordable Care Act (ACA), the Supreme Court described in some detail the circumstances of the American health care system and health insurance marketplace. *See King v. Burwell*, 576 U.S. ___, 135 S. Ct. 2480 (2015). As described briefly above in Chapter 7, at issue was whether federal subsidies that under the terms of the statute were available to individuals who purchased health insurance through an insurance exchange "established by the state" were also available to individuals who purchased insurance on the federal government's exchange. These subsidies were intended to assist individuals who otherwise could not afford to comply with the ACA mandate that they purchase health insurance. Central to the Court's ultimate disposition of the interpretive issue was its description and analysis of the economics of health care. The Court concluded that it was implausible that Congress had intended the terms of the subsidy provision to exclude the federal exchange and to cover only exchanges established by state governments, because that would render the ACA unworkable and could plunge "a State's individual insurance market into a death spiral." *Id.* at 2484.

Meanwhile, the many types of legislative history materials (as that term is used in its narrow sense) are sometimes categorized by their reliability. By way of overview, the reliability of legislative history materials that the legislature itself has generated is usually categorized as follows: At the top of the hierarchy of reliability come committee reports, which are the official work product of a set of legislative actors to whom the legislature has officially delegated institutional authority to understand and recommend individual legislative proposals. Among committee reports, the reports of conference committees are generally seen as the most dependable sources of legislative history, both because they represent the views of both houses of the legislature and because the members of each body are asked to vote on them (see Chapter 5). After committee reports usually come individual statements of the sponsors of a measure, explaining its purpose or operation. A sponsor's responsibility to shepherd a measure is seen as diminishing the chances that the sponsor's statements will be disingenuous or hyperbolic. Following far behind sponsors' statements are the statements, opinions, or explanations made by individual legislators in support of or opposition to a specific measure. Interpreters receive these materials much more skeptically (in fact refusing to consider them at all in earlier eras), as lacking much assurance that they are candid or accurate.

As for legislative history materials generated outside of the legislature itself—such as executive branch analyses or witness testimony—interpreters may assess their reliability or persuasive power partly on where in the legislative process those materials became relevant. Although these materials may also merit evaluation for reliability on their own merits, it is more important to determine how much of a factor these materials were in the legislative process, for instance determining whether they were a central component of an important committee hearing, or instead were merely an exchange of views with one legislator. But in every category of legislative history, reliability is a somewhat fluid characteristic, often depending less on the type of legislative history involved than on case-specific indicia of whether the particular content was likely to be persuasive to, influential on, reflective of, or relied upon by a critical mass of legislators.

2. INTRODUCTORY NOTE ABOUT OBJECTIONS TO USING LEGISLATIVE HISTORY IN INTERPRETATION

Before considering examples of how the primary categories of legislative history materials may factor in the interpretive enterprise, a reminder of the primary arguments for and against the use of legislative history in interpretation is in order. Jurists Antonin Scalia and Frank Easterbrook have been two of the most prominent contemporary critics of interpretation on the basis of legislative history, arguing repeatedly and consistently that because legislative history is not enacted law, it is entirely irrelevant as an authoritative indicator of meaning. "To be 'a government of laws, not men' is to be governed by what the law says, not what the people who drafted the law intended." SCALIA & GARNER, *supra*, at 375; *see* ANTONIN SCALIA, A MATTER OF INTERPRETATION (1997); *In re Sinclair*, 870 F.2d 1340 (7th Cir. 1989) (Judge Easterbrook). This is the essence of the Textualists' philosophical objection, discussed in greater detail in Chapter 8, to even inquiring about "intent" as a touchstone of interpretation (though Textualists are open to using legislative history simply as an example of meaning, to the extent that, like dictionaries, legislative history may simply provide some evidence of the ways in which words are used).

In addition to the philosophical objection that legislative history itself is not law, another primary objection to using legislative history as an aid to interpretation is a practical one, namely, that if interpreters rely on legislative intent, then legislators and their staff members can and will deliberately manipulate the legislative history by seeding it with content that might influence subsequent interpretation. This criticism often includes the refrain that a legislator who could not get a provision into the text itself (because the legislator was unable to persuade enough colleagues to agree to it) can instead simply plant the same idea somewhere in the legislative history. What is more, even staffers and lobbyists may similarly be able to influence the content of various types of legislative history much more easily than they could influence actual legislative text.

A third critique, which could amount to something of a hybrid between the theoretical and the practical objections, is that for many interpretive issues, the legislative history may provide material for a bevy of arguments on either side of the issue. This could be because of the difficulty of ascertaining one single intent for an institution composed of a multiplicity of actors, each with their own individual intentions. It could also be because that same multiplicity of legislators, in anticipation of the interpretive problem, have laced the record with arguments on either side. Thus, as Judge Harold Leventhal of the United States Court of Appeals for the District of Columbia Circuit is reported to have said, using legislative history can be like entering a cocktail party and looking over the heads of the crowd to pick out one's friends. *See* Patricia M. Wald, *Some Observations on the Use of Legislative History in the 1981 Supreme Court Term*, 68 IOWA L. REV. 195, 214 (1983).

Yet defenders of the use of legislative history to identify statutory purpose or intent respond not only that the will of the enacting legislature is what ought to matter most to the interpretive enterprise, but also that courts have the capability to at least seek to find that will. Although courts which undertake that search must be sensitive to the potential hazards of relying on extra-textual evidence of legislative purpose, they should not be precluded from a judicious exploration of all relevant evidence. Indeed, a balanced exploration, including a weighing of the reliability of each piece of evidence, is an activity to which the courts of our common-law tradition are well suited. This search is worth the candle, proponents argue, because legislative history may provide the best evidence of the legislature's intent. Furthermore, given the relationship among the branches, the legislature is always able to respond to an interpretation with which it disagrees by amending the statute.

Defenders of the use of legislative history in interpretation also argue that legislatures are constitutionally entitled to determine their internal operating procedures. If they decide to delegate much of their work to committees operating pursuant to internal rules and norms, then courts should respect that internal delegation. Thus, when committees, in compliance with these internal processes and expectations, report on their work to the full legislature, their reports are both authorized and, unless contrary evidence appears, appropriately presumed to be acceptable to the full legislature.

In addition, many legislatures increasingly seem to expect that legislative history materials will provide interpreters with additional interpretive context. Furthermore, the Constitution commands Congress to keep a "Journal of its Proceedings, and from time to time publish the same" (Article I, section 5), a requirement that some observers view as creating a justification for looking at records other than the statutory text to understand Congress's work.

Today, Textualist criticism of the use of legislative history is often credited with leading to what some commentators have called the **New Synthesis**, in which legislative history may have an important seat at the interpretive table, but is secondary in importance to the statutory text and must be carefully scrutinized for its reliability. On its face, this is a rather unremarkable proposition, even if it represents a position perhaps at odds with some previous approaches to interpretation. Yet even this proposition, under its surface, may raise contested questions of interpretive approach.

One recent case highlighting these lingering questions is *Exxon Mobile Corporation v. Allapattah Services, Inc.*, 545 U.S. 546 (2005), in which Justice Kennedy wrote a majority opinion discounting key evidence from a committee report as both irrelevant and unreliable, while Justice Stevens wrote a dissenting opinion arguing that the same evidence was relevant and reliable. Among other things, the majority opinion is notable for its claim that the committee report, which included language stating that "the legislative history was an attempt to correct [an] oversight" in the text of the statute itself, directly proved the Textualists' "worst fears" that legislative history would be used to circumvent the Article I lawmaking process. *Id.* at 570. Meanwhile, the dissenting opinion concluded that the very same portion of the report merely clarified that what was otherwise an ambiguous statutory provision should not be given an overly broad meaning. Justice Stevens' dissent is also noteworthy for this assertion: "I believe that we as judges are more, rather than less, constrained when we make ourselves accountable to *all* reliable evidence of legislative intent." *Id.* at 572 (Stevens, J., dissenting).

As the following discussion of each of the primary types of legislative history shows, this debate persists at both the federal and state levels (though at the state level it usually occurs with less developed legislative history materials), with most courts seeking to evaluate on a case-by-case basis which legislative history materials are relevant and reliable.

3. PRIMARY KINDS OF LEGISLATIVE HISTORY

Legislative history materials are usually categorized based on where they have been generated in the legislative process (as described in Chapter 5). These categories, in turn, tend to have different degrees of reliability. The discussion below begins with the category of committee reports because, as a general rule, they are seen as the most reliable kind of legislative history. But in any given interpretive problem, the reliability of each specific piece of legislative history must be considered on its own terms. Furthermore, as federal statutes have increasingly been the result of "unorthodox" lawmaking, these categories may have less significance. But they continue to form the backdrop for thinking about types of legislative history (and their significance may rebound at the federal level if under the Trump administration the country enters a post-gridlock era of more traditional congressional lawmaking).

a. Committee Reports

At the federal level, congressional committee reports are both the most reliable and the most widely used sources of legislative history. In substantial part this is because of the process that produces these reports and the role that the reports play within the legislature. Committee reports historically have been the result of a collaborative, bipartisan, regularized process designed to provide the entire legislature with the benefit of the committee's expertise. As discussed in Chapter 5, Congress has made a deliberate decision to rely on subject-matter committees to increase the efficiency of its work. In turn, each House of Congress expects that its committees will report back to the full body a reliable accounting of their thorough consideration of whatever measures they have been assigned. Formal written committee reports are the primary means by which committees fulfill this responsibility.

In many instances, members pay more attention to congressional committee reports than to the language of a bill itself. Although reports generally include the text of the bill, they also include other more user-friendly sections intended to assist legislators (and their staff) to digest and understand each measure. These sections include a summary of the bill, a section-by-section analysis, and the written statements of individual members who have opted to add their own concurring or dissenting views to the report of the committee majority. Reports must be distributed to the full membership at least 48 hours in advance of the floor debate, the body's formal consideration of the measure.

Throughout Justice Scalia's tenure on the Supreme Court, he consistently raised questions concerning the appropriateness of relying on legislative committee reports, in addition to objecting to the use of legislative history generally. But to some degree or another, his Supreme Court colleagues have continued to deploy committee reports in support of their interpretive conclusions, and the practice is widespread throughout the federal judiciary. The practice is also widespread at the state level, although many state legislatures do not regularly produce published committee reports like those that congressional committees produce. That has been changing, however, as more and more state legislatures adjust their processes and practices to make more materials available. *See* WILLIAM H. MANZ, GUIDE TO STATE LEGISLATION, LEGISLATIVE HISTORY, AND ADMINISTRATIVE MATERIALS (7th ed. 2008).

At the federal level, committee reports are often a primary means by which members of Congress communicate with each other. They therefore are obviously relevant to an interpreter who seeks to discern congressional intent. But how much familiarity with the details of a committee report is it realistic to expect legislators to have?

Consider the Senate Report to the 1976 Civil Rights Attorney's Fee Award Act, 42 U.S.C. § 1988, which provided for the discretionary award to a prevailing party of a "reasonable" attorney's fee. As guidance about what was a reasonable fee, the report stated that counsel should be paid "for all time reasonably expended on a matter"; referenced twelve factors that a Fifth Circuit opinion had described as relevant in computing a fee award; and cited three district court decisions that "correctly applied" these factors, even in disagreeing with dictum in the Fifth Circuit opinion. Did Senators voting for the act understand the interplay of these factors, and in particular what they might mean with respect to the circuit court's dictum that a contingency fee agreement imposed an upper limit on a "reasonable" attorney's fee under section 1988?

In *Blanchard v. Bergeron*, 489 U.S. 87 (1989), the Supreme Court relied on the Senate Report to conclude that the implication of these elements of the report was that Congress did not expect that a contingency fee agreement would impose a ceiling. Justice Scalia, early in his tenure on the Court, concurred in the result, but lambasted the majority decision for relying on the report:

> That the Court should refer to the citation of three District Court cases in a document issued by a single committee of a single house as the action of *Congress* displays the level of unreality that our unrestrained use of legislative history has attained. I am confident that only a small proportion of the Members of Congress read [the Report]; that very few of those who did read [it] set off for the nearest law library to check out what was actually said in the four cases at issue . . . ; and that *no* Member . . . came to the judgment that the District Court cases would trump [the language in the circuit court opinion] because the latter was dictum.

Id. at 98. Justice Scalia concluded his critique by opining that this portion of the Senate Report likely was written not to influence other Senators, "but rather to influence judicial construction."

Throughout his service on the Court, Justice Scalia maintained his staunch opposition to reliance on legislative history, including committee reports. Largely as a result of his influence, close observers have detected a decline in the Supreme Court's reliance on legislative history materials, and committee reports in particular. Nevertheless, over the past quarter century, Justice Scalia and Justice Thomas have been the only members of the Court who have steadfastly refused to ever consult legislative history for evidence of congressional intent. For the most part, reports of congressional committees remain widely respected and frequently used in resolving interpretive issues at the federal level.

Reports of congressional conference committees often have an even more exalted status than reports of each chamber's standing committees. The purpose of a conference committee is to work out differences between the two chambers after each has had a full opportunity to consider a proposal. Usually some points of disagreement remain to be resolved as part of achieving the agreement of both Houses on precisely the same text. Although conference committees are ad hoc committees, rather than standing committees, their members are especially trusted. They are appointed by the leaders of both chambers because of their extra familiarity with the subject of the conference and their ability to represent their respective house effectively in resolving remaining differences as a measure nears completion. Conference committees, by definition, also are joint committees of both Houses, and therefore speak on behalf of the Congress as a whole rather than just the House or the Senate. Furthermore, once the conference committee completes its work and refers its report to both chambers, each chamber then approves the same report if the measure is to become law. The content of conference committee reports thus can be especially probative in ascertaining meaning. The most noticeable weakness in conference reports is that they address only the points of disagreement, so any aspects of a measure on which the two chambers were already in agreement are not likely to receive much elucidation in the conference report.

For an interesting rejection of the apparent implication of a conference committee report, see *In re Sinclair*, 870 F.2d 1340 (7th Cir. 1989). There, Judge Easterbrook, perhaps the most prominent Textualist jurist other than Justice Scalia, explored the relationship between several amendments of the bankruptcy code added in 1986 for the benefit of family farmers, who then were in the midst of a difficult economic crisis. One provision created a new kind of bankruptcy proceeding—Chapter 12—specifically for family farmers. Another provided that the 1986 amendments would not apply with respect to cases filed under the bankruptcy code before the 1986 amendments. Yet another provision, which Judge Easterbrook did not reference, permitted the conversion to Chapter 12 of a bankruptcy proceeding begun under Chapter 11 or Chapter 13. The Sinclairs had filed for bankruptcy under Chapter 11 before the 1986 amendments, and under this third provision they desired to convert their proceeding to Chapter 12 once Congress created that option.

Judge Easterbrook ignored the tension between the provision permitting conversions to Chapter 12 and the provision prohibiting application of the 1986 amendments to proceedings already underway, seeing the latter provision as an absolute bar for the Sinclairs. But the conference report had clearly contemplated such conversions of pending cases, stating: "It is not intended that there be routine conversion of Chapter 11 and Chapter 13 cases, *pending at the time of enactment*, to Chapter 12. Instead, it is expected that courts will exercise their sound discretion in each case, in allowing conversions only where it is equitable to do so" (emphasis added). Judge Easterbrook dismissed this language of the conference committee report as inconsistent with the enacted text that prohibited applying the 1986 amendments to pending cases. Setting up a strawman argument (albeit one worth reading in its entirety for its delineation of the various uses of legislative history) between the statute and its legislative history, he concluded "the statute must prevail."

With respect to state statutes as well, interpreters may see committee reports as especially probative. However, at the state level it is much less common for legislative committees to issue written reports. Rather, legislative committees often fulfill their role as the entire body's delegate in a less recorded way (other than a committee's performance of its responsibility to "mark up" or revise the bill), for instance reporting orally in private conversations or caucus meetings that committee members have with other legislators not on the committee. But in states whose legislatures produce written committee reports, interpreters will readily look to them for interpretive guidance. Some states' legislative processes also may generate various other types of official reports, such as analyses by legislative drafting bureaus, joint study committee reports, or executive branch budget messages.

For instance, the New Jersey Supreme Court relied upon the report of the New Jersey Senate Judiciary Committee to construe the terms of the state's Products Liability Act in *Perez v. Wyeth Laboratories, Inc.*, 734 A.2d 1245 (N.J. 1999.) At issue was whether the "learned intermediary" doctrine relieved the manufacturer of the drug Norplant from tort liability for the drug's side-effects when the manufacturer had engaged in direct marketing of the drug to consumers. The state statute provided that "in the case of prescription drugs," an adequate warning of its potential dangers sufficient to avoid tort liability would be a warning "taking into account the characteristics of, and the ordinary knowledge common to, the prescribing physician." The committee report stated that "in the case of prescription drugs, the warning is owed to the physician."

The case is interesting in part because the statute at issue included an interpretive direction that committee statements "shall be consulted in the interpretation and construction of this act." In the view of the dissenting justice, both the statute and the committee report supported the view that the manufacturer was relieved of liability as long as it had informed the physician—the learned intermediary—of the potential side effects. But the majority concluded from a variety of evidence, including the committee report, that the statutory specification of what constituted an adequate warning reflected an earlier era when "drugs were then marketed to the physician," and did not provide a safe harbor against tort liability for drug manufacturers now marketing directly to the consumer.

b. Statements of Sponsors and Drafters

Although committee reports are generally seen as the most authoritative and reliable sources of legislative history, often it is a measure's principal drafters and sponsors who are looked to as best understanding the measure's purpose or intent. Sponsors and drafters will often find opportunities to make on-the-record statements about the meaning of some portions of their measures, typically in fulfillment of their responsibility to shepherd a measure's consideration by the full chamber. These opportunities most often include explanatory statements offered when introducing a measure, or colloquies (whether planned or spontaneous) with colleagues. As Justice Frankfurter said more than sixty years ago, "Whatever we may think about the loose use of legislative history, it has never been questioned that the reports of committees *and utterances of those in charge of legislation* constitute authoritative exposition of the meaning of legislation." *Orloff v. Willoughby*, 345 U.S. 83, 98 (1953) (Frankfurter, J., dissenting) (emphasis added). Nevertheless, interpreters must consider critical questions about the reliability of individual statements.

In construing the employment nondiscrimination provisions of Title VII of the Civil Rights Act of 1964, the Supreme Court relied on a number of floor statements uttered by the primary Senate sponsors of the measure. At issue in *United Steelworkers of America v. Weber*, 443 U.S. 193 (1979) (also discussed in Chapter 8), was whether Title VII's prohibition against racial discrimination in employment precluded a private employer from using a voluntary affirmative action program that benefitted members of racial minorities. Senator Hubert Humphrey, the floor manager of the bill, had described the purpose of the title as "to open employment opportunities for Negroes in occupations which have been traditionally closed to them." Relying on this and similar statements by other senators holding prominent leadership roles with respect to this measure, the Court concluded that Title VII should not be construed to preclude voluntary affirmative action programs.

However, the dissenting opinion concluded that other statements of key legislators provided support for the opposite result, including statements by Senator Humphrey that the bill "provides that race shall not be a basis for making personnel decisions" and "forbids discriminating against anyone on account of race." The House floor manager, Representative Emmanuel Celler, also had said on the House floor that the bill would prevent "employers from discriminating against or in favor of workers because of their race . . . ." As also described above in Chapter 8, the dissenting opinion thus saw in these sponsors' statements evidence that the purpose of the bill was to end all race-based distinctions in employment, while the majority opinion derived from other sponsors' statements that the purpose was to remedy the plight of minority workers. The majority opinion also distinguished the statements on which the dissent had relied as occurring at an earlier stage in the enactment process, before critical amendments to the bill had occurred.

Consider also *Hamdan v. Rumsfeld*, 548 U.S. 557 (2006), in which Justice Stevens considered contradictory statements of Senator Levin, on the one hand, and Senators Graham and Kyl, on the other. All three were sponsors of the Detainee Treatment Act of 2005, the retroactivity of which was at issue in the case. But the statements of Senators Graham and Kyl were less authoritative, in Justice Steven's view, because they were not uttered on the floor but instead were inserted into the Congressional Record after the fact (as all Members of Congress are usually allowed to do). Justice Stevens instead credited Senator Levin's actual on-the-floor statement that the act was retroactive.

In *United States v. Kosak*, 465 U.S. 848 (1984), a case roughly contemporaneous with *Weber*, the Supreme Court disagreed about another interpretive problem (involving the Federal Tort Claims Act), but this time over what reliance to place on an explanation of a *nonlegislator* who in the 1930s had the key responsibility of drafting the language at issue. The Court majority relied on a report prepared by this drafter, a Special Assistant to the U.S. Attorney General who would later serve as a federal judge, about the proposed measure, even though the Court had no evidence that Congress had been aware of the report. Justice Stevens' dissenting opinion argued in reply that "the intent of a lobbyist—no matter how public spirited he may have been—should not be attributed to the Congress without positive evidence that elected legislators were aware of and shared the lobbyist's intent." Justice Stevens also offered this advice from a 1902 English precedent: "[T]he worst person to construe [a statute] is the person who is responsible for its drafting. He is very much disposed to confuse what he intended to do with the effect of the language which in fact has been employed." *Id.* at 863–64.

For another example of interpretation in light of the statements of non-legislative participants in the drafting process, consider the dissenting opinion in *Circuit City Stores, Inc. v. Adams*, 532 U.S. 105 (2001). The case, as previously discussed in Chapter 9, involved the scope of employees covered by the Federal Arbitration Act. Although the majority opinion reached its result using a plain meaning approach, the dissent would have relied on an explanation of the American Bar Association committee that had pressed for the statute's enactment and statements of the Secretary of Commerce about the act.

Until relatively recently, the English rule for over two hundred years had been that "Parliamentary materials" (in other words legislative history) were not admissible in court to determine statutory meaning. But in *Pepper v. Hart*, [1992] UKHL 3, the House of Lords relied extensively on the equivalent of legislators' floor statements to resolve an interpretive problem. The opinion included an extended discussion of the arguments for and against modifying the English exclusionary rule. Central to the decision to admit these Parliamentary materials was the view that when faced with statutory ambiguity, courts should not "blind themselves to a clear indication of what Parliament intended," if they found that evidence reliable.

The Textualist critique, of course, is that legislative history is never reliable. In addition to Textualism's general criticisms that reliance on legislative history circumvents the lawmaking requirements of Article I and enables sloppy drafting, the use of sponsor statements is also subject to the particular critique that sponsors, more easily than entire committees, may deliberately include claims in their floor remarks strategically, precisely to provide arguments for a subsequent interpretive problem. When it comes to floor statements, the criticism runs, talk is cheap. Furthermore, the use of sponsor statements also is subject to the critique that not even sponsors are able to speak about a measure on behalf of the legislature as an institution; interpreters should not encourage this circumvention of the legislative process.

However, most non-Textualist interpreters will undertake an individualized look at each potentially relevant statement by a sponsor or drafter to see whether the statement bears sufficient indicia of its reliability. Underlying this inquiry is a sense of the importance to a legislative body of building and maintaining relationships of trust among its members. Colleagues may cease to trust one another if they engage in hyperbole or distortion at moments when others might expect to rely on their assertions, as in particular when sponsors are characterizing their own measures. Factors through which interpreters therefore seek to assess the reliability of individual member statements include: (1) Was the statement made under circumstances in which other legislators would have had full awareness of it? (2) Would other legislators have relied upon it? (3) Would other legislators have had an opportunity to seek additional information in light of the statement? (4) Is the statement consistent with other statements concerning the statute? Central to considering all of these factors is whether the statement likely expresses an understanding that is fairly attributable to the enacting coalition.

At the state level, courts frequently rely on statements of legislative sponsors, sometimes more so than on committee reports. In part, this may reflect the fact that transcripts of floor debate and committee proceedings are more common than published committee reports at the state level. In addition, and perhaps as a result, floor debate in state legislatures can involve a more genuine and substantive exchange of views and information than in Congress, as committee chairs are called upon to explain their committee's view on a measure for the benefit of all members. State court interpreters of state legislative output are therefore often quite willing to consider the views of the key proponents of a measure.

c. Floor Debate and Remarks at Committee Hearings

Distinguishable from statements made by sponsors, which although they have their own reliability issues nonetheless may carry with them some indicia of reliability, are statements made by other legislators during debate over a proposed measure. Statements made by legislators *opposed* to a measure are usually greatly discounted, again on the theory that talk is cheap in this context and opponents may readily overstate reasons for their opposition by mischaracterizing how a measure might operate. But occasionally statements made in debate by those in favor of a measure may have explanatory force, if the views can fairly be understood as representative of those who supported the measure. Likewise, interpreters may on occasion derive interpretive assistance by referring to testimony at a committee hearing.

As an example of the influence of floor debate on an interpretive issue, consider *BankAmerica Corp. v. United States*, 462 U.S. 122 (1983). One provision of the Clayton Act generally prohibited interlocking corporate boards, but excepted banks from its coverage. At issue was whether the exception allowed bank-nonbank interlocks, or excepted only bank-bank interlocks, which were regulated in a separate provision. An opponent of the bill had complained that the conference committee had produced a version of the bill that no longer prohibited bank-nonbank interlocks, although he understood the earlier versions from both the House and Senate to have done so. Two proponents of the bill, while agreeing that the conference committee version did not prohibit bank-nonbank interlocks, argued that this had also been true of the earlier versions. The Supreme Court credited this exchange to support its conclusion that the act did not bar bank-nonbank interlocks.

Another example of the use of floor debate is the Ninth Circuit's unpublished initial decision in *Montana Wilderness Association v. United States Forest Service*, which on request for rehearing the court subsequently withdrew and replaced. (The replacement opinion, which reached the opposite result but still contains a strong flavor of the withdrawn opinion's reasoning, is reported at 655 F.2d 951 (9th Cir. 1981).) In determining that a provision of the Alaska National Interest Lands Conservation Act that granted access to private lands within the National Forest System applied only in Alaska rather than nationwide, the circuit court's initial opinion noted that the act "was discussed endlessly on the Senate floor," yet the court could not find "one single suggestion [during that debate] that [the act] would affect access rights in the rest of the country."

This is an example of what is sometimes called **"the dog that didn't bark"** canon (or what Justice Scalia called the "Canine Silence" canon), after the A. Conan Doyle story "Silver Blaze," in which the fact that a watchdog didn't bark suggested that the crime had been an inside job. Similarly, when no legislator raises an alarm about a possible construction that ought to have raised an alarm in at least some quarters, legal interpreters often conclude that it is not appropriate to give the text that construction. And although the *Montana Wilderness* court did find evidence that a few members of the House of Representatives had viewed the provision as applying nationwide and had corresponded with the Department of Justice about this understanding, the court said that these "off-the-record views . . . are not attributed to Congress as a whole . . . . This is particularly true where, as here, there is no indication that the House as a whole was aware of the correspondence." 655 F.2d 951, 956 nn. 7 & 10.

As an example of the influence of testimony at legislative hearings, including testimony of non-legislators, consider the Supreme Court's decision in *FDA v. Brown & Williamson Tobacco Corp.*, 529 U.S. 120 (2000) (also discussed below in Chapter 12). The Court's opinion that the Food, Drug, and Cosmetic Act (FDCA) did not give the FDA jurisdiction to regulate tobacco products relied in part on the repeated instances in which FDA officials had testified at congressional hearings that the FDA lacked jurisdiction over tobacco products, even though the FDA had now changed its interpretation to assert such jurisdiction. Notwithstanding these prior agency interpretations, the dissenting opinion argued that both the plain language of FDCA and the purpose behind the act sufficed to establish the FDA's jurisdiction over tobacco.

d. Other Contemporaneous Legislative History Materials

Although committee reports, sponsor statements, and other remarks in committee meetings or on the legislative floor constitute by far the most widely consulted sources of contemporaneous legislative history, several other categories of materials receive occasional attention.

"Dear Colleague" letters. These are letters or memoranda from one legislator to another, typically circulated to all other members (or all committee members) in advance of a debate or vote. For instance, prior to the Senate debate on the Alaska lands act at issue in the *Montana Wilderness* case above, Senator Melcher sent a letter to his 99 Senate colleagues explaining why, during the committee's consideration of the act, he had introduced an amendment (which became section 1323 of the act) that would guarantee access to private lands within national forest system *throughout the United States*, not just in Alaska. The circuit court, which as described above initially construed the act to apply only in Alaska, apparently was never made aware of this letter. But had the letter been part of the briefing and argument, how much weight might it have carried? Perhaps the letter was not part of the legislative history before the court because it received almost no attention from Senator Melcher's colleagues in the first place, passing almost unnoticed through their mailrooms into their archives.

Correspondence between legislators and executive branch officials or private lobbyists. As discussed in Part I, many external influences shape the legislative process. On occasion, non-legislator participants may create records during the enactment process that shed light on legislative intent. Interpreters considering such evidence must of course exercise great care to use it only to ascertain what it was that the legislature meant, not what the executive branch or private sector lobbyists wanted.

For instance, in *Lindahl v. Office of Personnel Management*, 470 U.S. 768 (1985), the Supreme Court was guided by letters from the Director of the federal Office of Personnel Management to the chairs of the House and Senate committees considering the appropriate scope of judicial review of decisions concerning federal employees' disability retirement benefits. The Court wrote: "Yet while Congress' understanding of the enactment is of course our touchstone, in discerning what it was that Congress understood we necessarily attach "great weight" to agency representations to Congress when the administrators participated in drafting and directly made known their views to Congress in committee hearings." *Id.* at 788 (internal quotations omitted).

Presidential/gubernatorial vetoes and signing statements. Because the head of the executive branch is a necessary part of the lawmaking process in all fifty states and the federal system, the views of this participant might in theory be every bit as relevant as the views of a sponsor or other key legislator in understanding the intent behind a measure. On the other hand, except in the case of an executive veto, the President and governors do not have any official opportunity to participate in the lawmaking process until the work of the legislative branch is complete, making it very difficult for the other actors to respond to or rebut effectively whatever the President or a governor might say about a measure at that point. However, if the executive responds with a veto or "disapproval" when presented with a legislative measure, the veto is to be accompanied by a statement of reasons. These reasons can be especially influential in understanding the scope of the measure either if it is subsequently enacted into law in identical form notwithstanding the veto or if an alternative measure that responds to the objections is enacted.

For instance, in *United States v. Yermian*, 468 U.S. 63 (1984), the Court noted that President Roosevelt had vetoed Congress's 1934 attempt to amend the False Statements Act, 18 U.S.C. § 1001, because it did not do enough to expand the scope of the existing law. In response, Congress passed and the President signed a broader measure. The Court in *Yermian* invoked the President's veto statement to help construe the scope of the enacted measure.

On rare occasions, presidential signing statements have also factored into a court's interpretive reasoning. For instance, at issue in *United States v. Story*, 891 F.2d 988 (2d Cir. 1989), was whether the Sentencing Reform Act of 1984, as applied to criminal offenses that continued over a period of time, covered only criminal offenses begun after the act's effective date, or also covered offenses begun before but continuing after its effective date. The statute was ambiguous, but President Reagan's signing statement expressed agreement with floor statements of key sponsors of the measure that the act applied to conduct "begun prior to, but not completed until on or after" the act's effective date. The court relied on the signing statement as one of several sources of interpretive evidence, noting that while signing statements might often carry little weight, in this case the President's views were "significant . . . because the Executive Branch participated in the negotiation of the compromise legislation." *Id.* at 994.

Press accounts. In the federal system, it has long been the practice to publish in the Congressional Record a transcript of the proceedings of both houses of Congress, as well as to produce transcripts of most committee hearings and to require committees to publish official reports on proposed legislation. As discussed above, these materials form the bulk of the legislative history sources relied upon in construing federal legislation. But the analogous forms of materials are often non-existent in state legislatures. In those circumstances, press accounts are often the closest form of contemporary record of what occurred in a committee proceeding or floor debate. For instance, in *In re Jason W.*, 378 Md. 596, 602–04 (Md. 2003), the court relied on newspaper articles to understand the committee debate on a bill passed in 1970, an era before the state legislature routinely prepared committee reports or otherwise preserved committee records. It is worth considering when and to what extent interpreters might reasonably rely on press accounts of the legislative process to shed light on the legislative intent.

e. Post-Enactment Legislative Action and Inaction

On occasion, interpreters consider legislative activity that post-dates the enactment of the measure in question. To the extent that the interpreter's goal in doing so is to understand the intent of the enacting legislature, such an approach can be deeply problematic. That is because post-enactment, it can be even easier than during the enactment process for an individual legislator to make purely strategic statements or to attempt to characterize the purpose of a measure without much accountability. Thus, post-enactment explanations of meaning or purpose are usually greatly discounted. For example, in the *Montana Wilderness* case discussed above (considering whether section 1323 of the Alaska National Interest Lands Conservation Act, which provided for access to private lands within the national forest system, applied only to national forest lands in Alaska or instead applied nationwide), the Ninth Circuit dismissed Senator Melcher's statement on the Senate floor that the provision applied nationwide as an unreliable indicator of the full Senate's understanding because Senator Melcher made the claim eight days after the bill's passage. *See Montana Wilderness Association v. United States Forest Service*, 655 F.2d 951, n.8 (9th Cir. 1981).

Every now and then, however, some subsequent legislative activity does influence the interpretive process. For example, in a dramatic turnaround, the court hearing the *Montana Wilderness* case was sufficiently influenced by other subsequent legislative developments to grant rehearing and reverse the outcome. The subsequent history consisted of actions and explanations of the conference committee responsible for a different measure, the Colorado Wilderness Act. In the course of the conference committee's work resolving differences between the House and Senate versions of the Colorado Wilderness Act, the conference committee agreed to delete a provision in the Senate version that provided for nationwide access to private lands within national forest wilderness areas. The committee explained that it had deleted this provision "because similar language has already passed Congress in Section 1323 of the Alaska National Interest Land Conservation Act." The court also relied on floor discussion of this aspect of the conference report to reverse its previous decision that section 1323 of the Alaska Act had not provided access nationwide to private lands within national forest land. *See Montana Wilderness Association v. United States Forest Service*, 655 F.2d 951 (9th Cir. 1981).

Another occasional use of subsequent legislative activity is to determine whether the legislature, as a dynamic institution, has ratified or implicitly now concurs in a prior interpretation of an ambiguity. This use of subsequent legislative activity (or inactivity) may be less problematic, although reliance on this factor is also deeply contested by Textualist interpreters who view their role as solely to understand the text as enacted. The Supreme Court itself also has cautioned against the practice, observing that subsequent congressional activity "is a hazardous basis for inferring the intent of an earlier Congress." *Pension Benefit Guarantee Corporation v. LTV Corporation*, 496 U.S. 633, 650 (1990) (internal quotations omitted). Nevertheless, over the years a number of prominent Supreme Court decisions have relied on the notion that a subsequent Congress has acquiesced in previous judicial or agency interpretations of a provision.

A quintessential example of interpretation in light of subsequent congressional action is *Flood v. Kuhn*, 407 U.S. 258 (1972), also discussed above in Chapter 7. In *Flood*, the Supreme Court reconsidered an exemption from the anti-trust laws that its own previous decisions in 1922 and 1953 had granted Major League Baseball. The exemption had allowed the League's baseball teams to use a "reserve clause" to control their player rosters. However, by 1972, the underlying rationale that the Court had articulated when it first held that the anti-trust laws did not apply to professional baseball leagues—that they were not engaged in interstate commerce—was patently no longer accurate. Meanwhile, by 1972, a number of court decisions had refused to extend a comparable exemption to other professional sports leagues, including football, basketball, and boxing. So the time would have been ripe for the Court to overrule its prior decisions. Nevertheless, because Congress had been well aware of the Court's earlier decisions exempting baseball from the antitrust laws and yet had done nothing to reverse this exemption (indeed, what congressional action had occurred had been directed, though unsuccessfully, towards *expanding* the anti-trust exemption to other sports), the Court "concluded that Congress as yet has had no intention to subject baseball's reserve system to the reach of the antitrust statutes." The Court refused to rationalize this area of the law by overturning its earlier cases "when Congress, by its positive inaction, has allowed those decisions to stand for so long and . . . has clearly evinced a desire not to disapprove of them legislatively." *Id.* at 283.

In a similar vein, a few years after the Court in *Weber* had construed Title VII to permit a private employer's voluntary affirmative action program on behalf of racial minorities, the Court relied on what it saw as Congress's apparent acceptance of this construction of the statute to also uphold a public employer's affirmative action program on behalf of women employees. *See Johnson v. Transportation Agency, Santa Clara County*, 480 U.S. 616 (1987). The Court's underlying reasoning in *Weber* had depended quite substantially on two considerations not present in *Johnson*, namely the Court's understanding that the overwhelming purpose behind Title VII was to promote employment opportunities for racial minorities, and the Court's view that it should construe Title VII to not interfere any more than necessary with the prerogatives of private employers. Although neither of these factors was present in the facts of *Johnson* (because it was not about racial discrimination, and because it involved a public employer), the Court chose to follow rather than distinguish *Weber* because "Congress has not amended the statute to reject our construction, nor have any such amendments even been proposed, and we therefore may assume that our [*Weber*] interpretation was correct." *Id.* at 629 n.7. In dissent, Justice Scalia thought it "patently false" to use what the current Congress might desire as a measure of what the law meant as enacted by an earlier Congress.

An example of apparent congressional acquiescence in prior *agency* constructions of a statute is *Bob Jones University v. United States*, 461 U.S. 574 (1983), discussed previously in Chapter 8. There, the Supreme Court relied heavily on what it saw as Congress's acceptance, since 1971, of a pair of IRS rulings denying charitable tax exemptions to private schools that discriminated on the basis of race. At issue was the construction of section 501(c)(3) of the Internal Revenue Code, which provides a federal tax exemption to corporations "organized and operated exclusively for religious, charitable, . . . or educational purposes." Prodded by a district court injunction, the IRS rulings had announced that corporations receiving the exemption were expected to fit the common-law notion of "charity" and therefore to have a purpose not contrary to public policy. The IRS rulings concluded that because, by 1970, it had become "national policy to discourage racial discrimination in education," corporations that engaged in racial discrimination were not charitable under section 501(c)(3).

Bob Jones University had challenged these rulings as inconsistent with the plain language of section 501(c)(3). But the Court accepted the additional requirement the IRS had imposed that exempt charities not act "contrary to public policy." As part of its opinion, the Court observed:

> Nonaction by Congress is not often a useful guide, but the nonaction here is significant. During the past 12 years there have been no fewer than 13 bills introduced to overturn the IRS interpretation of section 501(c)(3). Not one of those bills has emerged from any committee, although Congress has enacted numerous other amendments to section 501 during this same period . . . . In view of its prolonged and acute awareness of so important an issue, Congress' failure to act on the bills proposed on this subject provides added support for concluding that Congress acquiesced in the IRS rulings of 1970 and 1971.

Id. at 600–01.

As a final example, it is worth reflecting on the way in which the Supreme Court relied on subsequent congressional activity to construe the Food, Drug, and Cosmetic Act (FDCA) in *FDA v. Brown & Williamson Tobacco Corp.*, 529 U.S. 120 (2000). Although the dissenting opinion and the FDA argued that the FDCA's plain language gave the FDA jurisdiction to regulate tobacco products, the majority opinion rejected this construction of the act largely on the basis that a number of congressional proposals enacted or considered subsequent to enactment of the FDCA quite clearly assumed that the FDCA had not given the FDA jurisdiction over tobacco products. For more on this case, see section D.9 of Chapter 12.

D. ADDRESSING INTERPRETIVE PROBLEMS THAT ARISE FROM DIRECT DEMOCRACY

The preceding discussion has been concerned entirely with issues of construing laws enacted by legislative bodies. But what about construing ambiguities in laws enacted directly by voters, rather than by their representatives? In the twenty-one states with a statutory initiative process (as described in Chapter 5, section E), citizens possess the power to create statutory law themselves. Precisely the same interpretive difficulties can and do arise in connection with these initiated statutes (and with popularly enacted constitutional amendments as well) as arise with statutes enacted by Congress or a state legislature. Determining the legislative intent behind a measure enacted by a majority of the 535 members of Congress, or by a majority of the members of a state legislature, can be difficult enough. But additional complexities may arise with respect to a measure adopted by all of a state's electorate through a popular initiative, rather than by legislative action.

Most of the intrinsic tools discussed in Chapter 9 can equally be brought to bear on the interpretive problems of direct democracy. *See* Jane S. Schacter, *The Pursuit of "Popular Intent": Interpretive*

Dilemmas in Direct Democracy, 105 YALE L. J. 107 (1995). But extrinsic aids available for problems of direct democracy look a little different and raise some new questions. The most fundamental one is how to ascertain the legislative intent behind a popular initiative. Subsidiary questions include whose intent matters, and what to include in the "legislative history" of an initiated statute.

For instance, in *Bishop v. Linkway Stores, Inc.*, 655 S.W.2d 426 (Ark. 1983), the Supreme Court of Arkansas reviewed a recent amendment to the state constitution adopted by popular initiative. The amendment, which was titled "The 1982 Interest Rate Control Amendment," contained two key provisions. One, headed "General Loans," capped interest at 5% above the Federal Discount Rate (FDR) "on any contract entered into after the effective date" of the amendment. The other, headed "Consumer Loans and Credit Sales," declared void as to both principal and interest "all contracts for consumer loans and credit sales" having a rate of interest above 17%. The issue before the court was whether a contract bearing interest at 15% for the purchase of home furnishings was subject only to the 17% interest cap on "Credit Sales," and thus lawful, or was also subject to the 5% + FDR (8.5% at the time) cap on "General Loans," and thus unlawful.

Employing a plain meaning approach, the majority harmonized the two provisions, viewing credit sales as a subset of general loans and treating the second provision as merely imposing an additional, absolute ceiling, regardless of how high the FDR climbed, on this subset of loans. But the dissenters, relying heavily on the context of the amendment, including the mischief it was intended to remedy and how it had been promoted to the voters, viewed the two provisions as independent limits covering separate categories of loans. The dissent argued that, to understand the measure, "all relevant evidence should be admitted," including statements of the amendment's drafters and newspaper articles and media broadcasts showing "what was communicated to the voters" about the amendment. These materials convinced the dissenters that the intent of the amendment was to establish one single lawful interest rate on consumer sales contracts. *Id.* at 432.

As the *Linkway Stores* decision suggests, a different variety of materials present themselves as *possible* sources of extrinsic interpretive aid in resolving ambiguities in an initiated statute (or constitutional amendment), most presenting unique issues about their relevance or reliability. These materials include: official summaries of an initiative, whether circulated while gathering signatures, incorporated into voter guides, or printed on the ballot with the initiative proposition; public statements of the sponsors and proponents of the measure made as part of the campaign; statements of opponents; campaign advertising materials; news media reports; public opinion surveys; and other aspects of the public debate about the measure prior to Election Day. But extracting meaning from these materials, much more than from committee reports or individual legislators' statements, can be problematic.

Divining reliable evidence of intent from these sources is complicated in part because there are so many more lawmakers—comprising all those who vote—than when a legislature enacts a statute. Furthermore, from among that group it is harder to identify those representative voices who can speak authoritatively about an initiated measure's meaning. Unlike in legislative lawmaking, no committees analyze and amend an initiated proposal, refining and clarifying the measure's language and meaning in the process, before it is put before the public. Moreover, unlike in the legislature, in which the identity of all of those who vote in favor of a measure are known, popular lawmaking involves no record of how any specific voter has voted, thereby making it even more problematic to know whether any one voter's (or one group of voters') assertions are reliable, rather than strategic. And because leaders of a specific legislative initiative may have little reason to seek to maintain any meaningful continuing relationships with other voters (in contrast to the kind of continuing relationships that exist among legislators who must negotiate with each other repeatedly about a range of legislative issues), their talk truly is cheap. The potential unreliability of statements made in support of or opposition to a measure therefore increases. All of these concerns are ones that a Textualist methodology avoids.

Nevertheless, when interpretive issues arise concerning a popularly initiated statute, courts could well examine all of these types of materials, weighing carefully whether they contain reliable evidence that might help them construe textual ambiguity. For instance, in *Evangelatos v. Superior Court*, 753 P.2d 585 (Calif. 1988), the California Supreme Court relied on a ballot pamphlet's description of an initiative to support its determination that the initiative did not apply retroactively. In practice, however, courts construing popular initiatives are usually reluctant to rely on extrinsic evidence. *See, e.g.*, *National Pride at Work, Inc. v. Governor*, 732 N.W.2d 139 (Mich. Ct. App. 2007) (refusing to consider sponsors' materials assuring voters that state defense of marriage initiative would not affect domestic partnership benefits).

Several commentators have urged state courts to develop distinctive canons of interpretation for initiated measures. *See, e.g.*, Jane Schacter, *In Pursuit of "Popular Intent": Interpretive Dilemmas in Direct Democracy*, 105 YALE L. J. 107 (1995). One proposal would be to interpret popular initiatives narrowly on the theory that they are arguably an exception to the ideal of republican government that the U.S. Constitution guarantees to each state. *See* Philip P. Frickey, *Interpretation on the Borderline: Constitution, Canons, Direct Democracy*, 1996 N.Y.U. ANN. SURV. AM. L. 477. Another proposal would be to interpret popular initiatives to accord with the will of the "median" voter, a political science construct whose identity and preferences it would require substantial effort to ascertain. *See* Michael Gilbert, *Interpreting Initiatives*, 97 MINN. L. REV. 1621 (2013). But state courts have done little to develop these ideas.

CHAPTER 11

AGENCY INTERPRETATION OF LEGAL TEXT

As Chapter 7 noted, many types of actors—from citizens to lawyers to judges to executive branch officials—must confront the task of legal interpretation. Nevertheless, as Chapters 8, 9, and 10 reflect, the primary focus of interpretive theory has been on how judges construe legal text, given the judiciary's role to declare what the law is. However, every bit as much (actually much more) official interpretation of statutory text occurs at the hands of agency officials, in fulfillment of their rulemaking and adjudicatory responsibilities summarized in Chapter 6, responsibilities that give rise to a host of agency regulations and orders. Meanwhile, agencies also must frequently interpret their own regulations and orders—a responsibility that is not always easy, given that agencies can be vast, complicated bureaucracies.

Although some of these agency interpretations will eventually come before courts for review under the standards discussed in Chapter 12, many agency interpretations will not, either because they are not appealed, or because by law they may be insulated from judicial review. In those cases, the agency's construction may effectively be the final interpretive word. It therefore is important to understand something about the distinctive way in which agencies in their own right may interpret legal text. This understanding then will also be a helpful prerequisite to considering how the judicial branch reviews these agency interpretations.

To that end, this chapter discusses several characteristics of agencies that relate to their implementation of statutory and regulatory language and their resolution of textual ambiguities. These agency characteristics include their delegated lawmaking authority, their frequently close working relationships with the legislature during the process of drafting agency legislation, their expertise, and their political accountability. It also briefly considers how these characteristics influence agency rulemaking, agency adjudication, and the principle of *stare decisis* with respect to administrative precedents. It concludes by summarizing key doctrine that affects which agency actions will or will not be subject to judicial review.

A. AGENCY DELEGATION REPRISE: LEGISLATIVE RELIANCE ON AGENCY IMPLEMENTATION AND INTERPRETATION

All lobbyists worth their salt know that even after a bill becomes a law, many opportunities remain to influence its implementation. This is primarily because the complexity of American law today regularly requires the promulgation of additional regulations to clarify and enforce the statute, and also relies on the administrative adjudication of a range of associated issues. Responsibility for promulgating these regulations and conducting these adjudications generally rests with the executive branch departments and independent agencies whose existence, organization, and function were described in Chapter 6.

Congress and state legislatures now routinely delegate to these organs of the administrative state the explicit authority to make rules and adjudicate controversies. In turn, these agencies, by law, conduct many of their most important proceedings in public meetings, formal on-the-record hearings, or notice-and-comment rulemaking procedures. The primary point of these processes is to help the agency collect additional information relevant to its execution of its responsibilities. Meanwhile, the public nature of these processes makes it easy for citizens and other interested parties to renew their efforts to affect the ultimate policy outcome, while also helping make the agencies more accountable for how they exercise the authority delegated to them.

As Chapter 6 explains, the nondelegation doctrine imposes some limits on a legislature's ability to give agencies unbridled discretion to make law. Nevertheless, agencies regularly construe and refine the statutes they are implementing in ways that create new legal rights and duties. Indeed, in the typical case of a delegation of authority, this is exactly what an agency is expected to do, as long as the agency's resulting rules and orders are consistent with its delegated powers. Congress and state legislatures often will enact measures that they know are ambiguous or insufficiently specified, with the expectation that the administrative agency will supply the clarifying interpretations when it promulgates regulations or adjudicates controversies.

Furthermore, agencies have the authority and responsibility to do more than just resolve ambiguities in the statutes they are charged to administer. Even in the course of implementing unambiguous statutory language, they also have the power to make subsidiary policy decisions, provided once again that their action is consistent with the overall policy established by the legislature. Additionally, from time to time agencies may need to construe, clarify, or otherwise refine their own previously issued regulations.

In all of these contexts, agencies are functioning as interpreters of legal text. But their interpretive role typically has some distinctive features as compared to the judiciary's interpretive role discussed in the immediately previous chapters. In particular, the most trenchant caution about the potential hazards of judicial interpretation—that in the guise of interpretation, courts may usurp the legislative function—is often less potent with respect to agency interpretation. Agencies regularly function in a quasi-legislative fashion, and in fact are expected to function in this way, within established limits and safeguards. Provided that these limits and safeguards have been observed, it may be no complaint that an agency has engaged in policy making, nor can it fairly be said that in doing so it has usurped the legislative role; rather, the agency has done exactly what the legislature tasked the agency to do when the legislature gave it lawmaking power. Furthermore, the agency is most likely to be in harmony with the legislative delegation if the agency is able to predicate its action upon a reasonable understanding of what it is that the legislature (or its key leaders) *intended*. In this sense, agencies arguably are functioning as both the legislature's faithful agents and its cooperative partners, within the sphere of their delegated authority.

Moreover, the interpreting agencies often will have been active, if behind-the-scenes, partners in the statutory drafting process. As a result, it not only may be appropriate (or even necessary) for agencies to identify and understand the legislature's underlying purpose, it also may be easier for them to do so than for courts. Thus, with respect to agency interpretations rendered in furtherance of an agency's delegated authority to implement a statute, the debate between Textualists and Purposivists may have less salience.

Furthermore, agencies exercising their delegated authority may be appropriately influenced—sometimes heavily—by two important factors: their own subject-matter expertise, and their adaptable political accountability. These factors, which deserve brief additional discussion in their own right, make agencies very different kinds of interpreters than courts.

B. TWO IMPORTANT AGENCY "VIRTUES"

In today's complex administrative state, two agency characteristics give agencies certain advantages, as a matter of comparative institutional competency, over either legislatures or courts: their expertise, and their political accountability.

1. AGENCY EXPERTISE

In substantial part, agencies are justified in serving as a cooperative partner of the legislature because agencies possess far greater expertise, expertise that the legislature often specifically seeks to tap. While legislatures prototypically consist of a cadre of generalists who legislate across the complete range of public policy issues, agencies are highly specialized in particular subject matters. Their normal functioning depends upon having a leadership team and a support staff who possess deep knowledge of and experience with their specific subjects.

Across the government bureaucracy, this expertise takes a variety of forms. It can include scientific training, engineering background, foreign policy experience, economic knowledge, military training, public budgeting and finance experience, and any number of other areas in which formal training or practical experience (or both) can be especially valuable. Indeed, one benefit of agency decision-making is that within a single agency, multiple kinds of expertise often can be brought to bear at one time on the same problem. Agencies in turn organize themselves around this expertise, seeking to ensure that they can contribute to whatever policy issues they confront.

The legislature may deliberately employ this expertise in at least three very different ways. One is by charging a particular agency to fill in the gaps of an enacted statute, on the premise that the agency is better suited than the legislature to specify the detailed rules that will best accomplish the legislative aim. A second is to allow the agency to adjudicate the application of the statute and its regulations to specific controversies, on the premise that the agency is better suited than the judicial branch to understand how the rules apply to the relevant facts within the agency's subject matter, especially in a complex or technical field.

A third way is for the legislature to rely on the agency's expertise during the drafting process itself, inviting agency personnel to the table to participate in the development of the statutory text. Indeed, agencies are often the primary behind-the-scenes drafters or architects of legislative measures; in many other cases, agencies may provide an invaluable source of technical assistance. *See* CHRISTOPHER J. WALKER, FEDERAL AGENCIES IN THE LEGISLATIVE PROCESS: TECHNICAL ASSISTANCE IN STATUTORY DRAFTING (2015). With this level of involvement in the legislative process, agencies frequently have an insider's perspective on the legislature's underlying purpose behind its enactment (including whether it is even fair to ascribe a specific purpose to a given legislative action). This perspective has obvious potential relevance to an agency resolving subsequent interpretive issues in both the rulemaking and adjudicatory contexts, provided the agency has a meaningful way to preserve its institutional memory of what transpired during the drafting process.

2. AGENCY POLITICAL ACCOUNTABILITY

A completely different reason that agency interpretation of statutes can be quite unlike judicial interpretation is that many agencies are to some degree politically accountable (though obviously less so than legislatures), in a way that federal courts are not. Executive agencies led by a cabinet secretary appointed by the President or Governor serve at the pleasure of that executive branch leader, and therefore must be politically responsive. To whatever degree these agencies have discretionary authority to fill in policy gaps when implementing and interpreting legislative statutes, they are likely to be mindful of public opinion and of the political impact of their choices. Typically, this is even truer of those state executive agencies that are led by an official who is independently elected in a statewide popular election, rather than one appointed by the Governor.

Courts, in contrast, are expected to make their decisions free from political considerations. In theory this is true even of the many state court judges across the country who must stand for election. Although these judges may be politically accountable for their judicial philosophy and temperament, the ideal of judicial impartiality usually suggests that they are not supposed to be politically accountable for any specific judicial decision, including ones in which they construe and apply a piece of statutory text. Agency officials, however, may very well expect to be indirectly politically accountable for each specific interpretive decision, and therefore to be responsive to the executive branch leaders to whom they report.

The extent to which agency officials are politically accountable for matters of textual interpretation may vary across agencies. For instance, political accountability may matter more for agencies with a single head, such as a cabinet secretary, than for multi-member boards or commissions. And political accountability is generally much more important for agencies within the executive branch than it is for agencies with a high degree of independence from the executive branch, as previously discussed in Chapter 6. The extent to which an agency is influenced by its sense of political accountability for a given issue may also be affected by the extent to which the issue involves technical, scientific, or other kinds of expertise the agency possesses that might trump any other bases for decision.

Of course, most agencies are politically accountable only indirectly, and therefore are not as politically accountable as are legislatures. But this mediated accountability may often allow agencies to be nimble in adapting to changing attitudes. Although some administrative processes are cumbersome, they are generally less cumbersome than the legislative process, and other administrative processes (such as issuing agency policy statements or interpretative rules) can be streamlined or relatively informal. The result is that assigning responsibility to an agency may often permit more efficient responses to new circumstances or concerns.

Moreover, the fact that agencies are more insulated from politics than are legislatures allows them greater leeway to rely on their expertise. Indeed, the idea of political accountability—a notion of public responsiveness, and that agencies might at least in some cases seek to respect public preferences—is potentially in tension with the idea of being guided by expertise—a notion that agencies should make decisions based on facts and expert opinion, not public opinion. Yet expertise and political accountability are both frequently identified as important features of the administrative state (and also, as Chapter 12 will discuss, as reasons for courts sometimes to defer to an agency's interpretation, even if the court might otherwise have reached a different result). In what circumstances political accountability should carry the day, and in what circumstances expert judgment should hold sway, may itself be an important aspect of an agency's discretionary power, except to the extent that a legislative directive may specify the proper basis for a particular agency decision.

C. IMPACT OF EXPERTISE AND POLITICAL ACCOUNTABILITY ON AGENCY ACTION

Administrative agencies' twin institutional competencies of expertise and accountability can be important in both the rulemaking and adjudicatory contexts, as well as in various other ways in which agencies offer guidance about the statutes they are charged with administering.

1. AGENCY RULEMAKING

As discussed in Chapter 6, federal agencies may engage in three distinct types of rulemaking processes under the Administrative Procedure Act: formal on-the-record rulemaking after a live hearing (quite rare today); informal notice-and-comment rulemaking, typically based on a paper record; and the development of interpretative rules, policy statements, and the like. Rulemaking proceedings can take months and even years. During this time, the agency has plenty of opportunity both to assay public opinion and to deepen its own expertise. Rulemaking is a quasi-legislative activity, by which additional legal text is promulgated. These rulemaking processes enhance the democratic legitimacy of the resulting agency regulations.

As part of the rulemaking process, agencies not only determine how to operationalize a legislative directive, but also fill in gaps and interpret ambiguities in legislative enactments. However, in doing so they must function within many more constraints than the legislature. These constraints encompass not only constitutional limits on government activities, including Due Process requirements, but also whatever limits the legislature has imposed through the agency's enabling statutes or other measures (often including requirements of conducting cost-benefit analysis), the limits of any applicable executive branch orders and directives, and the procedural requirements of the Administrative Procedure Act (or state law analogs).

At the federal level, the importance to agency interpretation of advancing the legislative purpose is implicit in the APA requirement that agencies incorporate within the text of their rules a "concise general statement of their basis and purpose." Agencies always tie these statements back to their enabling legislation, articulating a purpose for the rule that traces its pedigree to the congressional purpose and authorization of agency action. But subject to the constraints identified in the preceding paragraph, agencies otherwise have wide latitude to determine for themselves what rules to promulgate, based on their expert evaluation of the evidence in the record, their own evaluation of the public interest, and the legislative purpose to which they must remain faithful under their statutory mandate, consistent with the nondelegation doctrine. Their role as a cooperative partner of the legislature thus subsumes the element of also being its faithful agent, even while having substantial freedom within those limits.

As a normative matter, some recent scholarship has argued that within those limits, agencies are the superior governmental institution to exercise primary responsibility for the interpretation of statutes, largely because of their substantive expertise and democratic legitimacy. *See, e.g.*, William N. Eskridge Jr., *Expanding* Chevron*'s Domain: A Comparative Institutional Analysis of the Relative Competence of Courts and Agencies to Interpret Statutes*, 2013 WIS. L. REV. 411; Kevin M. Stack *Purposivism in the Executive Branch: How Agencies Interpret Statutes*, 109 NW. U. L. REV. 871 (2015). But the beginnings of these arguments about the comparative advantages of agency statutory interpretation trace back at least a quarter century. *See* Peter L. Strauss, *When the Judge Is Not the Primary Official with Responsibility to Read: Agency Interpretation and the Problem of Legislative History*, 66 CHI.-KENT L. REV. 321 (1990).

Recognition of the institutional competence and other advantages that agencies have in construing statutes also has produced an argument for a separate set of interpretive canons to guide agency interpretations. These include, for instance, "interpret to give energy and breadth to all legislative programs within your jurisdiction," "follow presidential directives," "use legislative history as a primary interpretive guide," and "engage in activist lawmaking." *See* Jerry L. Mashaw, *Norms, Practices, and the Paradox of Deference: A Preliminary Inquiry into Agency Statutory Interpretation*, 57 ADMIN. L. REV. 501, 521–23 (2005). To be sure, the advisability of some (or all) of these distinct interpretive tools for agencies is controversial. But all of these interpretive suggestions for agencies might be seen as inappropriate interpretive approaches for courts.

Of course, these arguments over how agencies might approach the interpretive enterprise quite differently from how courts do so are not necessarily reflective of what agencies actually do. As a descriptive matter, empirical research is only just beginning to explore which interpretive tools and approaches agencies in fact rely upon the most when construing statutes. At the federal level, early work suggests that agencies do rely heavily on legislative history materials, as well as on a few textual canons (primarily the Whole Act Rule, the ordinary meaning canon, and the *noscitur a sociis* canon, described in Chapter 9). Agencies also engage in statutory interpretation mindful of the way in which courts may review their work and the circumstances in which courts will most defer to the agency interpretation, as discussed in Chapter 12. *See* Christopher J. Walker, *Inside Agency Statutory Interpretation*, 67 STAN. L. REV. 999 (2015).

2. AGENCY ADJUDICATION

Problems of statutory meaning also regularly arise in the context of agency adjudications. As described briefly in Chapter 6, at the federal level agency adjudicatory processes, both formal and informal, differ dramatically from agency rulemaking processes. Yet agencies have few constraints for deciding which interpretive issues are most appropriate for resolution through the promulgation of an administrative regulation and which through the issuance of an adjudicatory order. As a result, agencies often rely on adjudicatory processes to establish new policies that arise through the agencies' clarification of ambiguities in statutes. *See SEC v. Chenery Corp. (Chenery II)*, 332 U.S. 194 (1947).

Legislatures task agencies with adjudicatory responsibilities in part because of the sheer number of cases that arise under the authority of the statutes and regulations that agencies administer, which would swamp the regular courts. But in many cases, agencies also are tasked with adjudicative responsibilities because agency adjudications may more efficiently produce reasonable outcomes, again because of agencies' institutional competencies. In formal agency adjudications, neutral Administrative Law Judges (ALJs), who are usually independent of the involved agency, are responsible for the vast majority of initial decisions or recommendations. However, the agency itself typically is then free to review the ALJ's determination *de novo*. In so doing, the agency may once again rely upon its own expertise, or be influenced by broader concerns about consistency or democratic legitimacy. Meanwhile, in informal agency adjudications agencies have even greater leeway to rely on these institutional competencies, often subject only to the requirements of Due Process.

As will be discussed in Chapter 12, when courts are called upon to review how an agency has construed a particular piece of statutory text, it usually makes little difference whether the agency interpretation has occurred as part of an adjudication or as part of a rulemaking proceeding. Both are avenues through which agencies adopt official positions regarding what the text means and how the agency will administer and enforce it.

D. AGENCIES' SUBSEQUENT REVISIONS OF INTERPRETATIONS OF STATUTES THEY ADMINISTER (OR THEIR OWN REGULATIONS)

An additional feature of agency interpretation is the flexibility that agencies have to revise how they have interpreted the statutes that they are charged with administering. As discussed in Chapter 7, the principle of *stare decisis* typically has extra strength with respect to judicial interpretations of statutory provisions, because courts are even more reluctant to overturn a statutory precedent than they ordinarily might be to overturn a common law decision or doctrine. By contrast, agencies have great freedom to overturn their previous constructions of statutory meaning.

Of course, it goes almost without saying that Congress should have the ability to revise its own handiwork; indeed, updating the law is a core legislative function. Agencies may also be able to make important contributions in this regard (within the accepted limits of the nondelegation doctrine), whether in response to changing public and political views, or in response to new information developed or evaluated by the agency experts. Agencies therefore not only are allowed to revise their own regulations (consistent with APA rulemaking requirements, which generally mean an agency must follow the same process to revise a rule that it used to promulgate it, *see Perez v. Mortgage Bankers Ass'n*, 575 U.S. ___, 135 S. Ct. 1199 (2015)), but also in many circumstances may be expected to do so when a regulation interpreting a statute has become outmoded.

A related but distinct feature of agency interpretation is that agencies have substantial latitude to interpret (or reinterpret) their own regulations whenever those regulations themselves have ambiguity in them. As Chapter 12 also will discuss, reviewing courts will generally uphold an agency's subsequent interpretation or reinterpretation of the agency's own rule unless the interpretation is "plainly erroneous or inconsistent with the regulation." *Auer v. Robbins*, 519 U.S. 452, 461 (1997). This is a highly permissive standard of judicial review, giving the agency great freedom to operate dynamically within the space delegated to it by Congress. Some commentators, including Justices Thomas and Alito and the late Justice Scalia, have worried that giving agencies this degree of interpretive freedom will encourage an agency to promulgate vague or ambiguous rules in the first instance, in order for the agency then to have more freedom when opportunities arise to interpret that regulation. Nevertheless, this remains the governing standard, as enforced through doctrines of judicial review to be discussed further in Chapter 12.

As also discussed further in Chapter 12, on occasion an agency may have the ability to re-interpret a statutory provision that a *court* has previously interpreted. *See National Cable & Telecommunications Ass'n v. Brand X Internet Services*, 545 U.S. 967 (2005). This power to have an agency interpretation displace a judicial interpretation is a dramatic feature that goes to the heart of agency delegation and judicial review thereof. It allows an agency in certain circumstances to undo a judicial construction of a statute that the agency is charged with administering even when the court itself would be unlikely to alter that construction because of the principle of *stare decisis*. Thus, in multiple respects this principle of adhering to past precedents may have a substantially different impact on agency interpretations than it generally has on court interpretations.

E. PRESUMPTION OF REVIEWABILITY

Finally, before turning to Chapter 12 and its consideration of how courts review agency interpretations of statutes and regulations, a threshold question lurks: Which agency interpretations are judicially reviewable, and which are not?

At the federal level, when Congress delegates rulemaking or adjudicatory authority to an agency,

Congress is free to specify whether or not the agency's use of that authority is subject to judicial review. Congress occasionally does so by including in a statute a preclusion of judicial review of specified agency actions, as for instance in a Department of Veterans' Affairs statute which provides that "the decisions of [the agency] on any question of law or fact under any law administered by the Veterans Administration providing benefits for veterans and their dependents or survivors shall be final and conclusive and no other official or any court of the United States shall have power or jurisdiction to review any such decision." 38 U.S.C. § 211(a); *see Johnson v. Robison*, 415 U.S. 361 (1974). Additionally, under the Administrative Procedure Act, certain agency actions may be unreviewable if they are "committed to agency discretion by law." 5 U.S.C. § 701(a)(2); *see Webster v. Doe*, 486 U.S. 592 (1988).

Often, however, a statute may be silent or ambiguous about whether a particular agency action is reviewable. For these circumstances, the Supreme Court has construed the Administrative Procedure Act to create a presumption that agency actions will be reviewable, absent strong evidence that Congress intended otherwise. *See Citizens to Preserve Overton Park v. Volpe*, 401 U.S. 402 (1971); *Abbott Laboratories v. Gardner*, 387 U.S. 136 (1967). Although at one time this standard required "clear and convincing evidence" that Congress intended to insulate an agency action from judicial review, the Court relaxed this standard somewhat in *Block v. Community Nutrition Board*, 467 U.S. 340 (1984).

Block listed five ways of establishing congressional intent to preclude judicial review: (1) clear statutory text; (2) specific legislative history; (3) a judicial interpretation to which Congress has acquiesced; (4) the collective impact of legislative history and judicial construction; and (5) inferences drawn from the statute as a whole.

When any of those factors persuades a court that an agency's authority to act is unreviewable, the agency becomes the final interpreter, even of legal meaning. Yet when what is at stake is the legal meaning of the words of a legislative enactment, courts are unlikely to find that the five *Block* factors overcome the presumption of reviewability. Instead, judicial review will likely be available, with the key question becoming just how much deference the reviewing court should grant to the agency's interpretation of a statute that it is charged with administering. Chapter 12 will now explore how courts conduct review in such cases.

CHAPTER 12

JUDICIAL REVIEW OF AGENCY INTERPRETATIONS

This Nutshell concludes with a chapter dedicated to one of the most important and difficult questions in the field of statutory interpretation: How should courts oversee or review the way in which administrative agencies interpret statutory text? In part, the question of the scope and relevant standards of judicial review of agency interpretation is important because of just how many laws today are interpreted and applied by the administrative state. But in addition to the widespread impact that the answer to this question will have, it is particularly important because it concerns the relationship among all three of the coordinate branches of American representative democracy. The legislative branch passes a law, but leaves to executive branch departments and agencies (whether deliberately or inadvertently) many elements of the statute's administration and enforcement, including ascertaining the statute's meaning in particular cases. Some of those administrative interpretations eventually come before the judicial branch for review. Reviewing courts then must decide how much to defer to the agency's determination, whether because of the agency's general expertise, its specific familiarity with the statute in question, its political accountability, or the legislature's explicit or implicit delegation of authority to it.

The question is a difficult one in part because it takes a basic problem of statutory interpretation and adds a second layer to it. It no longer is a simple question of what a reviewing court thinks the meaning of the statutory text is, but instead it becomes a question of what the reviewing court thinks of the administrative agency's interpretation. Thus, interpretation becomes a collective process, if not quite a collaborative one. It is also difficult because courts have struggled mightily to develop a consistent approach to this problem, particularly at the federal level.

Although this struggle is ongoing, in the federal system certain fundamental principles have emerged. These include the *Chevron* doctrine, which in certain contexts calls for judicial deference to the reasonable interpretations of agencies, on the basis of their expertise and democratic accountability, in light of either express or implied congressional delegations to them; secondary doctrines about when the *Chevron* doctrine applies; a set of other doctrines for various circumstances to which the *Chevron* doctrine does not apply; and the underlying principle that Congress retains ultimate control over the meaning of its enactments and the circumstances in which it allows agencies to be its partners in clarifying that meaning. Meanwhile, state level doctrine is different, generally granting agency interpretations far less deference.

This chapter offers an overview of each of these principles, acknowledging that the contemporary jurisprudence of judicial review of agency interpretations remains complex and fluid.

A. THE *CHEVRON* DECISION

In the federal system, the *Chevron* doctrine occupies the central position in contemporary discourse about how courts should review agency interpretations of statutes. This doctrine takes its name from the 1984 U.S. Supreme Court decision in *Chevron, U.S.A., Inc. v. Natural Resources Defense Council, Inc.*, 467 U.S. 837 (1984). In its thirty-year life-span, *Chevron* has become the most widely cited Supreme Court administrative law decision and the focus of an almost countless number of articles and analyses. Before considering the impact that the *Chevron* decision has had, it is important to understand both the basic interpretive question at issue in this case, and the Court's approach to its resolution.

1. STATUTORY ISSUE AND AGENCY TREATMENT

As amended in 1977, the federal Clean Air Act required "major stationary sources" of air pollution (not vehicles, in other words, whose emissions are governed by other federal laws), to meet new limitations on their emissions in states that had not yet attained previously established national air quality standards. In the nonattainment states, these limits applied both to newly constructed sources, and to modifications of existing sources if the modifications increased the emissions of air pollutants; the new limits did not otherwise require retrofitting of existing sources of air pollution.

The problem was that the act did not define what amounted to a "source." Did the term mean each device or apparatus that emitted a pollutant, or did the term mean each industrial plant, even if it might have multiple sources of emissions within it? If each smokestack were a "source," then every new smokestack, whether it simply replaced an existing apparatus or was part of an addition of new equipment to the facility, would have to meet the standards of the 1977 Amendments. But if each plant were a source, then a new smokestack or apparatus could be added without having to meet the new standards as long as some other source of pollution within the plant was eliminated (or its emissions reduced) so as to offset the new smokestack's emissions. Similarly, an existing smokestack could be replaced as long as the replacement did not increase total emissions from the entire facility. In effect, the plant-wide definition of "source" imagined a bubble over the facility, with one final smokestack, or "source" of pollution, coming off the top.

The Clean Air Act charged the Environmental Protection Agency (EPA) with administering the Act. Throughout the 1970s, in a series of rulemaking proceedings, the EPA had resisted industry calls to adopt a "bubble" definition of "stationary source" for all purposes of the Act (although the EPA had used the bubble concept for other purposes of the Act unrelated to the 1977 Amendments). But in 1981, under the deregulatory policies of the Reagan Administration, the EPA reconsidered its approach and issued a regulation adopting the plant-wide bubble definition for all purposes. The Natural Resources Defense Council and others then challenged this regulation as inconsistent with the language and purpose of the 1977 Amendments.

2. THE SUPREME COURT DECISION

Writing a unanimous 6–0 decision for the Court (with three justices not participating), Justice Stevens upheld the EPA's "bubble" regulation. In terms of its key doctrine, the opinion specified that the judiciary's role when it "reviews an agency's construction of the statute which it administers" involves two distinct steps: At what has become known as **Step One**, the court must determine, using what a footnote in the opinion called "traditional tools" of statutory interpretation, if the statute is ambiguous or silent with respect to the agency's challenged construction. The Court phrased this question as **"whether Congress has directly spoken to the precise question at issue."** If Congress has spoken, the reviewing court does not reach the second step; instead, "that is the end of the matter, for the court, as well as the agency, must give effect to the unambiguously expressed intent of Congress."

If, however, the court concludes that Congress has been silent or ambiguous on the interpretive question, the court moves to the next step. At **Step Two**, the court must determine **"whether the agency's answer is based on a permissible construction of the statute."** The *Chevron* opinion alternatively phrased this inquiry as "whether [the agency's view] is a reasonable one." If it is a reasonable or permissible construction, then under the *Chevron* doctrine a reviewing court is to uphold the agency's interpretation.

Since the *Chevron* decision, questions have emerged about when the *Chevron* framework even applies. Furthermore, many subsidiary questions have arisen out of each of the two steps identified in the *Chevron* opinion. The beginning of finding answers to these questions is to consider the way in which the Court applied these two steps to the EPA's "bubble" regulation in the *Chevron* opinion itself.

With respect to the Step One question, the opinion concluded that neither the text of the Clean Air Act

Amendments at issue, nor the legislative history of those amendments, answered the question of what a "major stationary source" was. (The opinion called the text neither "precisely directed" at the issue nor "dispositive," and the legislative history "unilluminating"). Instead, the Court simply found that the legislative history was "consistent with the view that the EPA should have broad discretion in implementing the policies of the 1977 Amendments." As for those policies, the Court found evidence in the legislative history that Congress had been concerned with both improving air quality in nonattainment states and fostering private industry's ability to make capital improvements at industrial facilities, and had sought some accommodation of these competing interests through the 1977 Amendments. But because "Congress did not actually have an intent regarding the applicability of the bubble concept," the Court concluded that it was up to the agency to adopt a permissible construction of the statute. So the Court moved to Step Two.

With respect to the Step Two question of whether the EPA's construction was reasonable, the Court was not at all troubled by the fact that the EPA had changed its position. As the opinion noted, prior to 1981, the EPA's regulations would have treated each smokestack as a stationary source for purposes of the 1977 Amendments. But as part of a new presidential administration's effort to reduce "regulatory burdens and complexities," the EPA had reevaluated its interpretation of the 1977 Amendments and adopted the bubble concept for all purposes of the Act. The Court described this reversal as justified by the results of an APA rulemaking proceeding concerning a "technical and complex" regulatory scheme. Moreover, the EPA was able to offer a "reasonable explanation" of its conclusion, explaining that adopting the bubble concept would serve both the environmental and economic objectives that Congress, without specifying exactly how, had "intended to accommodate."

The opinion might have ended at that point. Instead, however, Justice Stevens went on to distinguish the role of agencies from the role of courts in matters of statutory interpretation. First, he wrote that the EPA's resolution of the interpretive problem here was entitled to judicial deference regardless of whether Congress: (1) "consciously desired" the EPA to use its greater expertise concerning air pollution to reach an accommodation among the conflicting interests, or (2) "simply did not consider the question at this level," or (3) "was unable to forge a coalition . . . [and] each side decided to take their chances" with the agency's resolution. He then went on to observe that while courts may sometimes be required to "reconcile competing political interests," they must do so "not on the basis of the judges' personal policy preferences." In contrast, an agency may "properly rely on the incumbent administration's views of wise policy," as long as it acts within the scope of legislatively delegated authority. Accordingly, "federal judges—who have no constituency—have a duty to respect legitimate policy choices made by those who do."

Many commentators believe that Justice Stevens, and the Court for whom he wrote, had neither anticipated how important this declaration would become, nor even seen it as a break from the past. But the *Chevron* decision was to mark a significant shift in the way that courts treat and perceive agencies, as discussed next.

B. *CHEVRON* IN CONTEXT

In order to situate *Chevron* properly, it is helpful to know a little about the principal doctrines of judicial review of agency construction that had preceded *Chevron*, as well as how these doctrines continue to have some relevance after *Chevron*. Two cases from forty years before *Chevron* figure most prominently here.

1. *NLRB v. HEARST PUBLICATIONS*

In *National Labor Relations Board v. Hearst Publications*, 322 U.S. 111 (1944), the Supreme Court considered the interpretive issue of whether the term "employee" in the National Labor Relations Act (NLRA) encompassed "newsboys" who purchased newspapers on credit from the publishers and then resold them on the street at a price set by the publishers. The newsboys, whose compensation was the difference between the newspapers' purchase price and their sale price, desired to unionize and engage in collective bargaining under the NLRA. Although the publishers argued that the newsboys were not covered by the NLRA because they were independent contractors, not employees, the

National Labor Relations Board (NLRB) had treated the newsboys as employees and ordered the publishers to engage in collective bargaining with the newsboys' union.

When the Board's order came before the Court for review, the Court first answered what it saw as the purely legal question of whether the term "employee" in the Act should take its common-law sense, under which the newsboys would surely have been independent contractors rather than employees. The Court answered this question in the negative, and then turned to what it saw as a highly fact-dependent question of whether the term "employee," once untethered from its common-law meaning, applied to these newsboys. With respect to that issue, the Court found solace in the fact that Congress had created an agency to administer the NLRA—the National Labor Relations Board—and had assigned to it the task of determining "who is an employee under the Act." The Court observed that the Board's "everyday experience in the administration of the statute gives it familiarity with the circumstances and backgrounds of employment relationships in various industries," as well as with the extent to which the statute's collective bargaining provisions were well-suited to any given employment circumstance. The Court wrote that "the Board's determination that specified persons are 'employees' under this Act is to be accepted if it has 'warrant in the record' and a reasonable basis in law." *Id.* at 130–31.

Here was a theory of judicial review of agency interpretation that, very much like *Chevron*, depended on the Court first addressing, *de novo*, a purely legal question about what the statute meant, and then, if answering that question did not resolve the issue, deferring to the agency's resolution of the issue, provided it was reasonable. Furthermore, like *Chevron*, the Court's basis for deferring to the agency depended heavily on the fact that Congress had "assigned" to the NLRB the responsibility, as part of its regular "administrative routine," to determine to what employment relationships the NLRA applied. However, unlike *Chevron*, the Court articulated the key difference between these two questions not in terms of whether or not Congress had clearly spoken to the issue, but in terms of the difference between questions of pure law, appropriate for judicial resolution, and "mixed" questions of law and fact, more appropriate for agency resolution in light of the agency's role and experience.

In particular, mixed questions depend on "a specific application of a broad statutory term," with respect to which "the reviewing court's function is limited," as long as the agency's application has support in the record and is reasonable. In contrast, under *Chevron*, deference to the agency's resolution of the Step Two question did not depend on its being a mixed question of the application of law to fact. Rather, the *Chevron* Step Two question of whether the agency's construction is "permissible" or "reasonable" could involve an interpretive question of pure law, and still merit judicial deference. Nevertheless, *Hearst Publications* laid the foundation for the *Chevron* rule that courts should accept reasonable agency interpretations of interpretive questions that Congress had not directly addressed.

2. *SKIDMORE v. SWIFT*

A few months after *Hearst Publications*, the Court in *Skidmore v. Swift & Co.,* 323 U.S. 134 (1944), considered whether company employees serving at a company fire hall were entitled to overtime compensation under the Fair Labor Standards Act (FLSA) for their hours on-call when not attending to alarms. This time, the case came to the Court not from an agency decision but from a suit initiated in federal district court. As in *Hearst Publications*, this case again presented a "mixed" question of the application of law to fact. The record before the Court included informal rulings, an interpretive bulletin, and an *amicus curiae* brief of the Wage and Hour Division of the Department of Labor. In denying the employees' request for overtime compensation, the district court had disregarded these agency views as inconsistent with its understanding of the FLSA.

In contrast to its approach to the agency views before it in *Hearst Publications*, the Supreme Court suggested that no judicial deference to the agency conclusions expressed in *Skidmore* was required because Congress had not given the Wage and Hour Division authority to adjudicate violations of the FLSA, and accordingly the agency's expression of its views had occurred only in several non-binding interpretations. Nevertheless, the Court concluded that these agency views were entitled to "respect," and "constitute a body of experience and informed judgment to which courts and litigants may properly resort for guidance." In its critical passage, the Court's opinion continued: "The weight of [an agency] judgment in a particular case will depend on the thoroughness evident in its consideration, the validity of its reasoning, its consistency with earlier and later pronouncements, and all those factors which give it power to persuade, if lacking power to control." *Id.* at 140. The Court remanded the case to the courts below for reconsideration.

Thus *Skidmore*, like *Hearst Publications*, again suggested that how much weight courts should afford an agency's construction of mixed questions of law and fact would turn at least in important part on whether Congress had given the agency some formal authority over the interpretive issue. But *Skidmore* quickly gave rise to criticism that it was not clear what it meant for a reviewing court to show "respect" to nonbinding agency interpretations. It seemed to mean something more than merely showing the type of respect that a reviewing court might afford to any persuasive analysis of the issue before it, but how much more?

3. FROM *SKIDMORE* TO *CHEVRON*

Over time, federal courts in the pre-*Chevron* era came to rely on something of a sliding scale, in which the extent to which a reviewing court would defer to an agency's interpretation of a statute it was charged with administering would depend on the cumulative impact of a range of factors. These factors included not only those outlined in *Skidmore*, but also such other factors as precisely how much rulemaking or adjudicatory power Congress had given the agency; whether the agency's position was contemporaneous with the statute's enactment; how technical and complex the interpretive issue was; whether Congress had acquiesced in an agency's previous construction of a statute; and the extent to which following the agency interpretation would promote uniformity in the law. Furthermore, a multi-factor approach also came to characterize the courts' approach to the questions of whether it was reasonable to assume that Congress had intended to give an agency formal lawmaking powers, or that Congress likely would have expected the courts to defer to the agency.

For instance, in *General Electric Co. v. Gilbert*, 429 U.S. 125 (1976), the Supreme Court refused to defer to a guideline of the Equal Employment Opportunity Commission (which Congress had charged with helping to administer provisions of Title VII of the Civil Rights Act of 1964) that classified pregnancy-based discrimination as discrimination on the basis of sex, in violation of Title VII. Two factors of particular importance to the Court in discounting the EEOC's guideline were that (1) Congress had not given the EEOC authority to promulgate binding regulations, and (2) the EEOC had changed its position, so that its challenged guideline "flatly contradicts" the EEOC's own initial conclusion, reached much closer in time to the passage of Title VII, that pregnancy-based discrimination was not a violation of Title VII. As a result, the EEOC guideline "does not receive high marks" under the *Skidmore* standard, the Court wrote. In response, Congress then passed the Pregnancy Discrimination Act.

Meanwhile, in specialized contexts—for instance in matters of foreign affairs—the Supreme Court has sometimes created a special deference regime. Thus, a few years before *Skidmore*, the Supreme Court in *United States v. Curtiss-Wright Export Corp.*, 299 U.S. 304 (1936), showed tremendous deference to an executive branch construction of a congressional joint resolution (a measure equivalent to a statute) concerning the Chaco War then occurring between Bolivia and Paraguay. The Court upheld the President's declaration, made pursuant to the joint resolution, of an embargo on arms sales to South American countries, in part because of the President's constitutional role as the country's "sole representative with foreign nations." *Id.* at 319.

Finally, settled pre-*Chevron* doctrine was that reviewing courts would show no deference to an agency interpretation of a statute if the statute's meaning was "plain" to the reviewing court using traditional interpretive tools. But otherwise, by the time of *Chevron*, the standards for judicial review of agency interpretations were seen by many as somewhat incoherent. The *Chevron* decision then seemed, at least initially, to supersede the multi-factor sliding scale of deference that had grown up since *Skidmore*, and to return to something more like a clear rule-based approach, analogous to *Hearst Publications*. Indeed, the Court's *Chevron* opinion had described *Hearst Publications* as one of several key precedents establishing "well-settled principles" of judicial review of agency interpretation.

C. THE *CHEVRON* DOCTRINE

As previously noted, the *Chevron* opinion has become the most cited Supreme Court administrative law decision. Although in part this reflects the vast number of administrative interpretations that are the subjects of judicial review, at least two other factors help explain the *Chevron* opinion's continuing influence. One is its discussion of the comparative institutional advantages that agencies have over courts in certain aspects of statutory interpretation. The other is its articulation of a clear two-step framework for evaluating agency interpretations.

Well beyond the immediate decision, *Chevron* has spawned a cottage industry of analysis and reflection by academics, jurists, and practitioners, all striving to contribute to the jurisprudence of statutory interpretation and agency discretion. Several distinct questions have arisen concerning both Step One and Step Two. Meanwhile, questions about the threshold determination of whether a particular instance of agency statutory construction is even suited to the *Chevron* doctrine have given rise to the idea of a *Chevron* "Step Zero."

1. QUESTIONS ABOUT *CHEVRON* STEP ONE

An initial question is whether analytically the *Chevron* doctrine in fact involves only one step. That is, should the Step One question of "whether Congress has directly spoken to the precise question at issue" be understood as really just a specific inquiry relevant to answering the Step Two question of "whether the agency's view is reasonable"? If Congress has directly spoken to the issue, then under Step Two alone, any agency interpretation that departs from what Congress has said would be unreasonable, and not permissible. On this analysis, the sole *Chevron* question that a reviewing court needs to ask is the Step Two question of whether the agency's construction is a reasonable or permissible one. *See Entergy Corp. v. Riverkeeper*, 556 U.S. 208, 218 n.4 (2009).

Nevertheless, most courts invoking the *Chevron* doctrine continue to apply it in two distinct steps, first exploring as an independent inquiry whether Congress has clearly spoken to the interpretive question at issue or instead has left the issue for the agency to decide (within the limits of reasonableness). In large part the persistence of this first step of analysis may reflect the lingering influence of *Hearst Publications* and the desire to distinguish the judicial role of declaring what the law is (Step One) from the agency role of interpreting and applying that law to specific circumstances within its delegated authority, subject to judicially enforceable APA constraints (Step Two). It also may simply reflect how difficult it frequently can be for courts to resolve the Step One inquiry of whether or not Congress has directly spoken to the issue.

Indeed, how to determine at Step One the pure law question of whether Congress has directly spoken has engendered its own controversies, even though (or perhaps because) this question looks very much like the same one that courts have long addressed when interpreting statutes generally: Has the legislature made the statute's textual meaning clear? The familiar battle over Textualist versus Purposivist interpretation thus also continues to rage in the *Chevron* Step One context.

To some, the Step One requirement of determining whether Congress has directly spoken to the precise question at issue suggested a search for *textual* clarity. On this inquiry, Step One might be concerned only with whether Congress has "directly spoken" through the statute's text. Unsurprisingly, Justice Scalia adhered to this view. *See, e.g., I.N.S. v. Cardozo-Fonseca*, 480 U.S. 421 (1987). But this approach to Step One was certainly not compelled by the *Chevron* decision, which itself had relied on the legislative history of the 1977 Clean Air Act Amendments to resolve its Step One issue. Nevertheless, other courts occasionally thought of Step One as best resolved without resort to legislative history. *See, e.g., Bankers Life & Casualty Co. v. United States*, 142 F.3d 973, 983 (7th Cir. 1998) ("While this circuit has examined legislative history during the first step of *Chevron* . . . , we now seem to lean toward reserving consideration of legislative history and other appropriate factors until the second *Chevron* step."). This was never a widespread approach to Step One, however, and most courts have continued to use extrinsic aids (as discussed in Chapter 10) as part of the "traditional tools" of interpretation that *Chevron* approved for determining whether Congress had directly spoken to the issue.

One familiar intrinsic interpretive tool that has additional impact in the *Chevron* context is the canon of constitutional avoidance. The constitutional concern embodied in the otherwise moribund nondelegation doctrine (see Chapter 6) may in fact find life in at least some instances of Step One ambiguity, encouraging courts to construe the scope of delegated agency authority more narrowly to avoid raising a concern about an excessive delegation. For instance, in what is known as the Benzene Case, the Supreme Court reviewed a benzene exposure safety standard promulgated by the Department of Labor under the Occupational Safety and Health Act (OSHA). At issue was the scope of congressionally delegated authority to promulgate occupational safety standards "reasonably necessary or appropriate to provide safe or healthful employment or places of employment." Although the government contended that this delegation empowered the Department to promulgate any regulation reasonably calculated to improve workplace safety, the Court concluded that such sweeping power "might be unconstitutional" under the nondelegation doctrine. To avoid confronting this question, the Court construed the delegation to permit the Department to regulate "only where a significant risk of harm exists." *Industrial Union Department, AFL-CIO v. American Petroleum Institute*, 448 U.S. 607, 646, 652 (1980).

Meanwhile, a number of additional interpretive presumptions that are sometimes applied to reduce Step One ambiguity have been classified as a set of "nondelegation canons." These presumptions, many of which derive from the substantive canons of interpretation discussed above in Chapter 9, function to reign in the amount of authority that an agency might otherwise enjoy. *See, e.g.*, Cass R. Sunstein, *Nondelegation Canons*, 67 U. CHI. L. REV. 315 (2000). Some of these presumptions are briefly outlined in section D below.

As suggested by the deployment of the nondelegation canon and various substantive presumptions, another complication at Step One is that if courts can use all the traditional interpretive tools, in theory they might always be able to find a clear meaning, even for what may have appeared to be an ambiguous provision when considering the text alone. Indeed, on at least some interpretive theories, that is the purpose behind these tools—to allow the interpreter to identify the correct meaning with confidence. In that event, traditional statutory interpretation at Step One might lead to reaching Step Two only rarely. Even Textualists, relying on a more limited set of tools, might be prone to find a clear textual meaning. Justice Scalia had suggested something to this effect, observing that when reviewing agency interpretations, Textualists like himself are less likely to find ambiguity in the statutory text, and therefore are less likely to proceed to Step Two. *See* Antonin Scalia, *Judicial Deference to Administration Interpretations of Law*, 1989 DUKE L. J. 511; *see also INS v. Cardoza-Fonseca*, 480 U.S.

421 (1987); *EEOC v. Aramco*, 499 U.S. 244 (1991); *Christensen v. Harris Cty.*, 529 U.S. 576 (2000).

Furthermore, the Textualist versus Purposivist debate at Step One potentially involves an additional element not present in the analogous debate over matters of pure judicial interpretation of statutes. Some commentators have observed that an agency's position on the meaning of a statutory provision might itself be a relevant indicator of legislative intent, perhaps even a good indicator, for the reasons that the *Chevron* opinion offered to justify deferring to the agency at Step Two. That is, the agency's experience with the subject, often including the agency's participation in the legislative drafting process, may make it uniquely familiar with the statutory scheme, while at the same time the agency's political accountability also may help the agency better understand the underlying legislative intent. Of course, most Textualists reject this additional extrinsic source of interpretive guidance in resolving the Step One inquiry.

MCI v. AT&T. An important example of the tension between interpretive approaches at Step One is *MCI Telecommunications Corp. v. AT&T,* 512 U.S. 218 (1994), discussed previously in Chapter 7. At issue was whether the Federal Communications Commission (FCC) had the statutory authority to exempt "nondominant" providers of long distance telecommunications services from certain tariff filing requirements under section 203 of the Communications Act of 1934. That Act, enacted in an era when AT&T had long been the only provider of communications services, created a regulatory structure designed to ensure that rates for those services were "reasonable and nondiscriminatory." But in the 1980s, shortly after many "nondominant" providers had become competitors of AT&T in the late 1970s, the Commission had adopted a rule that made tariff filing optional for these nondominant providers. The Commission had relied on a provision of section 203, the tariff filing section, that gave it authority to "modify any requirement" of that section. AT&T argued that the FCC rule had not just "modified" the tariff requirement, but had effectively repealed it with respect to all carriers beside AT&T.

In a majority opinion by Justice Scalia, the Court agreed with AT&T and rejected the Commission's rule at *Chevron* Step One. The Court concluded that "modify" had a clear, *narrow* meaning of "to change moderately or in a minor fashion." The Court based this conclusion almost entirely upon various dictionary definitions of the term "modify," from both the present day and the time of enactment. After canvassing these definitions, the Court wrote: "We have not the slightest doubt that [the narrow meaning of modify] is the meaning the statute intended." *Id.* at 228. At that point, under the *Chevron* framework all that remained was for the Court to decide that the Commission's rule did not amount to a moderate or minor change of the section 203 requirement, and that it therefore was beyond the Commission's statutorily delegated authority.

In dissent, Justice Stevens asserted that the meaning of the term "modify," as used in section 203, was in fact ambiguous, and that the case therefore raised a *Chevron* Step Two question. With respect to this question, the dissenting opinion concluded that the Commission's rule was a reasonable application of its section 203 authority to modify any requirement of the tariff filing provision, in light of the changed economics in the industry. But the dissent is more important for its quite different approach to the Step One inquiry than the majority opinion's approach.

Although Justice Stevens also employed his own dictionary definitions, he cautioned that dictionaries "are no substitute for close analysis of what words mean as used in a particular statutory context." *Id.* at 240. In that regard, he considered the effects of the tariff filing requirements on AT&T's new competitors, and the apparently *de minimis* impact on the long-distance telecommunications industry of eliminating those tariff filing requirements. Those competitors had not existed when the 1934 act was passed, when AT&T had what the majority opinion acknowledged was a "virtual monopoly" on telephone service. Justice Stevens relied directly on the FCC's own explanations and analysis that, in light of the dramatic increase in competition within the industry, exempting nondominant carriers from the tariff filing requirement would do almost nothing to alter section 203's ability to fulfill its purpose of constraining monopoly power. In other words, the FCC's new rule was, on this way of understanding things, in fact only a minor modification. But all of Justice Stevens' argument to this effect was directed only to making the Step One point that Congress had not made the meaning of "modify" clear, leaving the Court to proceed to Step Two.

Several key questions emerge from these contrasting opinions in *MCI*. One is whether extrinsic sources of interpretation can be helpful, not to clarify an apparently ambiguous provision, but to reveal that a provision which appears to have a clear meaning actually may not be so clear. Another is to what extent a reviewing court might properly take the agency's own views and analysis into account at Step One, as part of determining whether Congress has made the meaning of the statutory text clear.

The Court's approach in *MCI* might suggest that the judicial branch should avoid construing broadly worded statutes *too* broadly. This reading is perhaps analogous to a presumption against allowing Congress to delegate too much authority to agencies. This approach departs from the basic *Chevron* principle of deferring to agencies because Congress expected it, suggesting that this delegation principle has limits when questions of great significance are at issue, at least if the intended delegation is not unmistakably clear. Thus, the approach in *MCI* arguably amounts to something of an implicit nondelegation presumption in "extraordinary" cases or cases that raise "major questions." See subsection D.9 below.

2. QUESTIONS ABOUT *CHEVRON* STEP TWO

At Step Two, the *Chevron* doctrine functions like a presumption that Congress has intended to delegate lawmaking authority to an agency whenever

Congress has not spoken specifically or clearly enough. The basis for this presumption is that the agency's resolution is preferable to the judiciary's, for any of several reasons, alone or in combination. In addition to the two previously mentioned notions of the agency's political accountability and expertise, other arguments for deferring to an agency sometimes include the agency's greater efficiency at developing national uniformity and consistency on an issue, and the agency's ability to adapt dynamically to changed circumstances.

Notably, the *Chevron* rationale did not require that the agency either rely upon its potentially superior expertise in resolving a given interpretive problem, or demonstrate any political accountability with respect to the interpretation in question. Nor did *Chevron* itself even require that the agency show that Congress had intended the agency to resolve the interpretive issue. Indeed, that itself is the critical presumption of *Chevron* Step Two, once the meaning of the statute is not clear at Step One. Thus, when *Chevron* Step Two is employed, the resulting judicial deference is independent of whether the agency in fact has capitalized on the agency's institutional competencies in resolving the particular interpretive problem. So once courts reach Step Two, the result in practice has been a highly deferential judicial willingness to accept with little questioning any reasonable construction of the statutory terms at issue.

Although the *Chevron* doctrine does not require the reviewing court to ascertain whether the agency actually in some way relied upon its greater expertise or its greater political accountability, commentators have raised alternative questions about whether some relatively crude proxy for these inquiries might be appropriate. These questions include, in particular: (1) whether *Chevron* deference is less appropriate for independent agencies, because they are less politically accountable; and (2) whether *Chevron* deference is less appropriate with respect to an interpretive issue for which expertise is less relevant than for an issue for which expertise is crucial. Although the U.S. Supreme Court has never explicitly modified the *Chevron* doctrine to incorporate factors like these, commentators have wondered whether they may sometimes be at play *sub silentio* in cases in which the Court has reviewed agency interpretations without mentioning *Chevron*. Thus, one Step Two question is whether *Chevron* deference is, or should be, more appropriate for those agencies with greater expertise or more political accountability.

A related Step Two question is whether, in order for the reviewing court to sustain the agency's interpretation as reasonable, the agency needs to have conducted an adequate process when deciding how to construe the statute. *See, e.g., Gonzales v. Oregon*, 546 U.S. 243 (2006) (rejecting one of agency's several proffered interpretive justifications because agency did not follow statutorily prescribed procedures). Here, judicial review of the agency's statutory interpretation also could implicate review under the Administrative Procedure Act, thus raising the question of whether there is a difference between a court reviewing the "reasonableness" of an agency interpretation at *Chevron* Step Two, and a court reviewing the arbitrariness of an agency action under section 706 of the APA (see Chapter 6). In a 2016 decision, the Supreme Court announced that it would not extend *Chevron* deference to an agency rule that resulted from a "defective" procedure, including failing to give adequate reasons for a rule under the *State Farm* decision discussed in Chapter 6. *See Encino Motorcars, LLC v. Navarro*, 579 U.S. ___, 136 S. Ct. 2117 (2015).

Many commentators have wrestled more generally with questions of how to reconcile or integrate APA review with *Chevron* Step Two deference. Arguably, APA review is more about process—especially **the facts** that this process is expected to bring to the agency's attention to support its decision—while *Chevron* Step Two is more about the reasonableness of the resulting interpretation of **the law.** Some observers have noted, somewhat critically, that with respect to APA review, the *State Farm* decision seems to say that courts need not be reflexively deferential to an agency's policy decisions, but instead should give them a "hard look." In contrast, with respect to an agency's interpretation of the legal meaning of ambiguous statutory language, *Chevron* tells courts to defer to any reasonable construction that the agency chooses. Arguably, these standards reverse what might be a more natural set of deference principles, in which agency expertise and accountability would justify deferring to almost any reasonable policy choices, while it would remain the judiciary's role to establish the legal meaning of a statutory provision. The primary explanation for this counterintuitive approach, once again, is the presumption that Congress intended to delegate interpretive authority to the agency.

The high degree of deference that a *Chevron* analysis affords agencies means that courts have only rarely invalidated an agency interpretation as unreasonable at Step Two. One recent study of federal circuit court cases found that agencies prevail more than 90% of the time at Step Two; in the U.S. Supreme Court agency losses at Step Two have been even more unusual. But in a significant development, in *Michigan v. Environmental Protection Agency*, 576 U.S. ___, 135 S. Ct. 2699 (2015), the Supreme Court in a 5–4 decision invalidated as unreasonable an Environmental Protection Agency's regulation of power plant pollution. The underlying statute had given EPA the authority to regulate power plant emissions if the agency determined that regulation was "reasonable and necessary," a standard that the Court acknowledged was very broad. Nevertheless, as discussed above in Chapter 6, the Court concluded at Step Two that the agency's interpretation was not a permissible one because the agency construed the phrase not to require the agency to consider the costs of regulation. Not only was this a rare example of a Step Two invalidation, but the holding (that it was impermissible for EPA to exclude cost considerations from its determination of what was "reasonable and necessary") has the potential to affect many other agencies and rulemakings.

Another Step Two question is how important or relevant traditional tools of statutory interpretation should be to the agency's interpretive process, if the point of *Chevron* is to permit the agency to use its expertise and accountability to resolve ambiguity however it wishes, within whatever space Congress has allowed. This delegated space allows the agency to act without regard to what Congress itself would have done within that space, or even would have intended the agency to do. In other words, most of the tools of determining congressional intent discussed in Chapters 9 and 10 are theoretically meaningless if the presumption is that Congress simply had no intent, except to let the agency use its own institutional competencies to establish the statutory meaning. (In fact, however, agencies routinely do employ many of the same interpretive tools that courts do, as Chapter 11 noted.)

On this reading, the *Chevron* doctrine effectively sees agency resolution of textual ambiguities at Step Two less as matter of interpretation and more as a matter of policy choice (a perspective that makes the difference between *Chevron* deference and *State Farm* "hard look" review all the more curious). *See, e.g.*, Peter L. Strauss, *"Deference" is Too Confusing—Let's Call Them* "Chevron *Space" and* "Skidmore *Weight*," 112 COLUM. L. REV. 1143 (2012). This perspective on an agency's exercise of delegated interpretive authority under *Chevron* potentially avoids the critique variously leveled at both Textualists and Purposivists (see Chapter 8) that their interpretive approaches mask the ability to engage in ends-oriented interpretation. It does so by acknowledging without embarrassment or shame that ends-oriented declaration of textual meaning is exactly what is occurring within the space protected under *Chevron* (but once again, only within the gap or space left by the legislature).

Still, questions linger within the academy and the judiciary about whether Step Two deference to agency interpretation of statutes either allows the legislative branch to shirk its institutional role of passing clear laws or usurps the judicial branch's role to declare what the law is, on the one hand; or instead appropriately involves the executive branch in declaring what the law is, as a "counter-*Marbury* for the administrative state." Cass R. Sunstein, *Beyond Marbury: The Executive's Power to Say What the Law Is,* 115 YALE L. J. 2580, 2589 (2006). These questions also relate to how readily an agency should be able to construe a piece of statutory text dynamically over time, or to supersede a previous judicial construction of the same statute with the agency's own subsequent interpretation, as discussed briefly in Chapter 11.

3. *UNITED STATES v. MEAD*: SUPREME COURT ACKNOWLEDGEMENT OF A *CHEVRON* "STEP ZERO"

For the first fifteen years after the *Chevron* decision, lower federal courts functioned as though *Chevron* was the principal framework for reviewing agency interpretations of statutes. The U.S. Supreme Court was not nearly so enamored with its own *Chevron* opinion, however, citing it only occasionally in its cases reviewing agency interpretations of statutory language. Yet it did little to clarify when or whether *Chevron* was ordinarily the appropriate framework for review.

That situation changed with the Court's 2001 decision in *United States v. Mead*, 533 U.S. 218 (2001). *Mead* has given rise to the notion that the *Chevron* doctrine necessitates a "Step Zero," a threshold inquiry about whether *Chevron* is even the proper frame for reviewing agency interpretations. As described in the following paragraphs, *Mead* established that a necessary condition for *Chevron* deference is that the agency have exercised "force of law" power, although *Mead* did not fully specify what would amount to "force of law" power. Meanwhile, a number of other cases have continued to wrestle with when *Chevron* applies.

Once again at issue in *Mead* (as in *MCI*) was a tariff matter, this time consisting of tariff classification ruling letters issued by the U.S. Customs Service with respect to imported "bound diaries" or "day planners." These ruling letters were not the result of any notice-and-comment proceeding, and instead were the product of a routine Customs Service responsibility to assess tariffs on specific types of imports. This responsibility typically resulted in some 10,000 to 15,000 ruling letters each year, "churned out" by 46 different Customs offices and having only limited precedential effect. *Id.* at 233. The issue before the Court was whether or not these rulings assessing specific tariffs were entitled to *Chevron* deference.

The Court concluded that *Chevron* deference was appropriate only when "Congress would expect the agency to be able to speak with the force of law." Because the Court here could find "no indication that Congress intended such a ruling to carry the force of law," the Court held that the type of tariff classification at issue "has no claim to judicial deference under *Chevron*." The Court observed that "the overwhelming number of our cases applying *Chevron* deference have reviewed the fruits of notice-and-comment rulemaking or formal adjudication," although the Court nevertheless left open the possibility that in future cases it could find sufficient "reasons for *Chevron* deference even when no such administrative formality" is present. But *Chevron* deference would not be appropriate when the agency's interpretation is "far removed . . . from any other circumstances reasonably suggesting that Congress ever thought of [them] as deserving [*Chevron*] deference." *Id.* at 221–31.

The Court might then have concluded that under *Chevron*'s terms the Customs Service action was not entitled to any deference. But instead the Court reinvigorated *Skidmore* as the appropriate framework for reviewing not only this case but the full range of agency interpretations, with the amount of deference "understood to vary with circumstances." The Court wrote that "*Chevron* did nothing to eliminate *Skidmore's* holding that an agency's interpretation may merit some deference whatever its form . . . ." *Id.* at 228, 234.

Writing a biting solo dissent, Justice Scalia argued that the Court's *Mead* decision had thrown judicial review of agency interpretation into chaos, and had resulted in "breathing new life into the anachronism of *Skidmore*." *Id.* at 250. In his view, until *Mead*, an agency's interpretation merited either *Chevron* deference or no deference at all, in which case "the court was free to give the statute what it considered the best interpretation." *Id.* at 239. But the majority opinion had complicated this clean bifurcation by resurrecting a mushy middle ground of *Skidmore* deference or "respect" (see subsection B.2 above).

Furthermore, in Justice Scalia's view the *Chevron* doctrine had been that "a reasonable agency application of an ambiguous statutory provision had to be sustained so long as it represented the agency's *authoritative* interpretation," whether or not the agency was exercising lawmaking power. *Id.* at 239 (emphasis added). He argued that previously under *Chevron* an agency was presumed to have congressional authority to resolve ambiguity in those statutes that it was charged to administer, whereas under *Mead* the presumption now was that an agency lacked such authority unless "[s]pecific congressional intent to depart from this rule" could be found in the form of a congressional grant to the agency of "force of law" power. *Id.* at 243. Justice Scalia worried that by dramatically limiting the number and type of agency decisions that now would qualify for *Chevron* deference, *Mead* would "lead to the ossification of large portions of our statutory law," because they would be construed by courts once and for all, whereas they previously would have been construed by agencies, remaining open for reinterpretation from time to time as the agency's views changed. *Id.* at 247.

As the dissenting opinion confirms, *Mead* is particularly important precisely because the majority opinion clarifies two aspects of federal court review of agency interpretation: First, *Chevron* deference is appropriate only after finding that Congress has given the agency power to speak with the force of law. Second, *Skidmore* deference otherwise remains the default mode of judicial deference for agency interpretations that do not flow from an agency's exercise of "force of law" power. Indeed, the Court's *Mead* opinion described *Chevron* as just an additional reason for deference, and almost seemed to characterize *Chevron* as but an exception to, or special case of, *Skidmore*. Justice Breyer has subsequently seemed to say as much in his opinion in *Barnhart v. Walton*, 535 U.S. 212 (2002).

Accordingly, since *Mead*, an essential component of *Chevron* analysis is to determine the threshold question of whether Congress has given the agency "force of law" power, either explicitly or implicitly. *See National Cable & Telecommunications Ass'n v. Brand X Internet Services*, 545 U.S. 967 (2005). But deciding whether Congress has intended to delegate lawmaking authority to an agency *with respect to a particular interpretive issue* is not always an easy matter. Consider an example.

Gonzales v. Oregon. In *Gonzales v. Oregon*, 546 U.S. 243 (2006), the Supreme Court faced a question of how much authority Congress had delegated to the

U.S. Attorney General in the Controlled Substances Act (CSA) of 1970. In 1994, Oregon had adopted a state statute (the Oregon "Death with Dignity Act") that legalized assisted suicide by exempting Oregon physicians from state criminal and civil liability for prescribing a lethal dose of drugs to a requesting patient, if they did so following state standards. Thereafter, the U.S. Attorney General issued an Interpretive Rule concluding that it was unlawful under the federal Controlled Substances Act for an Oregon physician to prescribe drugs covered by the Act for the purpose of assisting a suicide. The Interpretive Rule not only declared such action to be a federal crime, but also made it a basis for revoking a physician's authority to prescribe any controlled substances. The validity of this Interpretive Rule was at issue in *Gonzales*.

The CSA clearly reposed some lawmaking authority in the Attorney General. In particular, the Act allowed the AG to determine on which of five progressively more dangerous schedules to list prescription and other drugs, provided the AG did so by making required findings after notice-and-comment rulemaking procedures. The Act also required physicians who wished to prescribe these drugs to obtain a registration from the Attorney General, which the AG could deny or revoke if registration "would be inconsistent with the public interest," a standard that required consideration of five factors named in the Act. But the Act also gave other administrative authority to the Secretary of the Department of Health and Human Services, specifically providing that the Secretary and not the

Attorney General would have responsibility for certain medical or scientific judgments related to administering the Act, which the Attorney General was required to accept. Relying on an earlier regulation that required every CSA prescription to "be issued for a legitimate medical purpose," the Attorney General's Interpretive Rule declared that assisting suicide was not a "legitimate medical purpose."

After rejecting the AG's argument that his Rule was entitled to extra deference because it was an interpretation of the Justice Department's own prior regulation (see discussion of *Auer* deference in subsection D.7 below), the Supreme Court followed *Mead* in undertaking a Step Zero analysis of the Rule. The Court majority concluded that although Congress had undoubtedly given the Attorney General lawmaking authority with respect to certain aspects of the CSA, it had not given the AG lawmaking authority sufficient to sustain this Interpretive Rule. Specifically, the Court concluded that Congress had not authorized the AG "to make a rule declaring illegitimate a medical [treatment] authorized under state law," or to determine what is in the public interest except by reference to the five statutory factors, or "to decide what constitutes an underlying violation of the CSA in the first place." *Id.* at 245, 262. The majority opinion found the AG's asserted authority "inconsistent with the design of the statute" in fundamental respects, including with respect to the statute's delegation to the HHS Secretary of authority over medical judgments. *Id.* at 265. The Court thus did not see the case as appropriate for *Chevron* deference and invalidated the AG's Interpretive Rule.

Three dissenters, in an opinion written by Justice Scalia, saw the case as a clear call for *Chevron* deference. At Step Zero, the dissenters argued that the factors the AG was required to consider in determining whether to register (or deregister) a physician included "the public interest" and "public health and safety," factors intended to give the AG broad authority to regulate prescribing physicians: "Congress implicitly (but clearly) gave the Attorney General authority to interpret those criteria." *Id.* at 293. In turn, the dissenters saw the Secretary's responsibility for making medical and scientific judgments as limited to specific contexts and not "establishing a general principle of Secretary supremacy with regard to all scientific and medical determinations." *Id.* at 295. Having concluded that the AG had lawmaking authority with respect to the Interpretive Ruling at issue, all that remained was for the dissenters to conclude, at Step One, that Congress had not clearly spoken with regard to how the CSA should apply to assisted suicide, and at Step Two, that the Attorney General's interpretation was reasonable.

D. LINGERING CONTEMPORARY PUZZLES

After *Chevron*, *MCI*, and *Mead*, federal courts continue to wrestle with a panoply of issues about how to review agency interpretations of legal text. Like the essential question at the heart of the *Chevron* doctrine, these issues also all involve determining the proper scope of judicial oversight of agency action undertaken pursuant to legislative delegations of authority to make and enforce law. Many of these questions involve how to integrate some of the interpretive tools discussed in Chapters 9 and 10 into the process of judicial review of agency statutory interpretation. Nine categories of questions are summarized below.

One set of questions involves whether and how substantive canons should factor into judicial deference to agency interpretations. To the extent that these canons operate to protect constitutional values or otherwise constrain the scope of agency authority, their deployment in resolving matters of agency statutory interpretation can amount to a kind of "nondelegation canon." *See* Cass R. Sunstein, *Nondelegation Canons*, 67 U. CHI. L. REV. 315 (2000). Here, concern about granting an agency too much lawmaking power enhances the reviewing court's willingness to constrain the scope of the delegated authority. Five examples of questions arising out of the substantive canons include:

1. WHAT DEGREE OF DEFERENCE SHOULD COURTS SHOW TO AGENCY INTERPRETATIONS THAT RAISE SERIOUS CONSTITUTIONAL ISSUES?

Agencies, as much as courts, may face an interpretive problem one or more of whose otherwise plausible solutions may tread close to a constitutional limit or raise a constitutional concern. If an agency has chosen an interpretation that raises a serious constitutional issue, what role should the Constitutional Avoidance Canon (discussed in Chapter 9) play when the agency's interpretation subsequently undergoes judicial review?

Constitutional concerns could factor into a reviewing court's analysis at *Chevron* Step Zero, Step One, or Step Two. At Step Zero, one view is that Congress should be presumed not to have delegated authority to an agency sufficient for the agency to encroach upon constitutional limits. On this approach, a reviewing court would use the Step Zero inquiry to conclude that an agency's interpretation was simply not entitled to *Chevron* deference because the agency had acted beyond the scope of its delegated authority. The Supreme Court's decision in *Gonzales v. Oregon*, 546 U.S. 243 (2006), discussed above, partakes of something of this quality. The Court majority recognized that society was engaged in a "profound debate" about physician-assisted suicide, which could have constitutional dimensions. The Court refused to conclude that Congress would have impliedly delegated to the Attorney General the authority to construe a statute to implicate such a fundamental issue.

Alternatively, the Avoidance Canon can be employed at Step One, if a court concludes that what might otherwise amount to an ambiguous statute (appropriate for review at Step Two) instead must be judicially construed as having one clear meaning in order to avoid the constitutional question. For instance, In *Edward J. DeBartolo Corp. v. Florida Gulf Coast Building & Construction Trades Council*,

485 U.S. 568 (1988), at issue was whether a union's distribution of handbills in opposition to a construction company amounted to unfair labor activities in violation of provisions of the National Labor Relations Act. The handbills urged customers to boycott a shopping mall employing the contractor, while the Act prohibited labor organizations from "threaten[ing], coerc[ing], or restrain[ing] any person engaged in commerce." Noting that the union's free speech rights under the First Amendment might be at issue, the National Labor Relations Board nonetheless concluded that the union had violated the Act.

When the case reached the Supreme Court, the Court concluded that the rationale behind the Avoidance Canon required the Court to conduct an independent determination of whether the statute in question could be fairly construed to avoid raising the constitutional question. Concluding that such a construction was possible, the Court adopted that construction, effectively resolving the case at *Chevron* Step One and thereby avoiding any need to undertake the Step Two analysis of whether the agency's construction was reasonable. The Avoidance Canon thus took priority over *Chevron* deference.

The Avoidance Canon also can factor into judicial review even at *Chevron* Step Two. For instance, in *Rust v. Sullivan*, 500 U.S. 173 (1991), the Supreme Court reviewed regulations promulgated by the Department of Health and Human Services (HHS) construing provisions in the Public Health Service Act that prohibited using federal funds "in programs where abortion is a method of family planning." The regulations elaborated more specifically on the kinds of programs and activities to which HHS would not grant federal funds. Potential recipients of the funds challenged the regulations both as unauthorized by the Act and as unconstitutional.

The Court upheld the regulations at issue as an otherwise reasonable interpretation under Chevron Step Two, before then considering and rejecting the claim that the regulations nonetheless "must be invalidated because they raise serious questions of constitutional law." Observing that the invocation of the Avoidance Canon was "not . . . without some force," the Court noted that almost "any set of regulations [implementing the abortion limits of the Public Health Service Act] . . . would be challenged on constitutional grounds," and that the Canon therefore did not preclude upholding the agency's construction as a reasonable one.

2. WHAT DEGREE OF DEFERENCE SHOULD COURTS SHOW TO AGENCY INTERPRETATIONS THAT IMPLICATE FEDERALISM CONCERNS?

As discussed in Chapter 9, in recent years the Supreme Court has developed several substantive canons of interpretation that protect federalism values by refusing to construe a statute to intrude upon traditional elements of state sovereignty unless Congress has provided a "clear statement" that the statute should be read to do so. See subsection B.3 of Chapter 9. To what extent should a reviewing court rely upon these federalism values to trump an agency's statutory interpretation that might otherwise receive *Chevron* deference?

For instance, the Clean Water Act regulates the "the discharge of dredged or fill material into the navigable waters" of the United States, and empowers the Army Corps of Engineers to administer a permitting process for such discharge. The Corps asserted jurisdiction over an abandoned sand and gravel pit that was being used as a landfill site after it discovered that the site had also become a migratory bird habitat. In addressing the complicated issue of whether the Corps had jurisdiction over this landfill site as a "navigable waterway," the Supreme Court was influenced by the extent to which a broad reading of the act "would result in a significant impingement of the States' traditional and primary power over land and water use" and undercut Congress's own separate recognition of the rights of states to manage these resources. *Solid Waste Agency of Northern Cook County v. United States Army Corps of Engineers*, 531 U.S. 159, 174 (2001).

However, the decision also asserted that it was reading the statutory provision narrowly in order to avoid what it called the serious constitutional problems that a broad reading would raise. Although as a matter of constitutional jurisprudence it is questionable whether a broad reading of the term "navigable waterway" would in fact raise a serious constitutional question, the fact that the Court framed the issue this way leaves unsettled the extent to which federalism concerns alone, without an accompanying constitutional concern, might override *Chevron* deference.

3. WHAT DEGREE OF DEFERENCE SHOULD COURTS SHOW TO AGENCY DECISIONS REGARDING QUESTIONS OF FEDERAL PREEMPTION?

Another substantive interpretive canon discussed in Chapter 9 is the presumption against construing ambiguous federal statutes to preempt state law. Of course, many statutes unambiguously preempt state law, and such statutes will naturally give rise to implementing regulations that also preempt state law. But what about federal regulations that preempt state law as the result of an agency interpretation of a statute that is ambiguous about whether Congress meant to preempt state law?

It remains beyond the scope of this Nutshell to explore the legal complexities of federal preemption doctrine in any depth. But for current purposes it is worth observing that many of these same complexities serve as a predicate for the belief that courts, not agencies, should be the arbiter of whether an ambiguous measure has a preemptive effect, and that the question of any particular congressional measure's effect on limiting or preempting state law in the area is often not the kind of question for which either agency expertise or accountability is especially helpful. Accordingly, some jurists and scholars have been reluctant to extend *Chevron* deference to an agency's determination that a statute it administers should preempt state law when the statute is ambiguous on the point. The Supreme Court has not settled the issue.

However, the Court has found instances in which an agency's expertise has been an influential factor, a la *Skidmore*, in the Court's determination of the preemption question. For instance, in *Geier v. American Honda Motor Co., Inc.*, 529 U.S. 861 (2000), the Court confronted the question of whether a Federal Motor Vehicle Safety Standard that allowed automobile manufacturers to choose between airbags and seatbelts as standard safety equipment on their vehicles preempted a state tort action for failure to install airbags. In holding that the federal law preempted state law, the Court relied in part on the Department of Transportation's explanation, based on its "uniquely qualified" ability to understand a complex and technical subject, that allowing state tort suits for failure to install airbags would compromise the Department's long-term ability to accomplish its automobile safety objectives.

Meanwhile, just to complicate matters, on occasion the Court has said that a preemptive effect of an agency interpretation of an ambiguous statute does not alter the deference to which the agency is entitled under *Chevron*. For example, in *Smiley v. Citibank*, 517 U.S. 735 (1996), the Supreme Court reviewed the U.S. Comptroller of the Currency's determination that the term "interest" in a provision of the National Bank Act included late fees related to extension of a line of credit. Because the provision at issue did preempt state law, a broad agency construction would have the effect of preempting more state law than would a narrow construction. The Court concluded that this agency discretion to determine the preemptive sweep of the statute had no effect on the Court's willingness to afford *Chevron* deference to the Comptroller or the Court's evaluation of whether the interpretation was a reasonable one.

4. WHAT DEGREE OF DEFERENCE SHOULD COURTS SHOW TO AGENCY INTERPRETATIONS OF MATTERS INVOLVING FOREIGN AFFAIRS OR NATIONAL SECURITY?

Long before *Chevron*, and even before *Skidmore*, the U.S. Supreme Court had developed a highly deferential approach to reviewing executive branch activities "within the international field." Relying on the President's inherent powers under Article II of the Constitution, the Court concluded that in conducting foreign affairs and promoting national security the President needed a higher "degree of discretion and freedom from statutory restriction" than "were domestic affairs alone involved" (as noted in subsection B.3 above). *United States v. Curtiss-Wright Export Co.*, 299 U.S. 304, 320 (1936). This doctrine continues to have vitality after *Chevron*. When the Court invokes it, *Curtiss-Wright* deference extends to more than just issues of statutory ambiguity, and calls instead for upholding executive branch decisions involving military and national security matters "unless Congress specifically has provided otherwise." *Department of the Navy v. Egan*, 484 U.S. 518, 530 (1988).

Yet the Supreme Court has often reviewed agency or executive branch decisions involving foreign affairs or national security without invoking either *Curtiss-Wright* deference or *Chevron* deference. For instance, in *Hamdan v. Rumsfeld*, 548 U.S. 557 (2006), the Court considered the lawfulness of President Bush's determination that Osama bin Laden's chauffeur, a Yemeni national held by the U.S. since 2002 at the naval base in Guantanamo Bay, Cuba, should be tried by a military commission. Although the case turned on interpretations of both the Detainee Treatment Act and the Uniform Code of Military Justice, the Court in a 6–3 decision offered no deference to the President's interpretation of these measures.

5. WHAT DEGREE OF DEFERENCE SHOULD COURTS SHOW TO AGENCY INTERPRETATIONS OF ISSUES OF CRIMINAL LAW?

Occasionally an agency interpretation of an ambiguous statute will affect criminal law. For instance, the Attorney General's interpretation of the Controlled Substances Act in *Gonzales v. Oregon* (see pp. 515–518) redefined the types of physician conduct that could give rise to criminal liability. Similarly, the interpretation of the Endangered Species Act at issue in *Babbitt v. Sweet Home* (see pp. 276–277, 381–383) also affected who might be subject to criminal liability for "taking" an endangered species. A question that these sorts of agency interpretations may raise is whether the Rule of Lenity (see Chapter 9) should trump *Chevron* deference.

The Supreme Court has yet to resolve this issue definitively. Over the years, it has issued decisions on both sides of the question. *See, e.g.*, *Leocal v. Ashcroft*, 543 U.S. 1 (2004) (invoking Rule of Lenity in reviewing agency interpretation, without mentioning *Chevron*); *Sweet Home*, 515 U.S. at 704 n.18 (explicitly rejecting role for Rule of Lenity in deferring to agency interpretation); *see also Esquivel-Quitana v. Lynch*, 810 F.3d 1019, 1027 (6th Cir. 2016) (Sutton, J., concurring and dissenting) (arguing for priority of Rule of Lenity over *Chevron* deference); *cert. granted*, ___ U.S. ___, 137 S. Ct. 368 (Oct. 28, 2016). Meanwhile, several of the underlying rationales for the Rule of Lenity—namely, the importance of providing potential defendants with clear notice, and the risks of delegating to courts the authority to define crimes—are not present in the agency context, at least if the agency has followed notice-and-comment procedures or other public processes for adopting an interpretation.

* * *

Another set of questions concerning judicial review of agency interpretation involves problems unique to the agency context. Three of these issues are:

6. SHOULD COURTS DEFER TO AN AGENCY'S INTERPRETATION OF ITS OWN JURISDICTION OR THE SCOPE OF ITS DELEGATED AUTHORITY?

Separate from the *Chevron* Step Zero question of whether an agency is acting within the scope of its delegated authority when it interprets a statute is the question of whether to extend *Chevron* deference to an agency's interpretation of the reach of its own jurisdiction, or in other words whether the agency's interpretation of the scope of its authority is entitled to judicial deference. Just a few years after *Chevron*, a debate over this issue occurred between Justices Brennan and Scalia, without definitive resolution, in *Mississippi Power & Light Co. v. Moore*, 487 U.S. 354 (1988).

Twenty-five years later, in *City of Arlington, Texas v. F.C.C.*, ___ U.S. ___, 133 S. Ct. 1863 (2013), the Supreme Court appeared to resolve this question, for now. At issue was a provision of the Communications Act that required state and local governments to process wireless companies' applications for approval of cell tower sites "within a reasonable period of time." A Federal Communications Commission regulation interpreting this provision imposed specific time limits for different categories of applications. Municipalities challenged the regulation as outside the scope of the FCC's authority.

Justice Scalia, writing for the Court majority, wrote that for purposes of *Chevron* deference, it made no sense to distinguish between how the agency construed the scope of its jurisdiction and how the agency interpreted its resulting substantive authority: "[T]he question in every case is, simply, whether the statutory text forecloses the agency's assertion of authority, or not." *Id.* at 1871. Finding that the Communications Act did not foreclose the regulation at issue, the Court majority sustained it under *Chevron* Step Two as a reasonable construction of the FCC's authority. Chief Justice Roberts, joined by Justices Kennedy and Alito, dissented, arguing that *Chevron* deference logically depended on first concluding that Congress had delegated authority to the agency, and that it remained solely the judiciary's responsibility to determine whether such a delegation had in fact occurred.

7. WHAT DEGREE OF DEFERENCE SHOULD COURTS SHOW TO AN AGENCY'S INTERPRETATION OF ITS OWN REGULATIONS AND RULES?

Long before *Chevron*, the U.S. Supreme Court had called for a great deal of deference to an agency's interpretation of its own pre-existing regulations, at least in most circumstances. In *Bowles v. Seminole Rock & Sand Co.*, 325 U.S. 410, 414 (1945), the Court described these agency interpretations as "of controlling weight unless plainly erroneous or inconsistent with the regulation." Fifteen years after *Chevron*, the Court made clear in *Auer v. Robbins*, 519 U.S. 452 (1997), that the *Chevron* doctrine had not altered the *Seminole Rock* rule (although it is not exactly clear how much more deferential judicial review would be under a standard that for reversal requires plain error (*Auer/Seminole Rock*), rather than unreasonableness (*Chevron*)).

However, in *Gonzales*, the Court rejected the Attorney General's claim that his regulation prohibiting the use of prescription drugs for assisted suicide, because it was an interpretation of a 1971 Department of Justice regulation which required that prescriptions for controlled substances "be issued for a legitimate medical purpose," was entitled to *Auer/Seminole Rock* deference. The Court's opinion saw this 1971 regulation as merely parroting or paraphrasing the statutory scheme that it was implementing, rather than adding substantive content that reflected or incorporated the agency's expertise.

Gonzales suggests that *Auer/Seminole Rock* deference, in contrast to *Chevron* deference, does seem to depend on the agency having to some degree deployed its expertise, accountability, or some element of institutional competence in order to enlarge upon the statutory terms. Otherwise, the Court worried that agencies could bootstrap their interpretive authority in all manner of cases simply by adopting regulations at Time One that essentially did no more than restate the governing statute, and then subsequently construe those regulations at Time Two in whatever way the agency wished. The agency could then claim *Auer/Seminole Rock* deference for this interpretation. Some members of the Court have expressed concern about this possibility in today's era of widespread use of Interpretative Rules. For instance, see the concurring opinions of Justices Scalia and Thomas in *Perez v. Mortgage Bankers Ass'n*, 575 U.S. ___, 135 S. Ct. 1199 (2015).

Nevertheless, the Court has not been consistent on this point. For instance, in *Coeur Alaska, Inc. v.*

Southeast Alaska Conservation Council, 557 U.S. 261 (2009), the Court granted *Auer/Seminole Rock* deference to the agency's interpretation of its own previous regulation that had done little more than restate the statute on which the regulation had been predicated.

8. DOES *CHEVRON* DEFERENCE PERMIT AN AGENCY TO REVISE A PREVIOUS JUDICIAL INTERPRETATION OF A STATUTE THAT THE AGENCY WOULD OTHERWISE HAVE HAD CONGRESSIONALLY DELEGATED AUTHORITY TO CONSTRUE ITSELF?

On occasion, an agency confronts a statutory ambiguity that a court has also already confronted. Is the agency obligated to follow the judicial interpretation when, had the agency been the first interpreter, its interpretation would have been entitled to *Chevron* deference? This question of the *stare decisis* impact of a judicial resolution goes to the heart of the *Chevron* rationale.

In *National Cable & Telecommunications Ass'n v. Brand X Internet Services*, 545 U.S. 967 (2005), the Supreme Court resolved this question at least with respect to the lack of binding *stare decisis* effect of lower federal court decisions. The Court reviewed a circuit court decision that had relied on the circuit court's own precedent to trump an agency's subsequent attempt to obtain *Chevron* deference. The Supreme Court said that an agency could overturn a judicial precedent if it involved an interpretation of a statutory ambiguity of the kind that the agency could have resolved at *Chevron* Step Two. Even though a court may have already confronted that same question, the agency could revisit it just as the agency could have revisited its own prior interpretations. The Court saw this as necessary to honor the underlying principles of regulatory flexibility, and to prevent the "ossification" that Justice Scalia had worried about in his *Mead* dissent (see p. 514 above).

* * *

Finally, one overarching question concerning when the U.S. Supreme Court will find *Chevron* deference to be warranted is the following:

9. IS THERE A "MAJOR QUESTIONS" EXCEPTION TO *CHEVRON* DEFERENCE?

Another way of understanding cases like *Gonzales v. Oregon* (see pp. 515–518), and *MCI v. AT&T* (see pp. 502–505) is that the Supreme Court is simply not willing to defer to agencies in "extraordinary" or "major" cases. The Court's decision in *Brown & Williamson*, 529 U.S. 120 (2000), previously discussed in Chapter 10, might also be an example of the use of an implied presumption against delegation of extraordinary authority. There, the Court majority found at Step One of a *Chevron* analysis that, in light of a broad contextualized reading of the Food, Drug, and Cosmetic Act, "Congress has directly spoken to the issue here and precluded the FDA's jurisdiction to regulate tobacco products." *Id.* at 133. The statutory text was itself by no means clear on this point, but the majority concluded that the FDA's jurisdiction did not extend to tobacco because "Congress could not have intended to delegate a decision of such economic and political significance to an agency in so cryptic a fashion." *Id.* at 160. Likewise in *King v. Burwell*, described in Chapter 10 above (see p. 421–422), the Court explained that the question of whether Affordable Care Act tax credits were available on the Federal Exchanges was a centrally important question of "deep economic and political significance" that, "had Congress wished to assign" to an agency, "it surely would have done so expressly." 135 S. Ct. at 2489.

Although it is impossible to give a full definition of what might amount to an extraordinary case, as a rough explanation it may be a case in which the agency claims interpretive authority to undertake dramatic or substantial shifts in policy, such as authority to regulate tobacco products after decades of disclaiming such authority, or authority to interfere in the traditional state role of regulating the practice of medicine. Although Congress could authorize agencies to regulate in these areas, the Court at Step One has often rejected arguments that Congress has delegated such sweeping authority only implicitly, famously observing that Congress "does not . . . hide elephants in mouseholes." *Whitman v. American Trucking Ass'ns Inc.*, 531 U.S. 457, 468 (2001); *Gonzales v. Oregon*, 546 U.S. at 268.

* * *

After all this, what additional guidance can be offered to help students of agency interpretation of statutes master this complex area of the modern administrative state? As observed earlier in this chapter, the secondary literature is voluminous. But one potentially helpful approach is to think of judicial deference to federal agency interpretations as existing along a continuum. Specifying the full continuum is beyond the scope of this chapter, and individual observers might specify a deference continuum in various ways. But one helpful attempt is William Eskridge Jr. & Lauren Baer, *The Continuum of Deference: Supreme Court Treatment of Agency Statutory Interpretations from* Chevron *to* Hamdan, 96 GEO. L. J. 1083 (2008).

E. STATE DOCTRINE

The preceding discussion has focused exclusively on the federal doctrines of judicial review of agency interpretations of statutes. As previously noted, the number of cases and secondary discussions of this topic is extensive. Meanwhile, much less has been written about judicial review of agency statutory interpretation in the various state systems. A couple of helpful analyses or summaries of state practice include Aaron Saiger, Chevron *and Deference in State Administrative Law*, 83 FORD. L. REV. 555 (2014); and William R. Anderson, Chevron *in the States: An Assessment and A Proposal*, 58 ADMIN. L. REV. 1017 (2006).

Briefly, the *Chevron* doctrine is not yet widely followed in state courts. Instead, most state courts have maintained the doctrine that it is for courts to decide *de novo* what a statute means, even though in the course of doing so most state courts will consider an agency's construction. This approach is more like the federal pre-*Chevron* doctrine, in which courts evaluate in something like a *Skidmore* fashion whether the agency has offered persuasive reasons for courts to follow its interpretation. These agency justifications may provide the reviewing court with more than just good arguments, instead having greater weight or influence akin to that of expert witness testimony, or even functioning like non-binding persuasive authority from other jurisdictions. Still, in states employing this kind of *Skidmore* approach, the courts remain the final arbiter of statutory meanings.

However, a dozen or more states have now developed something like a *Chevron* doctrine, usually with far fewer of the complexities about when the doctrine applies than the federal counterpart. That is, the courts in these states more often simply make a threshold Step One determination of whether the state legislature has plainly spoken on the interpretive issue, and if not then uphold the agency's interpretation at Step Two if it is a reasonable use of the authority that the state legislature has delegated to the agency. Meanwhile, some commentators have observed a slow movement in the direction of *Chevron* in other state courts and in state administrative law jurisprudence generally.

Of course, given the flux in the federal jurisprudence of judicial deference to agency statutory interpretation, it is even harder to predict where state law on the subject is headed. Perhaps in the field of statutory interpretation, as in other fields, states can serve as laboratories of democracy, refining the complex relationships between the three branches of American government. In any event, it seems safe to assume that as long as federal and state government agencies continue to play the substantial and significant roles that they have increasingly come to play over the past century, issues of the appropriate extent of judicial deference to agency statutory interpretation will remain of central importance to American law.

APPENDIX

REPRESENTATIVE CANONS OF STATUTORY INTERPRETATION

The following examples of interpretive canons are only representative, not comprehensive. The list organizes the examples by general categories, drawing from a number of comparable but more extensive lists found in statutory interpretation casebooks and similar resources. These more comprehensive lists include, for instance, the Appendix in WILLIAM N. ESKRIDGE JR., INTERPRETING THE LAW: A PRIMER ON HOW TO READ STATUTES AND THE CONSTITUTION (2016).

The first three categories below are all types of "intrinsic" canons. The fourth category consists of "extrinsic" canons, a distinct set of interpretive tools not always even included in the family of interpretive canons. The fifth category consists of interpretive rules of deference courts sometimes deploy when reviewing how government agencies have construed statutory text.

Although many of these canons are frequently expressed in terms of the role that "Congress" plays in enacting the text at issue, the list below expresses many of the canons using the more universal term "the legislature" to reflect that these canons are also of potential use in construing state legislation as well as federal legislation.

A few of the canons could fit in multiple categories, and indeed many of these canons appear in several variations in some other lists, with the variants treated as distinct canons. The list below, however, has collapsed minor variations into a single more universal canon in many instances.

I. Examples of Textual Canons:

Plain (or ordinary) meaning canon: Rely on a term's ordinary meaning, unless a technical or other meaning is called for.

Dictionary canon: Follow dictionary definitions, unless the legislature provides its own definition. Specialized dictionaries are appropriate for technical terms.

Technical meaning canon: Interpreters may defer to experts to understand a technical term.

Settled meaning canon: Apply the settled meaning of terms that have such a meaning.

Common-law usage rule: Follow accepted common-law meanings of terms unless inconsistent with statutory purpose or the enacting legislature has specified otherwise.

Rule against absurd results: As an exception to the plain meaning canon, refrain from following the plain or literal meaning of a term where to do so would result in a patently absurd or unjust outcome, or when the text contains a "scrivener's error."

A. Linguistic Inferences:

Expressio/inclusio unius est exclusio alterius: The express mention or inclusion of one member of a class implies the deliberate exclusion of other members of that class.

Noscitur a sociis: "A word is known by its associates"; the meaning of an ambiguous term should be determined by the words associated with it in the statutory context.

Ejusdem generis: A generic term following a list of specific terms should be assumed to be limited in scope to the class of things typified by the preceding specific terms.

B. Inferences from Grammar and Syntax:

Punctuation & grammar rule: Presume that a legislature follows norms of grammar and punctuation.

Last antecedent rule: Absent an indication to the contrary, qualifying phrases refer only to the last antecedent.

May vs. Shall: "May" is ordinarily permissive and confers discretion, while "shall" is ordinarily mandatory.

And vs. Or: Presume that "and" is conjunctive, while "or" is disjunctive.

Singular vs. Plural nouns: Construe singular nouns to include the plural, unless otherwise apparent from the statutory context.

Gendered pronouns: Construe masculine pronouns to be gender inclusive, unless context suggests otherwise; female pronouns may be presumed to be exclusive, unless context suggests otherwise.

C. Textual Integrity and Continuity:

Whole act rule: Interpret statute holistically, reading each provision in light of the rest of the statute.

Title/headings rule: A statute's title, subtitles, and preamble may be considered in interpreting a statute.

Rule against surplusage: Avoid construing a statutory provision to be superfluous to other provisions of the act, absent evidence that a redundant meaning was intended.

Consistent structure/consistent policy rule: Construe a provision to be consistent with the structure of the statute as a whole and the policies reflected by other provisions of the statute.

Rule of meaningful and purposive variation: Construe same or like terms within a statute consistently throughout a statute; presume that variations in terms are meaningful and purposive.

Narrow exceptions rule: Narrowly construe provisos and exceptions.

Specific provision rule: Specific provisions targeting a particular issue supersede more general provisions; generic terms and language should be read broadly where the statute elsewhere uses more specific language on the subject.

In pari materia: Presumption that the same term used in similar statutes has a consistent meaning.

Acquiescence rule: Presumption that when a legislature does not amend a statute to respond to a court or agency interpretation of the statute, the legislature approves of that interpretation.

Re-enactment rule: Presumption that when a legislature reenacts a statute, it incorporates the statute's prior interpretations.

Borrowed statute rule: Presumption that when a legislature borrows a statute from another jurisdiction, it incorporates the other jurisdiction's interpretations of the statute.

II. Examples of Substantive Canons:

A. Generally:

Constitutional avoidance canon: Where fairly possible, construe statutes to avoid raising constitutional issues.

Rule of lenity: Narrowly construe punitive measures.

Non-delegation canon: Presumption that Congress does not delegate excessive authority to agencies (authority beyond that for which Congress has provided sufficient guidelines about its use).

B. Federalism Canons:

Rule against federal intrusion upon traditional state functions: Strong presumption against construing a federal statute to alter the federal-state balance or infringe upon traditional state regulation.

Rule against preemption of state law: Presumption that a federal statute does not preempt state law, absent actual conflict or evidence of congressional intent to preempt state law or occupy the field.

Rule against abrogation of state sovereign immunity: "Super-strong" rule against construing a federal statute to abrogate states' Eleventh Amendment immunity from federal lawsuits, absent explicit statutory language doing so.

Avoid construing ambiguities in a federal statute to authorize a state to engage in activities that would violate the dormant commerce clause.

C. A Few Subject-Specific Examples of Substantive Canons:

Environmental Law:

Construe environmental laws to further an underlying purpose of promoting a clean environment at reasonable cost.

Foreign Affairs/International Law:

Executive powers and foreign affairs rule: Construe statutes to avoid congressional and judicial interference with the President's core executive authority and inherent powers, including over foreign affairs.

International obligations canon: Presumption that U.S. law respects international obligations and that Congress recognizes the sovereign interests of other countries.

Habeas Corpus:

"Super-strong" Habeas Corpus canon: Statutory abrogation of right of habeas corpus must be explicit, not implied.

Indian Law:

Presumption against federal "diminishment" of Indian lands and rights.

Real Estate:

Settled property rights canon: Narrowly construe statutes that affect long-standing or firmly established property rights; construe in favor of the property owner a statute involving a government taking of private property.

Taxation:

Narrowly construe exemptions from federal taxation.

Veterans Benefits:

The veterans' benefits rule: Liberally construe veterans' benefits statutes in favor of their beneficiaries.

III. Examples of Procedural Canons:

Rule of severability: Presumption that unconstitutional provisions are severable.

Rule against retroactivity: Avoid construing statutes retroactively.

Rule against repeals by implication: Repeals by implication are disfavored. If two statutes cover the same subject, give effect to both if possible; infer a partial repeal only if the two statutes cannot co-exist.

Strictly construe statutes authorizing appeals.

Rule of sovereign immunity: "Super-strong" rule against construing a federal statute to waive the government's sovereign immunity, unless the statute clearly says it does so.

Liberally construe "sue and be sued" clauses that waive the government's sovereign immunity.

Presumption against private rights of action.

Rule against extraterritorial application: Presumption that a federal statute is directed to solely domestic affairs, absent a contrary statement.

"American Rule" canon: Narrowly construe statutes that provide for fee-shifting of litigation costs in contravention of the default "American Rule."

IV. Examples of Extrinsic Canons:

Statutory history (the historical evolution of the actual text of an enacted statute, as amended across time) is always potentially relevant to resolving interpretive problems.

Legislative history (contemporaneous documentation of how and why a statute was enacted and shaped) may be relevant to resolving interpretive problems.

Legislative committee reports are generally the most authoritative and reliable legislative history. Conference committee reports can be especially probative.

Floor statements, especially by sponsors, may be used to confirm apparent meaning.

The "dog that didn't bark" canon: Avoid construing a statute to produce significant policy change if legislative history lacks any evidence that the enacting legislature expected that change.

V. Examples of Agency Interpretation Canons:

Chevron deference: Courts should defer to an agency's reasonable construction of a statute the agency is charged to administer even if the construction is not the one the court would have adopted on its own.

A judicial decision affirming an agency's reasonable interpretation of a statute the agency is charged to administer does not preclude the agency, on grounds of *stare decisis*, from a subsequent reinterpretation of that provision.

Curtiss-Wright deference: Courts should be highly deferential to executive branch decisions in the international field.

Seminole Rock/Auer deference: An agency's interpretation of its own regulations is entitled to judicial deference unless "plainly erroneous or inconsistent with the regulation."

Skidmore respect: Courts should respect an agency's statutory interpretation based on factors such as the thoroughness of its consideration and the validity of its reasoning.

INDEX

References are to Pages